The Secret Police
and the Revolution

The Secret Police and the Revolution

The Fall of the German Democratic Republic

EDWARD N. PETERSON

PRAEGER

Westport, Connecticut
London

Library of Congress Cataloging-in-Publication Data

Peterson, Edward N. (Edward Norman), 1925–
    The secret police and the revolution : the fall of the German Democratic Republic /
Edward N. Peterson.
        p.   cm.
    Includes bibliographical references and index.
    ISBN 0–275–97328–X (alk. paper)
    1. Germany (East). Ministerium für Staatssicherheit.   2. Intelligence service—
Germany (East)   3. Germany (East)—Politics and government.   4. Internal security—
Germany (East)   5. Opposition (Political science)—Germany (East)   I. Title.
DD289.P46   2002
943'10878—dc21   2001016321

British Library Cataloguing in Publication Data is available.

Library of Congress Catalog Card Number: 2001016321
ISBN: 0–275–97328–X

First published in 2002

Praeger Publishers, 88 Post Road West, Westport, CT 06881
An imprint of Greenwood Publishing Group, Inc.
www.praeger.com

Printed in the United States of America

The paper used in this book complies with the
Permanent Paper Standard issued by the National
Information Standards Organization (Z39.48–1984).

10 9 8 7 6 5 4 3 2 1

Contents

Introduction

East Germans had the misfortune of moving without a real break from the National Socialist (NS) state of Adolf Hitler to the Communist state of Joseph Stalin. One provocative comparison is that the NS state was a genuine German product, which became ever more radicalized, whereas the Communist dictatorship, which was imposed from outside, became ever more soft. "The Third Reich was internally supported and overthrown from outside, while the DDR [Deutsche Demokratische Republik] was supported from outside and overthrown from within."[1]

Following this peaceful revolution of 1989 has come a scholarly revolution, because suddenly the secret documents of the DDR were under the control of the Bundesrepublik Deutschland (BRD), which had sufficient incentive to make public the secrets of a former enemy. With Germanic throroughness and deliberate speed, great masses of documentation were made available to scholars who had had scarcely a hope of striking it so rich. The new Russian State had less reason than the Germans to uncover its Communist past, but some bits of its vast documentation have been ferreted out with relevance to its former satellite. Memoirs from behind the Iron Curtain, through which one would formerly have to search for the grains of corn amid the mountain of chaff, have only the natural limitations of memories.

Researching the forbidden Secret Police documents in a dictatorship has a wonderful ring to it. When everything is supposed to be kept secret, these police should have kept the secrets. When the public was to know nothing, the Secret Police were supposed to know everything. Erich Mielke, the chief of the Ministry of State Security (known as the Stasi), made every effort to do precisely that.

My research of Gestapo documents in Bavaria, such as the Reports on Public Opinion, disclosed a divergence between the historians' image and the secret reality of the Third Reich. Although refused entry as a scholar to the dictatorship in the DDR, in 1964 I began 25 years of "family visits," with stimulating private conversations and depressing public observations.

Once the Berlin Wall came down, I happily began researching the central and local East German archives and found the Soviet correspondence useful to document the Soviet Occupation as the beginning of the DDR, showing a similar divergence between image and reality (as described in my *Russian Commands and German Resistance*).[2]

To document the DDR, I was first frustrated by the persistent obfuscation of reality in the Party sources, not to mention the anti-historical newspapers. Then in 1994 I gained access to the Ministry for State Security (MfS) documents, which were prepared in "The Gauck Office" in Berlin. I was shown the fascinating documents of the Central Evaluation Office (*Zentrale Auswertungs & Informationsgruppe*, or ZAIG), which was the integration of the local reports and described the worsening conditions and the increasing opposition in the DDR up to December 1989.

With a long-standing fascination with history, *wie es eigentlich gewesen*, that is, at the local level, I first returned to Leipzig. Despite its distinction as the center of the revolution, its files were relatively unrewarding. The keeper of its MfS documents, who had helped to occupy the building in December 1989, was aware that much had been destroyed somewhere else in that large building.

Having also researched the Soviet Occupation in Schwerin, I requested access to its holdings and discovered that this was the most completely processed local collection. The Bismarckian joke about Mecklenburg was that everything happens later there—in this case, perhaps, a delay in document destruction. With the excellent assistance of the staff, I could examine the very interesting local reports on which the Berlin reports were based. The subsequent opening of the archives to me in Magdeburg in 1998 offered a further perspective.

What emerges from the documents is a contemporary judgment that supplements the many unofficial contemporary views and the post-1989 analysis of that people's discontent. These reports of problems are the more credible because they were tabulated not by the enemies of the DDR but by its defenders, its "Shield and Sword." They are not accusable of hindsight or capitalist hostility.

The resulting wealth of detail of public complaints has enabled an explanation of the causes of the revolution, a bit like the *cahiers* of the French Revolution. The fall of the Republic came with such surprise to outside observers that it may come with even greater surprise that the Secret Police reported the conditions and the public reaction as already dangerous in 1987. These recognized elements led to the revolution, and the MfS can with some justification claim to have predicted it and, with less justification, claim that had the Politbüro heeded its advice, it would have saved a re-formed DDR.

The MfS reports are in sharp contrast to the rosy information that the DDR media presented the public, which found in most Socialist Unity Party (SED) documents, and even in the minutes of the Politbüro, an avoidance of bitter realities. Outside the MfS, no one was apparently admitting, except in the privacy of a few trusted friends, the serious problems until thousands of young people poured through the Hungarian Hole in the Iron Curtain, the first gap since the building of the Berlin Wall. The world, including most Germans behind the Wall, saw it all on television.

The Schwerin documentation evidenced that the local MfS, with "German efficiency," had created a very thorough system, which was accurately reporting the problems of Communism. Its agents were passing on reports of their unpaid "Unofficial Colleagues" (IMs), who were "telling it like it is." The local situation reports (*Lageberichte*) were also describing the fatal breakdown of the economy, not only as experienced by the citizens but as described by its spies assigned to factories and offices.

MfS members were the only ones who dared tell the truth because they could arrest anyone else who told the truth. No one would censor them because no free historian was ever to see what they reported. Behind the mantle of secrecy, the truth could be told.

The views of nearly every social group were reflected in the MfS files, especially farmers, workers, doctors and teachers. Thus, the MfS documents seem the best possible documentation of what masses of people were thinking. Memoirs can describe only a person's small circle. Foreign journalists could describe only the few whom they encountered, who could possibly whisper the truth. Even the Western intelligence would have limited access, primarily to those who succeeded in leaving. The MfS' many thousands of agents were in a position to know all corners of the country, from top to bottom, encouraged, rather than impeded, by the authorities. They and the hundreds of clerks who typed the reports were the unwitting friends of history.

The documents provide also a record of the collapse of the economy, which became the major concern of the spies, and Minister Erich Mielke occasionally passed on to the Politbüro a credible description of the core problems of the socialist economy. At the end the MfS made a frank admission of the weakness of the Secret Police, even the cherished Chekist techniques imported from the Soviet Union.

A further result of the research is the insight into how a dictatorial secret service operated, what it thought important to know, what it discovered, its problems, its weaknesses and its image of itself. It is fascinating just how its thinking evolved and how the thought of the old Erich Mielke differed from that of even his close assistants, like his successors, which led to their rebellion at the end.

Clearly, the MfS gradually moved from suppressing the opposition to joining it. There is even the interpretation that the Stasi was active agents in overthrowing Erich Honecker, the Minister President and General Secretary of the SED. This tracing of policies, procedures, successes and ultimate failure is an introduction to the limits of Secret Police power.

One can learn the nature of the problems that brought down the dictatorship and the nature of the Secret Police defenders, who began confidently and ended abjectly. The documentation permits an insight into the weaknesses of a dictatorship and insight into the reasons for the failure of a dictatorial socialism.

A remarkable part of the explanation was the undefeatables, those trying to emigrate (AstAs/Emigrant Applicants) who kept pushing no matter what the MfS did to discourage them. The story of this struggle of the irresistible versus the immovable shows how the police were being bent by their constant pressure, and how police obedience is altered into something akin to rebellion.

THE STRUCTURE OF THE FINDINGS

Rather than grouping the information flow by topics, I have left it largely chronological, as the MfS actually recorded and analyzed what happened, in order to show the flow of the commands and the reactions of the public and their keepers.

First discussed are the problems up to 1980, beginning with the relationship to the Soviet Union of Stalin, Nikita Khrushchev and Leonid Brezhnev. Next considered are the internal political problems of Walter Ulbricht and Erich Honecker's regimes and then the most serious problem of an economy's being led to the abyss by Honecker's economic tsar, Günter Mittag, who could not persuade Honecker of his folly.

Further background concerns what was presumed to be the solution to Communism's problems, the MfS—described officially as the DDR's "Sword and Shield" and described by the public, who feared and hated it, as the Stasi.

Then described are the stages of the coming revolution, the years from 1980 to 1986, then month by month, 1987 to 1989, first at the ground level, based on reports from the city of Schwerin and the small towns, villages and collective farms in its district. After this view from the grass roots, the focus shifts to the contemporary Berlin evaluations, the central judgments from the reports from all the districts, including their criticisms of the SED's Politbüro, although one of its members was the MfS leader, old Communist, Soviet-trained Erich Mielke.

The MfS reports describe much of the reality, but Mielke's policy was warped by his belief in the Soviet model, the Chekist devices to save Communism from its many enemies. Even so, his analysis, including long speeches to his generals and colonels, became toward the end also quite critical of the policies of his Politbüro peers.

These Secret Police reports will stand up in the court of history because the system's defenders reported and believed that the DDR had crippling problems that doomed it. This is not a hostile-negative (a favorite MfS adjective for critics) comment but that of the Stasi itself. This is what the believers in the system were forced to admit was the reality and what they at the end admitted had doomed what they had believed in.

Abbreviations Used by the MfS (Ministerium für Staatssicherheit)

BKG	die Bezirkskoordinierungsgruppe (district coordination group, created in 1975 to process the applicants for emigration)
BND	Bundesnachrichtendienst (West German Secret Police)
BRD	Bundesrepublik Deutschland (Bonn Republic)
CDU	Christlich-Demokratische Union (Christian Democratic Union, political party)
DBD	Deutsche Bauernpartei Deutschland (peasant political party)
DOSA	Dokumentensammlung (Document Collection)
FDGB	Freie Deutscher Gewerkschaftsbund (the workers' union)
FDJ	Freie Deutsche Jugend (Free German Youth)
HO	Handel Organization (state-owned stores, restaurants)
KPD	Communist Party of Germany (after 1946, only West Germany)
KSZE	Helsinki agreements for security and cooperation of Europe
LDP(D)	Liberale Demokratische Partei (Deutschland) (political party)
LPG	Landwirtschaftliche Produktionsgenossenschaft (collective farm)
NSW	Non-Socialist World
NVA	National Volks Armee (National People's Army)
SPD	Social Democratic Party of Germany (after 1946, only West Germany)
SU	Soviet Union
VdgB	Organization of cooperative help to farmers
VEB	Volkseigener Betrieb (a state-owned firm)
VEG	Volkseigene Genossenschaft (a state-owned farm)
ZK	Zentral Kommittee of the SED (central committee)

MfS Abbreviations about Itself

AGM	Arbeitgruppe des Ministers (Work Group of the Minister)
AIM	Archivierter IM-Vorgang (archived IM proceedings)
AKG	Auswertungs und Kontrolgruppen (Evaluation and Inspection Group)

AstA	Antragsteller auf ständige Ausreise (Applicants for permanent exit)
BdL	Büro der Leitung (office of the district leadership)
BV	Bezirks Verwaltung (district administration)
DE	Dienst einheit (service unit)
ELLKM	Evangelical Lutheran Landes Kirche Mecklenburg (Mecklenburg Land Church)
FIM	Führungs IM (leading IM)
GMS	Gesellschaftlicher Mitarbeiter für Sicherheit (social colleague for security)
GVS	Geheimverschlussache (secret matter)
IKM	Inoffizielle Kriminalpolizeilicher Arbeiter (unofficial criminal police colleague)
IM	Inoffizieller Mitarbeiter (unofficial colleague or informer)
IMB	Inoffizieller Mitarbeiter in unmittelbare Bearbeitung (IM in immediate assignment)
IME	Inoffizieller Mitarbeiter für einen besonderen Einsatz (IM for special assignment)
KD	Kreisdienststellen (county unit)
MA	Mitarbeiter (colleague)
MV	Mitgliedversammlung (membership meeting)
OG	Operativgruppe (operative group)
OibE	Offizier im besonderen Einsatz (Officer in Special Assignment)
OPK	Operative personen Kontrolle (operation about a person)
OV	Operativer Vorgänge (operational proceedings)
PID	Politisch-ideologische Diversion (political-ideological diversion)
PUT	Politische Untergrund Tätigkeit (political underground activity)
ZAIG	Zentrale Auswertungs & Informationsgruppe (Central Evaluation and Information Group)

All the italicizing for emphasis is that of the MfS.

Because the SED was the only party that mattered, it is referred to as the Party.

Since in the DDR the economic units were public, one can't refer to them as corporations or businesses. The word *Betrieb*, as in *Volkseigener Betrieb* (VEB), is translated as people's firm. Chemnitz is used instead of Karl Marx Stadt, the name used only during the DDR.

For simplicity's sake, dates in note citations are given using single digits (for example, 1.1.9 is used to indicate 1 January 1989). In rare references to the previous or following decade, a two-digit number is used for the year (for example, 77 for 1977 and 90 for 1990).

NOTES

1. Wolfgang-Uwe Friedrich, *Die totalitäre Herrschaft der SED: Wirklichkeit und Nachwirkungen* (München: Beck, 1998), pp. 136–37.

2. Edward Peterson, *Russian Commands and German Resistance* (New York: Peter Lang, 1999).

The Secret Police
and the Revolution

Chapter 1

The Dark Clouds Forming: 1953–1979

THE PROBLEM-FILLED STRUCTURE

Problems Imposed by the USSR

In 1949, when the Western Occupation permitted the German Federal Republic (BRD) its basic independence, Soviet leader Joseph Stalin responded by permitting a measure of autonomy to his German Democratic Republic (DDR), so declared in October 1949. By a more recent interpretation, German Communists, like Walter Ulbricht, pulled Stalin into a grudging decision to create it.[1]

There is substantial evidence that Moscow was never in full control of its Karlshorst headquarters, much less the some 17 million Germans whom the Cold War left under Communism.[2] Secret Police internal reports conceded that the East Germans remained largely unpersuaded of the Soviet style of Communism or the Russian style of living. Most Germans, although required to speak of the Soviets as "friends," considered them primitive, parasitical and latently violent oppressors.[3] (The much-oppressed individual soldiers were often pitied.)

This negative view was entrenched by the million-fold violence in 1945 to property and persons, primarily to women, and it continued with the billion-fold booty and reparations that had been shipped East. Soviet soldiers prevented revolt until 1989, but for those 44 years they were segregated from the population in order to reduce dangerous Russian action to Germans and dangerous German ideas to Russians. Soldier excursions were only in supervised groups. Officers were permitted contact, but if they had love affairs, they were quickly sent home.

Service in Germany was relatively pleasant for officers, who received 800–1,000 marks monthly, plus 150–250 marks for their families. With many more consumer goods available in German stores, families could accumulate substantial clothing and household goods.[4] Their purchases brought housewifely conflict when Germans experienced the shortages that seemed endemic in Russia. The general perception became ever more certain that to be in the Soviet camp was much more costly than it was for the BRD to be in the American camp.

Stalin had created a rule by the Communist Party, rechristened the Socialist Unity Party (SED), and had the apparent slavish loyalty of its leaders, especially the Moscow-trained Ulbricht. It is now evident that Moscow did not consider them obedient enough, that even their handpicked Communists behaved unreasonably German.

In early 1953 the Soviet Communist Party scolded the SED for the mass flight of its citizens through the open streets to West Berlin. The Soviet Secret Police said that 84,034 had fled by the end of March, but later research raised that number to 120,000. The Soviets thought that Ulbricht had pushed Communism too fast and had gone too far with collectivization. He had ruined too many artisans and small businesses, so that important groups had become more opposed to SED power.[5]

The Soviets blamed the desertion from the armed forces "on the low state of political work among them, but it is also due to a failure to provide personnel with adequate food and clothing. The Central Committee of the SED and the responsible state organs do not conduct a sufficiently active fight against the demoralizing work carried out by the West German authorities."[6]

After Stalin's death in March 1953, Moscow found itself in turmoil, including a bitter fight between its Secret Police (MVD), led by Lavrenti Beria, and its Party, led by Nikita Khrushchev. As part of this power struggle, Beria reduced his foreign intelligence service, recalling many from East Germany, soon considered a counterintelligence disaster; 1,700 of 2,800 officers were transferred, recalled or dismissed just prior to the Berlin uprising of 17 June.[7]

The speculation has been advanced that Beria was planning to reverse the policy of the two Germanies and to permit unification. Whatever Beria's policy about the need to reach a compromise with the West on a reunited Germany, his supposed power was limited. "The headstrong Beria ignored the obvious fact that the Soviet military would vigorously resist any experimentation that could jeopardize its hold on this piece of German territory, which represented sacrifices made during and since the war; and he should have understood the extent to which the Soviet intelligence services valued their stake in Germany as a base for foreign operations." In spite of his knowing how the Soviet power game was played, "he behaved in a reckless and naive manner," meaning that he should have known the extent to which the SED regime was disliked by East Germans.

Despite his murderous image, Beria seems to have naively believed that he could succeed Stalin by his control of the security forces. He underestimated the ability of the Party to protect its power. "He should have anticipated that his opponents had been hard at work planting their cronies in the system and for that matter in the armed forces. By attempting to rid the MVD of his enemies and build a brand-new service, he made it nearly impossible for the MVD and its German friends to cope with the June explosion that his political machinations had set in motion."[8] His mistake meant his quick arrest and execution by Khrushchev's allies, and it also meant the survival of the vulnerable DDR and Ulbricht.

Although the DDR line denied the reality of a serious revolution in June 1953, recent revelations suggest that it could have meant its collapse. Some 500,000 resisters participated in a nationwide strike, which involved almost 600 factories and 373 cities and villages, especially in Sachsen and Thüringen. Rebels in Görlitz stormed police headquarters and prisons, leading to "a complete collapse of the local structures." The rebels occupied 140 government buildings, including some of the Secret Police (MfS), opening nine jails and releasing about 1,300 prisoners. Martial law was imposed in 167 of 217 districts and counties; 6,000 demonstrators were arrested, and almost 100 were killed, among them 40 Soviet soldiers who refused to follow orders. The regime did not use its militarized police battalions, which were not sufficiently trusted, as a series of its officers and troops refused the command to move against the workers.[9]

Although Ulbricht has seemed the model of a Soviet robot, Russian suspicions of his being too independent could easily have caused his early downfall. The Soviets agreed with veteran Communists Wilhelm Zaisser and Rudolph Herrnstadt that Ulbricht, by going too fast, had created the uprising. On 7 July, in the DDR Politbüro, nine voted against Ulbricht; Erich Honecker and one other were for him.[10]

To Ulbricht's advantage, Moscow feared further trouble, and he played on this fear in July, when he flew to Moscow and got their crucial support. The Soviets did not want to show weakness to the German population, so on 20 July, longtime emissary V. Semenov told Herrnstadt that Moscow had decided to stick with Ulbricht. Among other punishments, Zaisser lost control of the MfS.

Many workers had been unhappy enough to act, but few intellectuals had. Because they accepted the propaganda that the DDR was antifascist and therefore sacred, 1953 represented a time of distance between intellectuals and workers. No debate preceded the spontaneous uprising, so it had neither program nor leaders.[11]

In 1956 there was an intellectual resonance in the DDR to the Khrushchev secret attack on Stalin and the resulting disturbances in the Soviet

Empire in Poland and Hungary. Ulbricht had alienated many medical and veterinarian students, plus young economists at Humboldt University. In the summer, Wolfgang Harich led an effort to democratize the state and to end the Secret Police. He seemed like Wladyslaw Gomulka in Poland and Imre Nagy in Hungary, but he had nothing of their support, only a faith in Moscow.

As a result of the collectivization campaign, about 40 percent of the wealthier farmers had fled, and 500,00 hectares lay fallow. In the spring severe food shortages combined with punitive taxation and decline in consumer goods.[12] Karl Schirdewan and Erich Wollweber (new head of the MfS) attacked Ulbricht for his incompetence. Famed dramatist Bertold Brecht denounced him as a dictator, alienated from the people. Again a power struggle in Moscow worked to Ulbricht's advantage. Despite Khrushchev's de-Stalinization, events in Budapest made him stay with Ulbricht. The young Erich Honecker delivered the indicting speech that led to Harich's 10-year sentence.[13]

Also, Ulbricht's reforms had been designed to turn workers against intellectuals. The work norms had been quickly moderated, and throughout the 1950s, almost everywhere, wages rose faster than productivity. As elsewhere in Communism, wage egalitarianism became a social norm. An implicit social contract restricted room for maneuvering in these supposedly totalitarian regimes, wherein East Germans had the highest rate of absenteeism in Eastern Europe and had the easiest flight into West Germany. Historian Jeffrey Kopstein observed, "The power of the totalitarian state to shape a new moral economy was extremely limited."[14]

The DDR suffered the most because the BRD's economic miracle of the 1950s was widening the gap in living standards, and Berlin remained an open city for "fleeing the Republic." Two million citizens fled in the 10 years before the Wall was built. In July 1961, Ulbricht told Khrushchev that he was forced to compete with the BRD and could not do it, because many more workers would leave.[15] Continuing an open border would bring the collapse of the DDR.[16]

A few days later Khrushchev said to go ahead with the Wall but to keep the preparations secret. That compelling symbol of the DDR as prison was begun, early Sunday, 13 August. Khrushchev admitted to BRD Ambassador Hans Kroll: "I know the wall is an ugly thing. One day it will be gone. Any other solution could have led to war with the U.S."[17]

With productive and ambitious citizens no longer able to leave, production increased the standard of living, faster than that of Russia. After Khrushchev was pushed out in 1964 by a conservative Brezhnev, Ulbricht adjusted again to Moscow but continued his "progressive" policy. Brezhnev visited Ulbricht secretly in October 1964 and complained bitterly that the DDR had become too caught up in its own economic affairs and was neglecting the Soviet Union, which had already cut exports. In 1963 certain types of steel, cotton, grain and meat were reduced by 25 to 35 percent. The Soviet Union had experienced a severe crisis, a bad harvest and food riots, and DDR imports further declined in 1965.[18] After Brezhnev lamented that the DDR was still not doing enough for the USSR, the USSR sent much less in trade than the DDR continued to send.

The further problem was that the DDR was to have links only to the inferior economies of Eastern Europe, the COMECON.[19] It had been pushed into specializing in shipbuilding, railroads and heavy machinery, for which it lacked the metallurgical basis and for which it could not get the necessary technology from the Soviet bloc.[20] Within these limitations, the DDR leaders were given far more autonomy than indicated in the conventional histories of the period. Ulbricht's economic reform appeared and disappeared not only because Moscow wanted it that way but because so did the East German elite.[21]

Further, Ulbricht irritated Moscow by constantly referring to his own more efficient system. Russian per capita production could not come close to East German production, and its draining off the German surplus was resisted and restrained. Ulbricht's misfortune was that his production did not grow as much as planned, and the economy developed serious disproportions between capital and consumer production. When in 1965 he could not get the needed raw materials and grain from the USSR, he initiated his own economic miracle by increasing investment faster than increasing the national income. The DDR would thus move further ahead and away from the always praised Soviet mentor.

The Ulbricht plan required a measure of cooperation with the richer capitalist BRD, which was fortuitously enabled by SPD chancellor Willy Brandt and his *Ostpolitik* to improve relations with the Communist East. In 1969 the perennial Soviet fear grew that Ulbricht was getting too close to the BRD. Brezhnev opposed this, but Ulbricht persisted. Despite their public displays of affection, sometimes to the level of public kisses, in 1969 Soviet Marshall Andrei Gretschko, commented, "The old one isn't worth much any more."[22] Moscow could shift to an Ulbricht supporter-turned-rival (Honecker) to regain a more compliant Berlin, for which the DDR paid a heavy price.

Economic Limits from the Soviet Union

Economic manager Günter Mittag blamed his massive problems on the Russians: "We were given by the Soviets the principles of the economy. We tried to modify them, in contradiction to the Soviets, but it did not suffice to create an efficient planned economy fitting to the highly industrialized DDR." Mittag calculated that the DDR had paid 727 billion marks in reparations, including 676 firms taken from East Germany, mostly in 1945–1946. Further, the DDR had to create two different export industries, one for the backward East and the other for the advanced West. (The USSR had primitively paid for complex machinery on the basis of weight.)[23]

Mittag lamented a crippling dependence: "It was clear that the DDR would not live without the help of the USSR, but because of its own problems, the [Soviet] tendency was to get from the DDR as much as it could. The real problem to them was that DDR living standards from the beginning were higher than the USSR. This had led to the dismantlings and delivering of what the Soviet Union needed."

The result was also an interdependent warping: "Our industrial structure was completely tailored to the needs of the USSR: shipbuilding, railroad cars, cranes. Some firms sent 80 percent of their production to the USSR, with pressure for more every year. The further demand was that the DDR must help to build the pipeline, so we did, leaving not enough saving for investment. Since 50 percent of industry was directed toward the USSR, not enough was left for trade with the West and Japan, so we had to sell whatever was possible. Thus we could not keep up, we could only try to keep up in some areas, like electronics."[24]

The Cold War also undermined the DDR economy. Already in 1953 the great pressure began for a military buildup, lasting into the early 1980s, when new investments went for missiles; 50 percent of the funds for highway construction went to build military airfields.[25]

Ulbricht's Internal Economic Problems

Although Mittag could blame Moscow, he was the man in Berlin who came to be blamed the most for the collapse of the DDR. Son of a Stettin worker, he had joined the Reichbahn and quickly worked his way up. When only 27, he was head of the Central Committee's (ZK) railroad department.

For almost three decades, this ambitious planner acted the master. He did not discuss, but merely gave orders and made it difficult to disagree. The system succeeded in organizing postwar reconstruction and modest growth but failed miserably in accomplishing the transition to high technology, which was revolutionizing the capitalist world. In the late 1950s, under Ulbricht's New Course, a tactical maneuver, conditions improved, but his drive for more DDR earnings did not lead to the hoped-for increase in efficiency and easing of the market. Rather, it heated up the struggle over dividing the scarce resources.[26]

The greatest internal barrier to improving consumption was the low national productivity. From its beginning with Marx, socialists had to concede the superior productivity of capitalism, but they had long dreamed of replacing the cruelty and uncertainty of the market with the justice and the security of "the Plan." Stalin had turned this vision into a method of a pressured industrial development and vast personal political power.

The Stalinist state therewith assumed full responsibility for the economy but could not properly reform it because that would have meant a loss of Party power. The government was absorbed by the economic problems and was constantly overextended. "The power proved to be a terrible burden." It was forced to motivate the people to work, and, lacking sufficient production, it could do little more than agitate. In Soviet parlance, the "subjective" (idealistic motivation) must dominate the "objective" (material realities and rewards).

The DDR's moving ahead was more of a miracle than the BRD, because it was forced to rely so heavily on practical intelligence from below. The necessary ingenuity included resorting to the black or the gray market. People necessarily developed a keen intelligence in working around the systemic shortages. It was not so much what you knew but whom you knew and how you used them. "Socialism without connections is like capitalism without money."[27]

Ulbricht's "New Economic System" (NES), begun in 1963, had elements of profit and rentability, reform of the price system, reduction of the subsidies and greater autonomy of the firms. It mandated an industrial price reform, the use of profit as the primary production indicator and revitalization of horizontal relations, "a system of economic levers." In short, there came a reworking of the ways in which enterprises were evaluated. As Soviet economist Evsei G. Lieberman had proposed, the DDR tried to repair the system through administrative and economic incentives.[28]

Besides its inner contradictions and diffuse concepts, the NES confronted two great opposition forces: the Party bureaucracy, because it would reduce the power of Party and its state, and the USSR, because it meant closer contact to the West to obtain the necessary new technology. The idea was to move ahead by using both Western technology and cheaper Soviet raw materials. The USSR soon showed itself unwilling and/or unable to provide more and cheaper materials, but the DDR was not permitted to get those materials from the West.[29]

The internal bureaucratic opposition that Ulbricht faced during the first years did not prevent him from modifying policies, and most of his measures were implemented. Many enterprises had become more independent, but this did not mean their success. "The primary goal of reform was to overcome the yearly plan mentality that neglected long range structural changes in technologies and production processes." But they did not manage to overcome the short-term perspective of plan fulfillment. "It bogged down in . . . bureaucratic infighting."[30]

At the top a vigorous controversy developed between Ulbricht and Erich Apel, who was leading the economic reforms. Its background was the unexpectedly low level of deliveries of raw materials from Russia. As Jeffrey Kopstein diagnosed the problem, the DDR's *Perspektivplan* quickly devolved into a series of never-ending planning rounds between the center and the productive units. "The planning organs felt at sea, as they had no way of assuring that the final plan would be balanced." By July 1965 the danger of serious disproportion in the long-range plan became so clear that Ulbricht held a special two-day Politbüro session, the essence of which was to show that the goals would not be met. "The reform had indeed decentralized planning and increased the potential independence of enterprises. Yet managers still played the well-established game of ensuring plan fulfillment by lobbying for more and more capital investment." Large firms with clout still got huge subsidies.[31]

Ulbricht had placed the burden of forced savings on the ordinary people in the form of higher prices for public transportation, goods and accommodations.[32] But he made the Planning Commission the scapegoat for the miserable failure (*Misere*). After Apel was found shot, in December 1965, Mittag's centralization was reinstalled.[33] At the 7th Party Congress in April 1967, the application of this New Economic System was dropped in favor of the "Economic System of Socialism." The planning organs and the ministries would step in and give special access to supplies and labor. These "structure-determining" projects initially received wide support among all groups in the economic elite, but easy access to supplies proved to be too strong a temptation to the ministries.

Ulbricht and Mittag's thinking in structural policy that summer was straightforward. Pouring much capital into selected projects, they hoped to catch up with the West. In chemicals, machine building and electronics, a selective great leap forward was to bring higher living standards than in the West. Ironically, a new force of central direction emerged. Enterprises found themselves increasingly obliged to fulfill centrally handed-down orders, while their formal freedoms became ever emptier for lack of resources or time to meet normal contract obligations.

Ulbricht's plan was little more than what the Polish government had tried: massive borrowing from the West with the promise of repayment from the profits earned. By 1969 Ulbricht had grown reckless, and shortages in consumer goods and the energy sector quickly led to mass discontent, evidenced in monthly MfS reports from the various districts.[34]

Together with the "Prague Spring" warning against permitting social democracy, this meant the end of reform experiments, formally on 8 September 1970. The blame was placed on "disproportions in incomplete planning."[35]

The Politbüro meetings were long and raucous, with objections raised by Honecker, Stoph and Neumann. The 14th SED plenum in December 1970 provided a dramatic public forum for criticism of Ulbricht's economic policy. Neumann honestly admitted: "Everything is disorganized. . . . This has not been completely planned and balanced. . . . The economic organs are working according to the principle of economic accounting and not according to state and national economic standards." Thus was laid the groundwork for recentralization.[36]

Ulbricht's Overthrow by Brezhnev and Honecker

Erich Honecker, a member of the KPD (Communist Party of Germany) from the Saarland, had climbed near the top, as Egon Krenz would 20 years later, by becoming the closest supporter of the man whom he would replace. He had shown loyalty at key moments, like helping against the opposition in 1956. Ulbricht thus trusted him with the Secretariat and the security realm.

Politbüro member Günter Schabowski wrote that Honecker was not well regarded in the SED. He was seen as a youth leader, wearing the blue shirt of the Free German Youth (FDJ), delivering his monotonous speeches in a high voice. He seemed colorless. "We terribly wanted someone who would make the DDR look good." Otto Grotewohl, Ulbricht's nominal peer, had described Honecker's "very limited ability to develop." Mielke had denounced him to the Soviet Secret Police chief Yuri Andropov. The anti-Honecker group usually had Willi Stoph, the Minister of Defense, in mind.

Yet when it came to a power struggle, Communist-style, Honecker proved himself the more expert. Schabowski admitted, "We were mistaken, behind the scenes he had been working, very much goal-oriented on establishing his power. He had his concept and knew how to get people to commit themselves to him just as had earlier the Ulbricht crew." Schabowski conceded that Honecker was not a cynic but believed he was right. He had stayed away from the economy, but by 1970 he involved himself, at first behind the scenes. With Ulbricht's supply crisis, he saw his chance. Schabowski added, "Atheists needed a cult figure."[37]

The Soviets acknowledged that they were fed up with Ulbricht's dream of overtaking the West while simultaneously accumulating a debt to it. Brezhnev resented Ulbricht not only because the old man held up his country as a model but also because he suspected that Ulbricht was prepared to sacrifice relations with the Soviet Union in order to settle the German question. Brezhnev told Honecker that the Soviet Politbüro would like to see him removed from office. With the Soviets dissatisfied and the SED provincial and district leadership fearful that the economy was headed for the rocks, Ulbricht's rivals felt secure in preparing his ouster.

In Moscow and East Berlin the hostile forces organized, finding wider DDR support. As Kopstein crystallized it: "Those opposed to the reform for practical reasons could now find common ground with those opposed to it for principled ones. Bureaucratism became political opposition."[38]

In July 1970 Brezhnev again expressed his dissatisfaction with Ulbricht's independent ways. Honecker expressed the fear that Ulbricht would make Mittag his successor. (The irony is that Mittag became Honecker's closest aide.) Brezhnev said that since the DDR had been won with Soviet blood, it was also its affair, and there must not be a process of approaching the BRD. Instead, the ravine between the DDR and BRD was to be made even deeper.[39] Honecker got Brezhnev's support, also by promising that he would be less arrogant toward the other socialist countries.[40] (Another irony to be.)

When in August 1970 Ulbrecht boasted to Brezhnev that the DDR would catch up with the United States in technology, this was also an arrogance that the DDR would be even further ahead of the USSR. As though he wanted to reinforce the Soviet opposition, he described his cooperation with Willy Brandt. "If we do not take maximum advantage of the opportunity of having a social democratic government in Bonn, the people would not forgive us, nor would the Russian people." Then, when he said that he would create a true German state ("We are not Belorus. We are not a Soviet State"), he had sealed his fate.[41]

On 8 September the Politbüro, in the absence of Ulbricht, discussed the fact that between March 1968 and September 1969 the Planning Commission had invested 30 billion marks, which increased the problems of supplying private consumers. They modified the economic policy closer to the Soviet pattern. Honecker, having the support of 13 of the 20 members and candidates, then argued that Ulbricht had violated the September decision, endangering relations to the USSR, which on 21 October warned Ulbricht against more cooperation with Brandt.[42] When Ulbricht appealed for more help with resources, the cool Soviet answer was: "Our production will not enable more help." This represented both Soviet political strength and Soviet economic weakness.[43]

At the 8th Party Congress, Honecker presented a credible domestic and foreign program.[44] Honecker ally Werner Lamberz got Brezhnev's final approval for the coup on 1 May 1971 on a secret flight on a Soviet military airplane, when supposedly giving a speech. Honecker worked out every detail with Brezhnev; then when Ulbricht was ill and absent for months at Döllnsee, he called the DDR Politbüro together.[45] A few weeks later Brezhnev told Ulbricht of the discontent in the Politbüro, and doctors kept him in the hospital. He tried to fight back but was permitted very limited activity, for which he had to accept Politbüro terms.[46] Mielke used trusted agents to control Ulbricht during the takeover and was promoted to general.[47]

Honecker rewarded his people by moving them into the Politbüro: Lamberz in 1971, Mielke, Werner Krolikowski, Harry Tisch, Gerhard Schürer, Werner Felfe, Joachim Herrmann, Inge Lange, Konrad Naumann and Heinz Hoffmann in 1973, then Egon Krenz and Horst Dohlus in 1976, when he also restored Mittag and Stoph.[48]

Stefan Bollinger observed that under Honecker the Central Committee lost its character of discussion.[49] Typically, at a Politbüro meeting the men arrived promptly (most were there a half hour before the beginning of the meeting). Each tried to discover the mood of the day from Honecker on his way to the room in hopes of winning some allies. One minute before 10:00 A.M. the general secretary entered the room. Everyone stood up and then sat down only after Honecker was seated. The office manager read the minutes of the last meeting and on Honecker's instruction took up each point of the agenda, for which the invited guests and experts were called in one after the other. To these were addressed the shortest questions. As Schabowski reported, "It was very much like the atmosphere of a classroom, tiring and boring"[50]—a fatal flaw in 1989.

Honecker moved to a new formula that sought to establish a separate DDR identity on the foundation of a different, richer socialist lifestyle.[51] Yet another irony is that this man from the Saarland would be irresistibly pulled to the rich BRD brother, because this was necessary for any DDR economic advance. By 1980 most of those who had helped Honecker were worried about this adventurous policy away from Moscow. Stoph and Mielke expressed fear of his reliance on Western capitalism. Stoph also called for sharp cuts in social programs, but Honecker, having more allies, blocked them.[52]

Honecker thus settled on a socialism of comfort. Such a strategy seemed viable as long as the regime could live off the accumulated investments from the Ulbricht era and be kept afloat by Soviet cooperation and easy terms on international capital markets. The revolutionary changes in commodity prices and terms of trade during the 1970s rendered such a strategy dangerous.[53]

How Honecker Multiplied the Problems

Honecker inherited an intact economy, although not one to compare with that of the BRD.[54] In 1971, with the basic reconstruction from the war accomplished, he began his policy of socialist welfare. He promised an end to the emphasis on heavy industry and shifted the priority to consumption and social services under the slogan, "The unity of economic and social policy." If it were impossible to compete with the BRD in economic power, the DDR could claim to be the better "social-state." The reason for the existence of a second German state would be that it was fundamentally different from West Germany; the poor, not the rich, would get richer.

Thus, in contrast to Ulbricht's investment at the expense of consumption, Honecker aimed to increase consumption. Cynically put, the people were to be bribed to keep them loyal. In June 1971 one of Honecker's first acts was to import food and clothing.[55]

Mittag realized that the social improvement by the state would mean more Demand (consumption) but not more Supply (production), and, in fact, the Honecker policy quickly meant that people consumed more than they produced. The appeal to the citizens to tighten their belts was impossible from the beginning because of the limits of the system's power.[56] The policy could have survived only if technology had excelled, but cut off from the West, it was falling ever further behind.

Initially, this Communist Keynesianism spurred some growth, but social spending that used more than it was producing created a growing gap between limited means and unlimited aspirations. Honecker also changed from the "Achievement Principle" (*Leistungsprinzip*) to the "Social Principle," the emphasis on satisfying people's needs.

The Ulbricht investment had not been in apartment construction but, rather, an emphasis on repair. Honecker's highest priority of housing meant that prefabricated, standardized, newly built (*Neubau*) apartments sprang up like mushrooms.[57] They could be mass-produced and centrally controlled, but they seemed deadly monotonous and ill built, as in Russia, where this style of cheap construction had begun by 1960.

From 1973, massive housing construction increased every year to 1989. "Whereas throughout the 1950s and 1960s, lower levels of housing construction added to the overall housing stock, during the 1970s and 1980s, the marginal return on this investment declined precipitously." The new suburban additions were canceled out by the decay of the old inner city. This increasingly obvious misery of the old city added to the opposition.

A housing brigade's achievement more often reflected the local director's access to concrete and other materials. Even when workers' poor performance could be documented, managers were hesitant to lose scarce labor, so evaluation of the work was subject to a leveling. As good bureaucrats, clever county Party secretaries knew how to manipulate the rules to undertake projects that were formally prohibited by the center, but the locals did not have the power to reverse completely the effects of central policy.[58]

To assure popularity, Honecker rolled back rents and introduced day care, child support and maternity leave. The 8-billion-mark subsidies in 1970 rose in 1988 to 53 billion. When Schürer's planning commission in January 1972 said that the DDR could not afford so ambitious a welfare program, he was attacked by Honecker allies.[59]

The Honecker team dismantled the Ulbricht edifice of technocracy in a deliberate recentralization. Enterprises lost their right to accumulate capital for investment, and the procedures for securing credit were (formally) tightened and recentralized, as were prices.

To enable this central control, business was further centralized into giant combines. In 1971 East German private and semiprivate enterprises still employed 470,000 people, accounting for 11.3 percent of production. A secret export weapon had been their highly flexible ability to produce specialty machines and consumer goods on short order. To the extent that DDR industry remained internationally competitive at all, it had been due, in large measure, to the goods produced in this sector.[60]

Honecker quickly sacrificed the export and the public's needs by taking control of the small private firms and artisans.[61] Mittag eliminated 10,000 medium-sized firms, merging them into the conglomerates of similar factories (*Kombinate*). Since all shoe factories, for example, were combined, the reason to compete was reduced to a minimum. These had been very often led by the former owners or managers, which had meant they were more productive. Therewith would disappear from the market "the 1001 things," the myriad of items that central planners could not imagine in their plans and that would be increasingly missed. The flexible individual processing according to the wish of the consumer also largely disappeared, except for those with connections.[62]

The planners tried to control 167 centralized combines and 90 district combines; a combine had as many as 100,000 employees, as few as 2,500. The model combines, like Zeiss in Jena, shipbuilding in Rostock, and clocks in Ruhla, were copied, but, because the facsimile was not natural but ordered from above, the new combines did not function as well. It was soon clear that many combines had been put together wrong; many were composed of scattered small firms, and many measures of integration remained on paper.[63]

Creating "combines" appeared to render the planning system more manageable in the short run but could not forestall the decay of the capital stock, the increasing indebtedness, decreasing competitiveness and falling living standards. They pushed through wage increases for several classes of workers, but that could not cure shortages.[64] Kopstein observed that the technocratic thinking of the Communist 1960s had moved away from the shop floor technocracy of the 1950s. Such a shift had the logic of confronting working-class resistance.

With Mittag came the search for new approaches to information processing and production forecasting, such as cybernetics and Western organization and production theory. He worked hard to implement Honecker's unity of economy and social policy but claimed to have known that it would lead to disaster sooner or later. After three years he was replaced by Werner Krolikowki when, in 1973, Honecker pushed him into the less important job as deputy minister president.[65]

Honecker's early 1970s was the DDR's best time; there were more consumer goods as the DDR imported large quantities of Western products, but the indebtedness to the West during the second half of the 1970s increased by more than 20 percent a year from 1975–1980. Enterprises continued to hoard labor and materials and seek less demanding plans. Plan fulfillment continued to be frustrated by shortages, often small amounts of critical supplies.

Krolikowski's secret report in 1973 showed the disproportion between consumption and investment. Honecker said to destroy every copy and pushed him aside. Already the Politbüro was indulging in an ostrich policy toward the economy. Subjectivism, the Soviet principle that motivation could be achieved by propaganda, remained more important than the objective reality. There was to be an increase of 4 percent in the people's income, so Honecker blithely assured, "We'll promise workers 4 percent and they will work harder."[66]

The hope was that the increased production would cover the costs, but many necessities to increase production were lacking. Consumption went up but, contrary to the plan, debts also went up while investment went down. Honecker prevented price reform, reduction of subventions and the increase in the firms' autonomy. In the spring of 1974 the USSR informed the DDR of its dramatic price increases, which, though modified through high-level negotiation, added to pressures on prices.[67]

The evidence confirms similar observations in the USSR that the local Party organs played an active role in procurement of supplies but little evidence that Party intervention added to the Plan's rationality or effectiveness.[68] "The planners didn't learn but kept up the ritual of a big man helping out the little boys." The decisions about where to invest were very important, but local officials had little power to attract and less power to resist.[69]

Notwithstanding the various campaigns, the district and county Party leaders seem to have had very little success in their struggles with enterprises in the provinces. "In the fascinating politics of central versus local authority, the three player game, between branch industries, local authorities and the population was perhaps the most important cleavage in Communist society."[70]

To reconcile contradictory orders and permanent shortages, individual companies were forced to become self-sufficient and produce everything that they needed. Such autarky led to the firms' hoarding raw materials and to bartering between firms. Since there were no local taxes to support an infrastructure, the factories had the further need to provide child care, sports facilities, cultural entertainment and vacation resorts.

Managers developed a production mentality that neglected not only competitive use of technology but the competitive drive to higher quality and lower cost. "Since rewards were based on apparent fulfillment of plans rather than on sales, it was a wonder that anything worthwhile was produced at all."[71]

In 1976 Mittag was recalled to keep the system running somehow. He resorted to an extreme personal centralization and placed his agents in the firms so that the firm managers could scarcely resist. Because the oil price shock and the arms race made international borrowing difficult, he also stressed technological innovations, relying on special access to the leader. To attempt to bring the DDR into the computer revolution, he selected 12 firms for the development of electronic equipment, their contracts ranging from 4 million to 135 million marks. The helpful MfS got 10 million DM to develop its electronic equipment.

Mittag assumed extra powers to solve the special tasks assigned him, for example, the infamous "KoKo" (*Kommerzielle Koordinierung*), meaning secret selling of whatever to whomever. He used it from 1977 to make whatever deals possible to paper over the money gaps. It was entrusted to the mysterious Alexander Schalck-Golodowski, who was later accused of gigantic corruption. One problem was that some of his foreign deals were contrary to DDR law; foreign firms, including Toshiba, had been taken to court. If what they were doing was made public, it would lead to an "extraordinarily high foreign political and financial damage to the DDR and danger to the security of a number of persons." Therefore, it must be kept quiet, and who better for that than the MfS?[72]

Mittag seemed to be the closest thing to a Honecker friend, but he could never persuade him to change policy and blamed him for a blindness to the economic reality that he was trying to explain. Fellow economic expert Gerhard Schürer also warned Honecker early about coming trouble but had even less chance to persuade him.

As the economy became more imbalanced, its precariousness should have been discussed at the top, but it was not. Honecker's Politbüro was like a royal court: no criticism allowed, only harmony and rosy colors.[73] Politbüro members at meetings just reported on their spheres, so there was no real discussion, and they rarely met outside the formal meetings, although they lived as neighbors.[74] When in 1977 Schürer again sounded the alarm that the DDR debts were held by many banks that were not willing to delay payment, Honecker was able to keep the topic off the Politbüro agenda.

When reality failed to live up to the Plan, Mittag used indoctrination and censorship to maintain the appearance of success. His power was also that he controlled the flow of information. Mittag's assistant, Carl Janson, blamed him for worsening the economy, although conceding that Mittag's massive problems had begun with reparations, the lack of raw materials except for potash and brown coal, the loss of qualified workers to the West, his being blocked from the advances being made in the West and the chronic DDR shortage of capital. Because he had cut his officials out of the decision making, Mittag's planning led to disaster. The worse the situation became, the more he concentrated information and decisions only to himself.[75]

In late 1978 Schürer and Mittag told Honecker that the DDR already had problems taking care of the interest on the foreign debt. Mielke was assigned the task of assisting Mittag's work, not only to keep the problem secret. Secret Police were sent in to push the economy and in selected areas even to push technology. After these first panicky meetings, the next year a similar alarm came from the Party apparatus, also without effect.[76]

The results (1976–1980) were catastrophic, the trade deficits the highest in DDR history. Instead of the planned reduction of the debt, it continued to mount. Innovations in COMECON failed due to the foreign debts and the Polish crisis. Instead of using imports to stimulate modernizing, more than a third of the imports were in the form of grain provided from the United States. The slender domestic investment funds were exhausted by the shift to brown coal and the 14 billion marks stuffed into microelectronics.[77] The system was designed to avoid confronting realities, but those at the sheltered top could have been the most ignorant.

Stefan Wolle suggested that the famous deceiver of Catherine the Great, Prince Potemkin, would have been the appropriate national saint of the DDR. The streets of East Berlin through which Honecker's auto cavalcade drove each day were not only watched most intensively but better provided than elsewhere, including better painting of the facade, especially what could be seen from his car windows. "So the General Secretary spread miracles and good deeds, wherever he wandered." It may always be a secret whether he was ever curious what the world outside that habitual route looked like, but he never asked to turn into a side street or come unannounced and spend 15 minutes in a corner bar. "The stiff Byzantian ritual left no room for side trips, although it would have given the old man perhaps a small piece of the people's love for which he yearned."[78]

The calcification of the system went almost unnoticed. "Those in the East fell happily for the policy of distributing bonbons and those in the West wanted stability above all else."[79] Those at the bottom would be offered some amusement.

The Social Repression Reduced

Honecker softened the regime and reduced the politically sensitive sphere in which conformity was enforced. He moderated the repression of the young and lightened up in little things like the grimness of the newspapers. He tolerated long hair, blue jeans, rock music and Western TV. He allowed more citizens, including some SED members, to visit relatives in the BRD.

There was even hope for a new Prague-like Spring or, for most conformists, a better life, and for intellectuals, "a small park to play in." Tolerated were quite a few clubs in Berlin, which indulged in much discussion.[80] As for the FDJ celebrations: "The young people differed little, other than for their obligatory blue shirts, from their contemporaries in the west. That they provided the scenery of a political production they accepted as part of the deal."[81]

Wolle described Honecker as "The man of little compromises, the master of the quiet retreat and of 'just pretend' " (*So tun als ob*). Western TV was not directly forbidden, not directly allowed. "Behind the foggy curtain of mini-liberalising, which carried few risks and brought much approval, he took a regressive course. He was the man of the MfS and his accession brought the culmination of the rise of Erich Mielke to top level of power."[82]

Honecker's real interest and skills were in personnel politics, for which purpose he stayed close to the MfS. As soon as Mielke left a Politbüro meeting, the telephone rang for his assistant Hermann, who was given the line for the day.[83] The MfS, having both the Gestapo and the KGB as models, had arguably the best control of any state in the East, but it had the greatest problem, the closeness of the West.

Honecker was also striving for an adherence to the Western norm (or its appearance), which would make the DDR accepted in polite company.[84] To be accepted as a European state, the DDR needed BRD tolerance, which meant that it had to tone down the attack on Bonn and appear to reduce the clash in values, in short, to be more "German." He desired, in particular, to be honored in his Saar homeland.[85]

The resulting treaty with the Brandt government was signed in 1972, with the MfS-planted superspy Günter Guillaume helping the Soviets in their poker game in negotiations lasting six months. The selling of prisoners began in 1969 and reached a high point in August 1974, by which time 265 million marks had been paid by the BRD. The DDR put some criminals, even agents into the deals, and the BRD did not publicize these ransomed prisoners. "One kept silent and paid—50,000 marks per head."[86]

From the beginning of the 1970s, a culture opposition had emerged led by singer Wolf Bierman and Robert Havemann. It was predominantly composed of Marxist-trained young intellectuals who wanted to get some legal maneuvering room in the official culture enterprise. They were encouraged by the Helsinki agreement of 22 November 1972 and by the admission of the DDR to the United Nations (UN) in 1973. That the DDR was being accepted into the family of nations was matched with the fact that it was becoming economically ever more wrapped into the family of Western capitalists.

If "Prussian Communism" had become more regimented than its Russian model, the old German sense of civil society was also increasingly asserting itself. The traditional German values were only partially submerged by their Soviet style-masters. Daily life provided many more hiding places from the regime than the neat organizational schemas implied. Although the Party denounced such behavior as bourgeois consumerism, the people, rather than for the common good, searched continually for personal advantage, for which they were repeatedly stimulated by Western TV.

In August 1972 dissident Oscar Brüsewitz burned himself to death, and in November Bierman was expelled.[87] The exodus of known artists and young intellectuals in the cultural opposition showed that the mid-1970s meant the end of the SED hope that there would be a uniform socialist view, instead of the inclusion of the progressive traditions of German history from the Reformation, through Prussia, to the present. So in the summer of 1979 there was a massive disciplining of writers.[88] The state suppressed the physicist Haveman, who was brought to trial and house arrest.

Masses Vacuumed into Party and Police

The system relied also on mass support by means of organizations, to the extent that every third person had come to be organized. Of 2.2 million SED members, 500,000 had some paid function in the Party, state or economy. Of functionaries, the SED had 691,000; the FDGB (union) had 590,000; the government had 185,000; there were 270,000 propagandists; 133,000 elected representatives at some level, including 50,000 in the MfS; army and police had about 40,000 officers, plus the myriads of Battlegroups *(Kampfgruppen)*, a militia organized in factories, offices and collective farms.

The SED membership profile had stabilized at 37 percent workers, 22 percent intelligentsia, 7.7 percent employees, 4.8 percent farmers; the percentage of intelligentsia had doubled since 1967, and women had risen from 24 to 35 percent. Of these potential cadre, 1.9 million members had been exposed to indoctrination at a Party school for at least three months.[89]

The Soviet way, rule by the Party, meant, in fact, rule by top Party leaders. SED functionaries were forced to an enormous expenditure of time in meetings, which were used only to entrench decisions already made from above. They had then to institute and defend policies on which they had no apparent influence. The insistence on obedience drove out the local ability to deal with a crisis and, to take a personal initiative, much less take a personal risk. The underlings lived with a constant uncertainty because of the high demands for absolute loyalty, in a condition of dependency and guilt, with always an opening for some disciplining from above. That officials were conditioned to wait for orders from above would cripple the local authorities when confronted by the revolution.[90]

Corruption existed at the top, and privileges existed in the middle, and some personal advantages remained for those cadre (leaders) near the bottom.[91] The Party could offer mostly psychological rewards, a fullness of medals, honors and titles, the illusion of having risen into the elite. The privileges were actually modest, much less than the burden of office holding, which included the loss of free time in the many sessions, up to five evenings a month, being shunned by colleagues and denied West contact, which came to mean the loss of West money.

These "cadre" were exposed to limitless demands, their lives supposedly dedicated to service to Party and state. They could at any time be disciplined for sins of omission or commission. They also suffered the fear of sinking back into the working class.[92]

The top leaders could distribute privileges according to loyalty, and there had come to be a limited upward mobility, which had accelerated until the Wall, because so many skilled persons fled and left openings for others to climb into. In principle, everyone could become everything if he or she was presumed to be loyal; the worker's child could gain higher education, but the pastor's (class enemy) child could not. Work was guaranteed unless the person was politically incorrect.

Thus, a loyalty had been created to "the Social State," but the DDR did not adopt Janos Kadar's motto in Hungary: "Who is not against us is with us." Instead, Mielke was assigned the task to crush the slightest opposition; everyone must fear the "Stasi," so the DDR was "a quiet land," thoroughly authoritarian.

By 1980 it had come to trust more to propaganda than to threats, fearing that more public repression would strengthen more private opposition.[93] The other weapon was infiltration with loyal IMs. Partly because the MfS infiltrated opposition groups, which lacked resources and organization, it had little direct access to the masses.

The opposition's two positive elements were motivation and a personal network. A semi-independent church provided a small opening for opposition, providing not so much a pulpit for direct attack as a basement room for quiet meetings. It enabled taking a moral, non-Communist principle, but it avoided affirming political opposition. Church members per se were no more involved than nonmembers in opposition.[94]

The state deliberately manipulated the church, but dissent could crystallize around the issue of peace, which the authorities had difficulty opposing. Young people began to form peace circles and to use the church spaces for discussion and experimentation. The State assumed that church leaders could restrain them, and the MfS targeted churches as its major battleground.

All such political dissent was second in importance to the worsening economy. From 1945 to 1980, the individual by extra efforts and training had a real chance to acquire a richer life. This opportunity was clearly declining in the DDR's last decade.[95]

Thus, Mielke's Secret Police had the heavy double duty of maintaining Honecker's weakening Party control and maintaining Mittag's weakening economy.

THE STASI AS SHIELDING UMBRELLA

Glorified as "the Sword and the Shield of the Republic," the Ministry for State Security (MfS) had its origins in the *Kommissariat 5* (K-5), created on 16 August 1947. It arrested so many "enemies" that concentration camps (KZs) had to be opened or reopened. Not surprisingly, K-5 acquired a reputation as bad as that of Stalin's Secret Police and worse than that of the Gestapo. At least with the Nazis, albeit fanatically racist, their victims did not suddenly disappear into the gulag.

With the MfS officially created on 8 February 1950, the Soviets worked to make its every detail correspond to their system. Appointed was old Communist Wilhelm Zaisser, who had been the imposing "Gomez" in the Spanish civil war and survived the Stalin purging. He had been arrested on his return to Russia but then during the war was put in charge of prisoner of war (POW) reeducation at Krasnogorsk. He came to the zone only in February 1947 to become head of the *Volkspolizei* in Sachsen-Anhalt. Closely linked to the Soviet Secret Police chief, Lavrenti Beria, in 1949, he was chosen to train the new police troops.[96] Erich Mielke, also active in Spain, was made his state secretary and insisted on the Chekist methods of his adored founder of the Soviet Secret Police, Felix Dzerzinsky.[97]

In September 1952 the Soviets inspected the MfS and blasted its serious shortcomings, including its inadequate operational preparation, its poor quality staff, its very slow penetration of the West; it was getting little help from the SED. In March 1953 the Soviets still found it unable to cope, because of inadequate training, lack of experience and weak political preparation. When it was reported as especially inept in placing agents among the intelligentsia, it selected 239 college-educated persons, but those above suspicion were narrowed down to 6.[98] Its failure was evident in the uprising, which might have toppled the regime on 17 June.

That rebellion showed that the DDR had in no way come close to enthusing the public with the idea of socialism and that its SED leaders had no instrument to deal with demonstrations and disorder. It had no soldiers, and the leaders knew that the many varieties of police, including some who resembled an army, were not a reliable support to the regime. Thousands deserted, made easy by the open city of Berlin.[99]

Zaisser and Rudolf Herrnstadt, who, like the Soviets, had criticized Ulbricht as the cause of the uprising, became the scapegoats. Mielke accused Zaisser of calling for rapprochement with the BRD, which was also the accusation in Moscow of the executed Beria. A purge of the MfS in July included the arrest of about 30 of the 100 officers who had demonstrated against Ulbricht. Placed under Willi Stoph in the Interior Ministry, the MfS was to be subject to close Soviet and Ulbricht control. It was forbidden to spy on the SED, so that there would be no way for the Secret Police to go against the Party.[100] Khrushchev similarly got the MVD under Party control to prevent more Stalin-like purges of his Party.

The Soviet inspectors concluded that the MfS also remained incapable and insufficiently cooperative. This was compounded by the strict compartmentalization of departments, in Moscow down to the Karlshorst military command and the corresponding MfS departments. A chaotic state of affairs seriously hindered the work. The mass DDR arrests of "West

German agents" were criticized in Moscow as done only for publicity and as counterproductive.[101]

The Soviets' military command at Karlshorst had not sent agents out in the field often enough, so in May 1954 the KGB created offices in each district's Kommandantura. Although they were required to submit regular reports, "The reports tended to be uniformly upbeat and uncritical; to report critical comments would have invited follow-up and investigation." KGB offices were further impatient with the growing reluctance of German officials, particularly those in the MfS, to follow orders without question. "This shift in attitudes was apparent at all levels of Soviet–German interaction."[102]

To effect an improvement, the Soviets installed Ernst Wollweber, a German Communist who had escaped the Nazis to Denmark and was assigned to sabotage freighters headed for Germany, Italy and Japan. In 1940 he fled to Sweden to do the same and was arrested but somehow got to the USSR.[103] Favored by Soviets because he was not so loyal to Ulbricht, he was brought in to bring the MfS up to Soviet standards.

He was not so personally ambitious, had a wider horizon and was much more able to communicate, being a talented speaker, as shown when he had been in the pre-1933 Reichstag. His regime was one of the hardest, but he took over an organization that in many ways was unstable and lacking in qualified personnel.[104]

The associated Battlegroups (*Kampfgruppen*), a militia of workers in factories, farms and offices, were formally created in December 1953. Volker Koop judged that contrary to the propaganda, these "fighters" were ill motivated, avoided their training whenever possible and were not noticeably socialist. The public was given a fuzzy picture about what the Battlegroups were to do, as were they themselves, but implicitly they were to be used against the public, as they were in 1956 and 1961. For most, it was an accepted social obligation; for many, a welcome diversion, providing the feeling of comraderie.[105]

Wollweber reported to Ulbricht that the Battlegroups appeared more like "robber bands." The typical Battlegroup comment: "We don't have any democracy, instead the SED and that is a dictatorship." Further, the militarized police were in a desolate condition, with massive discipline cases and orders not carried out.[106]

Although Ulbricht thought Wollweber too coarse and outspoken, he was given the task of finding the nonexistent conspirators of 17 June. He utilized no show trials as in other Communist countries or executions, perhaps because the DDR was frightened of an adverse reaction in the BRD.[107] Wollweber managed to satisfy the Party's wishes without filling its vengeance quota with wholly innocent victims. Further careful maneuvering made his an independent ministry.[108] It was also independent of the local

Party, when the local SED was cut out of the reporting system by Soviet pressure.

In September 1953 came the first clear statement of MfS duties, from a panel of Wollweber and Mielke, plus Hermann Matern (for Ulbricht) and Malenkov's agent Pitovranov and his deputy Ivan Fadeikin. Wollweber in November said that it had no strategy of a concentrated attack and would make no mass arrests of enemies and agents. In contrast, Matern spoke of intensifying MfS work, quoting Ulbricht, "We must make the DDR a hell for hostile agents."

The KGB with vetoes and instructions increased its power. Wollweber instructed on 13 December 1953, "If a Soviet instructor orders something and you disagree, tell him you disagree but do it. No measures should be taken contrary to the view of our Friends." (The Friends was the politically correct term for the Soviets.)

The constant Friendly criticism (1953–1957) concerned the lack of personnel qualifications, in particular, the lack of work with informants. Ulbricht, to get rid of Wollweber, was saying much the same thing, probably taking it from the Soviets, including the criticism from the Soviet Communist Party in May 1956.[109] The KGB disliked Wollweber's mistress, Clara Vater, who had ended up in Stalin's labor camps and thought him too nationalist.

In the early years, the methods had been more influenced by the Soviet instructors than by the Party apparatus. These brutal interrogation methods changed so that after 1956 there were fewer forced confessions, and the police were supposed to present some evidence to a judge. Wollweber tried to improve the public image, even holding press conferences. He kept the DDR quiet in 1956, destroying student oposition in East Berlin, but the credit went to Ulbricht.[110]

The basic decisions in 1955 came clearly from the Soviets, including restructuring the apparatus and setting the priorities of work in the West, rejecting the DDR plans. Wollweber assigned 50 percent to West agents, a move that was used as an excuse later by Ulbricht to fire him, although Wollweber did not hide that fact that this was at the expense of internal controls, which naturally concerned the unpopular Ulbricht.

In February 1955 KGB chief Serov advised the Moscow Central Committee of problems with Ulbricht, who had ordered his MfS to increase repressive measures against persons whom he suspected of "wrecking" and sabotage; for example, in the Agricultural Ministry "at least 10–12 percent were enemies." Ulbricht had ordered suspects to be arrested, even if the MfS had no proof. He wanted similar action in other ministries. Wollweber thought that the law should be followed, but Ulbricht wanted longer detentions. Serov warned that innocents could thus be damaged.

From Mielke, Ulbricht gained direct access to the cases being handled, sometimes before Wollweber saw them. At the end of January 1957 Wollweber rejected the Ulbricht criticism of laxity. Pitovranov refused to accept the Ulbricht views, and this became similar to the Ulbricht battle with Zaisser and Kobulov in 1953, in a vehement rejection by Ulbricht of the concentration on "West Work." He pushed for a stronger basis in the large firms and the increased responsibility of the territorial branches of the MfS, with both linked to Party control. The new chief adviser Alexander Korotkov paved the way for this to be the orders of the Soviet Politbüro, an indirect criticism of the other Soviets whom Wollweber had followed.

The 1956 Moscow "Thaw" had little effect in the DDR, with discussion crushed by Ulbricht, presumably justified by events in Poland and Hungary. Mielke charged Wollweber with contacts with BRD ideological subversion and on 1 November 1957 Wollweber resigned for ill health.[111] Korotkov reported Ulbricht's elimination of opposition and a growing DDR assertiveness.[112] He facilitated the power of Mielke, who made himself so loyal that he received the Order of Lenin six times. Even so, Ulbricht did not put Mielke on his Politbüro.[113]

Ulbricht was obsessed with crushing any opposition and had been angered that he had to take Wollweber instead of Mielke. The Soviets had trouble tracing Mielke's past. After leaving Spain in 1939, he had been interned in France; when the Germans invaded, he allegedly escaped, but the length of his stay in the camp and date of his escape were not known. He was reportedly arrested by the Germans in 1944 and worked in the labor battalions of the Todt Organization and in May 1945 appeared from the American zone.[114]

A suspicious Soviet Intelligence supervisor noted that Mielke had not reported the death of a brother in West Berlin. "He is crafty and insincere to everyone, including the Soviets, even though he plays the role of a good friend. It would be best if you chose one of your best district first secretaries to be minister and let Mielke or Markus Wolf be his deputy."[115] Ulbricht did not obey.

In November 1958 the Soviets reduced their adviser apparatus in the MfS from 76 to 32 officers. Mielke at their farewell party said cryptically, "It will not be easy for many of those of us who were accustomed to rely on the advice of our Soviet comrades." Yet the MfS attained only a limited autonomy from the KGB, particularly in espionage, where the Soviets had immediate access and influence up to the 1980s."[116]

The MfS was supposedly the loyal agent of the SED. Almost every MfS person was a member (93 percent in 1959) except for its guard regiment, but the Party organization had scarcely any involvement in the operatives' work, none in the sense of involvement in their authority. Its instrument was the ideological forming of the MfS personnel and the implementation of its cadre principles. The Party could discipline MfS personnel for violating Party rules.[117]

As for ideological purity, the belief in the West was that the former

Gestapo became Stasi. When Jens Gieseke tested the common phrase, "First Brown [NS], then Red" (brown was a term that meant Nazi), the MfS orders were that there would be no NS party member, nor active HJ (Hitler Jugend/Youth)/BDM (Bund Deutscher Mädel). Perhaps some exceptions in the more hectic 1950s occurred, as with some IMs. "In the Ministry there was not a single example of a personnel continuity between the NS terror organization and the professionals in the MfS. They copied the Soviets not the Gestapo.[118]

Mielke's Monster

Thus developed an East German police state that made it nearly impossible for clandestine organizations to carry on a resistance, "the largest, best equipped and most pervasive police state apparatus ever to function on German soil."[119] It created "the best police state," one well organized and disciplined, with no visible rivalries, as were found elsewhere in the Soviet world.[120] Yet without a Wall, they would have lost control already in 1961.

Mielke had thousands of farmers in 1959 arrested for resisting collectivization, but that many more fled, necessitating the Wall, begun on 13 August. Ulbricht remained unhappy with the lack of Party propaganda effort. Although the Battlegroups were described as getting stronger, barely 50 percent took part in the training, including commanders. The number in June 1962 declined by 10,475 from 187,359, because orders were that those not completely loyal must be thrown out, an order taken too far by local organs.

Although the MfS expressed the fear that not letting the disloyal citizens leave would intensify resistance, it could, in fact, relax until 1975, when Honecker signed the Helsinki Agreement on Security and Cooperation in order to be more acceptable in the world. Soon 10,000 more MfS officials were created, and measures became tougher in the "Guidelines 1/76" manual of procedures.[121]

By 1979 Mielke had a system of internment camps, which by 1984 had 24 designated locations. General Josef Schwarz perfected six categories of those to be arrested, with numbers into the tens of thousands. The Twentieth Main Directorate (XX-HVA) under Lieutenant General Paul Kienberg was to combat underground political movements, using some 1,800 officers stationed in the 15 district offices. Each supervised at least 30 regular informers (IMs), a total of more than 54,500, for each handler about 55 clandestine monthly meetings.

The Twentieth Directorate's closest collaborator was the Second Main Directorate for domestic counterintelligence, which included 4,400 agents inspecting the mail. Every post office had MfS officers, and all letters and parcels sent to, or received from, a non-Communist country were to be opened. (This reportedly evolved in the last three years into mail robbery of 6.5 million West marks; of 20 million parcels from the West, 200,000 did not reach their destination.)[122]

Lieutenant General Günther Kratsch, head of Counter Intelligence, was slavishly devoted to Mielke and reported directly. His power was therefore more than for most, as Mielke ordered all to cooperate with him. His staff of 2,350 had IMs who totaled 2,500 to 3,000. In the Third Directorate, under Major General Horst Männchen, 6,000 officers tapped telephones, although against the law. This included phones used by U.S. installations in West Berlin, half of the day manually, half by computer.[123]

At the Autobahn border crossings, the pass photo and information were sent electronically to Berlin, while the visitor inched along toward customs. The visitor remained under frequent control, with an observation point stationed every 10 kilometers; every Autobahn rest stop had a unit, with almost everything, including toilets, watched by cameras.[124]

The Magdeburg District, which had jurisdiction over the major road and railroad entries from the West, had 2,500 permanent employees, 800 in pass control on the border; its yearly budget was 100 million marks, of which salaries took 63 million. It used 5,000 IMs, and 1,200 residences for contacts, with 52 bungalows for vacations. General Müller had risen from poverty, joining the SED in 1949. He wrote later that his reports were accurate, and he had assumed that Mielke would take care of the reported problems.[125]

As early as 1950 the MfS had assumed the task as a protector of the economy. On the local level in the county organizations, the economy was either first or second priority. In 1969 Mielke assumed responsibility for the New Economic Policy and its technological advance, in particular, its computerization. Although they were not supposed to interfere, MfS agents were in every firm and combine to keep the economy going.[126]

The MfS also spied on its government. In August 1960 Mielke linked with Stoph to arrange IMs in some ministries and the Planning Commission. His Department III should investigate economic problems, in particular, the supply of spare parts. In December 1961 a Colonel Walter gave examples of incorrect reports, showing that even leading officials had manipulated theirs. Mielke added that his MfS had given useful suggestions and must inspect their implementation and promptly signal which cadre were unsuitable for their command positions in the economy. "This the MfS had neglected to do in the past." He very strongly criticized the Agricultural Ministry and the Planning Commission, which had no clear conception of the technical equipment used. The MfS got many in the ministry fired.

Therewith, the MfS tried to be the "Grand Inspector General," not only to force back the hostiles but to oversee how well the presumably loyal economic leaders did their jobs. Suckut judged that it did not mean to be a state within the state but an eager implementer of SED policy. The Central Committee regarded the MfS as "Comrades for the rough work." These "Comrades" were often too impulsive, violating therewith the laws, often undisciplined and ignoring the praised socialist morality. Instead of being scientific, they were rather practical and pragmatic. Some boasted, "With money and women we can do anything!"

Matern, for Ulbricht, in December 1962 criticized the MfS for having arrested too many without court involvement. "The circle of citizens who were investigated was very large and in many cases had nothing to do with the discovery and liquidation of hostile activity." The SED criticism was that the MfS had ignored any destabilizing effect and had equated discontent with hostility. Matern continued that the training in class warfare, which sharpened the repressive measures, as well as the hard punishments, equaled a dangerous dogmatism. Every day a multitude of citizens were interrogated by the MfS about other citizens, sometimes in an unprofessional manner. The MfS rather should concentrate on the real enemies, those linked to foreign imperialism or those who for other reasons were organizing political crimes against the State.

Mielke, displaying an amazing amount of self-will, rejected the criticism but agreed to reduce his information gathering insofar as the state and economic apparatus improved. Predictably, the apparatus needed more, not less, supervision.

The MfS did not have a monopoly of information; the SED had its own network, including 44,000 functionaries in the firms. The SED criticized, "The energy and the time invested in the meeting with the IMs were in no proportion to the actual results."

Despite the constant professions of loyalty to the Party, there were many instances of collisions and rebellious behavior of MfS officers, especially Mielke. Regarding criticism in October 1967 about being unscientific, he strongly rejected it. The SED reaction: "In his statements he became very vehement and unobjective and polemicized about problems which had not been raised." The Party conclusion was that Mielke simply had not been able to understand certain problems.

The SED Central Committee's Department for Security proved itself weak when confronted with the frequent MfS arrogance and the belligerent and easily exploding Mielke, presumably because of his relationship to Ulbricht, then Honecker, the only ones Mielke really listened to.[127]

Although Honecker's era seemed secure, the number of Stasi doubled, growing each year by 3,000 until it reached the limit of DDR resources. His organization grew steadily to 100,000 full-time employees. (The Gestapo had significantly fewer for a nation with four times more people.) Organizing along military lines, General Mielke had 27 generals reporting to him.[128] John Koehler figured one Stasi for every 66 persons, counting the IMs; this was four times the ratio in Russia.[129] Of the 13 major and

20 independent departments, the most important office for control of the population had files on 6 million persons, one for every second adult, on shelves that would stretch for 125 miles.[130]

The Dzerzinsky Guard Regiment was expanded to division strength and equipped with heavy weapons and helicopters. It had a direct line to the districts and the 211 county offices. Its duties included protection of the elite's housing compound at Wandlitz, outside Berlin.[131]

Hauptverwaltung Aufklärung, the major department for spying, both domestic and foreign, was created by a much-admired Markus Wolf, who made it into the elite branch. The son of Communist dramatist Friedrich Wolf, he grew up in the USSR, where somehow he and his family were among the few intellectuals who survived the purges. Markus returned in 1945 as journalist, and even he was surprised when he was named chief of foreign espionage in 1953 and given a staff of 1,000. He was much more creative, tactful and flexible than Mielke, who kept him from the Central Committee.[132] Mielke had opposed Wollweber and Wolf's emphasis on espionage in the BRD as against spying in the DDR itself.[133]

Of spies in West Germany, Wolf sent 80 percent, and the army the rest. Joachim Gauck estimated that at least 20,000 West Germans spied for the MfS. He scored major successes, including infiltrating the famous aide to Willy Brandt (Guillaume). A female mole prepared the daily top secret report for Helmut Kohl. Dr. Gabriele Gast in the West German counterpart (the BND), 1969–1990, sent the best information, which, after being somewhat falsified, was used to weaken the BRD.

The office for espionage engaged in torture of "enemies," aided rightist extremists, supported efforts to sabotage nuclear plants, spread disinformation and recorded BRD politicians' phone conversations. Klaus Kinkel, when head of the BND, was a particular target.[134]

Although the MfS leaders described their work as a sacrifice, the leaders had perks, payoffs up to hundreds of thousands of marks, cars immediately for their sons, even hunting lodges where game was maneuvered by old hunters.[135] Power led to abuses: when a woman discovered that her husband was MfS and opposed it, in a few weeks she was divorced, and he had the three children; she had to leave the apartment and lived in a single room without conveniences.

Especially theology students were spied on, harassed and arrested, forbidden to study.[136] Karl Fricke, one of its victims, wrote knowingly of the many MfS crimes, like kidnapping a defected border officer and ordering a death penalty for espionage. The MfS attained several death sentences of MfS officers for West contact. Mielke dismissed resistance to executions as nonsense (*Käse*). He had allegedly ordered the death of a soccer player who left Mielke's Dynamo team for the West.[137]

The MfS boasted of its ability to divide and destroy and had penetrated the most intimate circles. It was trying to control the groups, and their notorious rifts were partly due to the intended suspicion. The MfS planted rumors of alleged collaborators. Gerd Poppe learned later in his 12,000-page file that his wife had been targeted for an extramarital affair and that his son had been turned against him at school.[138]

With détente came more concern with appearances. Instead of open persecution by arrest, the MfS used stronger preventive measures, attempts to intimidate and to break up active opponents by "operative Actions."[139] The MfS gradually shifted from physical intimidation to psychological manipulation. It penetrated dissident circles so effectively that every fourth member seemed to be in its pay.[140]

The core purpose was to know the public's opinion so there would be no more surprises. The SED tried to achieve security from what it saw as a hostile West and unreliable population by the maintenance of blanket surveillance, which meant another primary duty was to decide who got important jobs. The "Stasi State" was as much a massive system of vetting as it was an apparatus of persecution.

The very sense that the Stasi was watching served to atomize society, preventing independent discussion in all but the smallest groups. In this sense it was far from being a secret service and might best be described as the Party's public scarecrow. Potential terror seemed as effective as real terror until 1989.[141] The MfS was limited in its options, because after Hitler it was difficult to employ the death penalty; it was used little after the 1960s and then not for political opposition.[142]

As external pressures hit the DDR the hardest, its security police became more aggressive, even though imprisonment rarely followed. Markus Wolf's criticism: "Everyone who ever became suspected of doing anything in opposition was spied on. This is the core of the false security doctrine of the Ministry."[143] The information system had become so complex that it became inefficient; efforts to modify the system with computers were only beginning. "Tasks increased year to year and not only for state security. The demands for tightest conspiracy and independence, and the separation of each unit from another made an ending of the condition impossible."[144] This criticism was accepted by the man who replaced Mielke in November 1989, Dr. Wolfgang Schwanitz.

Mittag also complained that the Stasi was too blown-up. "It had a monopoly of information, which is the bread of politics. The others did not know what was necessary for them to do their jobs."[145] Arguably, the MfS also did not know enough.

The Insufficiency of Collaborators

The best-known agents were the unpaid "Unofficial Colleagues" (IMs). Their spying became increasingly important in the economy, 30–50 percent of the total IMs. Although many agents were assigned to the 300 combines, they were also thick in the army in order to know what men of certain ages thought.[146]

For a higher quality of effectiveness, there were full-time professionals, "Officers in Special Assignment" (OibE), 2,448 officers who were sent as spies to various organizations, domestic and foreign, of whom 582 were assigned to the BRD. These OibE increased the MfS power in the ministries.[147] Most important were officers Mobis with the Council of Ministers, Burghart in the Foreign Office and Bahnig in the army. With them, Mielke created a "shadow government . . . in order to do everything better."[148] A special category was the Unknown Colleagues (UMI), those who spied on MfS persons, past and present, spies of spies.[149]

The MfS agents were supposed to be professional and accurate in their reports, and IMs had to assume that others would report on the same subject, so they had to be careful in what they said. Many did not know that they were considered IMs: "They were just having conversations."[150] One can distingush those who merely regularly conversed with MfS from true IMs; the latter signed a commitment, met secretly, did not report this to superiors and provided potentially harmful material about someone.

All contacts were to be secret, but as soon as the public was involved, plans were discovered and the information was banalized. "The much affirmed omnipotence of the MfS apparatus had limits in every phase of its operation."[151] Mielke had already criticized the IM work in 1969, criticized it even more strongly in 1971 and in 1972 found "serious deficiencies and weaknesses." This he described as the most important problem of the organization. Particularly the expectations for the GMs (Geheimer Mitarbeiter) were disappointed.

The Berlin complaint of local reports was that they were only statements and frequently described only the public mood. No less than 90 percent of the information was judged unusable. Quantity was given too much importance, as Mielke complained again in July 1974. He ordered a revision of the IM program in December 1975, which became four years later the cited revised instructions.[152]

As for the sources of IMs, people were rarely forced to spy. Like any secret service, the MfS knew that compulsion was no stable base; using force would take more than it was worth to control the source.[153] Volunteers came sometimes from idealism, sometimes from persons desiring something special in life or a special importance. Annette Maennel described five women who had volunteered, beginning with "Brigitte," who had married an older man and then found out that he was an IM. When he died, she needed someone to talk to and found her sessions with her contact rather romantic. Some officers supervised their informers with almost loving solicitude.

As another example, Petra was a devoted and energetic teacher who reported that colleagues got rid of poor teachers by giving them medals and making them administrators. She had the sense that with the MfS she could finally speak honestly from the heart. When she was recruited, her handler offered a remarkable justification: "The MfS wanted to get on the table their awareness of the calcification of the Central Committee. These old men live on the moon, and our job is to wake them from their winter sleep. . . . He said that the time had come that the class enemy was approaching for his major attack. The enemy wanted to break the DDR into pieces. The indications were of a coming storm and if we did not react and tried to refloat the ship which was already sinking, and did not give the people honest answers to their questions, then everything would be lost."[154]

As the ones "who could get things done," Mielke's men saw themselves as the problem solvers of the DDR and expanded their involvement far beyond the normal service of a Secret Police, even into the economy, as though Secret Police could compel production and technological advance.

The drive was to know everything about everybody, but knowledge did not suffice. The MfS came to know the system's inefficiency and the public's discontent, but all the spies could not control it. It came to know "the Enemy" but could not destroy it.

NOTES

1. Wilfried Loth, *Stalin's ungeliebtes Kind: Warum Moskau die DDR nicht wollte* (Berlin: Rowohlt, 1994).

2. Norman Naimark, *The Russians in Germany: A History of the Soviet Zone of Occupation, 1945–1950* (Cambridge, MA: Harvard University Press, 1995).

3. Edward Peterson, *Russian Commands and German Resistance* (New York: Peter Lang, 1999).

4. Margarita Mathiopoulus, *Rendezvous mit der DDR* (Düsseldorf: Econ, 1994), pp. 214, 217.

5. Peter Christ and Ralf Neubauer, *Kolonie im eigenen Land* (Berlin: Rowohlt, 1991), pp. 19, 25.

6. David E. Murphy, Sergei A. Kondrashev and George Bailey, *Battleground Berlin* (New Haven, CT: Yale University Press, 1997), p. 134.

7. Ibid., pp. 160–61.

8. Ibid., p. 181.

9. Mathiopoulus, *Rendezvous*, p. 224; Ehrhart Neubert, *Geschichte der Opposition in der DDR 1949–1989* (Berlin: Links, 1997), p. 82.

10. Manfred Schell and Werner Kalinka, *Stasi und kein Ende* (Frankfurt: Ullstein, 1991), p. 73.

11. Christian Joppke, *East German Dissidents and the Revolution of 1989* (New York: New York University Press, 1995), pp. 57–59.

12. Jeffrey Kopstein, *The Politics of Economic Decline in East Germany, 1945–1989* (Chapel Hill: University of North Carolina Press, 1997), p. 35.

13. Joppke, *East German Dissidents*, pp. 62–63; Bruce Allen, *Germany East: Dissent and Opposition* (Montreal: Black Rose, 1991), pp. 37, 42.

14. Kopstein, *Politics*, pp. 37–40.

15. Ibid., p. 43.

16. Jürgen Weber, *Der SED-Staat* (München: Olzog, 1994), pp. 18–19.

17. Hans-Herrmann Hertle, *Der Fall der Mauer* (Opladen: Westdeutscher, 1996), p. 23.

18. Kopstein, *Politics*, p. 51.

19. Günter Mittag, *Um Jeden Preis* (Berlin: Aufbau, 1991), p. 44.

20. Ibid., p. 215.

21. Kopstein, *Politics*, p. 47.

22. Theo Pirker, *Der Plan als Befehl und Fiktion* (Opladen: Westdeutscher, 1995).

23. Mittag, *Um Jeden Preis*, pp. 213, 216, 352.

24. Ibid., pp. 169–73.

25. Ibid., pp. 203, 217.

26. Christ and Neubauer, *Kolonie*, pp. 29, 31.

27. Peter Bender, *Unsere Erbschaft: Was war die DDR—was bleibt von ihr* (Hamburg: Luchterhand Literaturverlag, 1993), pp. 43–46.

28. Kopstein, *Politics*, pp. 49–50.

29. Hertle, *Der Fall der Mauer*, p. 23.

30. Klaus Schroeder, *Der SED-Staat: Partei, Statt und Gesellschaft, 1949–1990* (München: Hanser, 1998), p. 180.

31. Kopstein, *Politics*, pp. 57–58.

32. Ibid., p. 73.

33. Schroeder, *Der SED-Staat*, p. 180.

34. Kopstein, *Politics*, pp. 64–69.

35. Schroeder, *Der SED-Staat*, p. 181.

36. Kopstein, *Politics*, p. 70.

37. Günter Schabowski, *Der Absturz* (Berlin: Rowohlt, 1992), pp. 109, 114, 119.

38. Kopstein, *Politics*, pp. 71–72.

39. Hertle, *Der Fall der Mauer*, pp. 24–25; Stiftung Archiv Partei und Massen Organization (SAPMO), ZPA, JIV 22/A/3196, 28.7.70.

40. Schabowski, *Der Absturz*, p. 200.

41. Hertle, *Der Fall der Mauer*, p. 27.

42. Peter Przybylski, *Tatort Politbüro*, Band II (Berlin: Rowohlt, 1992), p. 22.

43. Hertle, *Der Fall der Mauer*, pp. 26–27.

44. Schabowski, *Der Absturz*, pp. 109, 114, 119.

45. Mathiopoulus, *Rendezvous*, p. 221.

46. Przybylski, *Tatort Politbüro*, p. 34.

47. John Koehler, *Stasi: The Untold Story of the East German Secret Police* (Boulder, CO: Westview Press, 1999), p. 71.

48. Hertle, *Der Fall der Mauer*, p. 29.

49. Stefan Bollinger, *1989—eine abgebrochene Revolution: Verbaute Wege nicht nur zu einer besseren DDR?* (Berlin: Trafo, 1999), p. 45.

50. Mathias Judt, *DDR Geschichte in Dokumenten* (Bonn: Bundeszentrale für politische Bildung, 1998), p. 49, cited in Manfred Uschner, *Die zweite Etage* (Berlin: Dietz, 1993), pp. 69–70.

51. Kopstein, *Politics*, p. 73.

52. Przybylski, *Tatort Politbüro*, p. 59.

53. Kopstein, *Politics*, p. 74.

54. Christ and Neubauer, *Kolonie*, 29–32.

55. Kopstein, *Politics*, p. 103.

56. Christ and Neubauer, *Kolonie*, pp. 34–37.

57. Dietrich Staritz, *Die Geschichte der DDR* (Frankfurt, a.M: Suhrkamp, 1996), p. 94.

58. Kopstein, *Politics*, pp. 182–85.

59. Ibid., pp. 81–82.

60. Ibid., pp. 75–77.

61. Wolfgang Rüddenklau, *Störenfried: DDR Opposition, 1986–89* (Berlin: Basis, 1992), p. 17.

62. Christ and Neubauer, *Kolonie*, pp. 46–47.

63. Carl Heinz Janson, *Totengräber der DDR* (Düsseldorf: Econ, 1991), pp. 111, 124.

64. Kopstein, *Politics*, pp. 74–75.

65. Konrad Jarausch, *The Rush to German Unity* (Oxford: Oxford University Press, 1994), p. 99.

66. Pirker, *Der Plan*, pp. 298, 305.

67. Kopstein, *Politics*, p. 86.

68. Ibid., p. 140.

69. Ibid., p. 177.

70. Ibid., pp. 173, 181.

71. Jarausch, *Rush*, pp. 97–98.

72. ZAIG, 2240, Sekretariat des Ministerium, pp. 6, 18.

73. Schabowski, *Der Absturz*, pp. 111–14.

74. David Childs and Richard Popplewell, *The East German Intelligence and Security Service* (New York: New York University Press, 1996), p. 68.

75. Janson, *Totengräber der DDR*, pp. 10–13.

76. Kopstein, *Politics*, pp. 86–89.

77. Wolfgang-Uwe Friedrich, *Die totalitäre Herrschaft der SED: Wirklichkeit und Nachwirkungen* (Munchen: Beck, 1998), pp. 101–6.

78. Stefan Wolle, *Die heile Welt der Diktatur: Alltag und Herrschaft in der DDR, 1971–1989* (Bonn: Bundeszentrale für politische Bildung, 1998), p. 163.

79. Ibid., p. 45.

80. Rüddenklau, *Störenfried*, p. 18.

81. Wolle, *Die heile Welt*, p. 164.

82. Ibid., p. 44.

83. Schabowski, *Der Absturz*, p. 122.

84. Elizabeth Pond, *Beyond the Wall* (Washington, DC: Brookings Institution, 1993), p. 77.

85. Bender, *Unsere Erbschaft*, p. 62.

86. Hanns-Heinz Gatow, *Vertuschte SED-Verbrechen* (Berg am See: Türmer, 1991), pp. 204–6, 217.

87. Ehrhart Neubert, *Geschichte der Opposition in der DDR 1949–1989* (Berlin: Links, 1997), pp. 209 ff.

88. Ibid., p. 345.

89. Hermann Weber, *Grundriss der Geschichte DDR* (Hannover: Fackelträger, 1991), pp. 180–83; J. Weber, *Der SED-Staat*, pp. 6–7.

90. J. Weber, *Der SED-Staat*, p. 14.

91. Ditmar Gatzmaga, Thomas Voss and Klaus Westerman, *Auferstehen aus Ruinen* (Marburg: Schüren, 1991), p. 21.

92. J. Weber, *Der SED-Staat*, pp. 8–11.

93. Bender, *Unsere Erbschaft*, p. 37.

94. Karl-Dieter Opp and Peter Voß, *Die volkseigene Revolution* (Stuttgart: Klett-Cotta, 1993), pp. 159, 181, 236.

95. Johannes Huinink, in Hans Joas and Martin Kohli, *Der Zusammenbruch der DDR: Soziologische Analysen* (Frankfurt: Suhrkamp, 1993), p. 158.

96. Childs and Popplewell, *East German Intelligence*, pp. 39, 47.

97. Karl Wilhem Fricke and Roger Engelmann, *"Konzentrierte Schläge": Staatssicherheits aktionenen und politische Prozesse in der DDR 1953–56* (Berlin: Links, 1998), pp. 4–5, 13; Koehler thought that Mielke was involved in purging Trotskyites and possibly had Ziemer, his fellow murderer in Berlin, killed. Koehler, *Stasi*, p. 48.

98. Murphy, Kondrashev and Bailey, *Battleground*, p. 134.

99. Volker Koop, *Armee oder Freizeitclub: Die Kampfgruppen der Arbeiterklasse* (Bonn: Bouvier, 1997), pp. 7–20.

100. Childs and Popplewell, *East German Intelligence*, pp. 56–59; Koehler, *Stasi*, p. 61.

101. Murphy, Kondrashev and Bailey, *Battleground*, pp. 286–88.

102. Ibid., pp. 289–91.

103. By one account sent to Russia in 1943 after Moscow claimed he was a fugitive for embezzlement. Koehler, *Stasi*, p. 50.

104. Fricke and Engelmann, *"Konzentrierte Schläge,"* pp. 30, 33.

105. Murphy, Kondrashev and Bailey, *Battleground*, pp. 286–88.

106. Koop, *Armee*, pp. 22, 52–53, 59.

107. Childs and Popplewell, *East German Intelligence*, p. 43.

108. Ibid., pp. 59, 61.

109. Siegfried Suckut and Walter Süss, *Staatspartei und Staatssicherheit* (Berlin: Links, 1997), pp. 51–54.

110. Childs and Popplewell, *East German Intelligence*, p. 64.

111. Koehler, *Stasi*, p. 63.

112. Murphy Kondrashev and Bailey, *Battleground*, pp. 294–300.

113. Walter Süss, *Das Verhältnis von SED und Staatssicherheit* (Berlin: Bundesbeauftragte, 1997), p. 7.

114. Murphy, Kondrashev and Bailey, *Battleground*, p. 130; Koehler thought that the Todt organization would not have hired him in France. He got four Soviet medals perhaps for service behind enemy lines. Koehler, *Stasi*, pp. 48, 51.

115. Murphy, Kondrashev and Bailey, *Battleground*, p. 292.

116. Ibid., pp. 56–71.

117. Ibid., pp. 110–12, 128.

118. Ibid., pp. 133–38, 148.

119. Ibid., pp. 126, 129.

120. Manfred Uschner, *Die zweite Etage* (Berlin: Dietz, 1993), p. 43.

121. Koop, *Armee*, p. 59.

122. Koehler, *Stasi*, pp. 141–44.

123. Ibid., pp. 265–66.

124. Pond, *Beyond the Wall*, p. 140.

125. Dietmar Linke, *Theologie-Studenten der Humboldt-Universität* (Neu-kirchen-Vluyn: Neukirchner Verlag, 1994), pp. 56, 80, 102. Mielke picked up the tab for the entire KGB operation in East Germany, staff of 2,500, including all family facilities. Koehler, *Stasi*, p. 74.

126. Hans-Hermann Hertle and Franz Otto Gilles, in Klaus-Dietmar Henke and Roger Engelmann, *Aktenlage: Die Bedeutung der Unterlagen des Staatssicherheitdiensts für die Zeitgeschichtsforschung* (Berlin-Links, 1995), pp. 118–21.

127. Suckut and Süss, *Staatspartei*, pp. 152–67. The MfS prediction was that building the Wall would mean that troublemakers could no longer leave and would be a greater problem.

128. Joachim Gauck, *Die Stasi-Akten* (Hamburg: Rowohlt, 1991), p. 61.

129. Koehler, *Stasi*, p. 9.

130. Uschner, *Die zweite Etage*, p. 47.

131. Karl Wilhelm Fricke, "Schild und Schwert," Die Stasi, Deutschland Funk, 7 Okt. 1992.

132. Pond, *Beyond the Wall*, p. 126.

133. Koehler, *Stasi*, p. 64

134. Karl Wilhelm Fricke, *DDR Staatssicherheit: Das Phänomen des Verrats—Die Zusammenarbeit zwischen MfS und KGB* (Bochum: Universitäts Verlag, 1995), p. 3.

135. Pond, *Beyond the Wall*, p. 140.

136. Linke, *Theologie-Studenten*, p. 22.

137. Karl Wilhelm Fricke, *MFS Intern* (Köln: Wissenschaft und Politik, 1991), pp. 62–65.

138. Joppke, *East German Dissidents*, pp. 109–14.

139. Süss, *Das Verhältnis*, pp. 29–30.

140. Jarausch, *Rush*, pp. 35–38.

141. Childs and Popplewell, *East German Intelligence*, pp. 61, 63.

142. Ibid., p. 95.

143. Fricke, *MfS Intern*, p. 47.

144. Fricke, "Schild," p. 21.

145. Mittag, *Um Jeden*, p. 50.

146. Gisela Helwig, *Rückblicke auf die DDR* (Köln: Deutschland Archiv, 1995), p. 125.

147. Fricke, *MfS Intern*, p. 53; Süss, *Das Verhältnis*, p. 32.

148. Schell and Kalinka, *Stasi*, pp. 111–12.

149. Fricke, *DDR*, p. 69; David Gill and Ulrich Schröter, *Das Ministerium für Staatssicherheit* (Berlin: Rowohlt, 1991), pp. 79, 91–92.

150. Neubert, *Geschichte*, pp. 33–37.

151. Ibid., p. 70.

152. Henke, pp. 67–72.

153. Peter Siebenmorgen, *Staatssicherheit der DDR* (Bonn: Bouvier, 1993), p. 73.

154. Annette Maennel, *Auf sie war Verlass: Frauen und Stasi* (Berlin: Elefanten, 1995), pp. 90–91.

Chapter 2

Distant Rumblings:
1980–1986

SCHWERIN

Widespread discontent in this northwest agrarian district can be traced back in the MfS reports to the beginning of the DDR. In the 1950s the great problem had been the DDR's trying to collectivize agriculture, an Ulbricht push possibly contrary to Stalin's wishes.[1] Reports show that the Plan was to get 50 percent of the farmers into the collective farms (LPGs) by 1960: "A hard fight in all counties, the most difficult conditions, the hard class warfare."

In Ludwigslust and Hagenow Counties, "The stagnation shows that the work of the state apparatus, as well as the Party, in the Intelligentsia, in the bitter fighting with the negative forces has failed. The leadership, dominated by sons of Big Farmers, who are not controlled, has been a complete failure. Some join LPGs to escape their quota deficits, then quit the LPG."

The MfS described the weaknesses in the three categories of collectives, based on the wealth on entry: "In Type I, [farmers who had had more land] the farmers are directly hurting themselves. In Type II, there is a direct enemy activity, including the destruction of socialist property. In Type III (the near landless), the chairmen are often unqualified and immoral, and are not capable of understanding the job."

The perennial problem "is the drunkenness in the LPGs, the chairman sitting in the bar or driving around. The big problem is the big farms that have gone to the dogs [those taken from private owners]. Many members are unmotivated and there are troublemakers, who glorify the West and try to end the LPGs."[2]

In Rastow the LPG III chief was a former NS and an estate secretary "who always agitates, calls our friends 'Russian serfs.' He greets with a fascist salute and sings fascist songs, like *'Deutschland über alles.'* The chief is competent but spends most of his time in inns and with other women. Most of the other LPG farmers do the same. Despite the shortage of labor, the wives go to work for "the Big Farmers" and the LPG does nothing to stop it." There is waste from neglect. "Constantly animals are lost. These conditions are considered normal, and nothing is done to change it." The MfS had "a hard conversation" with the chief; fearing arrest, he cried and promised to change and actually did stop his drinking and adultery.

Problems in other villages were also reported. "Former fascists, now CDU, keep farmers from joining an LPG. One 'Big Farmer' told his LPG chief, 'When the times change, you'll be hanged.' Farmers who join LPGs are threatened with hanging, and called traitors to the nation. The district has 2,662 'Big Farmers.' " A MfS confession of weakness: "We don't have enough secret informants among the large and middle farmers."

The MfS lacked agents as instruments of rural power. "We have 25 IMs among "Big Farmers"; none in Güstrow of 162 "Big Farmers," or in Parchim of 262, Hagenow, only 6 of 518, 1 in Perleberg out of 614 Big Farmers. In one community we compelled one man to be an IM, but he does not come to the contacts; another only defends the Big Farmers and the county unit doesn't change it. The IMs who are left on their own don't do anything."

Sabotage was the preferred explanation for the failure of production. "For the spring planting, even the tractor stations service the private farms first. Some LPGs have nearly 100 percent earnings, others lose 50 percent. 'The Enemy' has his hand in the game. Sabotage: they set the plan at less than they produce and the locals don't stop it; in the Schwerin district are 75,000 fewer swine than the program demands. An example is a field brigadier, who is completely under the influence of his wife, and her father, who is a Big Farmer."

Socialist agriculture was failing. "The People's Estates [VEGs] constitute only 2.8 percent of the land. . . . Of 36 VEGs, only 12 are viable, with losses as much as 609,000 marks; others have 'planned losses.' In these there is not the required 'leading role of the Party.' The political work is minimal. The Pritzier VEG director has connections to the CIA [Central Intelligence Agency]. He is a dictator, as are two others."

Even SED farm leaders were rebellious. "The managers are more capitalist than socialist. Although SED members, they say they will hang the SED functionaries. The directors met in 1957 near Berlin, watched BRD farm films, and most spoke against the DDR economic system. One VEG director said those who created the DDR should be punished and told his secretary to join the SED to spy on it."

Deception and incompetence reigned. "The IMs are not functioning, they are extremely ineffective. The tractor stations are led by former officers or

Big Farmers and report doing more work than is actually done. An agronomist has no ability; when many piglets died, he simply said, 'Fine, we have more food for the rest.' He was appointed although known to be an incompetent, a person who needed someone to direct him, but he was sent out on his own."

Corruption, opposition, and resignations were widespread. "There are many cases of old tractors bought, fixed and then sold to Big Farmers. The head of the Farmers'Aid (VdgB) in the district works contrary to VdgB policy. Most farmers quit the SED." Reports of problems in socialism continued page after page, describing how the system was failing. The LPG members declined from 1957 to 1958 from 40.9 to 33.5 percent. "In 1945 there were 450 Junker estates; in Güstrow, they were reported reduced to 33 but the count is, in fact, 82; the 24 in Gadebusch now number 48. We know of 94 cases of Junker networkings."[3]

To break such farmer resistance and to keep the unhappy LPG members down on the farm, the Berlin Wall had to be erected in 1961. Reports thereafter reflect, if not contentment, at least more manageable problems.

The Ill Wind from Prague

The stability enabled by the Wall was disturbed when the Czechs moved a step away from Communism. In the dangerous "Prague Spring," echoes of liberalism reached as far north as Mecklenburg, whose 6 April plebiscite was to create an image of democracy. "An IM working for the postal service reported that the popular view was that no plebiscite was necessary, 'It was only a big hullabaloo.' "

Two FDJ (youth organization) leaders did not support the plebiscite and were fired. A member said he would never vote "Ja." The mayor did not answer, and the meeting was abruptly ended. "A secretary for rural youth resigned saying that no one would come for indoctrination. He refused to follow the order to work every day on it, saying two sessions were enough. He had tried to avoid orders with obvious excuses." Having listened to the Czechoslovak Soviet Socialist Republic (CSSR) radio station, he had doubts about the DDR opposition to the liberal regime there. "He said the BRD had succeeded in isolating the DDR, which was mostly the fault of DDR leaders."

There were frequent arguments with FDJ functionaries about the necessity of ideological work. One said, "If Thälmann could see the conditions in the DDR, he would faint. . . . We're not like Czechs, we're still occupied by Russians."

Those involved in *Kultur*, like the State Theater's Dr. Wohlert, were strongly negative and critical.[4] Students criticized the Prague intervention in August: "The DDR goal is just to get one over on the BRD. To defend our socialist Fatherland with weapons is nonsense." They said that the plebiscite was held "because those people up there need a campaign from time to time." A doctor said that even the high functionaries in Berlin are sick of plebiscite propaganda. "The people are treated like idiots." The analysis of the mail showed that the more education the person had achieved, the more the person criticized; some got Western publications via the CSSR.

The church was always the problem. "The Mecklenburg Lutheran Church reactionaries regard the constitution as atheist." The MfS was concerned that only 64 percent of the Protestant pastors voted, and 57.4 percent of the Catholic.[5]

People panned the celebrations, like the 30th anniversary of the Liberation; the journalists were getting little reaction "because it has already been talked about so much. . . . Nothing was happening, often because of conflicts of leaders." The complaint was that the celebration was like last year, when everyone was ordered to be there at 8:00 A.M., but things were not started until 10:45 A.M. "On 1 May, there was also poor organization, they waited up to 2 hours because the speaker had given wrong information. People didn't care about the occasion, they only liked the day off."

About that "Liberation," a caller raised a provocative question: "Did Stalin command his troops to plunder for 3 days?" Dr. Sorgenicht of the Central Committee did not deny the plunder but did not know of such an order.

The SED paper praised several persons not with proletarian, but with bourgeois, backgrounds who offered to work harder to fulfill the Plan. "In contrast the production and technical leaders showed absolutely no initiative, saying working extra would not increase pay because the plan would not be fulfilled anyway."[6]

Already the numbers wanting to exit the DDR were viewed with alarm, as was the image of their being mistreated. The Berlin decree, of 2 November 1976 ordered legal restraint in the arrest of these Emigration Applicants: "They must have shown enemy activity, and that you are preventing more such hostile behavior. Your action must show true humanism; do not arrest a mother with small children until there is a hearing. Try to link them to enemy organizations."

A long series of regulations were to project this image of legality. "You can cancel their telephone only if it was misused. A meeting does not constitute 'a group.' Never form groups or provoke. It is not illegal to visit the BRD embassy. Do not anticipate what you will find. You can not use their letters to the UN and embassies. Never let MfS control of the mails be evident in the hearings. Prove that the initiative came from the enemy and not from internal conditions. Never turn it over to the police."

The MfS also had to camouflage its effort to divide the opposition. "The art of differentiation must be commanded as the expression of our higher humanity." Yet in July the MfS had to admit that the Schwerin Emigration Applicants were still increasing.[7]

Already in August 1977 the church was giving employment to these "enemies." Educated applicants were being helped with low-paying jobs as cemetery workers, porters; some medical personnel were transferred to church medical positions; most had "arrest records" (for trying to leave).

Official Dishonesty and Public Discontent

Rostock reported a general unhappiness with the 7th SED Party Congress. The public was critical and pessimistic, with negative attitudes of the various classes, in particular workers and employees. "In part, it is the doubt about the realism of the Politbüro report and the speech of Comrade Schürer, mostly in connection with the insufficient supply of goods."

The official dishonesty was apparent even to the MfS. "The picture in the press of the economic conditions does not correspond to the real productivity. There are greater difficulties in tractor parts and other farm machines." The MfS agreed with the recurring complaint: "Despite assurances of price stability, prices rise under the name of improved quality, which places a greater burden on the people."

The MfS decried this dishonesty: "The time has come when the firms' leaders should finally send realistic reports to their superiors and not their pipe dreams." Orders were being avoided: "The ordered measures for saving auto fuel are not being implemented in the firms, and the effectiveness of the management must be increased." The marginal comment: "That's true." The Mfs accepted: "Supply and demand do not match. The talk on TV is of improving supply but nothing has changed."

The public criticisms included the Intershops, where only foreigners could buy better products with Western money: "Everyone would like to have such good things." (The MfS defensive comment: "We don't have enough.") Then the core problem: "The DDR can not maintain price stability and the social-political program can not be attained, because the foreign debts are too great."

The socialist states were also a drag. "The expenditures for international solidarity are too high. The economy must bear heavy burdens because it is being exploited by the Soviet Union." (The margin's criticism: "This is openly anti-Soviet.") The public view: "Everything is only gray theory. When you go into the stores, you can get nothing." (Hostile marginal reaction: "Who has the initiative, the representative of this enemy ideology?")

The Party's constant pushing was too much for the public to bear. "That plus the call for competition is driving people too far. The drums are always beating and no one gets any rest. There are always demands for more effort but no higher wages." As for the acclaimed "socialist" competition: "The call for competition of firms was a waste of time; no one pays any attention."[8]

Enemies were at work. In August 1979 Mielke's assistant Mittig warned the locals that there was an active undermining of the cadre, including the liberal propaganda to work more closely with the BRD. "This operates under the concept of the so-called 'cultural community' " (meaning Germany). "The intent is to pull us away from the Soviet Union."

Mittig noted that Mielke's restrictive edict still stood. "The use of criminal law can not replace political work." He lamented that the SED preferred to push their problems off on the MfS rather than to solve the problems with persuasive activity. "We must avoid having our efforts spread too thin." Mittig was also unhappy with some IMs. "There are numbers of IM who provoke hostile action or knew of it and did not report it. This is a very serious problem."[9]

The MfS described honestly the economic failure in 1979, that there had been a very small growth in investment and that dishonesty was everywhere. "The gaps in Supply are increasing." This dishonesty was compounded by incompetence ("In the DDR, 30 percent of the food supply is destroyed") and deception ("The illegal building, the manipulation and other frauds, which are discovered in every firm and branch of industry, have worsened the problem"). The task was: "We must know Who is Who, who causes the economic problems and what can be done to punish them." IMs must spy on their bosses to increase production.

To improve that IM system was also a problem. "In that network we observe a great two-tonguedness of a large number of our IMs. They say one thing at work and something different when they talk with their handler." Reports were causing problems with the SED: "Often we give such information on to the SED and then get into a complicated situation *vis-à-vis* the Party. These attitudes affect our operative colleagues, up through the intermediate cadre leaders, to the leaders."

There were also reports of MfS incompetence. "A number of the operative colleagues are not competent to deal with the political and operative problems of the time. . . . Only in the rarest of cases have we been able to cover it all and secure a classic presentation of evidence. Because of this the elimination of damaging conditions is delayed and often the criticism is raised against us. This is the work of the enemy."[10] The "enemy" would seem to be within.

Public discussions were almost entirely about shortages. "The shortages in consumer goods have led to 'Hamstering' " [scrounging for food]. Policy led to waste: "Bread prices were kept so low, that one finds in the garbage half-eaten loaves." The problem would be reduced by raising prices, including for alcohol: "There is too much drinking, which is limited only by increasing prices." The MfS could report a success: laws had reduced laughter. "Since the law had clamped down, fewer political jokes are being told."[11]

Another Celebration, Another Complaint

Communism had too much celebration: "We are celebrating the 30 years anniversary, and we just finished the 60 years of Red October. It is getting crazier and crazier.' "[12] The anniversary was reported as unsatisfactory. Its problems were blamed on insufficient political ideological work. "Orders were not followed, in July–August, there had been no schooling in the counties."

The MfS solution was to have one IM in every unit of 50 marchers. "The key positions in the leadership already had IMs; also in the marching groups and special formations the close contacts by IMs will be strengthened. They are to prevent attacks or infiltration of alien persons in the parade and to maintain an orderly march, especially near the reviewing stands. To deal with any negative, decadent youth, there are the Battlegroups and the police."[13]

Even so, the MfS had problems controlling the torchlight parade. "There were many and varied appearances of negative-hostile and criminal behavior, of a lack of discipline and rejection of the social conditions in the DDR." There was loose talk: "The participants' many sources of information included scandalous love affairs. They glorify the west, glorify the NS times, and are much influenced by the church." As for the grievance, "It concerns the supply problems and the subsidies, and selling things 'under the counter.' So we plan to talk to 300 youth ahead of time."

The District MfS made a long list of dangers to avoid in celebrating the 35th anniversary in 1984.[14] "We arrested 460 negative decadent-criminally endangered youth to secure the 30th Anniversary. After giving 313 of them long talks, 228 were held longer."[15]

The MfS was still expressing confidence in itself: "From the standpoint of our operations comes the impression that every general confrontation or every divergent noticeable behavior will be erased."

But the MfS reported a negative reaction toward Honecker's liberal policy toward criminals. It was not thought fair that the amnestied were given housing when ordinary citizens could not find any. "Many citizens don't understand the amnesty.... The streets will be unsafe." A social worker predicted cynically, "Let me pick them up from jail, otherwise, they will be drunk before they get home." An IM in the Justice Office said, "Much work will be necessary but there is no assurance that those released will be integrated; almost everyone thinks that those released will be arrested soon again." The better-educated people supported the amnesty and regarded it as a "clever tactic." A technician observed, "We amnesty criminals but lock up people for political jokes."[16]

There was also a growing divergence potential in the SED against old leaders from the beginning of the 1980s. In 1984 the *Ostsee Zeitung* published a realistic economic analysis that was picked up by the West and enraged top SED. The editor was called to Berlin and told, "We permit no discussion of mistakes. You are party hostile."[17]

Both the public and the MfS reacted negatively to the growth of expensive *Exquisit* (luxury) shops: "Prices are set high to drain off savings. Prices are also up in Poland and CSSR, so they come to buy here where our prices [of basics] are kept down. In exchange for worthless foreign goods, ever more high-value consumer goods are bought here." Meanwhile, "Western imports are being blocked." More hostile negativism: "Our IM says that people regard the media as ineffective. There are also a significant number of negative expressions, particularly involving higher education and medicine."[18]

There was general discontent about textiles, auto parts and tires, contrary to the Central Committee's rosy report. The MfS was also upset: "When one reads that report, one must assume that the flow of information does not reach that high level and they have no idea what the situation is regarding supply. How can one publish such statistics where everyone can see that the supply has gone down steadily for two years and the prices have gone up? Where are those goods that allegedly have been produced? There are supposedly three classes of merchandise but only the expensive ones can be seen." MfS personnel, as consumers, were agreeing with the critics.

Contrary to the happy collective-farmer propaganda, mismanaged LPGs continued to be the reality. In Wendorf and Klein Siel, personnel were drinking on the job. Other misdeeds included ignoring veterinarians, lacking temperature control, losing track of mothers, leaving calves to lie in excrement and in dangerous drafts. This had meant a 30 percent loss of calves.

As described in the banned Orwell's *Animal Farm*, a worker said: "The human being in socialism is only a workhorse." Some were more equal than others: "Some leaders have 1 or 2 *Dachas* [Russian vacation homes]. It would be better if everyone had one proper house."[19]

Production problems had become more serious, like the MfS investigation into why the electrification of the railroad was not being completed and the serious discrepancies in the realm of finances. "Needed are leadership cadre who can control the process, so that deadlines can be met with technological discipline for sufficient quality and quantity of the foundations as promised." The material stimulus for the leadership cadre was regarded as insufficient. Little was done in July and August for lack of pylons, and there were serious difficulties in producing the necessary software. "We can't finish this year, so we will have to go back to steam locomotives which will cost more money."[20] Knowing the deepening discontent, the MfS ordered an increased alert against agitation.[21]

Troubling Resistances

Although decried by anti-Communists, because of Bonn's *Ostpolitik*, treating the DDR as sovereign, the BRD was getting significant concessions. By 1984 the Western journalists thus permitted to operate in the DDR were already recognized as a danger: "40 percent of them don't give journalism as their jobs; 90 percent were W. Germans, who came well-prepared and equipped, and usually created long relationships. They contacted the politically ambivalent, especially Lutz Rathenow and Rainer Eppelman. The IMs countering such enemies were not satisfactory."[22]

In July 1986 Colonel Kralisch wrote a long report of the increasing resistance problems. He emphasized the BRD's Green Party, the efforts at partnerships of East and West cities, and the International Peace Committee, which he linked to the Trotskyites. He had already sent Berlin a 15-page indictment of those guilty of high treason, but the SED leadership had decided not to prosecute. "The central point has come to be 'human rights,' which has meant telling massive lies about the DDR."

Kralisch saw "increasing signs of public resignation, and a disappearing participation in Party work," as well as more hostility: "The Mecklenburger Basis Group was hostile. . . . In Güstrow, the 'hostile-negative forces' had succeeded in getting an absolute majority in 'the Peace Work Group.' " Pastor Heiko Lietz presided, with Dr. Karin R. as deputy. Involved were Pastor Jürgen R., delegate of the Church Council, and Dr. E. of Schwerin. "In the underground activity of the church, the person of the bishop is most important. Stier was better for us than his predecessor, Heinrich Rathke. We have been able to prevent certain decisions and recommendations, which could have brought conflict with the state. So for the past two years, there have been no significant attacks on us."

Spying on the church had its problems. "Our IMs, for the past 5 years with the same personnel, are wearing out." But the attack must continue: "All units have been ordered to identify candidates for the election of the new Synod in 1987 and do all possible against the hostile-negatives."

The MfS still thought it was winning: "Through operative measures and the disciplined influence of state authorities, it was possible to continue successfully the process of dividing up the pastors. An evident result in the past year is the continuing diminishing of the number of pastors, who are prepared to defend the underground political activity. . . . Naturally they still oppose but they are less likely to act."[23]

Remarkably, the District MfS made a fundamental admission about weakness of the system that it was serving. "Socialism as an achievement-oriented society places too great a demand on humans. . . . The constant pressure to produce is human-hostile, and in recent years has produced increased signs of resignation, leading to such problems as alcoholism and 'dropping out.' " It also hindered freedom: "The communist raising of children and youth hinders a free personal development."

This criticism of conformity was coincidentally also the theme of a hostile group, mostly from the State Theater. Under the camouflage of a birthday party, they rented a room at an inn and for about 30 persons presented a "Tin Can Theater." With tin cans hanging from ropes, they mocked a "demonstration for Socialism." Gray cans, the mass of the demonstrators, marched by a presidium in lockstep. The presidium was colored cans, the major figure a blown-up larger can. Anyone different was pushed away. "Our IM judged the audience to be mostly persons who were failures, homosexuals, dropouts and church youth workers."

Young people were showing some excitement, but for amateur dance bands, which were out of control. The MfS admitted some admiration for them: "With great personal efforts and with substantial financial investment for musical instruments and technology, they have created presentable groups, which enjoy great popularity among the young." On the downside, "We socialists have not been involved in this. Performances are scarcely organized so our influence equals zero." But the MfS conceded that they had positive aspects: "Their negative image is not justified; at a recent gathering in a barn, everyone had to sign that they had voted, and that misuse of alcohol would lead to immediate expulsion."

The colonel saw reasons to worry about security. "We must increase the protection of our IMs. The 1985 efforts of our enemies to uncover our sources have not relented." The 67 new IMs must be better prepared. In addition, "There must be much improvement in using them."

In 1986 the MfS work on the many church leaders, who were protecting the underground, had made some progress. "The necessity of the goal-directed assignment of IMs for our political activity is proven by its work on the so-called youth work in Schwerin's Paul Church, which is a modified form of political underground. Here we were able to make the leaders of the organization so insecure that in the past year, only one of the programs with political-negative content occurred, where before there had been monthly programs with sometimes over 100 participants. Alternative actions and provocations did not get beyond the planning stage and the major organizer applied for a position in a different Land church."

But the security problem was still serious: "Yet with every emphasis, I must insist on the increased need for security of our IMs." The irony was that "The IMs must be close to the opposition, which comes up with destructive ideas which we would never have thought of. By arresting two from the stage crew, we made the others less secure."[24]

The MfS was also frustrated with "political-tourism," West Germans coming with subversive intent, "including the idea of Germans belonging together and the glorification of the BRD." In 1985, 8,500 persons in 212 groups had come. "Most of the groups meet on the other side for up to 3 days to be trained against the DDR. They were told where to go in Schwerin, how to meet groups, and how to avoid DDR controls." It was malice aforethought: "Tourist Group Travel was systematically being ordered with the long-range intent to undermine our social fabric relationships."

About this attack the MfS was getting much too little information and considered that an IM could be used. It specified important visitors who needed to be watched. The top category was to be consistently watched; the next category, watched not as much as possible but as much as necessary. The MfS noted, "The less important the [BRD] person the more likely they are to keep contact."

Nationally, 25 percent of BRD citizens had DDR connections, of whom 83 percent sent letters, and 85 percent sent packages; of these 25 percent complained that theirs had been lost in the DDR mail. The MfS worked hard to keep down Schwerin's contact with its partner city, Wuppertal.[25]

An MfS major complained that since 1980, enemies had also been using protection of the environment as a weapon against the DDR, sending in ecology agents; nonsocialist reporters were cooperating. Among a long list of security breaks, a BRD citizen had been shown the meteorology office: "It should be kept as a state secret." The major did not show concern for environmental problems, only how to keep them secret.[26]

Even workers were difficult, because of "the lack of political ideological preparation." The workers' state could not get former railroad workers to return to work. Lacking were 818 workers, unhappy about salaries and about railroad wagons being trashed and other old wagons bought from the BRD, and the problem would be to get replacement parts. Some rejected working overtime. In Güstrow, "They say that a salary policy known to be false was adopted to anger the workers."[27]

Yet a greater problem existed: "One observes unmistakably that the people stand behind Gorbachev." This despite the DDR efforts to keep Gorbachev's reforms away from the DDR. Sadly, his *Glasnost* meant that Germans were shocked to learn that the model socialist country had difficulty feeding its own people.[28]

BERLIN

The Trouble-Filled Soviet Connection

Soviet Secret Police chief Yuri Andropov, who brought Gorbachev to Moscow, saw at the end of the 1970s that deep reforms in Communism were necessary because the West was so much ahead technologically. Worse yet, the East was becoming ever less competitive.[29]

By 1981 the Soviets were no longer able to do economically what they had done when necessary in 1953, 1958 and 1960: bail out the SED. Instead, in August Brezhnev said that because of three consecutive bad harvests, they must reduce oil shipments by nearly 2 million tons. This hurt, because the DDR had invested heavily in refineries to process and export cheap Soviet oil, so Honecker refused to accept the cuts.

Schürer warned the Soviets that the DDR would have to borrow another $3.5 billion by 1985, violating the recent promise to reduce the dependence on the West. His counterpart Baibakov candidly lamented, "We have so many to help. Should we give away S.E. Asia? Angola, Mozambique, Ethiopia, Yemen? We carry them all and our own standard of living is extraordinarily low. We really must improve it."[30]

The DDR also wanted to improve. Honecker went to Andropov's successor, Konstantin Chernenko, on 15 July 1984 to get 19 million tons of oil, rather than 17 million. "I beg you, Comrade Konstantin Ustinovitsch. We are helping Cuba with 1.5 billion marks, Vietnam with 1 billion, various Solidarity funds with 1.7 million, Nicaragua, Angola, and Mozambique, a cement factory in Ethiopia, an oil mill, a textile factory."

But Chernenko talked instead about his own problems, including China, "who made demands with every Soviet effort to improve relations." Describing his money problems, Chernenko seemed almost to ignore what Honecker needed but questioned, "Are you sure, Comrade Honecker, that your visit to the BRD will not be used for an upswing in the feeling for German unity and the creation of more differences between the DDR and the Soviet Union?"[31]

In the past, Brezhnev had wanted the DDR to help contain Poland, so he permitted this double-dealing with the BRD. In 1980 Honecker had been the most vociferous for a Warsaw Pact invasion of Poland to stop the Solidarity revolution.

Until the mid-1980s, major DDR personnel changes were cleared with the Soviet Communist Party. High NVA (National Volks Armee) officers told Schabowski that Soviet advisers had the last say in the ministry down to the division level until the end of the regime.[32] Ambassador Abrassimov was demanding reports and appearing as though he were still high commissioner in an occupied land. He was always ready to criticize any variation from the Soviet norm.[33] On his side, he complained that Honecker would listen politely but then do what he wanted. Although Moscow preferred to keep its DDR isolated, Honecker wanted contact with the BRD, also because that brought in the needed West money. He became ever more irritated by restraints.[34] His greater problem was not having enough to sell to repay those debts.

The Secret Police to the Rescue of the Economy

Despite Mittag's push to increase exports at any price, the DDR did not possess viable exports. The foreign deficit problem was insoluble because the DDR's industrial product was not of world-market quality. Further, the effort to autarky, doing without imports, created disturbing price rises and a more disturbing unrest from shortages.[35]

The catastrophic results were declining exports and growing debts. The hoped-for push for innovation in Eastern Europe, COMECON, did not happen, as the economies in all its countries were in a desolate condition.[36] This bleak reality was kept secret not only from the public but also from the leaders.

Even the supposedly well-informed MfS leadership was shocked to learn that the DDR economy was near bankruptcy and that Mittag's house of cards was threatening to collapse. This mind-boggling information went in 1981 to Kleine, who turned pale and sent it to Mielke, who called his assistants irresponsible for saying such things. They dutifully recanted. Mittag knew better and called on Schalck-Golodowski to delay the collapse with whatever possible deal to get hard currency.[37]

In 1982 Mielke had come to recognize that the DDR was living only by borrowing and that Mittag was deceiving the Politbüro. He assigned Kleine's department to be, in principle, a shadow government.[38] As liaison, he set up a "workgroup" with Mittag, Gerhard Beil, Foreign Trade Ministry, and Schürer, of the Planning Commission.[39]

Mielke-Mittag constituted a personal foreign trade apparatus to get hard currency anywhere and from anything. In April 1982 weapon shipments went via Rostock to Iran and to an unidentified partner. This meant serious reductions in the MfS holdings of weapons and munitions. In 1983 Mercedes tank transports were used to ship "Art und Antiquities" to Saudi Arabia.[40]

As for "normal" trade, the forced exports to the West were more like those from an underdeveloped country, two-thirds being raw materials. To earn 16 billion valuta marks, Mittag had to spend 65 billion paper marks.

Much that was lacking had to be bought in the West, but Western banks, because of their costly Polish and Romanian experience, had put on the credit brakes in 1981. Mittag was desperate enough in 1982 to send in agents to sell millions of DDR marks before the rate could change.[41]

In a further blow from the East, oil prices from Russia increased 650 percent, and DDR's industrial prices much less, so the DDR had to ship much more to the USSR to stay even.[42] At the end of June 1982 Stoph told the Politbüro that the Planning Commission must reduce consumption, to which Honecker answered: "These words we want never to hear again." Whether the Politbüro heard the words, it did not act, so the problems only escalated.[43]

As Mittag remembered: "When in the early 80s the price of oil went up 8 to 10 times, we had to export large amounts of consumer goods and reduce oil consumption by 5 million tons. It would have meant chaos in supply and collapse of production. We turned to barter deals, mostly for purposes of modernizing." He had also to move from oil to coal. Coal mining cost more, and it poured more sulfur oxide into the air, which pollution became another source of discontent, particularly in Leipzig, which was also being invaded by the coal mines.[44]

Mittag later made an honest confession: "The debt was not the cause of the collapse of the DDR economy, it was the symptom. We could not compete at world standards if 70 percent of our exports went to the COMECON, so we had to get capital from the West." More painful honesty: "It was not . . . exploitation by western banks."[45] Keeping the debt until 1986 at 28 billion marks meant also that imports were cut to the pain level of consumers.[46]

Kopstein noted the political importance of consumption: "East Germans understood their own citizenship rights largely in economic terms, which in the 1980s had come to mean a middle-class life style." Thus, the Honecker strategy: "For years the SED had desperately fought Western conceptions of political rights with an image of a package of economic rights, present only in a socialist society."[47] This cherished DDR image was beyond its means.

The foreign loans had enabled more goods, but repaying the loans meant having much less to consume. Mittag, trying to obscure the reality, reported "increased value" produced, which meant the same quality at higher prices. Since all of this must remain hidden, one could not publish the real problem or the solution.[48] Mittag offered a startling defense of that secrecy: "We had to hide the cooperation with the BRD from the agitators Schabowski, Krolikowski and others. We were working toward confederation (with the BRD), another purpose of the barter business."[49] The secret Mittag solution was his form of economic unification!

Almost inevitably, he also chose a greater centralization. Mittag, who had written Ulbricht's treatise on reform in 1962, now speeded up the recentralization begun by his successor Krolikowski, including centralizing the combines. He liked the few productive units so that he could promote computer hardware and brown coal production. Some economists thought that the combines might be able to resist Berlin, and it could mean more worker loyalty, because bigger companies could do more for workers. Indeed, the MfS watched smaller firms because they assumed less loyalty there.

Yet a Central Committee department head thought that the formation of combines actually changed nothing because their managers were so overwhelmed that they left it to subordinates. Many combines remained little more than paper entries. Constant shortages and supply constraints forced managers to employ a form of "import substitution," that is, between firms. A do-it-yourself approach was appealing, but the lack of specialization made it less efficient. "The essence of the combine reform was to raise an objective tendency of enterprise autarky in the economy to a matter of principle." East Germans therewith learned that a directionless "recentral-ization" would not solve the problems.[50]

Control was attempted by Central Committee seminars led by Mittag twice yearly that all combine directors had to attend. Being invited was a matter of pride, but being personally attacked and humiliated by Mittag was the price.

Obsolescence was another price. The rationalization officials spent 20 percent of their time modernizing machinery, 20 percent on repairs and the remaining time substituting for unavailable imports. Thus, although the initial impact of the rationalization divisions was rather impressive, the marginal returns decreased dramatically after a very few years. Applied research got ever less time and less money. As overall investment declined, the capital stock deteriorated, and the use of scientists as repairmen intensified.[51]

With the economy falling behind ever more, industry alone would have needed an investment of 220 billion marks. Whereas in 1967 the gross domestic product per employed person was 67 percent of the West German, the proportion had steadily declined to 40 percent.[52] The MfS admitted its low worker productivity: using the DDR as 100, the United States was 157; the BRD 139; the USSR 79, and the production of machinery was worsening.

In its agriculture, old machines had not been replaced since 1979; up to 65 percent were worn out; 50 percent of the equipment was obsolete; 42 percent of the dairies had overaged machines. In construction, 30 percent of the machinery was written off, as were 63 percent of the mobile construction machines. Spare parts production equaled 20–30 percent of demand. Production conditions were nearly everywhere catastrophic.[53]

Mittag's assistant, Carl Janson, observed a staggering number of problems beyond the foreign debt, low productivity and efficiency: an inability to use scientific progress, inadequate capital accumulation, a centralized command economy, an overbureaucratized planned economy, a shortage of motivation and creativity, the lack of a willingness to produce, low worker morale, social policy at the wrong places, an overproportioned social superstructure and repression apparatus, unproductive personnel everywhere, the liquidation of property at any price, consumption not accumulation, an emphasis on new housing and disregard for older building substance, the high military and sport emphasis, plus the extra social measures to appeal to the young.[54]

Mittag also blamed Krenz for wasting millions on his gigantic sportfests. "The economy was burdened with too high expenditures for other [political] purposes. That is the truth." He also blamed his superiors for the untruths: "One can not avoid the accusation that they [the Politbüro] really lied to the people." This was by implication a criticism of the MfS: "In the style of Stalin, the solution would be to find someone else who is guilty. They hid the truth until it became overwhelming."[55]

Mittag mostly blamed Honecker, with whom he was not as close as he pretended and as was generally assumed: "I did spend some time with Honecker but there were very basic differences." Honecker just didn't get it: "He probably did not understand the extent of the problem at the time. Probably due to his illness, he no longer seized the initiative. One could talk to him but he changed none of those things, which were crucial. For a long time it was difficult to discuss anything with him that did not fit into his long-held scheme of things." He might have leaped over the boss: "My mistake was not to go directly to the Politbüro."[56]

Mittag blamed the Politbüro as well. "From 1980, the Politbüro did everything to poison the atmosphere and to worsen the situation. They did not care about trade with the West, but used 15 billion marks to supply the population." He was isolated: "I lacked allies to make the necessary changes."[57]

Fellow Politbüro member Schabowski blamed Honecker's lack of economic knowledge but also Mittag's desire to dominate the housing program, then the chemistry program, the auto program and robot technology. Mittag tried to do it all himself. In the vicious cycle, by saving foreign exchange, quality went down, and the DDR became even less competitive. The first 256-byte computer chip cost 536 marks to produce and sold for 16, double the world price. There were bigger holes in the Plan every year.[58]

Already in 1982, the situation had reached crisis proportions. Shortages of basic goods constituted a regular feature of the monthly SED district leaders' reports. "The Politbüro issued a number of secret emergency measures for ensuring the DDR's liquidity, the most important of which was a series of approvals for 'temporary' releases of weapons, ammunition and raw materials."

Only in 1983, after a secret meeting of Schalck and Franz Josef Strauss, did West German banks receive BRD government guarantees and resume lending to the DDR. Then other foreign banks resumed lending.[59] Strauss emphasized that his objective was to prevent another war in Europe. To get the 1 billion credit, Honecker secretly promised that children under 14 and, later, retired persons would not be forced to exchange money at the border. He would think about stopping the automatic border guns, and there would be friendlier border controls later. Schalck judged that "the credit delayed the fall of the DDR until a more propitious time."[60]

Mittag praised Soviet leader Andropov for understanding the DDR's problem, which Soviet economist Daschitschev thought part of an East European problem, which was insoluble. "I wrote Andropov on 27 July 1982, that the $80 billion loans had not led to the desired increase in efficiency and quality of production in Eastern Europe but would be a heavy burden." The expert prediction: "Our project of top scholars in East

Europe concluded, in 1982–83, that the economic weakness of Eastern Europe meant that with its inefficient productive system, the Soviet foreign policy had no chance to succeed in its confrontation with the West."[61] In June 1985 Gorbachev expressed this concern that the Soviet Union had lower living standards than other socialist countries, partly because the West applied new science and technology so much more quickly.

The DDR hoped to meet the Plan for 1986, but costs had increased 16 percent because of frequently interrupted production, high inventories, transportation and storage losses, poor quality and selection and failure to meet deadlines and contracts.[62] In May 1986 Schürer was given the task of finding a solution to the falling economy, but the only possibility would have killed Honecker's sacred cow, "the unity of economic and social policy."[63] This program, to make the DDR appear to be comparable to the BRD, had to be financed by more loans from the West, which meant spreading more deliberate seeds of DDR destruction.

The economy was moving along the edge. "Like the limousines of the prominent going through the new housing, there was a thin line of order in the general chaos." The thin line was held by Mielke's troops. Previously, when the Plan had failed, violence and terror were used, but passive resistance had become too widespread.[64] The MfS had become an ever more imperfect instrument.

The Secret Weaknesses of the Secret Police

The MfS admitted secretly an increasing disorder even in its own house. Its Berlin Party organization in 1982 had dealt with 360 cases of lapses from Party discipline and had expelled 69; in 1983, that increased to 422 cases, with 87 expelled. "Dishonesty, cowardice and unpreparedness had created extreme danger points," as did immorality: "MfS agents have recruited IMs for their own personal gain, to get goods not common in the DDR and, without any operative necessity, to have a sexual relationship. That is bad when the IMs realize the purpose. Because of inexact accounting, the agents can use operative money for personal use, and in substantial amounts."

Corruption coursed through the MfS collectives: "The problem is so serious that the entire collective, or large sections of it, from leader to employee are involved or the entire collective knew or should have known, by comparing their life style with their salaries, that their comrades were misusing the people's property. The tip-off came not from within but mostly from people outside. The concentration of negative characters and political-ideological weakness indicates that these comrades did not just happen to end up together, but were there because of government and party leaders."

The report judged the leaders also corrupt: "Some 119 elected party functionaries were involved in all kinds of criminal acts, including the worst." MfS democracy failed to stop abuses of power: "These get elected because the people are not kept informed. This comes from cowardice, habit and careerism. They have the idea that the office will protect them. There is no sign of improvement as these people are re-elected. There are 50 such leading cadre. Some really think of themselves as completely untouchable so that they neither should nor can be disciplined by the Party. Many of them say so openly . . . and pay no attention to Party decisions, the Minister's commands or society's values. They simply use money, time and colleagues for personal uses and for alcohol."

The president of the Control Commission blamed the system's secrecy. "As long as this can not be discussed openly, this leads to doubts that we are serious when we say that Party discipline is the same for everyone." The policy had been to let MfS get away with it: "Party action is less harmful than Party inaction. The tendency is to sweep everything under the rug." Poor superiors worsened the problem: "Among other things, weakness of leadership is covered up. We content ourselves with many half-truths in these cases."[65]

From such internal problems followed 407 party trials and over 500 warnings or criticisms in group meetings. "These were usually limited to a formal handling, and did not achieve the necessary improvement in behavior. Some trials don't succeed either because they are not properly prepared or because the necessary open criticism and self-criticism are inadequately developed. Worse are the alcohol problems and the petty bourgeois ideas. They are using MfS materials and MfS social advantages, without the full development of their own productive capacity. Party members must be made responsible for their MfS duties."

The Secret Police were insisting on their freedom: "Many are opposed to the military-chekist discipline. They don't want to give up their gifts from the West. Their leisure time or weekends at home is when they often meet politically-negative persons and listen to BRD broadcasts. They meet an unsuitable partner and categorically refuse to leave him/her. Some are able to hide their true beliefs in their collective; some steal MfS property. Drinking leads to fights, which hurt Party and MfS and there is adultery."

Of those tried, 73 were SED functionaries; 29 had already been disciplined, mostly for theft and drunken driving. The top-heavy list included 35 soldiers, 190 noncoms, 149 lieutenants and captains, 28 majors and colonels.[66]

In 1985 there were 359 cases and over 560 warnings, of which 111 resisted the decreed punishment. "In not a few cases the leaders and membership meetings tolerate extremely superficial and vague responses. No check exists on what change if any takes place, and if he thereafter performs his Party duties."

A lack of ideological loyalty existed. "25 percent of the trials have to be implemented because of politically unprincipled behavior, abandoning the Party's position and the class standpoint, and in defeatist behavior. But the MfS members pay little attention. If pushed to do something, they refuse to stay in the SED and MfS. They are not prepared to consider doing what is required in their choice of partners. They can not be motivated; they show a lack of comradely concern; they make all sorts of excuses; 30 percent violate discipline. There is an increase in adultery." Crimes were committed in 25 percent of the cases, involving 53 leaders, 181 officers and 219 noncoms.[67]

In 1986 the MfS Department for Cadre and Schooling reported a continuing deficient implementation of Party decisions, a persistent subjective problem and a lack of thoroughness, continuity, responsibility, creativity and discipline. It ended up quoting the Scriptures: "Not all seed fell on fertile ground."[68]

Hans Modrow, Dresden's Party leader, reported the MfS tendency "to arrogance, snobbishness, and knowing everything better." Its General Böhm treated colleagues that way. "We must have a discussion with Böhm, to demand that he behave like a Chekist and Communist."[69] Not coincidentally, Honecker had Böhm spy on Modrow, but Markus Wolf, who supported Modrow as a leader-to-be, tipped him off.[70]

The IM spies were indispensable, but a Stasi major described them as a problem: "Very few of the IMs were real sources of information. We often had more trouble with them than operative usefulness. The sources were undependable. We waited hours for them often and they came late or didn't show up. And the assigned tasks were not completed or only partially."[71]

The Party itself was aging. Long tenures in SED office were the policy; the average tenure as district leader was 13.6 years by 1985. The average age of a district's leader was just over 60 years.[72] Only the dissidents were getting younger.

The "Hostile Negatives"

New in the 1980s was not so much the discontent but the changing organizational forms and orientations of political activists. Also changing was the domestic political context of their actions, including the growth of spaces within which they could act, the changing response of the state, and the changing international context.[73]

Dissent crystallized around the issue of peace, as young people began to form "peace circles." These groups were tied closely to the community structures, as a form of its spiritual life. Although they could not stop the armament, many persons were prepared to make a sacrifice and did so ingeniously. "In the wide variety of actions, church services, Blues-masses, demonstrations, bicycle tours and tree plantings were thousands of people."

Just one of them, the Swords to Plowshares, involved almost 100,000 persons.

The communication among the groups was stabilized with a stronger integration of oppositionists with various orientations. They showed a greater professionalism in contact with the public and the media. The MfS registered that recruiting agents in these groups became more difficult and in many groups they had infiltrated no IMs at all. The MfS judged there to be 20,000 to 25,000 activists and many incidents were not reported. The high point was 1982–1983. More students would have maintained an interest but except for theology students, all knew that their careers depended on political conformity and men students were pressured to serve as reserve officers.

With the SED effort in 1983–1984 to destroy the Peace Movement, Bärbel Bohley and Gerd Poppe were arrested but released when they refused to go West. Almost the entire opposition agitated under the roof of the churches, which meant serious conflict with the loyalist pastors.

The DDR was under money pressure from the BRD to permit more travel and contact and under diplomatic pressure from Moscow not to endanger détente, so thousands were permitted to leave. The remaining opposition was not subject as much to arrest, but the attempt was rather to use disciplining measures in the workplace, in organizations and state offices and increased efforts to divide.[74]

The SED reacted nervously, caught between its pacifist rhetoric and its militarist practice. The MfS prided itself prematurely on its demoralization of the Peace Movement and its co-option of compliant church leadership, but MfS repression of these peace activists transformed dissent into a question of civil rights. In 1985 Bohley, Gerd Poppe and Lotte Templin organized the Initiative for Peace and Human Rights.[75]

The MfS was more alarmed by the Women for Peace and in 1985 began a systematic and coordinated attack, Operation Wasps. They infiltrated IM women and used IM church leaders, but the women continued, maintaining 15 groups, most actively in Berlin, Halle, Leipzig and Magdeburg. All groups could mobilize for the meetings and achieve good contacts with peace groups in the West.[76]

The MfS worked especially hard to infiltrate the church. Catholics were less of a problem because they numbered only 1 million and because of their deliberate withdrawal from public life. The bishops held strictly to political abstinence. The MfS could persuade no Catholic Church leaders, with two exceptions, to a real conspiratorial cooperation, that is, with conversations without the knowledge and approval of their church superiors. Despite all efforts, church personnel policies remained autonomous, no placing or transferring of persons, and in only one instance did a draft of a pastoral letter show a state influence. By gathering IM information, the MfS could sometimes create confusion, intimidate individuals and destroy trust and solidarity. Interestingly, no Catholic priest lost his life in the DDR, and fewer than 20 briefly lost their liberty. [77]

The 8 million Protestants had become more cohesive. Younger theologians turned to social action and worked to democratize socialism. The MfS recognized that the opposition, like Havemann, Heym and Eppelmann, had power because they were the true socialists.[78] Churchman Manfred Stolpe told Eppelman that he and Havemann represented the DDR fear—true Marxists in the only institution not completely controlled by the state.

Eppelmann wrote a delightful account of his life of resistance to the MfS, beginning when, as a teenager, he could not take the stupidities of a politicized school, but as a bricklayer he found freedom in a handworker collective. Most workers did not open their mouths to criticize the system, although it would have meant little risk. "What could they have done to workers? They needed them." Eppelmann observed, "The extent of freedom was wider than commonly assumed. If you did not cross the lines, if you surrendered the right to call Ulbricht or Honecker a criminal, little would happen to you."

Instead of military service, Eppelmann became a "construction soldier," which the DDR had grudgingly permitted. The memories of the war meant that the state could not directly attack religious pacifism, and it was strongly denouncing the BRD as militaristic. As Eppelman learned, "The SED system could be enormously inhumane, but it could also be much less bad. It depended mostly on what person sat in what chair and had the power." It also depended on what kind of person sat in the resister's chair. "Very much depended on whether you had civil courage and were decent." More profoundly, "it concerned human weaknesses, which had made the DDR regime possible, along with indifference, laziness, cowardice and the drive for a career, prosperity and privilege."[79]

The MfS limited itself and insisted that its operations were constitutional: "Arresting people because of their political position is not legal in the DDR, therefore there are no political criminals or political prisoners. There must be some deliberate action breaking specific laws, violations of the sovereignty of the DDR, peace, humanity and human rights." The SED Secretariat warned the county leaders of danger and presented the solution: "The enemy, with his ideological influence on a part of our citizens, continues to be listened to, so people are still trying to leave without proper reasons. This includes also highly trained cadre in important economic positions. This development must be vigorously opposed in everyone's effective individual political-ideological and educational work, in the elimination of disturbing factors, and through a comradely behavior to prevent the wish to leave or to reverse the wish."

The MfS attacked BRD "provocation" of DDR travelers: "Chicanery, repeated illegal seizure and damaging of vehicles, and deliberate pressure on the visitor. . . . Especially skilled persons persuade them to treason and remaining in the BRD. There has been a particularly massive increase in the attacks from its secret service [BND] and other imperialists trying to get DDR citizens to commit treason. This goes from openly provocative statements, putting persons under pressure, and going as far as lengthy, planned covert action." On the positive side, "Our tactically clever action forced the BRD to react to our demands."

Unfortunately, DDR citizens were admittedly vulnerable: "Experience shows that often petty bourgeois thinking and behavior, the drive for property, consumer-thinking, theft, and moral weaknesses present openings [for the enemy]."

The MfS report for 1986 indicates the variety of hostile violations:[80]

Agents	81
Agitation	18
Crossing the border	1,322
Diversion and sabotage	2
Economic damage	60
Espionage	27
Public insults of DDR	453
Resistance and rowdyism	1,918
Smuggling persons out	17

The greater danger of subversion came from the East, not the West. Gorbachev began in 1985 his *Glasnost* (openness) and *Perestroika* (reconstruction). The great irony was that these, the first popular Soviet ideas to hit East Germany, had to be banned. Honecker set up a special committee to comb the Soviet press for offensive reformist articles and to prepare critical commentaries.[81] Not only capitalist but also Communist ideas had to be kept from the DDR.

In May 1986 Stoph gave the Berlin KGB a packet of materials for Gorbachev, outlining the real economic situation. It was directly critical of Honecker and especially Mittag, but Gorbachev refused to take sides. Foreign Minister Eduard Shevardnadze told SED leaders that Gorbachev was determined not to intervene outside the USSR but dared not say so because the Soviet Party and state were opposed. BRD Foreign Minister Genscher had picked up on the opportunity, but the United States resisted a different policy as "too soft," being skeptical of a Gorbachev who seemed to waver between change and continuity.[82]

The amazing DDR problem was that Gorbachev would take the USSR toward a freer society and permit the DDR and its neighbors to do the same. He moved faster "toward the West" in the Soviet form of socialism than Honecker would follow. The opposition to Honecker's "Stalinism" could use Gorbachev to attack him, so Honecker forbade Soviet liberal propaganda. The DDR, while still repeating the holy chant, "To learn from the Soviet Union is to learn to be victorious," in fact was trying to prevent its people from learning about the new Soviet ideas of freedom.

NOTES

(Unless otherwise noted, every source is from the MfS archives at Görslow, just east of Schwerin.)

1. Wilfried Loth, *Stalin's ungeliebtes kind: Warum Moskau die DDR nicht wollte* (Berlin: Rowohlt, 1994), p. 193. The difficulties on the land are described in my *Russian Commands and German Resistance* (New York: Peter Lang, 1999).

2. Schwerin (hereafter Sch), BdL, DOSA 400376, 10.6.58, pp. 3–13. The types of LPG varied from I, for those having had more land and subject to more restrictions, to III, those as poor farmers, therefore given some privileges.

3. Sch, BdL, DOSA 400376, pp. 20, 27–43, 65, 83.

4. Sch, Abteilung (hereafter Abt.) XX, 53, Aktion Optimismus, pp. 50–61, 68.

5. Abt. XX, 53, pp. 64–86.

6. Abt. XX, 114, Information Bericht, pp. 3–11.

7. BKG, 646b, pp. 3–21.

8. Thomas Ammer and Hans Joachim Memmler, *Staatssicherheit in Rostock* (Köln: Deutschland Archiv, 1991), signed Mittag, 2.12.77, pp. 80–84.

9. KD, Sternberg, 4544, 6.9.79, pp. 9–18.

10. Ibid., pp. 4–9.

11. Abt. XX, 114, Information Bericht, pp. 42–44.

12. Letter, Mittag to Oberst Ammer, 2.12.77, pp. 80–84.

13. Abt. XX, 114, Information Bericht, pp. 42–44.

14. Ibid., pp. 104–13.

15. Ibid., pp. 54–56, 101.

16. Ibid., October 1979, pp. 46–52.

17. Kai Langer, *"Ihr soll wissen, dass der Norden nicht schläft": Zur Geschichte der "Wende" in den drei Nordbezirken der DDR* (Bremen: Temmen, 1999), p. 84.

18. Abt. XX, 114, Information Bericht, pp. 54–56, 101.

19. KD, Bützow, 10115, June 1980, pp. 15–16.

20. Sch, AKG, 07, 8.1.6, pp. 3, 6.

21. DOSA 401150, 22.12.1.

22. Sch, 25g, pp. 5–7, 18.

23. Sch, DOSA, 400918, 22.7.6, pp. 8–12, 20–21, 27–31.

24. Ibid., 17.7.6, pp. 34, 37, 43–48, 50–52.

25. Sch, DOSA, 400931, 29.8.6, pp. 14–31.

26. Ibid., 400974, 31.12.6, pp. 3, 6, 9.

27. Sch, 07, 8.9.6, pp. 8–9, 123–24.

28. KD, Hagenow, 5143, 19.3.6, p. 3.

29. Ralf Georg Reuth and Andreas Böne, *Komplott: Wie es wirklich zur Deutschen Einheit kam* (München: Piper, 1993), p. 7.

30. Jeffrey Kopstein, *The Politics of Economic Decline in East Germany, 1945–1989* (Chapel Hill: University of North Carolina Press, 1997), pp. 90–93.

31. SAPMO, DY30, IV 2/2.035, Büro Axen, p. 57.

32. Jürgen Weber, *Der SED-Staat* (München: Olzog, 1994), pp. 94, 182.

33. Günter Schabowski, *Der Absturz* (Berlin: Rowohlt, 1992), p. 207.

34. Margarita Mathiopoulus, *Rendezvous mit der DDR* (Dusseldorf: Econ, 1994), p. 222.

35. Carl Heinz Janson, *Totengräber der DDR* (Düsseldorf: Econ, 1991), p. 102.

36. Wolfgang-Uwe Friedrich, *Die totalitäre Herrschaft der SED: Wirklichkeit und Nachwirkungen* (München: Beck, 1998), pp. 101–6.

37. Peter Christ and Ralf Neubauer, *Kolonie im eigenen Land* (Berlin: Rowohlt, 1991), p. 48.

38. Manfred Schell and Werner Kalinka, *Stasi und kein Ende* (Frankfurt: Ullstein, 1991), p. 69.

39. Uwe Bastian, *Auf zum letzten Gefecht: Vorbereitungen des MfS auf den Zusammenbruch der DDR-Wirtschaft* (Berlin: Forschungsbund, 1994), p. 2.

40. MfS, ZAIG, 2240, Sekretariat des Ministerium, p. 29.

41. Peter Przybylski, *Tatort Politbüro*, Band II (Berlin: Rowohlt, 1992), p. 64.

42. Christ and Neubauer, *Kolonie*, p. 40.

43. Janson, *Totengräber*, p. 102.

44. Przybylski, *Tatort Politbüro*, p. 64.

45. Günter Mittag, *Um Jeden Preis* (Berlin: Aufbau, 1991), pp. 38, 40.

46. Gisela Helwig, *Rückblicke auf die DDR* (Köln: Deutschland Archiv, 1995), pp. 122–24, 126, 130.

47. Kopstein, *Politics*, p. 191.

48. Janson, *Totengräber*, pp. 84, 91.

49. Mittag, *Um Jeden Preis*, pp. 99, 106.

50. Kopstein, *Politics*, p. 97.

51. Ibid., pp. 95–98.

52. Ibid., p. 160.

53. Janson, *Totengräber*, pp. 72–76, 79.

54. Ibid., pp. 103, 274–76.

55. Mittag, *Um Jeden Preis*, pp. 31–32.

56. Ibid., pp. 20, 23–24.

57. Ibid., pp. 41–42.

58. Schabowski, *Der Absturz*, pp. 124–25.

59. Kopstein, *Politics*, p. 94.

60. Alexander Schalck-Golodowski, *Deutsche-Deutsche Erinnerungen* (Hamburg: Rowohlt, 2000), pp. 291, 296, 305.

61. Wjatscheslaw Daschitschew, "Sowjetische Deutschlandpolitik in den achtziger Jahren," *Deutschland Archiv*, January 1995, p. 56.

62. SAPMO, DY/30 IV 2/2.039, 26, pp. 5, 32.

63. Manfred Uschner, *Die zweite Etage* (Berlin: Dietz, 1993), p. 59.

64. Heiner Ganßmann, in Hans Joas and Martin Kohli, *Der Zusammenbruch der DDR: Soziologische Analysen* (Frankfurt: Suhrkamp, 1993), pp. 174, 177.

65. MfS, 15891, SED Kreisleitung 510, 22.3.4, pp. 953–93.

66. Ibid., Kreis Partei Kontrol Kommission, pp. 11–18.

67. Ibid., pp. 35–42.

68. ZAIG, 4833, 24.12.6, pp. 91–94.

69. ZAIG, 5353, 8.10.6, pp. 51–53.

70. Schell and Kalinka, *Stasi*, p. 338. (Böhm committed suicide in the beginning of 1989.)

71. *Ausgedient, Ein Stasi Major erzählt* (Halle: Mitteldeutsch, 1990), p. 40.

72. Kopstein, *Politics*, p. 125.

73. Uschner, *Die zweite Etage*, p. 201.

74. Ehrhart Neubert, *Geschichte der Opposition in der DDR 1949–1989* (Berlin: Links, 1997), pp. 465–97, 499–500.

75. Konrad Jarausch, *The Rush to German Unity* (Oxford: Oxford University Press, 1994), pp. 35–36; Uschner, *Die zweite Etage*, p. 201.

76. Neubert, *Geschichte*, p. 581.

77. Dieter Grande and Bernd Schäfer, *Kirche im Visier: SED, Staatssicherheit und Katholische Kirche in der DDR* (Leipzig: Benno, 1998), pp. 102–3, 108.

78. Jarausch, *Rush*, p. 37; Armin Mitter and Stefan Wolle, *Untergang auf Raten* (München: Bertelsmann, 1993), p. 542.

79. Rainer Eppelmann, *Fremd im eigenen Haus* (Köln: Kiepenheuer, 1993), pp. 33, 48, 87, 187.

80. ZAIG, 5353, 21.7.6, pp. 47–50, 56.

81. Kopstein, *Politics*, p. 101.

82. Alexander Fischer and Günther Heydemann, Hg., *Die Politische "Wende" 1989/90 in Sachsen* (Koln: Böhlau, 1995), pp. 32–33.

Chapter 3

The Winds Rising: 1987

SCHWERIN

The local MfS also regretted support for Soviet reforms, conceding that "Those with higher education are more interested in Gorbachev." But his *Glasnost* was raising doubts: "The reform has led to questions, such as how was the Soviet government elected before? Why weren't these weaknesses discovered earlier? What good did Brezhnev accomplish?"[1] Then they reflected, "We too have lackings in planning and in supplies, problems are similar. It would be good if we would talk about this in a more open fashion, because everything is described as being too smooth."[2]

The MfS thought itself to be smoothly functioning. "Only in Bützow and Schwaan had dissident publications appeared. Attendance at church services had not increased." Of nine pastors, only one voted publicly, three did not vote, five used voting booths, signs of dissent.[3]

A number of "hostile-negative" activities were reported, "all without impact on the public." Pastor Lietz's "subversive" Peace Circle group had a total of 21 persons in 10 subgroups. "His lack of concept and preparation meant that several left early. . . . It has also financial problems, trying to get contributions." But the "hostiles" were not dumb: "Begun in December 1986, they have been very careful and clever."

The MfS was also pleased that Lietz's "Olof Palme Peace March" did not reach its hoped-for goal of a mass march because of a lack of church support and little resonance in the BRD. The MfS enjoyed a pastor's frustration: "Now we are stewing in our own juices, without decisions, concept and constructiveness."[4]

An IM helped the MfS thwart a homosexual group, exploiting the group's fears; the homosexuals were suspicious of each other as possible MfS but never suspected the real IM. "They think they are clean, but they are being moved in the right direction. Through IMs in the leading positions, it is assured that all planned activities will be known in time and all necessary preventive measures can be initiated. So we are secure on the homo scene."[5]

But not on the drama scene: the theater called off a ballet evening because the soloists did not have shoes. Agriculture was lacking much more: "The shortage of materials leads to accidents, lack of fences; the lack of security reduces production." A veterinarian said he would rather give up his cadre position and 200,000 marks than his contact with the West: "With West money, one can live well at the Intershop and in hiring craftsmen."[6]

Continuing noncompliance was observed among LPG cadres: "The reports are written only to calm the state leaders and Party county leaders. In actual practice little work is done. Sometimes people here do not even know what the Party policy is. Others know the policy, but don't believe it's correct."

Many people were asking, "What is the use of science and technology, if I can't get the basics, fodder, fuel and spare parts?" It was not only the people: "The middle cadre increasingly agree. We're operating from our core substance without any reserve." A reform had not helped. "Separating LPGs into animal and plant production was a big mistake." Legality and leaders impeded their work: "Achievement is too little rewarded and in the many security regulations one can not increase production. . . . In addition to the missing materials is the poor leadership in some LPGs."[7]

February

The MfS still had successes in breaking up groups, like a self-help homosexual group, which was trying again to organize. "The creator wanted to keep it internal, and avoid difficulties with the state, but already he has career difficulties. He was not permitted into the Vietnamese worker barracks, so he can't be a leader any more. Our IM said the measures taken against him have frightened him. Church Prior G. M. was not disappointed; he did his job and has one problem less."

Speaking for "the hostile-negative forces," Land Youth Pastor J. L. expressed his disappointment with the church: "Their view is that 'hollow heads without backbone' are determining the church's youth work. Church leaders want to quiet them. We are studying how we can best operatively utilize this division." J. L. soon left church service; he refused a pastorate, saying that he must emigrate because he could not find work outside the church in the DDR. His wife divorced him, and the MfS considered how it might also exploit the divorce.[8]

The MfS was pleased that it had also defeated clergyman C. W., who had organized "the Cellar Meetings" in Schwerin's Paul Church. "On the basis of our long-standing measures to divide them, W. gave up as social deacon. We were able to defeat his plans for an Open Youth Work in Schwerin, Neubrandenburg and Rostock; nothing seems realizable. This will probably affect such ideas all over the DDR. It was done by forcing internal church differences, along with our operative working on a series of leading church officials."[9]

Farmers were less easily manipulated. "In almost all LPGs are many people with pessimistic and negative positions about developments."[10] In general, "The public's reaction to Soviet developments is the hope for more popular influence on the state, less SED dominance in the economy, and the hope for a new generation of socialists. They were very disappointed with Honecker's speech."[11]

March

The public was pleased with a Gorbachev speech on peace but observed critically, "Reagan in 1981 offered a similar solution but the Soviets turned it down. That was too bad, the DDR could have invested that money and material in other areas." Draftable men were also for peace; none took a belligerent position.[12]

An MfS internal speech was a 71-page attack on the BRD's dangerous seduction of DDR citizens in the subversive misuse of travel. Among the tricks to get them to go West was giving money to DDR visitors (a necessary generosity because the poor DDR permitted its citizens to take only 15 marks). They got "Greeting Money," plus gifts, special programs and free tours, even a trip to the Karl Marx house in Trier. Some could also get offers of lucrative jobs.

The MfS lamented that DDR officials gave only a superficial inspection of those wanting to emigrate. An applicant's boss, assuming that the police would say no and that the police would confront them, automatically granted permission.[13]

An inspection of an LPG found not only improper safety measures but great disorder, like 15–20 recently emptied schnapps bottles. The master could only say that drinking was not allowed; the LPG used to have a drinker, but he had been sent home.[14]

April

From postal intercepts it was reported: "Internal church leader correspondence shows that the church leaders believe the developments in the Soviet Union and the constructive dialogue with western states will enable the churches to expand and achieve their own goals. There have been a series of efforts by church officials to mix in state business and misuse church buildings." They were getting many invitations from BRD and NSW (non-socialist world) churches.

The editor of the Lutheran paper, Pastor Beste, spoke extremely provocatively against censorship as contrary to the constitution. Land Bishop Christoph Stier spoke against the increased pressure of the MfS on church workers and laypersons but spoke "positively" at the synod. On the other hand: "The church receives letters from those who got to the BRD, thanking them for their help."[15]

In May the MfS reported that its long-standing measures against "Initiators and Organizers" were still having effect. "Negative meetings show the crippling effects of our internal IM work. There has been a decline in the Paul Church Cellar meetings with increased appearances of asocial elements. With the continuing development, as guided by our operative, the church will not be able to avoid closing down these meetings."[16]

June

A rising dissidence was evident in the block parties. On 30 June Schwerin county leaders reported that some county organizations were not in agreement with the coalition policies.[17]

MfS tasks also included diminishing contacts with Schwerin's partner city, Wuppertal. Their joint meetings had increased: 1986 was up 12 percent from 1985, 1987 was up 16 percent from 1986; their professional meetings were up 139 percent. Checking out Wuppertal contacts on their central computer file, they found 25 persons who had done "spying things."

The MfS was having problems in investigating DDR citizens who were "secret carriers," like teachers. Among the problems, 36 percent of its IMs provided only small bits of information for the computer. "Some comrades do not read the distributed literature and say they can not work on the opinion reports." Keeping up is difficult: "A serious problem in our informational activity about public opinion is its frequent obsolescence. . . . This obsolete information delays our work."[18] So did the dishonest reports about production, a juggling of figures tolerated or ordered by firm managers.[19]

July

LPG problems were similarly unrelenting. "The messy offices show lack of leadership as do other indications. Among the cadre problems can be seen the strong LPG-egoistic thought and behavior, as well as their prestige and political-ideological positions. Leaders could solve this but they blame the others." There was an attitude problem: "The attitude is defensive, pessimistic and negative; they still believe LPGs [animals and plants] were

better when kept together; the integrative councils have too little power."
And those ubiquitous shortages: "Not only do we not get technology but
we do not get nails, screws and bolts. Since we haven't solved the parts
problem for years, we must doubt the planned economy."[20]

In analyzing those applying for their first visit to the West, 21 had already met someone from the West while visiting socialist countries; 32 were
"weak in the faith."[21] The MfS complained that even "secret carriers" were
getting permission to go West for family reasons.[22]

August

In a "hostile-negative" peace seminar, Bishop Müller, Pastor Lietz and
the "Wanderer" [code name] organized a 24-page information sheet on
how to resist military service. "It goes far beyond religious matters to massive attacks on the DDR defense policy. This continues the confrontation
against the state. . . . The state efforts to prevent writing this sheet were
blocked by Stier and Müller."

Churches were abusing the desire for peace. "The contents of their Peace
Network and a number of internal church documents prove that the question of refusing military service has become a central position in the attacks
on the social state, just as the peace theme and human rights have been
pushed to center stage by hostile-negative forces. This can also be seen as
a kind of substitute solution for the non-credible peace demagoguery."[23]

The MfS still expressed its pleasure that the "internal enemy" was not
having success. "It was clear that in their [the dissidents] peace campaign
they did not care about people, but just wanted to oppose." Yet the dissidents admitted that a woman had reduced her work as a doctor in order
to do more peace work.

The MfS proudly noted no church efforts to revive the churches' "Open
Youth Work"; the church, although not saying so, was "pleased," because
what had frequently occurred in youth work was illegal. "That problem is
solved—next comes the environmental problem."[24] (This meant the environmentalists as the problem.) Lietz wanted to accept a BRD Green Party
invitation; Stier supported it, but Müller, "realistic and juristic," said that
it was a political, not religious, kind of action. This result was viewed by
the MfS as their successful "differentiating" process.

Poets were less realistic and showed hostility at the sponsored 17th Poets
Seminar. Contrary to Party policy, they did less political-ideological
"schooling," or indoctrination, than poetic schooling. They displayed a
lack of discipline, drank too much alcohol and asked provocative questions
in an undignified manner; wine bottles in their hands, they did not stand
up or give their names. This behavior met no counteroffensive; the FDJ
sponsors did not maintain order. "One could not recognize this as a FDJ

meeting. There was no control of the leisure time, rather they had intellectual discussions into the morning hours."[25] Poetic license.

September

The monthly evaluation of MfS operations began with problems in protecting secrets in a plant breeding institute; putting in an IM had not sufficed. BRD buyers were considering a new DDR fertilizer spreader, but it had serious technical problems and had to be withdrawn; although conceding the defect, the MfS thought that the BRD wanted to discredit the DDR land machines.

Suspicion was also directed at Volkswagen: when it said that it would invest in a DDR firm, this could be spying on the firm's capacity. Another dubious case: a BRD customer of the People's Beverage Combine in Schwerin tried to get its director to come to the BRD to make a deal, "although they knew he was not travel cadre" [leaders permitted West].

The MfS alleged two other examples of BRD firms spying or sabotaging but admitted a core internal problem: "In a large number of firms exists a tense economic situation. This is connected to the manifold material supply problems and deficiencies in the planned growth of management's ability, which was to be achieved by scientific-technical progress and rationalizing the infrastructure. It is partly from a shortage of technically and politically qualified cadre and a management which does not fit the new, changing requirements. Many times the leaders discuss for months the impossibility of the central plan rather than fighting to accomplish it."

The MfS conceded another growing problem: "More and more IMs/GMs in all branches are reporting manipulation, the sending of false reports and painting a false picture. Even though we can't prove that this manipulation is from hostile sources, it does discredit the SED."

The railroad situation was also worsening; the worn-out equipment presented a permanent danger, "but some cadre did not do their duty, and retreated from the complexity." Therefore, losses of hundreds of millions of marks were occurring, which the MfS could not prevent. "Our operatives [IMs] in the economy are not satisfactory."

Nor were the controls satisfactory over the many postal and telephone officials who traveled to the West. "There exists a greater need for defending against spies." More defenses were needed against an expanding opposition: "There was a greater variety of opposition groups. Although a close contact among groups and persons was not permitted, they succeeded in creating and upgrading an inter-city communication network. Many go to Berlin to meetings and have many personal meetings with exponents of the political underground in their homes."

MfS achievements included liquidating two important positions in the Mecklenburg Land Church, people who were organizing an underground;

a social deacon who had been trying to set up an "alternatives" center in the Paul's Church resigned. It got a woman in church youth work in Schwerin fired; the peace group was further reduced, and the Schwerin Women's Group became inactive. This was only a partial success: "There are still enormous numbers of subversive church newspapers in the synod. They emphasize travel, resistance to military service and expanding the partner-city contacts. They are now pushing for adopting the policy development in the Soviet Union." For the church to use Gorbachev against the DDR was a low blow.

Stier and Müller were trying to improve relations with the state. "We should continue to try to put loyal people into church leadership." However, there was outside interference: "The BRD is trying to get in some CDU [Christian Democratic Union] educational materials, which are subversive, as is the political-tourism." Political tourism concentrated on the Evangelical Church in Ludwiglust and the Dom (Cathedral) in Schwerin. "They are also trying to leave the tour members more free time so it would be harder for us to keep track of them. We stopped their contact with the Paul's Church Cellar." On another front: "More IM should be used to gain control over the State Theater."

There was dissent in the SED's militia: "In the workers' Battlegroups, we have infiltrated 13 IMs, including 3 commanders, and a staff chief. One member tried to commit suicide, another refused to use a weapon, 2 tried to get across the border and 2 did not come back from a West trip."

As a success, the MfS was still stopping efforts to cross the border; in 1987, there were 21 attempts, and in 1986, 14; 75 percent were captured before they reached "the dead zone." Of 35,911 applications to visit the West, 2,258 were turned down; in 1986, of 16,901 applications, 961 were turned down. "We got IMs into key positions in the police so the border work should get better."[26] Sadly, the police had to be checked to reduce the risk of their flight.

The MfS noted an increased willingness to take risks to escape; a man drowned while crossing the Elbe on two air mattresses. People came with maps, pliers, knives, ropes and compasses; 72 percent were factory and farm workers whose efforts to emigrate had been turned down.[27]

October

Colonel Kralisch warned of Reagan's "Star Wars" [the words used]. "The imperialists were using technology to get ahead." He boasted, "They wrongly assume that the socialist countries can not keep up. After their theory of killing us with rearmament, they are trying to replace it with a goal of strangling us." This was dangerous because "[w]orker productivity of Soviet industry is circa 55 percent that of the U.S., and in agriculture, 20 percent.... Much in our economy does not increase as we have planned. . . . Therefore we are using Chekist measures in the battle to achieve our economic goals" [spying and manipulation].

As Berlin had ordered, the district gave its staff secret economic information. "Mielke wants everyone to understand economic strategy." And the problem: "Of 85 plans for firms, 19 were not realized, ergo a deficit of 113 million marks."

Mittag told them not to blame this or that group, but September had seen the lowest growth in years. In Güstrow there was a deficit of 11.6 million marks in jeans and leisure goods. "Computers and robots haven't freed enough labor. The shortage of 40,000 workers meant a loss of 2 to 4 billion marks in production. The winter cost 4 billion marks and accidents cost 2 billion more. The oil price fell, so our processing didn't earn as much; we need 5 billion marks to cover our obligations. How are we to get it? We must reduce imports 10 percent and save 500 million in energy. In the plan for 1988, national income must increase 5 percent and production 9.3 percent, therefore we must use Chekist methods."[28]

The MfS was being mobilized to counter economic officials and leaders. The district statistical office did not report the truth: "We confront in our work, again and again, many ways and methods in which the leading cadres do not present the achieved results realistically and sometimes deliberately falsify them. Most of the time this falsification occurs with the knowledge and the permission of their superiors, and even on their command. Therewith an unreal rate of production growth is described. The existing shortages and bad conditions in the internal production process are covered up so Party and government leaders are wrongly informed." Bookkeeping lying persisted: "We are confronted with double counting, when something is shipped both sender and receiver count it; unfinished goods are reported as finished."

SED leaders were also resisting the MfS. "Our operations have shown that the discovery and the overcoming of manipulation and falsification of the results is an extremely complicated process, in which we must confront serious resistance from the superior economic authorities and we do not experience the necessary understanding by Party functionaries. Despite that, this is our task. It requires the installation of qualified expert IMs in the central bookkeeping domain and in the economic directorates. Such information must be checked and proven. The manipulation of the plan, the breaking of the law and regulations must be proven, which must be emphasized. We must have official proof, which requires control agents in the firm"—the Secret Police as prosecutors of the state.

Spying on managers was necessary because of the increased public dissatisfaction with consumption as compared to the BRD. "There is the general sense that the people create the wealth but others use it. The criticizing gets worse in late afternoon and early evening." Then followed this MfS admission: "The price policy led to bad consumption habits, like the misuse of bread, which policy keeps it cheap, because it is a necessity."

The fertilizer spreaders sent from the VEB Güstrow to the BRD were breaking down. "The official investigation said there were recognizable production mistakes, which were very harmful to export." Yet such failures were somehow to be kept secret: "In dealing with the West, we should be careful that they do not see our economic weaknesses, which they will use against us unscrupulously." On the veterinary front, an informant reported that a BRD chemical liaison was using bribery to sell its medicaments.

The Parchim Metalform Firm lied about robot effectiveness: "The work began late and has in no way reached the needed effectiveness. . . . It was only 75 percent of the previous production, plus lower quality. A second robot complex has in 2 years worked only 3 weeks, yet it was reported as effective. . . . Obviously this is deliberate deception of the state."[29]

In contrast, the costly accidents were not deliberate; MfS investigations did not discover any foreign or domestic sabotage, just negligence and often actions of children. The solution was predictably to get more IMs. "Particularly serious is the fact that in Bützow, Güstrow, Lübz and Sternberg Counties, we do not have a single agent in the realm of the economy. We lack qualified IMs for such technical questions." The MfS needed more spies, but there, too, was a problem: "We should know more about our IMs, including their wives." IMs should spy on IMs.

The report further lamented IMs as being poorly placed and prepared. "In addition, we lack IMs who have contact with the hostile-negative circles, people who are firmly integrated in such target groups. In our supply of IMs, there is a large number of so-called leader cadre, too many SED members and progressive workers, whose operative possibilities and abilities are very strongly limited. . . . The few qualitatively good new recruits to the IMs with perspective are outweighed by the many who doubtless are not up to the increased demands of the job."

These demands were also multiplied by the awful Applicants: "We must concentrate and analyze more, but so much of our time and energy has to be used to deal with the people trying to emigrate."[30]

Even some SED reports to Berlin were permitting themselves a restrained criticism of the problems. "The public notices the contrast between the public descriptions and the daily reality." A remarkably frank report spoke of the failure of the plan to improve life in the villages but mentioned the worn-out equipment: "Special aspects will not be solved either soon or in the coming years. . . . In many LPGs the necessary facilities to improve life and work conditions have not been installed . . . The planned equipment can not be achieved."[31]

November

When greeting Estonian guests, district SED leader Heinz Ziegner reacted to Gorbachev: "From a mountain of questions on the table, particularly new questions, there is a resulting ideological confusion."[32] Other voices were saying that Gorbachev was making too many compromises. "His motivation is not based on the unity of socialism, but on the economic problem of the Soviet Union, which cannot maintain both military parity and their economic strategy. The progress made is primarily due to the desire for peace of the USA and NATO [North Atlantic Treaty Organization]."

On the local level, there was a special desire for the end of the Cold War: "The relationship of the citizens to the Soviet comrades and their families stationed on our territory has worsened. This derives from the lack of clarity in the thinking that the stationing of Soviet troops here is necessary." People were commenting on the increasing collapse of the confiscated houses that had been taken by the Soviets and the daily damage to the environment from their tanks and helicopters and their increasing purchases in the stores.[33]

Dissidence was still not worrisome. "There are groups of presumed Intellectuals coming from Berlin, Wismar and Schwerin, but they present no problem to public order." Nor did homosexuals: in Schwerin there were inns for homosexuals and those with jail time. "When the inns get that reputation, others avoid them."

The young were a greater worry. "Youth organizations with a firm structure do not exist any more." Instead, "There were a few music formations, which are registered but some are 'illegal.' . . . A punk group, calling itself 'First Ass' [the English words used], sing politically negative texts. They perform mostly in small towns and villages. Two such groups got frequently into fights, so they were forbidden in Bützow County. Some tried to have private gatherings but we prevented that." At a meeting appeared the sign: "I feel like I am locked up."[34]

Dissident Eppelman misused his visit to his mother in the BRD to get support for his opposition. A long report concerned Jehovah's Witnesses who were trying to avoid laws, smuggling in brochures on their bodies, in letters or in soap boxes.[35]

The MfS was pleased at the small Sunday attendance at village churches during the "Peace Decade." The sessions were strictly religious, nothing hostile; even fewer came for evening service; a total of 100 children and mothers marched on St. Martin's Day, substantially fewer than in 1985–1986.[36] MfS progress.

Officer Korth ordered more listening: "Many citizens are not working sufficiently hard to fulfill the plan in their firms and often express their displeasure concerning the supply of goods. Therefore the MfS should follow public opinion very exactly and so report."[37]

An inexact SED report began with the assurance that everybody believed in the Party ever more and would work harder, but it soon admitted, "The results are completely unsatisfactory. Again and again we confront the position that achieving the implementation of the key technologies in the economy is to be doubted. To counteract that we are working hard to explain to the comrades that its implementation is a matter of life or death of our society." Further sobering lessons: "Our experience is that the local organizations succeed only if they go after concrete projects, involve the government leaders and the workers, so that the technology brings quick results."[38]

After claiming 100-plus percent production, the SED admitted that in Schwerin and Bützow, one could get one's TV set repaired only 35 percent of the time, 15 percent in Güstrow and 17 percent in Sternberg, and washing machines could be repaired only 7 percent of the time in Gadebusch und Güstrow. Of auto parts, for Czech Skodas the percentages were only 25 percent; for Russian Ladas 40 percent; Trabant and Wartburgs 75 percent. "There are long lines to get scarce goods. Schwerin supposedly had the largest growth rate, with 7.2 percent, but it has more gaps in the stores."

Everywhere shortages were worsening problems; having so little children's clothing worsened the conflict between German and Russian mothers. "There is no bitumen for the streets, no bricks for chimneys. A construction crane is so old it is dangerous to use." In response to the constant questioning, "management can't explain why more is produced but less is available" or why "farmers were getting less of the meat they had produced."

Scarcity had undermined socialist ideology: "There are no collective feelings to be seen, every one is out for himself. Among the young there seems to be no sense of the honor of work."[39]

Failure was noted again in December. "There is a deficiency in the leadership and management of the economic progress in a number of firms, as well as increasing apathy, and neglect of duty on the one hand, and a great impatience of class-conscious workers and leaders against the manipulation and neglect of duty on the other side."[40]

The intensity of economic dissatisfaction had increased in recent weeks, pushing political matters into the background. The MfS raised the question: "Why ask the public and then pay no attention to what the public says?"[41]

BERLIN

When 1987 began, a group of DDR experts had already recognized that the DDR economy would not be able to survive and that somehow the BRD would have to help. Predicted already was that the necessary secret dealings with Chancellor Kohl would mean more open borders, so that, in effect, the Wall would fall.[42]

The Cold War was also at risk. The Reykjavik meeting of Gorbachev and Reagan meant to Mielke a greater need to resist the United States and its "Star Wars." The MfS would need more IMs to help keep DDR technological research and production secret. "Like capitalism, communism must keep its business secrets." Yet Mielke also protested his organization's overuse of secrecy: "Too many in the MfS use the classification of 'confidential' and 'only for official use.' "[43]

Mittag maintained extreme secrecy about everything, including the fact that he had lost a leg in 1986. By strength of will, he could appear in public and walk. Then he lost the other leg.[44] Perhaps symbolic of his economy.

February

Mielke's further priority had come to be fires after a 36-million-mark loss at a paper factory. The suspicious MfS ascertained the cause as socialist negligence and incompetence, not capitalist maliciousness.[45]

Mielke's 168-page speech, lasting nearly five hours, described MfS weaknesses within the economy. "I must say again that the success in the political-operative work stands or falls with qualified IMs. Now it is clear that a substantial number of our IMs in the economy do not possess the necessary qualities and are not in a position to obtain the necessary valuable information."

He recognized the failure, as was reported from Schwerin: "The problem is of selecting, preparing and placing IMs. Our principle is that quality comes before quantity. The core problem is that the IMs we have scarcely offer us the opportunity to influence and remove the limiting factors in the economy."

The IM problem was made worse by poor internal procedure. "The weaknesses in operation are erratic meetings, not staying with a subject until fully cleared, the lack of written reports from IMs and not making sure of a minimum documentation. We have many people trained in economics, but the less competent and younger people are assigned to handle the IMs."

He saw that other insoluble problem: "Emigrant Applicants are increasing in number, despite all our efforts. Of visitors to the BRD, three times as many now don't come back. A high percentage are the top qualified, 8,793 higher education cadre; most of these when they arrive in the BRD tell them all they know in order to have a better start there."[46]

Mielke quoted Honecker that the MfS must look beneath the surface to know exactly the morale, feelings and views of people and to influence them properly. "IM should be in key positions and clearly improve their qualifications. They should be honest and willing to solve whatever problems." On the other legal hand, "No one may be limited in his rights as a citizen without reason."

Then Mielke criticized the internationalizing of the human rights efforts to stir up trouble, including "misusing" the Helsinki Agreement in order to conduct a comprehensive slander campaign against the DDR. "For the first time oppositional elements from the DDR, the CSSR, Poland and Hungary are actively involved in pamphlets and petitions. Their goal is to create an independent peace and human rights movement."

These enemies had been curbed but remained dangerous. "A series of persons, who are known to us, are insecure and at present inactive, but hold fast to their known political positions. Spectacular provocative-demonstrative actions are not in the foreground now. Their meetings are to clarify their positions, to consult on practical measures. There is a hard core, particularly in Berlin, who have the strings in hand to create a network. The concentration point is their effort in a demagogic fashion to transfer to the DDR the movement of the USSR and to bring a new political thinking and action in international relations. They use the hostile terminology, 'more human rights and freedom,' and try to force an independent political dialogue of party and state."

Evangelical activism was worse than Catholic abstinence. "Reactionaries in the church are opposing the progressive elements. As they have done consistently, the leadership of the Catholic Church in the DDR uses the tactic of distancing themselves from the government, the avoidance of any official position to basic political questions. The policy set in the 1950s was to forbid the activity of the clergy in political parties and social organizations. One can now expect a similar development as in the Evangelical Church."[47]

The hostiles were misusing the law: "They push to get enemies out of jail and to get expanded legal room for their activities." For this they were using the figure of Soviet dissident Sacharov. The commander of the Berlin MfS said that he usually could not arrest on political grounds; rather, he would build up a case for later, when it would be necessary. "Under other conditions one could arrest them all quickly." He noted, "There was an increase of political misdeeds, such as meeting someone or insulting the state."

Against such misdeeds, the MfS mounted yearly 4,000–4,500 "operations," 60 percent of which were without result; 2,600 resulted in "preliminary proceedings." The 1,000 cases of flight constituted the bulk of its work; 10,000 persons were under "sharp observation." More thousands came to the MfS offices trying to leave.

There were 85 percent more applications to leave than in 1985, mostly from Dresden, Berlin, Chemnitz, Gera, Leipzig and Erfurt; the fewest came from Suhl and Schwerin. Fewer applicants were reconsidering their decision; in 1984 it was 1 of 3.3, and in 1986 only 1 of 4. Dresden, Chemnitz and Berlin had the most who did not come back from family visits, "which shows officials there have been too soft."

Mielke told his leaders of his concern about "resettlement" to the BRD; he said that he wanted suggestions, because the serious problem required new measures. "Without any reason, important cadre were falling to western propaganda. We need a political offensive by which, as good comrades, we will reduce the problems that bother them, until they are integrated solidly in our society. Help them solve their problems. Bring in important persons with authority and experience to impress them."

If there followed any suggestions or any discussion, it was not recorded, and he finished as though he had learned nothing. The top four leaders took the recess by themselves rather than mingling for underlings' ideas.[48] Emigration applications continued to rise, to 87,000.

Bernd Eisenfeld estimated that 25,000 persons were in active opposition. Most disturbances were in Chemnitz, Leipzig and Dresden and occurred without the MfS having an idea of them before they happened.[49]

May

The Politbüro should have known of the staggering problems. For example, Bitterfeld's horrible pollution was reported and, a few days later, Mielke passed it on to Honecker, Stoph, Krolikowski and Mittag as a danger to life of the workers and the area residents. There was a shortage of workers because many left. If Bitterfeld, the pharmacy center of the DDR, could not supply its 4,000 products, this would cripple wide areas of the economy.[50]

The Central Committee also received appeals from people: 24 percent concerned housing and 22.5 percent concerned travel. It concluded that there were some "heartless leaders" who had not solved the justified desires of citizens, mostly concerning repairs, about the decay of old housing. Even the new housing had problems of leaky roofs.[51]

Salaries of some DDR workers were increased by up to 2,500 marks, but that led other workers to demand more. "To plug a particularly painful hole in the economy, one took measures that led to 21 smaller holes, which also grew larger every day."[52]

Henke concluded that the MfS had taken on an impossible task. "In trying to reduce the effects of the structural flaws in the economy with their traditional conspirative instrument, it was generally without effect." Its many spies produced information, most of which duplicated what was already reported. "Many an industry minister rubbed his eyes in wonder to find on his desk a top secret report about conditions in his area which he well knew."

This MfS information did not lead to decisions, partly because it was all supposed to be top secret; therefore, the unhappy public would not be

mobilized for change. Secrecy also limited the power of its monstrous bureaucracy. As Mielke told the Volkskammer in October 1989, he had reported everything; alarming reports alone could not stop the collapse.[53]

September

The MfS reported accurately that just trying to supply life's necessities
"has created in all circles a significant increase in critical discussions."
There was much to be critical about: "There are more evident bottlenecks,
gaps in variety, lower quality, in clothing, technical goods, auto parts, even
basic foods. There is more skepticism of official reports, including that of
the Central Committee's fourth meeting. It is ever more difficult for functionaries, particularly in Neu Brandenburg, Leipzig, Dresden, Magdeburg,
Chemnitz and Frankfurt, to deal with these doubts and with the question
whether leaders really know the conditions."

Even in the rural areas, "Food is also a serious problem. . . . This has
stimulated discussions, with the greatest sharpness, expressing the lack of
understanding and deep disillusionment that such a supply situation has
been permitted. People even tell visitors from the BRD about the 'Berliner
rage to waste.' "

Around DDR fringes, many raged. "In Suhl anger is high because border
areas are supposedly to be better supplied. It is worse in the countryside
because of the saving of gas, and because the transport vehicles are terribly
worn out. The lack of warehousing means many goods are ruined. There
is a lack of cooling and proper equipment, the lower qualification of retail
personnel and the improper handling of goods, mostly in the county seats."

The result was a lack of fresh goods. "The workers in Chemnitz, Magdeburg, Frankfurt and Rostock complain about the lack of fresh fruits and
vegetables. It is the worst supply in years, and people don't understand, 'If
the problem is bad weather, why not import?' " Discontent reached from
top to bottom. "This has a negative impact on leadership cadre and commercial workers. They think firms and combines develop too little initiative.
Too much goes to export and to Berlin, the latter is the subject of many
letters, which are getting more bitter. There is increasing corruption and
bribery, which the state must do more to stop."[54]

When, for the 750th anniversary of Berlin, the DDR tried to present East
Berlin as a "World City," the extra deprivation of the rest of the DDR
greatly annoyed the non-Berliners. Dresden truck drivers struck against
bringing Berlin its cucumbers; Berlin autos had their tires stabbed, and
Berliners sometimes were not sold gas.

The MfS foresaw conditions worsening: "The problems for winter will
be severe with the brown coal production suffering from lack of parts,
obsolescence of transport, violation of technological discipline, lack of pro-
vision for parts and replacement for worn out machines." More earthly

problems: "There is the inability to deal with the increasingly complicated geological requirements." Then an ominous secret: "There are problems in the power plants, including the nuclear plant at Greifswald."[55]

The MfS admitted its own many serious problems: insufficient clarification of "Who is Who in the Opposition," the lack of planning and analysis, the nonrealization of planned assignments, the insufficient location of IMs and their use, the inadequate IM investigation of residential and leisure-time areas, unrealistic goals, a lack of supervision at the district level, insufficient cooperation with the officers in Special Assignment, inadequate chekist training, especially of those in the economy, the lack of long-range assignment of tasks, a lack of stability and low-quality cadre in the economy, especially in the combines, too few qualified cadre, overly burdened middle cadre, inadequate guidelines for IMs and operations, a lack of the leaders' influence on the evaluation and informational activity and the lack of adjustment for the complexity of the combines.

The list of insufficiencies goes on and on. More flexibility was needed against the capitalist spies, saboteurs and "hostile centers in the economy," especially in key development industries. Again the complaint: "There are too few IMs with useful information; we get too much unimportant information. There is a serious deficiency of IM work with travel cadre. Our punch card system has a limited value. The sum of information for the central data bank is very limited. Our priority must be to realize the Plan in science and technology, those matters with high economic usefulness."[56]

Yet MfS responsibilities were increasing, as some DDR laws had to be relaxed. So that Honecker could make an official visit to Bonn, the DDR eased travel passage, reduced inspections of those going to Berlin, removed the compulsory change of money for children under 14 and reduced it for retirees. It approved partner cities and removed the automatic shooting devices on the border. Honecker permitted 20,000 dissidents to leave, and 100,000 more promptly filed for emigration.

Despite the MfS assurance of legality, the procedure to get permission to exit remained demeaning, even under the best circumstances. Fulfilling mysterious regulations and their arbitrary interpretations required countless visits to the local police and other offices. Filing for emigration meant the loss of one's passport and de facto confiscation of real estate, bank accounts and other personal property. While the application was pending, would-be emigrés were reassigned to onerous tasks, such as scrubbing toilets, or were simply fired. Friends and acquaintances would break off social contact out of fear of being associated with subversives.[57]

While Applicants were thus being kept from the West, Chancellor Kohl was agreeing to back a loan of 950 million deutschmarks to a shaky economy. The other irony was that although Gorbachev was getting closer to Reagan, Honecker's getting closer to Kohl was taken as an affront to the

USSR and brought a harsh reaction. Honecker also irritated Moscow by speaking against nuclear missiles stationed in Germany.[58]

For the Kohl visit in October, the MfS ordered isolating him ("Protect him and keep people away from him") without permitting him to be aware of the isolation: "These measures should be very thorough but so organized that Kohl and party do not notice it or anyone knows what has been done. Also prevent any hostility being shown Kohl. Make his crossing the border the quickest possible, object to nothing, charge no fees and force no exchange of money."[59] That is, make it unreal.

What could be considered a thaw to enable Honecker's visit to the BRD was changed when the Stasi on 24 November raided the Environmental Library and then arrested its leaders, an action that set off a wave of protests in various churches.[60] The church leaders faced the danger that they would no longer be taken seriously by their membership. Still alive were the old traditions of individualism and that theologians could appeal to conscience.[61]

The Catholics stayed out of it, as though they were sure that their church would outlast all oppressors. Jehovah's Witnesses suffered the most pressures but had a strength that was often missing in the mainstream churches: a preparedness to suffer.[62]

The bourgeois parties were showing a beginning of ambivalence toward the SED but were judged under control: "All cadre in important positions are appointed only after the MfS says it has no objection." On the other hand, "The influence of the CDU in the church is small; CDU members are scarcely represented in church leadership. The mass of church workers reject the CDU; pastors that happen to be CDU are pushed out of church leadership; only 15 percent of CDU members are active Christians."[63]

The shift in the Berlin dissident scene toward human rights got a push from Gorbachev. The Human Rights group (IFM) published *Grenzfall* in mid-1986; until then East Germany had produced virtually no *samizdat* (self-published) literature, partly because West German material was so available.[64] In Berlin a subgroup existed of this human rights organization, some of whose members were IMs who denounced each other to their handlers. Herewith the Stasi was the victim of its own tactic.[65]

November

The MfS was further foiled in its task of raising production: "The problem concerns insufficient Plan discipline, manipulating the Plan or false reports of results. It concerns the lack of leadership, including the ignoring of justifiable criticism, as well as ignoring worker suggestions." Yet the faith in spying continued: "Our providing information will take care of the subjective causes of the economic problems."

Yet further in the same report, the MfS recognized its failure in increasing factory production: "In 1987 we made no substantial progress. As before we did not succeed to the necessary extent to produce information of a complex character, for example, to inform about a great problem area, to create useful generalizations about . . . shortages and bad conditions, their sources and their connections. The tendencies are to a certain routine which no one can really observe, but with justifiable criticism of the workers and an irresponsibility and indifference of certain functionaries. Only Leipzig, Halle and Frankfurt are doing it satisfactorily. The MfS must be better informed about the economy."[66]

December

This month occasioned another worried analysis of the justifiable public reaction to the shortages: "It is the dominant theme of many meetings at work and in neighborhoods. It is increasingly critical and sharp in the statements, and reflects a growing anger and dissatisfaction, in particular at the increasing gaps in the variety of selection; the discontinued deliveries of different commodities; the low quality of industrial and technological goods; impossibly long waiting times in the service departments, particularly for auto repair, which lacks spare parts; the unjustifiable prices in the *Delikat* and *Exquisit* [luxury] stores. Here goods which used to be sold at a lower retail price are now sold only in these stores without any improvement in quality." The MfS was accepting these popular complaints.

The MfS also shared consumers' other grievances: "There are also price increases of new or imported goods, TVs, furniture, electrical appliances, clothing, shoes, and added costs for cars. Anger is everywhere. Food complaints come also from small towns and rural areas. A senseless closing of retail stores forces rural persons to full-day trips to county seats. There is a shortage of illustrated magazines, no subscriptions for daily newspapers, a lack of home improvement items, such as electrical cords, cement, lime, bricks and guttering." The MfS was joining in these negative sentiments.

Shortages led to further waste and even aggression. "There are more group protests to the authorities and increasingly workers take hours off to look for goods, which absenteeism is known and approved [by management], because later in the day the items would not be found. There are lines of people waiting, particularly for children's clothes and shoes, often without their knowing what is in the store. Repeatedly the police must be used to support the sales personnel in controlling the flow of customers. There are reports of increasingly aggressive behavior by customers who do not get the demanded goods. Frequently heard are angry observations of customers." Shortages were undermining public order.

Shortages were also undermining socialism. "The present supply situation does not help to make socialism more attractive. These problems can not be swept away by talking about the stable prices of basic foods. The

SED has not kept its promises. If conditions do not change soon, we can no longer enthuse people about socialism." How remarkable for the Sword and Shield to admit such things!

The danger to socialism was made worse by travel. "One will have to expect the worst, if the 'backwards development' is not stopped soon. Progressive people note that people returning from the BRD speak at work of the overwhelming variety of goods there, the great cleanliness and order in stores and towns, about the punctual and comfortable travel with the BRD railway and they compare this to the negative conditions in the DDR. They also found DDR products [in the West] at much lower prices. The question is why are not those goods here when people work hard?"

Skepticism was increasing of the DDR's ever succeeding: "Everywhere people doubt the ability of regional and central organs to solve supply problems. So often one hears expressions that conditions are as bad as they were long ago, a sad thing after 38 years of the DDR."

The people were explaining such problems as the incompetence of the authorities, the inability of socialist industry and commerce to adjust to the needs of the people and too much being put into the Berlin celebration. "Or the manipulated reporting from the bottom to the top, which leaves the Party and government leaders ignorant of the real situation." Again the MfS report did not challenge these popular accusations.

Further defined as a cause of problems was the arbitrary intervention by central organs (meaning Mittag) to increase exports at the cost of the domestic market. The policy could not be defended to the public. "Those on the inside are under ever greater pressure to explain the problem and to name those responsible, no matter what their position is, and hold them responsible. They have ever more difficulty explaining this to the workers. Many say that Party functionaries, state and economic leaders in the factories or the territories, avoid discussions with the workers. If there is a discussion, the workers get the impression that the functionaries don't understand, or are not in the position to answer questions or to suggest acceptable solutions for the indicated problems. Many times they try to divert from the actual questions and the problems and discuss only 'the great Party Line.' "

Depression reigned inside the system. "Commercial functionaries point worriedly to the increased evidence of resignation among their colleagues, who show an unwillingness and disinterest in their work, as well as quitting, or threatening to quit, with the explanation that they are no longer prepared to be scolded by customers because of missing goods."

Disaffection was diminishing production. "Experienced workers perceive among the functionaries a lack of strength to make a decision, their rejection of responsibility and avoidance of confrontations. . . . There is a decline in work discipline and morale, in the willingness to accept responsibility, and to work overtime."

Production might improve if only the truth were told the workers. "There is increasing doubt that the leaders are informed about the real situation. A primary target of exceptionally critical expressions is the media policy of describing everything in rosy colors, which is in sharp contrast to the realities of daily life. It is emphasized that the people of our country are mature enough also to deal with uncomfortable truths." Instead, statistics had become a joke: "Progressive forces stress that the monthly statistics elicit ever more ironic comments and are generally ignored or rejected by the population."[67]

Another December report denounced the state's lies: "The lack of basic materials is such that those in the know do not believe the conclusions of the Farmers' Congress. There has been a manipulation of reports. Sometimes in reports about the filling of the Plan the figures are deliberately falsified, in order to pretend that the central objectives and commitments have been achieved. That has been even tolerated by their superior officers." The lies were poorly defended: "Local functionaries can't answer questions and only change the subject."

The report also emphasized the worsening public reaction to DDR policy. "The people like the peace policy and the Gorbachev meeting with Reagan, but progressive forces fear that the DDR compromises could have long-range negative effects on the consciousness of elements of the population. The agreements with the BRD will mean a deepening and a broadening of contacts in all sorts of ways and levels, including increasing travel."

Broadening travel was broadening the anger: "In the countless discussions about the state of crisis in the economy can be seen the significant impact of the travel in the West. Thus among the politically engaged non-party-members, including many factory workers, and the intelligentsia, new and higher demands are being made."

Even the MfS was dubious about the possibility of socialism: "The serious disturbances in production have reached such an extent that the well-founded doubt became much stronger about the viability of the socialist planned economy in the DDR. This comes from leaders all over the economy. They describe the physical and moral erosion of factories, equipment, machines and transport as catastrophic."

The MfS had come to the conclusion that Gorbachev, rather than Honecker, should be followed. "The DDR must do as the Central Committee of the USSR is doing, more openness, through a more critical approach and a solving of problems. It is the general belief that the problems of the system, as now acknowledged in the USSR, are the same in the DDR." Flagrant examples: "More and more of clothing needs are being met in the illegal ambulant street sales, in front of the train station and where there are Polish workers."

Even Politbüro member Mielke made a strongly critical statement to his staff that the economic reality was the opposite of the official report of the Central Committee. "I told Comrade Tisch during the State Hunt, that everyone sees these problems and speaks against the development, but have no concept how it can be solved. To try to counter this development with administrative [police] measures, I find unthinkable. This problem is certainly solvable only with a fundamental change in the price structure."

Mielke then criticized another Honecker policy: "Here are the substantial causes of our problems: 66 billion mark subsidies should not be distributed, but used for the development of increased productivity." An inflation was coming: "The people's income in 1987 grew faster than the goods that could be purchased, 2.7 billion marks are lacking. I recommend that you do not pass on this information." Mielke's top aides signed in support of this criticism: Grossman, Neiber, Schwanitz, Felber, Kleine, Braune, and Kienberg.[68] [The insistence on secrecy was as though the worker did not know the problem.]

At year's end, lagging productivity and increasing price subsidies had depressed the nominal growth to 2.5 percent. Creeping inflation had wiped out real gains. Mittag wrote later that he realized then that the game was up. "The East was unable to help and I could not turn to the West because of latent political resistance in our own ranks." The 2.5 billion marks annually transferred from Bonn for highway construction or personal visits eased the problem.[69] The DDR was selling anything movable, from dissidents out of the jails to cobblestones out of the streets.

Although the USSR was beginning a critical examination of its development, the SED refused. Honecker scornfully dismissed *Perestroika* as a person repapering a room because a neighbor did it.[70] The Party, which had heretofore claimed to learn from the USSR, refused to learn from Gorbachev.

NOTES

1. Sch, 10121, KD Bützow, Stimmung, pp. 1–4.
2. SAPMO, DY30/vorl. SED, 40906.
3. Sch, 49a, Bützow, 2.1.7.
4. Sch, Abt. XX/7, 16.1, 18.1, 29.1.7, pp. 118, 120.
5. Sch, AKG 48c, Abt XX, 6.1.7, p. 29.
6. Sch, Abt. XX/7, 10121, KD Bützow, Stimmung, pp. 1–2.
7. Ibid., KD Bützow, 10121, pp. 13–16.
8. Ibid., pp. 112–15, 128.
9. Sch, Abt. XX/7, p. 130.
10. Sch, 10121, KD Bützow, Stimmung, pp. 11–12.
11. Sch, Abt. XX/7, p. 115.
12. Ibid., pp. 19–20.
13. Sch, DOSA, 400 983, 11.3.7, pp. 35, 65.
14. Sch, 10121, KD Bützow, Stimmung, 12.3.7, p. 21.

15. Sch, Abt. XX/7, 8.4.7, pp. 87, 95–98.

16. Ibid., 2.5.7, p. 88.

17. Kai Langer, *"Ihr soll wissen, dass der Norden nicht schläft": Zur Geschichte der "Wende" in den drei Nordbezirken der DDR* (Bremen: Temmen, 1999), p. 81.

18. Sch, 49h, 24.6.7, pp. 6–7, 20.

19. Sch, AKG, 08b, 15.6.7, p. 129; Langer, "Ihr soll wissen," p. 81.

20. Sch, 10121, KD Bützow, Stimmung, 1.7.7, pp. 35–38.

21. Sch, AKG, 49d, 30.7.7, p. 3.

22. Sch, 47, 21.8.7, p. 23.

23. Sch, Abt. XX/7, pp. 88–89.

24. Ibid., p. 86.

25. Sch, AKG 48c Abt XX, pp. 44–45, 51–54; Abt. XX/7, 24.8.7.

26. Sch, DOSA, 401048, GVS SWN 22–166/87, pp. 6–12, 32–36, 51–53, 66.

27. Ibid., 401044, 13.10.7.

28. Ibid., 401049, 23.10.7, pp. 7–18.

29. Ibid., pp. 22–23, 43, 52–53, 64, 72.

30. Ibid., pp. 107, 132–33.

31. SAPMO, DY30/vorl. SED, 40906, 16.10.7; 40906, 5.11.7.

32. Ibid., 30/40905—BL Sekretariatsitzungen, BL Schwerin, 12.11.7, p. 10.

33. Sch, DY 30/40905, Parchim 10.11.7, pp. 22–24.

34. Sch, 11a, 14.11.7, pp. 85–88.

35. Sch, AKG, Leiter 2b, 2.10.7, pp. 33, 58.

36. Sch, 10121, KD Bützow, Stimmung, pp. 64–65.

37. Sch, DOSA 401060, 26.11.7.

38. SAPMO, DY 30/40905,12, Parchim 6.11.7, p. 16.

39. Ibid., pp. 26, 49.

40. Sch, AKG, 08b, 10.12.7, p. 25.

41. Sch, 30,18.11.87, pp. 3–7.

42. Margarita Mathiopoulos, *Rendezvous mit der DDR* (Düsseldorf: Econ, 1994), p. 62.

43. ZAIG, 4833, pp. 14, 27, 30–33.

44. Carl Heinz Janson, *Totengräber der DDR* (Düsseldorf: Econ, 1991), p. 235.

45. ZAIG, 4833, p. 87.

46. ZAIG, 8703, 13.2.7, pp. 7–9, 30.

47. ZAIG, 8728, 13.2.7, pp. 96, 117, 126, 133–45.

48. ZAIG, 8702, 12.2.7, pp. 8–13, 34.

49. Bernd Eisenfeld, "Vortat, Widerständiges und oppositionelles Verhalten im Spiegel von MfS Statistiken," *Archiv*, February 24, 1994, p. 5.

50. Klaus-Dietmar Henke and Roger Engelmann, *Aktenlage: Die Bedeutung der Unterlagen des Staatssicherheitsdiensts für die Zeitgeschichtsforschung* (Berlin: Links, 1995), p. 133.

51. SAPMO, DY30/JIV2/50, 22.2.7.

52. Henke and Engelmann, *Aktenlage*, p. 136.

53. Ibid.

54. ZAIG, 3605, 14.9.7, pp. 1–5.

55. ZAIG, 3614, pp. 1–8.

56. ZAIG,14422, pp. 60–65, 72–80, 93–94.

57. Konrad Jarausch; *The Rush to German Unity* (Oxford: Oxford University Press, 1994), p. 18.

58. James McAdams, *Germany Divided* (Princeton, NJ: Princeton University Press, 1993), pp. 156, 160–62, 175.

59. ZAIG, 8707, 7–8, 26.

60. John Torpey, *Intellectuals, Socialism and Dissent* (Minneapolis: University of Minnesota Press, 1995), p. 105.

61. Ehrhart Neubert, *Geschichte der Opposition in der DDR 1949–1989* (Berlin: Links, 1997), p. 70.

62. Ibid., p. 85.

63. Armin Mitter and Stefan Wolle, *Untergang auf Raten* (München: Bertelsmann, 1993), p. 513.

64. Torpey, *Intellectuals*, pp. 93, 97.

65. Neubert, *Geschichte*, p. 71.

66. ZAIG, 14474, pp. 22–27, 53, 64.

67. ZAIG, 5353, pp. 78–85.

68. Ibid., pp. 86–102.

69. Jarausch, *Rush*, pp. 100–102.

70. Hermann Weber, *Grundriss der Geschichte DDR* (Hannover: Fackelträger, 1991), p. 183.

Chapter 4

The Lightning Striking: 1988

___

SCHWERIN

In international relations at the personal level, Russian wives, who were buying clothing without "even trying it on," faced irate German women. "Obviously the present situation does not promote thoughts of friend-ship."[1]

As for Honecker's prestigious visit in France, "People assume the French pressured him for more human rights, but young people hope for French autos. The workers are little interested." As for their jobs, "At work the attitude is never to put out, only to do what one is told, never take any function or responsibility."[2]

Few people were willing to help prepare for the elections in May. Communal problems continued to play the dominant role, like finding materials for streets and homes.[3] For example, the Jessenich VEB director didn't get the 2 million marks that he had earned to improve operations: "So he was forced into 'illegal deals,' but he is unable to create better conditions and therewith improve morale."[4]

Conditions meant that workers were also finding personal solutions rather than increasing production. "There are ever more questions about the truth of the economic information, so workers look out for their personal needs. Work time is wasted," as were pressures to produce. "In the Schwerin cable works, planning discussions concentrate on working conditions rather than on increasing production. They only receive orders from above, because the equal voice they used to have in planning doesn't exist anymore."

Instead, workers' voices were ridiculing the Plans: "In the Boizenberg

Metal Construction firm, the numbers in the Plan are considered ridiculous and impossible. The workers wonder how the production Plan was achieved when actually production declined. This leads to apathy." The system was dictating failure: "Those responsible for construction in Parchim County say that a non-fulfillment of the Plan is programmed in, by the lack of materials, machine and worker capacity."

The people saw more clearly the danger of the system's deceptions. "The cynicism is that if the Plan is not fulfilled, the Plan will just be 'corrected.' There can be no real planning if one must always report that the Plan has succeeded. The manipulation of results at the district level means that at the central level, false conclusions will be drawn about the capacities, which means that increases in export will be planned and made firm in treaties. Then comes the drive to fulfill these at all costs. From this came 'The Selling Out of the DDR' " [Mittag's selling whatever valuables he could find].

The missing technology had led to a missing involvement. "Workers explain it as the old problem of missing parts and materials, the obsolete machines, and now the lack of computer capacity, by the absence of the achievement principle, by too much administration and bureaucracy, therefore the frequent breakdowns and the low quality. Everything else is only a pipedream."

Breakdowns of machines meant a breakdown of morale. "In almost every firm come these breakdowns in production." What was worse, "The workers are no longer fighting to overcome shortages." Thereto the missing leadership: "At the top, despite constant signals of the serious problems, nothing has been done to help. When we exert pressure, the people just run away."

Instead, management had learned how to cheat the system. "In the Hydraulic Factory, after the introduction of the production-based wages, they manipulated the worktime and therewith achieved production of 124 percent, which meant paying the highest wages. In other firms, they are stopping 20–30 minutes early because the quota was achieved and any more production would not bring any increased pay, but which could mean that the less productive workers would suffer a reduction of pay." A further deception was the fraudulent recording of overtime hours.

The MfS writer reflected sadly on the instability in the socialist world and the lack of a DDR flexibility. "There is more to be thought about than the leaders of the Party and state apparently are willing to consider."[5]

Socialist guest labor also did not work according to plan, particularly the Mozambicans. "In one department, the work was not satisfactory; some refused to work, not being paid as much as promised. One can not get them up to 100 percent norm." They also rejected involvement: "In their free time, only football interests them. Efforts at getting them involved in other things, as at Christmas, failed. They don't come to union meetings. The political work of their leader Neves is very unstable."

Asians were better: "There was no problem with the Vietnamese, who unlike Mozambicans were well prepared and adjusted easily. They are mostly older with career training. Most have families at home and say, 'We have to make money.' They are disciplined, hard working and polite."[6]

February

Some natives were none of the above, like the alienated Heavy Metal, Skinheads, Punkers or Trampers (so named in the reports). "They have been pretty well restrained." The Skinheads did go to work but were often racist and fought each other; their negative behavior was mostly as football fans. Trampers were often close to the church and were not aggressive.[7]

Even the "responsible citizen" was causing more concern. In the Redefin LPG/P [for plants not animals], the poor leader, although just elected, was unpopular. "He drinks in working hours; he lost his driver license, but still drives. Many occasions lead to alcohol consumption and the farmers believe there are too many unexplainable festivities with excessive costs, and too much being spent on the leadership and canteen personnel." There were also reports of adultery: "The technical leader, also SED secretary, had illegal affairs for a year with several women. His wife is trying to stop his drinking. When drunk he makes advances and once ran naked though the LPG office."

At another collective, "The leader is weaving his web of intrigue in the dark," creating Party problems. He was linked to the drowning of a child. "He neglects youth work and sport." Two other LPG leaders were reported drunk on the job. The next report complained about drinking in yet another LPG; drunken workers had even run over animals. Five more LPGs were reported with poor stall equipment and permitting smoking on the job.[8] "In Tramm, the delay in road construction will have a negative effect on the election. Already people are resigning from all voluntary responsibilities and raising their own animals instead."[9]

Many violations of regulations were also occurring at the Schwerin cable factory, although their reports blamed technical problems. "Department heads don't fulfill their responsibility to the director, who is therefore forced to decide on minor matters. Therewith ideas for solving complicated problems are not implemented. On the average, 100 workers are lacking each day."

Because of the 1987 amnesty, 300 prisoners were lost at the plant in Butzow, so engineers sometimes had to drive the machines. "Forty amnestied men working there sometimes wander around unsupervised and are often missing from their stations. There is always a brigade of alcoholics." If that were not enough, "Lacking is leadership, competition and youth activity."[10]

Fraud added salt in the wounds of incompetence: the synthetic wool plant reported a plus of 8,000 marks, when it was actually 784,000 marks under the Plan, which was then changed to the advantage of the wages.[11]

Loyalty was also being lost, even in the schools: "Teachers say it is hard to reach youth, who have been impacted by the western media. The DDR media react much too sluggishly and too late."[12] Western journalists were understandably winning: "Our DDR publications do not compare to the massive agitation campaign of the West media."[13]

As a result of the money-compelled concessions, these journalist-spies-agitators were everywhere. When district churches sent four Lutherans and three Catholics to the Ecumenical Meeting for Justice and Freedom in Dresden, "There were lots of West media, a series of interventions in state business and hostile-negative attacks on our socialist state. There were provocative signs made for the West media and a chanting, 'Down with the Wall! Erich give us the key! We Germans are one nation.' When 6 were arrested, 100 protested. The West media were well prepared for the planned provocation with long lists of stimulating themes."[14] Western journalists immediately attended even a demonstration in small-town Ludwigslust.[15]

More worrisome were the DDR citizens, who were being permitted to see the West, although the MfS reported, "Christians see that human rights are violated in both systems, such as the homeless in the West."[16] Even so, "Emigration Applicants are usually those who have visited the BRD. This is a real problem. Their bosses agree to their applications without any questions."

People frequently asked, "Where is the attractiveness of socialism? People get money, but not color TVs, autos and attractive travel."[17] As for Mittag's hailed plan for electronics, "Doubt exists whether the DDR can keep pace in hard and software."

Similar cynicism greeted a Honecker speech: "People are pleased that he mentioned real problems, like sloppiness and shortcomings in production. As for those who avoid work, the DDR should change the labor laws. The practice has been, however, that little or nothing happens to these people." Inspectors are deceived: "The cadre get involved only when some higher personage from Party or State is coming."

More Honecker involvement would lead to more mistakes. "As for his corrections of the Plan, this usually means that the firms are favored rather than favoring increased production." A farmer asked a simple question, "Why can't they just admit that the Plan was not met?"

Others added bitterly, "More production will go for more export, thus there will be no more for workers. They have to buy some goods during working hours, because they won't be there when work is over. Workers said that Honecker had finally given up on promising more production, as the store windows keep getting emptier. Everyone sees the lack of organization as the core problem."[18] The presumably "overorganized" state lacked organization.

An educator lamented: "It is an absurdity that Honecker in a major speech has to talk about production of shoes; the minister should be fired for such failure." Teachers wished that local leaders were as enlightened as Honecker's speech. On the other hand, "There was criticism that he minimized the role of the parents, who were encouraged to do better only at their jobs."[19]

From Raben Steinfeld came this cynicism: "They promised goods in 3 price levels, but only the higher priced can be found because that way they can fulfill their Plan better. Too much was produced for the warehouses [meaning producing what people would not buy]. Valuable raw materials were thus turned into junk."

More threatening was the unhealthy state of medicine: "Equipment is over 20 years old; the medical technique is hopelessly out of date; patients often wait a half year for an operation; the doctor's offices are often in danger of collapse."[20] The issue was not only money: "Doctors say if they get extra money now it will be useless if they can't buy autos. More money doesn't balance their lack of freedom and won't stop them from staying in the West." More than doctors were missing: "Already the shortage of nurses means that some operations are delayed more than a year."[21]

April

The MfS accepted the common view that changes had been only for the worse. "For consumer goods, citizens are increasingly aggressive and demanding. Even those in the State apparatus expect no improvement this year. Those with higher income are angry with the *Exquisit* stores; the DDR products there lack the high quality of imports. Just providing the basics is no longer enough. It is unworthy that a country in the top 10 of industry has the worst fruit and vegetables in 20 years." The problem was also the personnel: "Any sales person in the West who behaved as do those in the HOs [state stores] would be fired in 3 days."

Despite Honecker's censoring him, people thought Gorbachev's reforms were inevitable: "Many believe that the DDR does not want to accept the necessity of such a course, but it will have to follow the same road."[22]

The MfS itself criticized that the DDR was learning neither from West nor East: "The DDR is not picking up on the changes in the rest of the socialist world." Bad policy meant bad behavior: "There is anger at 'new secret rules,' which block travel to the BRD. People behave very badly and say they will quit their jobs. Workers at the Transport Firm are angry that Modesalon Yvonne calls up wives of functionaries to tell them of new arrivals and gives them special times to take their pick."[23]

Even cadre and engineers were saying, "You can't hide the problems of housing because anyone trying to find housing knows that you are forced to wait more than 2 years to get any." The MfS learned the low percentage of goods being delivered as compared to the Plan's promise, the worst being shoes and leather, being able to provide 16.8 percent, and clothing only 13.2 percent of needs. "The public is especially angry about children's clothing and the doubling of the prices of washing machines and freezers."

Letting some people visit the West angered the rest. Such treatment encourages deceit: "Many people fabricate 'relatives' to visit. Everyone can go, except the ones who are trustworthy." The arbitrariness of the situation was resented: "People protest when a trip is refused the day before they planned to leave."[24]

That the Applicants were defeating the MfS was evident in its half-surrender: "We must concentrate on those where there is a real chance of keeping them, so that before their applications are refused, they will withdraw the application. But to prevent difficulties, the following broad categories should be allowed to leave:

a. Those with negative attitudes and who have gotten organized.

b. Those who have behaved provocatively or have been inclined to do so.

c. Those who have been active in various ways, like quitting their jobs, or have written the UN.

d. Those with jail time or who are unteachable.

e. Those likely to be active.

Let those who refuse military service go, but prosecute those who try to organize Emigrants. Act vigorously to avoid difficulties with Emigrants, but avoid the impression that there is a campaign."[25] Were this the known policy, the exit door would revolve wildly.

The MfS could keep some "hostiles" from coming in. Stier and Stolpe wanted former BRD Chancellor Helmut Schmidt to come for the church days in Rostock and were using underground activities to change his being banned. "So on 15 April, both bishops were thoroughly instructed, but even the bishops could not stop the hostile-negative ideas."[26]

The MfS could also not stop the apathy of supposed leaders: "There is a lack of initiative of leadership cadre at all levels, as well as workers, in quantity and quality. There is a lack of cooperation of LPGs in Zolkow and Mestlin; they have met only twice in 6 months. In Zolkow, such a poor leader means much dissatisfaction. There is a lack of effort and interest of the leadership, as well of individual ideas and activities, and a lack of inspection." In two other LPGs the animal count was manipulated, like selling animals but keeping them on the books.[27]

Nor could the MfS break the disruptive power of the West mark: "There is a chase for West Money. The country has become two classes; those who have some and those who have none. There is also criticism of the extra money to doctors and teachers, who already get more." Then the hated restrictions: "People dislike the arbitrary decisions of the police about travel. Often letters from the BRD with documents get lost, maybe postal employees open them for West Money."[28] The MfS shared but could not prove this common assumption.

Even disarmament raised doubts about careers in the army, so extra recruiting efforts were necessary. "Only 1/6th are willing to serve in the border troops, it is too dangerous and they might have to kill someone trying to escape."[29]

It was also difficult getting volunteers for May Day. Instead, the MfS was afraid that civil rights people would show up with their signs. Youth were negative, saying, "Nothing happens here. The parade has become only a funeral march, getting sadder every year."[30] Workers would also march unhappily. "Many workers regard this as a burden. Some refuse and go to church instead."

The Soviet mentor (teacher) would be shunned: "There will be no pictures of Gorbachev, some say the SED is afraid. There will be more security measures this year."[31]

May

MfS statistics explained its concern with the protesters: of the increased number of placards, 20 percent were written by Emigration Applicants, 17.7 percent by those under the influence of alcohol, 15.5 percent under BRD media influence; 2.5 percent were linked to the church; 50 percent of the cases were solved in 1986, only 40 percent in 1987. Attacks on conditions in the DDR were up from 54.1 to 62.3 percent; of these 37.4 percent were directed against the Wall; 10.6 percent wanted Soviet-style changes; statements against leaders were 11.4 percent, of which 79 percent attacked Honecker. They were mostly written by persons under 25, working in groups of two to three.[32]

Of those returning from the BRD, "Quite a few feel themselves completely thunderstruck and have problems in evaluating their superficial impressions correctly. They don't explain the DDR advantages when they are in the BRD." Internally they have already emigrated: "Intellectually the Emigration Applicants are already living in the BRD, while they are materially taking advantage of all the DDR social achievements. There is a big increase in contacts of organizations with the BRD, some initiated in the DDR, as when Dömitz went for a partner city."[33]

The situation in Poland was another cause for MfS worry; reduced supplies and drastic price increases had led to provocative demands and strikes. "Some think the Poles are to blame for their own problems and that other socialist states have done enough to help them. Their politics reflect their economy. Some think the DDR will also become radicalized."[34] In addition, "Some say the situation is like 1953, with trouble starting first in Poland.

The sense is that the people at the top are undecided, which weakens their authority, and could stimulate more opposition."[35]

On another ill-managed farm, "The LPG in Zachun for years has had a lack of leadership. The chief lets his department heads decide everything. He takes no political position and exerts no political influence."[36]

June

The Gorlosen LPG had a great shortage of labor, housing and stalls. "The Lüblow LPG's leader was alcohol-sick; his substitute does not have control, so there is confusion and disorder."[37]

Control was also being lost in the factories. The Parchim Hydraulic management used manipulation to fulfill its quota. "For example, they recorded 6 hours with 120 percent, plus 2 hours of machine breakdown, and came up with a result that they had exceeded the Plan, whereas the actual production was less than 100 percent."

A continuing lack of effort was reported: "Their management style is not to use workers fully, having an ineffective conduct of intermediate leaders, and too many coffee breaks. There is early quitting and conducting private work on the side, a negligence or even avoiding of taking measurements [of the productivity of each worker]. The necessary authority of the master is missing and workers take advantage of the late and night shifts with much alcohol. Nothing is done without a financial reward. Workers say quotas are either too high or too low and extra production is not paid for. There is insufficient support for research and development; the preparation of the engineers is inadequate. The directors are aware of all of this. No one knows how the many existing problems can be solved. The Party and the union have little influence. The required competition is mostly ignored."[38]

DDR-produced machines caused problems: "Because of the hydraulic pumps coming from Chemnitz, there are problems with the cranes made by KGW Schwerin, so they could not deliver as promised to the USSR. The cadre leader was fired." And elsewhere, "The DDR's hydraulic industry has problems. They will have to get some pumps from the west; the KGW can not reach the world standard."[39]

What the MfS was reporting in secret was common knowledge. "From all classes comes serious, comprehensive criticism; the economy has come to a halt and must have immediate measures to get out of its stagnation." Nor was it hidden from the public: "For lack of fan belts, buses and postal autos can't be used."

Honesty would be the best policy: "The Central Committee will have to tell the public the truth, which the public sees every day anyway. They must have more freedom to create. Many people simply stay in their positions in order to get their pensions. They do not measure up to the increased demands."[40] A regional conference needed 35 men ushers to protect the microphone from unplanned speakers.[41]

Too many citizens were not returning from BRD visits, especially doctors and university cadre. The MfS was again ordered to analyze better the Applicants, public opinion, the churches and West travelers. All unit reports should be turned in, because the top State and Party leadership must be given more accurate information on the economy.

The MfS looked suspiciously at a "well-known member" of an American Intelligence unit, who came for his 10th wedding anniversary "to the prettiest town in the DDR." They gave him a sales pitch on Schwerin "as a model of economic and social policy." They fended off his probing questions and those of his Berliner wife, both obviously prepared to ferret out problems between the central and local governments.[42]

July

There was an increasing difference in central and local attitudes toward the Soviet changes. "People like Gorbachev's free, self-confident, goal-oriented style. He is credible because he does not try to persuade using dry ideology, but with the material and intellectual possibilities of life."[43] Yet "Progressives" complained that "Gorbachev can't call 70 years a mistake. . . . Up to now he has only created problems." The DDR had to face problems in the construction of the Russian gas pipeline; Soviet promises had not been kept, so the result was "mud and dirt."[44]

The MfS, following Mielke's order to spy out the problems in the domestic economy, found many, including some very serious pollution. In Kuchelmess, everything was stagnating, with very serious urine and feces problems. "The bad ground water probably explains the children's skin disease. In the gravel pit, it stinks 15–20 meters down."[45]

There were other problems. "LPG leaders are not good about accident control. . . . Cattle get poor feed; their weight has gone down. . . . In two places people repeatedly use machinery while under alcohol's influence, although the leader knows it. In Parum, the leader is tyrannical, with no interest in other people's wishes." More generally: "Capable cadre are lacking. The SED grassroots organization remains ineffective."

The MfS was joining more often in the criticism: "One must be amazed that work continues at all despite this miserable spare part situation. What is the value of technology without spare parts? That problem was partly that the county has no reserve, missing also is management."[46]

The MfS was again accepting the public's doubts about socialism: "Frequently in all layers of society occurs now the argument that in the present development in the DDR and the other socialist lands, if one leaves out the social political achievements of the DDR, it is difficult to prove an increase in the attractiveness of socialism or the Marxist Law of the collapse of the capitalist social order."[47]

Similar doubts were disrupting the 40-year party block: "The 'friendly parties' are showing in an aggressive and impatient fashion, an increase in criticism of the series of unsolved problems for years in the implementation of centrally assigned tasks." The MfS showed increasing concern about the communal elections in May 1989. "The functionaries of the block parties, when in small circles, argue that they do not get sufficient help from the local SED on how they should react to these problems and above all, how they should respond when confronted by their members concerning the evident changes taking place."[48]

The dangerous democratic socialism was raising its head: "Some of the friendly parties are discussing a socialist democracy, with more power to the elected leaders. The voting is increasingly seen as a formal act, which does not represent a real election. Liberalism and indifference have grown."

August

The MfS saw contradictions again and again between news reports and reality. Its own long internal report had most of the pages underlined for emphasis, highlighting the MfS' increased concern for openness and getting rid of unqualified Party and state leaders, which it described as "the compelling need, if there is not to be a massive discontent."

Specific claims in the SED paper were "known to be factually false. We are actually short 9,300 windows and 47,000 doors." The wood had not been sent from the Soviet Union, which said that since the DDR sent wood to the BRD, the Soviet Union should not fill the gap. Workers rejected overtime (if the wood should arrive) for fear they would later be unemployed again. The workers knew that "higher productivity does not mean higher earnings."

Education had ever more serious problems: a lack of basic school supplies, paper and pencils; 100 teachers quit, and 44 more were talked out of it. "This is mostly due to the heavy load and stress in instruction and extracurricular activities. They would take less money, if given less responsibility. The pupils are, in part, fresh and undisciplined." The problems were mostly in the sciences, foreign language and sport.

Teachers had other strains. "Many teachers are young mothers, whose husbands have little understanding for teaching." There were further limitations on teacher travel: in 1987, to the teachers' requests to visit the West, rejections increased by 65 percent; in 1988, of 863 who applied, 398 were refused, many of whom said that they would leave the profession. "They don't understand the refusals and morale suffers." They were also angry at working Saturdays.[49]

There was also a decline in discipline on the farms. "People don't show up for their safety instruction. Empty beer and schnapps bottles are found on tractors and in work stations. Repairs on fencing are delayed a long time. All milking stations have unsanitary conditions, with the lack of cooling and proper machinery. Valuable machinery is left unprotected in the weather."[50]

Failures were observed at Parchim's mechanization factory: "By taking on large contracts, without the real possibility of meeting them, it was often penalized. The leadership was not stable, the director lacked vision and was taken advantage of by some of his specialists, who did not fulfill their promises energetically and he didn't keep track."[51]

As for the sewing machines produced in Wittenberge, DDR citizens had to wait four to five years to get any, which angered many: "With the county leadership cadre, one can no longer have a reasonable discussion about the economic situation. Everyone becomes abusive."

The Vietnamese made no problems, "but the Mozambicans still care about only football and disco; offers of going any place are rarely accepted. They have the problem of drinking before work, but their work habits are getting better." A couple of attacks on women had occurred.[52]

Increasingly, people were saying about the Applicants, "Let them go." One was taken from jail and quickly sent to the BRD, which made other Applicants envious: "We should break the law and get sent out." The MfS was puzzled: "Somehow everyone quickly learned about what happened."[53]

September

Still more insecurities were reported. "The public is annoyed with the non-workers on the Pieck Platz and fear to take their earnings past them." This was linked to the asylum seekers ("Why don't the police do something about them?") and the unwelcome Friends: "Poles drive big cars here and buy up goods. Russians are also buying up everything."

Discontent found more expression. "No new tendencies in opinions but problems are discussed more openly." Doctors expressed more opposition to the State because of the personnel and materials shortage. "The extra 100–200 marks for them is not enough."[54] Teachers complained that school leaders were only receivers of commands from above.

The public was ever more alienated. "The people feel abandoned in uncertainties, no one listens to their problems. They are turned off." About the high price for a Wartburg auto: "Are we not the worker and farmer state?" No trucks or tractors were getting to agriculture. "At Banzkow, functionaries were talking such nonsense that the Party secretary marched out of the room. With strikes to the east, there will soon be unrest here."

The DDR policy on wages was "a total running away." In exporting so cheaply, "We are simply giving away our products."[55] This was particularly true in farm products, one of the few areas where quality was exportable.

Because the DDR said that it was for peace, people could get away with arguing for it. To avoid longer military service, very many used DDR slogans like, "My work place is my fighting place for peace." They also asked, "Since we are disarming why should I serve longer?" The MfS regretted, "The military gets less recognition than civilian careers. Those who are candidates for officers and non-coms are not the most capable individuals. We have tried but failed to reverse the trend, sometimes because of relatives in the BRD. A growing number of youth appear as Emigration Applicants and demonstrators."

It was a lost generation "who often don't get answers to economic and international policy questions, especially changes in the Soviet Union. There is much discontinuity in FDJ functionaries; most FDJ leave when they finish their apprenticeship; only half the youth in Schwerin-South are organized. There is clearly more materialist interest and less willingness to serve society. They are obviously influenced by the enemy's ideology." The new BRD radio stations directed at DDR youth broadcast much international music, good reception and short political comments.

Pastors had similar problems with the young. "The churches have free discussions but youth soon learn that churches can't offer social and political alternatives. Some clergy are also carriers of diversion." As for schools, "One can prove that the students just say in school civics and history what is politically required. Their real political beliefs are often only expressed in private circles. Party positions and arguments are only laughed at, as they refer to the West media."[56] The complaining was growing about banning *Sputnik*, the Soviet humor magazine that carried the Gorbachev heresy.

Youth organizations were breaking down. "Of 57 state youth clubs, with 2 full-time leaders, at most 50 percent are viable, those which are attached to some institution, like a firm or school and not with the FDJ itself."[57] In Güstrow County, of 166 FDJ organizations, "The 30 in the schools are functioning because of teachers' interest, but if the FDJ activity seems like teaching, they turn off or don't show up. For city and village youth, it exists only on paper. FDJ leaders lack experience; only 30 percent of FDJ leaders are SED members. Many accept membership in the SED but avoid responsibility. Membership is sought for reasons of career. They join a Battlegroup, although they have only a very weak class consciousness."[58] Unfortunately, they had strong inclination to drink: "In these Battlegroups, the enjoyment of alcohol is harming their training again and again."[59]

Western spies had become more successful. "There is increased BRD spying on political, economic and military aspects. Their priority is to get reliable agents. They are aided by Detente and the cultural exchanges, also by Western embassies and correspondents. They are able to get much top-secret information. Our unit doesn't have the necessary IM to inform on this." The MfS did not report any spy being caught.[60]

October

Increased efforts to flee the Republic were described as "attacks on the border." In 1980, 117 persons had tried to flee; the number declined steadily to a low of 34 in 1986 but had climbed to 98 already by June. The reasons for the failure of border controls included a false evaluation of the signals and insufficient attention both there and in the home community. In summer, escapees started in the Elbe away from the border and swam several kilometers downriver to where it became the border.[61] In 1987, 3 of 11 efforts had succeeded, and in 1988, 8 of 12.

Police control was weakening. "The responsible officers of the border troops and the police do not understand how to motivate their people properly. . . . Several do not exhibit the necessary involvement in solving this task and have not recognized the necessity of securing the border. The reporting in and out of the patrols and therewith the control of the volunteers is still not thoroughly accomplished. The use of volunteers for patrols is very limited during the harvest season."[62] Sadly, "Those who get out add much to the criticism of the DDR economy."

The ideas crossing the border were worsening the morale of the militia. "Battlegroups are exposed to more political-ideological diversion; they have more contacts with the West. There is a decline in the participation in training, although still 91.4 percent, and an unwillingness to take on other jobs or to join the SED." Some were saying, "If I must join a Battlegroup, I'll leave the Party." The 11-mark addition to their pensions was not worth it. "More are going to the West, although not any commanders. Many had joined because they liked the uniforms and days off work."[63]

Kralisch listed 10 gatherings for "hostile activity," to which the MfS tactic was to split the church into the loyal versus the reactionaries and to polarize the environmentalists and other alternative groups. "The response should be the infiltration of IMs into hostile groups. One must also check out the personnel in the government and the other parties."[64]

The MfS sent many reports of popular scorn. "Some say Honecker is Moscow's marionette. 'Whether Erich goes to Moscow or not, he is told exactly what he has to do.' " Opinion was that Moscow was profiting from DDR technology: "What they send us is not as high level."[65]

All classes were critical of the DDR's social, political and economic developments and unsure of the Russian experiment. "They always compare DDR developments with what is happening in the other socialist countries, and as what will likely happen here. The socialist planned-economy is no longer attractive. Most important, the DDR will still help the USSR, so we should be able to take on their policies. If it is weakened, everyone will be affected." In a correct perception, "The west media see *Perestroika* and *Glasnost* as an alternative to real socialism."

The DDR planning was judged senseless: "Everywhere Demand exceeds production. Criticism is particularly about leader cadre who have become indifferent and follow their private interest and preferences." Instead of planning, "planlessness" had developed: "Some say discussion of the plan lost its meaning because orders keep coming from above. The 1989 Plan is unrealistic, not worth discussing because production has declined so much. Despite constant signals of serious problems, nothing is changed." The MfS was agreeing with the critics.

The other core problem was that the authorities could not compel compliance: "People just run away if we make greater demands and we are held responsible." Commands were known to be ineffective: "People doubt that the responsible state organs command the planning process. The cadre say the planners think only of what should be and not of what actually is. They know the local firms are ordered, come what will, to produce more for export. This is seen as the selling out of the DDR."

A forced self-sufficiency meant a forced inefficiency: The Wittenberge sewing machine factory had to make its own parts because other producers did not deliver any. "The discontinuity in production has become a daily occurrence."

The system led to a waste of time. "The plastics factory director just goes home at 2 P.M.; when production stops, workers go shopping or do other personal errands, even using the firm's machines and materials, particularly in construction. Bosses often send the workers on personal errands. The old stimulus is gone, the fighting atmosphere to overcome existing shortages and bad conditions has eroded because of the negative experiences."[66] Similar waste was reported at the furniture factory in Bützow: "They quit early, thinking that otherwise the quota would be increased, with no more pay."[67]

The system also led to drunkenness on the job. "Customers came to the Schwerin construction factory and found three employees who were drunk, and who just sent them to the office. After 20 minutes they tried another building and found three other drunken men, who sent them to another building, where they found one man too drunk to help. A young man not quite drunk did help them. . . . They saw two more drunks, and were told by others that this was often the case, because these men could trade goods for alcohol." Heavy drinking included the women in the offices.[68]

Poor organization increased worker resistance. "There was a refusal to work night shift at the VEB Elbewerft and most workers sympathize because so much is not in order: bad supplies, slow reaction from leaders, sloppiness, bad working conditions, general indifference, worker suggestions being ignored; less merit pay; the increased price of the Wartburg [auto]; a general agreement that the workers are not listened to, lower wages than in the south; losing workers because of the poor housing." In the LPGs, one could add a humiliation: "They write relations in the BRD to get fan belts for their mowing machines and many tractors are not working."

Local political failure added more anger. "The morale is negative, partly from the bureaucratic behavior of communal organizations. . . . An entire street got no sewer connections, so they say they won't vote. There is a continual reduction of the cultural and gastronomic niveau. There is less SED interest in serving on the city council. The Friendly Parties are pushing for more voice and more seats. Many office holders will quit, including many mayors."

Local FDJ leadership was described as tense and uncollegial. "The cadre are lacking and unqualified; only about 55 percent of the youth are in the FDJ. . . . In many clubs there is only a core. Many inns oppose having dance evenings for the young. They get little support from the councils, meaning a lack of improvement of the facilities; it is mostly discos and excessive alcohol." The cadre conference had also too much alcohol. "The political diversion is the glorification of the West from the media."[69]

Sternberg had 211 employees, with 51 secret holders, "all of whom get the lecture, but pay little attention. . . . So many are now going to the BRD, even their wives are betraying information."[70] Hagenow reported 7,842 travel applications, 5,854 approved. "That they can convert less money had little effect on their interest. . . . They keep trying; they quit organizations, and keep up a tough pressure on officials. A few don't return, or do return for strong family reasons."[71]

The MfS reported increased unhappiness with "the selling of the DDR," and the persistent official deception: "Statistics were being manipulated, which is sometimes ordered by the government. A leadership change is needed, like those occurring in other socialist states."

The MfS had begun to worry about DDR survival. "The question is how long can this economic development continue, before it leads to damage in all economic and ideological realms."[72]

November

Of 28 Youth Clubs in Schwerin County, 8 were judged very good; 12 met only sporadically and then only disco-danced. "The others existed only on paper. The school FDJ had to stop activities because of the school buses. The pastors also were trying to work with the youth, but few have much success."[73] Likewise, "The churches are not having much luck with young people either."[74] The MfS was having similar difficulties: "There are few cases of opposition from the youth, but with our young IMs, we do not command the situation. There has been a decline for the past five years in the recruitment of IMs, younger than 25."

The MfS was further worried because "the Human Rights Agreement" created more openings for internal enemies, who were "using nationalism, the church and the media." What was worse, "Demagogues are misusing *Glasnost* and *Perestroika*." The public wanted a choice: "From all classes, the demand is rising to change the election practice."[75] Hagenow's police conceded, "Mistakes were evident in the Party election, so that scarcely a speaker could talk without being interrupted by criticism." The new SED leaders got 42 negative votes.[76]

There was increasing enemy activity for peace and passage through the Wall. "An Emigrant Applicant demonstration on 6 March, Women's Peace Demonstration, and demonstrations on 1 May and on 13 August. In an effort to create a group on Civil Rights, 40–70 persons presented the Department of Internal Affairs with demands and threats." Tanks were graffitied. The peace problem rose again: since the summer, 20–60 persons had demonstrated each Wednesday at noon at the Schwerin Market as a "peace prayer."[77]

New emigration applications increased 17.5 percent, to 552 persons. "The withdrawal of applications is 30 percent, for some this is a tactic to drop out of sight. We cannot yet speak of the desired Change (*Wende*). The situation is serious and will remain serious and will demand of us much struggle, work and commitment." Thereto troublemakers: "We must be prepared for a quick increase of externally initiated provocations. . . . We must keep the situation under control, no matter what it costs." One cost was indicated in a long description of MfS counteractions.[78]

Escapes had increased 43 percent, the highest for years. An increase of 150 percent in border violations involved more groups of two to five persons, bringing cutters and skin diving and surfing equipment. "They are more willing to take risks, flying a balloon, swimming the Elbe in winter. They sneak into the dead zone and avoid communities. Despite our efforts we don't get more help from residents; only 15 of the 110 arrests to October came from such tips. Where are our IMs?"[79]

Mielke criticized a general laxity in Schwerin: 60 percent of all operative cases in the DDR had led to some action, but in Schwerin only 38 percent. "A problem is that of new IMs, 10 percent are no longer used two years later; in Schwerin it is 13 percent." It was a numbers game: "We are trying to get quality not quantity but we have a long way to go. There are supposed to be 'contacts' in secure locations, but many aren't; 15 cases were failures, they left the DDR, 7 of whom were IMs."[80]

The district dared criticize Mielke's policy: "The motto, 'Movement is everything, the goal is nothing' has to stop. We must also stop simply passing on IM reports. We must analyze each IM more." In a concession of laxity, "IMs must be extremely critically evaluated by their handlers. There should be 'meetings' before and after travel, but often none take place. Over 50 percent of IM trips occur without any preparation and their reports are often only oral." The writer referred frequently to another Mielke motto: "The Law is subordinate to Policy."[81]

The IMs in the church had some success: the reelection of the "progressive" Peter Müller as president was 35 to 7. "The effort has to be made to use internal sources in the church to resist the hostile/negative forces in the Cathedral, and Lietz in Güstrow." Six churchmen came from Rostock and Wismar with a bedsheet that said, "Better three church papers unpublished than one paper censored." Church leaders quickly accepted the state's demands and sent them home; 17 of the 44 Mecklenburg church papers were stopped because of objectionable articles and for mixing into state business. Bishop Stier, who got his son out of the DDR, was discredited by that favoritism.[82]

It was not so easy to raise quality of production. "The serious problem is that leaders and workers are getting accustomed to this lower quality of work." The agriculture cadre were saying, "Without a decisive change in technology and parts, everything will collapse. Our animal stall technology equals junk." The subjective factor: "In the Grain VEB, the deputy is permanently working against the director, creating a lack of leadership."[83]

The director of the plastic factory mismanaged; therefore, little was done during the week, then he piled on overtime on the weekends. Some workers were commenting very cynically about people who had risen in the firms: "Under today's conditions, the one who succeeds is the one who pretends to have scruples, builds up a network of connections, does black-marketing, utilizes gaps, shortages and mismanagement, creates many west contacts for himself, never performs any regular or disciplined activity, belongs to no collective, and works only for himself." Those who visited the West reported a perfect organization of labor, very clean firms, where the materials were ready, and the most modern technology was in place.[84]

In contrast, DDR exports were increasingly defective. "As part of the deficit to the West are the many returns by customers of defective production, which has reached major proportions in recent months." The source was attitude: "The damage done to many machines and facilities is because of indifference."

Such an attitude was a "subjective" problem but one that derived from the objective realities. "VEB House-Construction engineers complain they are not able to fulfill plans, because of so many objective and subjective problems. Workers in the WGK firm say that it does not pay to work. Only when there is responsibility in the management and honesty in the accounting will the combine get out of the red."

The supposed local involvement in planning had withered away. "At the telephone office, there is no discussion of the Plan any more. Because of lack of time the figures are sent immediately back to the headquarters in Berlin." But Berlin was not paying attention to plan results. "People are upset, they didn't make the 1988 goal and the 1989 goal is higher." At the

SHB furniture factory, "The Plan is of increased production of 12.6 million marks, but 40 percent of that will be realized by increasing prices and lowering quality. Some furniture, to be assembled, was sent without instructions." At the household goods factory, "In 1987, 200 gas stoves were produced; in 1988: 500 were planned, but only 70 were delivered. The need is for 1,000."

Unproduced tires were crippling production. In the animal fodder VEB, "Of 22 vehicles, 10–12 are functioning; tires are so short that they go out without spares." So was missing labor: "So many people are leaving the land, with earnings too low, that often they can't keep regular working hours on the farm."

Yet the media kept to the false picture. "The constant praising of the system displeases the people . . . the workers, knowing how bad the conditions are in their branches, know the truth."[85]

For consumers there was only regression: "In the 1960s and beginnings of the 1970s, one could notice a clear development forward, but now clerks will often say, 'Have it sent to you from the West.' To get children's shoes, mothers must often wait outside in the rain, because so many are waiting inside. One can say, 'Already the children learn that in socialism, you have to wait in line.' "[86]

The result was disillusion in the schools: "Teachers report that optimism about a victory of socialism is disappearing." The 11th and 12th graders were saying, "Communism is an unrealistic dream."[87] The FDJ was worse: "There are no behavior problems with students, but some provocative questions, which shows West media's influence." There was a "happy byte" club (the words they used), but mostly with computers that were gifts from West relatives.[88]

Most young people preferred the English music lyrics, saying, "In the DDR one can't describe people's problems."[89] This was a further reaction to the censorship: "With the present information policy, there are ever more rumors, speculations, half-truths, political jokes and disinformation."

The Honecker policy meant subsidized waste. "People ask how the state can buy up so much fruit and vegetables at high prices and sell them at lower prices and how processing plants can feed cucumbers and beans to the hogs, and yet there is frequent scarcity in the stores, and how the price of grain is higher than the price of the bread."[90] In Parchim, warehouses of Christmas oranges were partly rotting; the Berlin order had been not to sell them until 5 December. "This was discovered by police who became angry."

All of this would affect the elections in May. "Efforts of progressives to defend the system have no listeners and are made fun of. . . . All agree that the coming election will be the most difficult and complicated in DDR history." Many community leaders would not run again, "because they get nothing done. The population demands a change in the methods; since everyone here is a worker, elections could be open."

There was more grumbling in the block parties. CDU in Hagenow said it had 79 members and only 4 seats, whereas the SED with fewer members had 16 seats, the DBD with 12 members also had 4 seats. Regarding SED corruption, "The functionaries are more untouchable than ever; in Güstrow, leaders were building bungalows on the lake."[91]

The DDR trade plight had led to a newfound interest in Jewish memorials, "part of a considerable effort to get better trade with the USA, where Jews have economic power." Then the devastating line: "The DDR is now seen as the land of the cheap." Opinion remained bitterly negative about banning *Sputnik*: "It was another Honecker mistake and he should go."[92]

December

The drumbeat of dissatisfaction continued. "Everyone recognizes that the DDR and SED are exposed to a great ideological pressure. We must push the BRD back and clarify our party positions." There were dangerous thoughts ("The question being raised is whether the many forms of socialism are the equivalent of political pluralism?") followed by noncommunication from above: "Many think that Honecker spoke of the problems, but gave no indication of how to solve them. . . . The Central Committee reports and those of the Friendly Parties were in language that went right over the heads of the average citizen."

Colonel Korth further deprecated the MfS ineffectiveness to his district leaders: "My deputy and I will rigorously no longer tolerate units which do not show the necessary commitment and perseverance in the battle. Only because of that do we have these real surprises and breaches, even some that later become very expensive. There are more attempts to cross the border and in the approach to the border, there are serious problems and gaps, with too few arrests. There is also hostile activity involved in West export und import." The confession: "We are weak in analysis and suggestions."

Although they claimed to have arrested more BRD spies, "In our IM work, we have not achieved the necessary capability. With 600 IMs, of which 50 are assigned to combat spying, we have too few agents. Further successes in the battle against the enemy, who is almost inside our house, have not occurred." Little information meant little power: "We have too little actual knowledge. We need IMs with real ties to the enemy."[93]

A long-standing SED production policy was being ignored. "Socialist Competition in the Plastic VEB . . . exists only in the drawer of the manager and is unknown to the workers. If any one asks about it, they are rudely dismissed." Education was being wasted: "University graduates say that their abilities are not being put to use."

Worker imagination was also frustrated. "The workers in Parchim have reached the production limits of the methods they have available. There are clever ideas on how to produce but they face a lack of materials and intellectual potential. Again and again, the Achievement Principle is not being properly applied. What is needed is a harder consequence to those who do not do their duty. Too often, their supervisors simply avoid confronting them, and prefer to get out of their way."

Shortages even led to obscenity. "When people discuss the bad organization, they often use words which are not repeatable in polite company. For example, for more than a year at the cable factory the radiation network can not be used, because a device from the Soviet Union still does not work. International cooperation should not lead to this."[94]

MfS reports hit another note of desperation. "The reserves are used up, we are living from hand to mouth. No one wants to hear about the real problems. The local farms and businesses have somehow to survive. Too many are leaving agriculture, but we can't improve the LPGs, because we don't have the money." Nor were there willing workers: at the TEGA factory, "50 percent of the oxygen production stopped so that everyone could get in their vacation."[95]

Quality, as well as quantity, was sinking all around. "The new Wartburg has frequent motor and transmission problems and there are still no spare parts. Construction workers doubt that the housing problems can be solved by 1990. . . . The quality of the finished housing clearly continues to sink."[96]

The Housing Combine described a leadership failure: "The situation is chaotic. The Plan will not be met and the combine is incapable of paying, but they still do not get the needed new director. We are clearly standing in front of a failed SED economic policy. Motivation is lost, particularly in the construction cadre. If we changed the rent rules [allowed rent to rise], it would reduce the under-usage of residences."[97] It could also have enabled some owners to initiate much-needed repairs, the lack of which had condemned a majority of rented buildings to decay.

The banning of *Sputnik* brought more pages of criticism. "The 40 years of ideological education in the DDR would appear to have no results if the people can't be trusted to read it. More people say they miss it than had ever read it." Five Soviet films were also banned. The "organized" writers also sent a protest, although about half voted against protesting for "tactical reasons."[98]

Perleberg reported that since the amnesty of December 1987, the persons amnestied had committed 23 crimes, of which 10 were property crimes, 3 were insults and acts of resistance; 14 avoided reintegration and did not work.[99] In the year 1988, district border violations totaled 84 incidents with 121 persons, almost double that of 1987.

The MfS reported public pleasure at the relaxed rules for visiting the

BRD, but this worsened its task of preventing them from going. "The Cabinet ordered us to train people to do it, using a work collective, more informants, and recognizing in time who is at risk."[100] Teachers were angry that they could travel only during vacation and may be restricted as to where. "We who are properly trained can't travel, and the *Dummköpfe* can."[101]

With such unhappiness, one might wonder why it took nearly a year to effect the change already seen as necessary even by the Secret Police.

BERLIN

During the traditional January State Hunt, Honecker told Ambassador Kotschenmassov that the DDR would ban the word *Perestroika*. He prophesied, "If Gorbachev continues, he will in two years destroy the Party and the country." Kotschenmassov was already embarrassed at Soviet failure: "I was sometimes ordered to ask for deliveries of millions of tons of potatoes or meat or butter [from the DDR]. When a deputy of Ryshkov told me to ask for some thousands of tons of pickles, I said I was too ashamed. The DDR filled all requests correctly and promptly."[102]

Aware of the DDR's problems with the West, Schürer discussed with Schalck the plan to work for a confederation with the BRD, "because there was no longer any chance for the DDR being able to pay its debts." Included was the recognition that the DDR must permit more of a market economy.[103]

Schalck in his memoirs wrote that the DDR had to keep the living standard or improve it, although that was impossible, so Schürer had a constant struggle with unrealistic ideas of the Politbüro. If he said that something was impossible, it was not treated as a material problem but as a political problem. So his planning commission was an apparatus to statistically carry out unrealistic goals. It tried to force a basic discussion, but this was interpreted as a power fight against Honecker and Mittag.

In this complicated situation, Honecker often provided surprises. Reports from the districts or MfS, from Politbüro colleagues or stories from Honecker's family caused precipitous decisions in the Politbüro. When Honecker's daughter went to the Charité hospital, a doctor told her of shortages of gloves, bandages and syringes. She told her father, and he pushed the alarm button. The shortages must be solved. "So I took 16 million marks to get them—instead of doing it rationally, it had to be done immediately."

In the government hospital where the big shots were treated, Hager made sure that shortages did not exist. "To shield Honecker from stories which might set him off, we began at 6 A.M. to prepare the spin on stories which Mittag had by 8 in order to fend off Honecker."[104]

Seeming to ignore all warnings and the MfS reports of massive discontent, Honecker continued to reject the Soviet-style reforms, such as separating Party, state and economic organs, term limitations, a truer political competition, discussion of candidates, changes in the Central Committee, public meetings for cleaning up the Party, subordinating the bureaucracy to the elected leaders, reducing the secrecy, stronger guarantees of personal rights and recognition of different forms of socialism.[105]

The rest of that socialist world had left the DDR blowing in the wind. The DDR resisted the liberalization in the Vienna agreements. Mielke planned to prevent their implementation. On 11 January he wrote Minister Fischer, personal information for his eyes only, about his talks with Soviet Foreign Minister Shevardnadze and an MfS resistance to Soviet policy: "The compromises in Vienna go the limits of the possible, and have partially exceeded them. They present us with complicated problems. One has to say openly that the responsible authorities of the DDR are presented by these far-reaching compromises with the extremely complicated task, to divert or limit as much as possible serious damage to the socialist state and society. Considering the basic political and security demands, we in the DDR cannot agree to the expansion of the Helsinki inspection groups, including the 'rights of the individual.' Decisive is that legalizing the activity of such forces in the specific situation of the DDR can not be tolerated without serious internal and external results."

He noted that the DDR had the special problem with the BRD: "There are millions of border-crossing contacts between the citizens of both countries, as evident in reciprocal visits and many other kinds of communication. Over 10 million persons traveled for the purpose of family relations in 1987. We are already very generous in humanitarian matters, so that contacts are increasing and deepening. There exists a massive ideological influence through the channels of communication, with their pseudo-pacifist solutions and human rights demagoguery."

Bonn was leaving them no peace. "The international law violations, led by BRD politicians and secret services, are part of a massive attempt to organize state-hostile groups and forces inside the DDR under the cover of protecting alleged human rights. They wish to undermine the DDR and to lead our citizens to abandon the republic and settle in the west. In the International Society for Human Rights are known agents, like the traitor and renegade Agrusov, who are not so much interested in leaving as in putting pressure on the DDR, to cause internal trouble and damage its reputation. To comply would lead to a situation where unusual measures would have to be taken to maintain stability."[106]

Domestic tranquillity was challenged by the activism of the few handfuls of bright citizens, while the many citizens grumbled but made do. Some members of the political elite shared the concerns of activists, at least at lower levels and in provincial areas, if not at the top of the party.

After 1987 practically every political movement of the SED was accompanied by oppositional activity, which meant that the long-exercised MfS methods would be the measures of last resort. "Since the traditional social guiding instruments increasingly failed, the MfS power tools were used as a substitute for regulated political procedures to solve problems, without ever dealing with more than the symptoms." As weak as they seemed, the oppositionalists had the issues of freedom, peace and ecological prosperity. "The SED was so much pushed on the defensive that it relied almost entirely on a conspiratorial splintering of the opposition." Its advance element was the ecology movement.[107]

The BRD Green Party maintained contact, mostly in Berlin, but went elsewhere and, where possible, participated in the demonstrations. In November 1987 the state suffered a defeat. The MfS could not criminalize the Ecology Library or destroy it because the international public was watching. Instead, there was a wave of openings of similar libraries for ecology or for peace in all the important cities.

The MfS could not reach many activists in the church structure, and it did not perceive clearly that out of these misfits, the most important, ideologically unintegrated group was able to attract ever more recruits with an expanding list of *samizdat* publications. All they needed were some stimulus and maneuvering room.[108]

When the Initiative for Peace and Human Rights (IFM) published a brochure, five leaders were arrested, and the activist core was thus dispersed to the BRD. There was already a split of dissidents between those who wanted to emigrate and those who wanted to stay and push for reform. Estimates were up to 500,000 of those who wanted to leave, vastly more than the group pushing civil rights, which added to its weakness.[109]

Part of the explanation for the excellence of some pastor-dissidents is that nonconformity had meant their nonadmittance to the usual higher education. An exception existed in seminaries, so careers open to freer thinkers, commensurate with their talents, were possible within the church. There was also the increased importance of women's organizations, such as Bärbel Bohley's, within the church.

By excluding them, the state had inadvertently created a cluster of able young adults who were committed to greater honesty, open debate and discussion. They could look a bit like "the flower children" of the late 1960s in the West. The MfS had rather easily controlled their "Peace Decade" by working on the older church leaders and using a critical presence of IMs and "reliable social forces."[110]

From late 1987, both sides were aware that church leaders were losing any control that they had over the dissidents, whose forces for reform had developed more sophisticated forms and tactics. The MfS responded with more open and visible repression and heavy-handed tactics, arresting Bohley, Stefan Krawczyk and Vera Wollenberger and increasing the pressure on the church.[111] Further discouraging to the dissidents, Bonn politicians seemed to accept the permanence of SED leadership.

The dissidents' tactic was to use early KPD leaders, in particular, the martyred Rosa Luxemburg, in her time a voice for dissidence from Leninism. The MfS took sharp measures to suppress "the provocative anti-socialist" activities planned in her memory for 17 January. The dissidents selected disturbing texts from her writings, and although forbidden on 13 January, they persevered. "Our 'social forces' stopped them from displaying banners for the BRD television teams that had appeared."

Arrested were 118 persons, 93 from Berlin, who were given a scolding; 105 other persons were arrested on the way, including 30 women. The social breakdown: 46 skilled workers, 16 employees, 19 intelligentsia, 8 church employees, 2 students, 4 housewives, 2 self-employed, 7 unemployed, including a doctor; 15 were over 40 years; 84 were Applicants, of whom 19 were quickly given permission to exit the DDR.[112]

February

As a solution to the increase of Applicants from 72,900 in 1986 to 105,000 in 1987, Mielke ordered more vigorous action, including arrest. "They are trying to create conspiratorial connections, as they say, 'to start a ground fire.' Everything points to their creating a permanent potential force, which can at any time attack the government with effective public actions. The events of recent weeks are a visible result. They are planning demonstrations on 28 February. I emphasize, if there is any threatened illegal activity, immediately arrest them. Push it through so that the arrests and fines are accomplished immediately. Use one judge and up to one year imprisonment or fines of 1,000 to 5,000 marks."

Dissident young men should be promptly drafted but carefully assigned: "Of these Applicants, call into army service any male 18 to 26. The plan is to put them into units that are primarily involved in physical activities, which means the engineering units of the army. These are to be taken already in May. Do not take those who would present a danger to the army. Put them together and arrange political-operative counter-action in these units. Infiltrate Applicant groups with IMs; emphasize any contact with the BRD and prevent any public provocation with all means."

Whatever part of this was implemented, the MfS would soon admit that Applicants were too tough and could not be dissuaded. As for those dissidents whom the BRD bought out of jail: "The resettlement of those released will no longer be done in buses." It had added to the bad impression. Mielke also warned against BRD "political-tourists." For example, the Konrad Adenauer Foundation had organized a travel group to Suhl, schooled with a set of questions.

The Politbüro noted the destabilizing of travel; only 0.23 percent stayed, but these were highly qualified. So they tightened the rules; couples with children could not go. Mielke instructed: "We are now making public the Politbüro decision of no more approvals for a visit to an uncle or aunt, cousin or farther relationship, or for any birthday celebration before the 50th, then only those of 60, 65, 70th birthdays."[113]

This arbitrary action created much bitterness because of the strong emotional attachment to family, as well as the desire to see the West. The Bonn liaison Bräutigam warned Krenz that there must not be a serious decline in travel.[114] The permitted visits to the West increased from 60,000 in 1985 to 500,00 in 1986, to 1.2 million in 1987, and 1.3 million in 1988.[115] To be more acceptable in Bonn, the DDR also abolished the death penalty and introduced the right to appeal.

Mielke again held forth on 26 January, this time for 142 pages, to emphasize that the DDR was on the defensive against an aggressive NATO.[116]

March

In the new two-front ideological war, the DDR was also on the defensive against the Soviets. Bernd-Lutz Lange, Leipzig cabarettist, described the importance of Gorbachev, with dangerous facts and arguments coming from the East. "At the moment when the DDR rejected Gorbachev, it was already lost, because suddenly people had courage who never had courage before." In Leipzig signs appeared from his quote. "We need openness and democracy like air to breathe."[117]

Mielke reacted angrily to a talk with Shevardnadze: "The Vienna treaty is a dangerous mixing into our internal affairs. . . . The BRD is continuing a large-scale libeling campaign, like the Liebknecht-Luxemburg demonstration, directed from outside. The question arises what would happen if these hostile forces could operate legally, with an official position as a so-called dialogue partner of the state, putting pressure on Party and State leaders and, by continuing disturbances, to damage the international image of the DDR."

As if that fright were not enough, "The church is being pushed into the role of a legal opposition. This is justified by linking the church concern with caring for souls, that 'all those in need' should receive help and support."[118]

Mielke documented the growing problem with statistics of crimes, largely illegal border crossings, acts of antisocialism and recidivism after the amnesty. Border crimes included 3,668 persons, an increase of 45 percent not coming back from visits mostly to the CSSR and Hungary.[119]

April

The most ominous cloud to the DDR was rising over Hungary, which brought reformers into its Politbüro, a liberal action that Gorbachev had welcomed. His adviser, Daschitschev, was becoming a major force for German unity, but DDR leaders assumed that Gorbachev would fall to conservatives, who would support Honecker.[120] Conservative Soviet officers in the DDR probably furthered this optimism.

The greater danger remained DDR's unpayable debt. Manfred Uschner, assistant to Politbüro member Hermann Axen, recalled: "The Politbüro dragged a report out of Mittag, which was intentionally presented in an almost unreadable format, the rows of numbers contained no gaps after three figures. We had to strain ourselves, and in great haste, to try to learn the magnitude of the indebtedness. Then it was completely clear to us: the DDR was totally bankrupt, and there was no way it could get out of the new fatal circle."[121]

Reformer Schürer tried again to get around Mittag's obscurantist tactic, giving Honecker a paper that outlined problems and solutions. He urged reducing Mittag's high investment in electronics and the subsidizing of food and housing, keeping the rents low. In order to stop the rate of foreign debt growth, DDR needed a 6.5 billion-mark trade surplus per year. "The Republic is going bankrupt."

These logical changes would have killed Honecker's sacred cow of "the unity of economic and social policy." Mittag used every device to destroy the argument, and Schürer's warning was firmly swept off the table. He was surprised that "the non-communist" parties also opposed change.[122]

May

Mielke accused the capitalists of using technology to subvert Communism. "In addition to their secret services, they are using firms and scientific organizations, plus increasingly diplomats, journalists, scientists, experts, in a systematic misuse, therefore greater SED diligence is needed." Businesses were also attacking: "There have been the extremely criminal business practices of capitalist firms. I take, as example, the deliberate disinformation in dishonest negotiation and the shoving of all financial and material risk onto the DDR partner, the pushing of the delivery beyond our abilities. This leads to production problems, so we must use Chekist methods."

He perceived a wider, viciously clever attack: "The capitalists use various methods, from targeted contact activity, to corruption and a rigorous exploitation of every mistake made by our cadre. We know they are concentrating on certain groups of people, like those who approve travel, cadre who have the right to travel, highly qualified scientists and experienced specialists in the key areas of research, development and production. They are looking for agents, trying to create traitors. . . . To be frank, they keep finding corrupt [DDR] persons. They look to subvert able young people who will rise to leadership positions."[123]

On 5 May Bonn Minister Wolfgang Schäuble threw an overwhelming argument on the table. The sum of assistance for five years would increase from 525 to 890 million marks annually, but he made clear that this depended on a continued improvement of the travel regulations. Both sides hoped that this would release the pressure but the emigration numbers exploded.[124]

June

The exit efforts were worst in Gera, with many university or technical school cadre, as at the Zeiss Combine and Jena University. The most serious losses were doctors. "There must be a broad effort to beat them back. We learned of 200 plans to leave."[125]

Mielke again criticized his district leaders, beginning with Cottbus, about the ineffectiveness of their IMs. "With the modern complexities we can't rely on the original Chekist tasks." The MfS must be more creative. "The political-operative situation can change radically and sudden turns cannot be excluded as possibilities. The local leaders need more time to guide the IMs. It is necessary to have more specialization and productivity."

He also criticized Magdeburg's dealings with its IMs: "Characteristic is a formal approach." Even worse, "In Stendal, Col. Neumann has also no concept of what problems to concentrate on, how and through whom, how the task can be accomplished other than increasing the number of IMs. The process must concentrate more on IMs from whom the operatively most valuable results can be expected. This is not what the system is producing now, which is measured only by the number of contacts and quantity of reports."

The handlers were losing control: "There is the problem of IMs applying for visits to the BRD, which shows this aspect was not known to their handlers. The IMs have not been required to come to the handler before leaving. They are not prepared on how to handle interrogations in the BRD. There is no follow-up report and examination of the IM on his return. Our study of materials and interviews demonstrated that the IM handlers and the middle echelon cadre did not give enough importance to the IMs' protection and security. A major reason was the insufficient imagination about the actual enemy attacks on the IMs and their effects."

The handlers needed to know their IMs better: "Our examination also showed that there was no objective analysis of the knowledge of the IMs, a lack of study of documents concerning them, an insufficient concern with the IMs' possible treason. These must be checked before and after visiting the West."[126]

Mielke found even more problems in his bureaucracy: "Weaknesses are in the middle cadre, who often change very grudgingly the practices in their work. An immediate reaction to imperfections follows only occasionally. They seldom use their opportunities to exert a direct influence on their colleagues, in particular in the preparation, implementation and the evaluation of the contacts."

His regional leaders were poor examples: "They too seldom provide the model of how IMs should be handled. Still too frequently it is a formal approach, without sufficient attention to the political-operative situation and the total personality of the IMs." Following faulty assembly came faulty analysis: "Too often there is no critical evaluation of the evident information and instead idealistic stereotypical statements are used. Important problems are insufficiently considered or even left unmentioned."

Despite his repeated commands, his subordinates were still showing a lack of thought and intelligence: "Thus results a too uncritical view by handlers of the IMs and the middle echelon. They do not prepare solidly enough for a contact, about the expectation and the related problems. They don't consider how the personality of the IMs could be used, so some IMs in complex tasks ignore the assignment or even threaten to quit cooperating. The contact is so often done without thinking of how to get more from the IMs. Since they usually don't tape, the interviewer can put his own perspective into the report."

The head of the MfS kept reporting that his much-feared organization was badly organized and lacking in skills. Therefore, the poor result: "Only a few IMs bring significant information. Too many offer only general information about persons, problems of the firm and the reaction of the population. There is not enough Chekist action. Also noticeable is the change in handlers, every two or three years. Too many contacts occur in the IM's work area, or rooms set aside for the purpose in firms, and in autos. There is not enough consideration to the secrecy necessary to the IMs. Sometimes the report of the circumstances of the contact is not truthful. Reports are very incomplete and general after IM visits to the West."[127] Yet increasingly, the MfS described these IMs as the heart of their operations, including efforts to control dissident behavior. The MfS had no better idea.

Mielke had come to recognize the dangerous political situation and ordered MfS to inform the SED at each level. He did not want anyone to say that the MfS had been surprised as in 1953.[128]

July

Mielke described more problems in his local units, including the continued expansion of the tasks given these offices, which could not be accomplished with the persons and materials at hand. As already reported in April: "This has led to superficial solutions to all the assigned tasks or completion of only some of them." He had also received complaints that MfS operating space had been reduced. "The criticism is further that the advanced training gave insufficient knowledge about the basic operative procedures."

The middle-echelon problem surfaced again: "There must be improvement of the intermediate leadership. These often take on the tasks of their colleagues. They often still work with too many IMs/GMs and have too little time for leadership. In large counties the leadership can work only on the most important points. The complaint from small counties is that often the district administration simply passes on instructions without differentiating [among them]."

Even the Berlin direction was admitted to be a problem: "The local leaders report again that they are no longer in the position to know the many rules in MfS instructions and in a position to obtain the compliance of their subordinates." Despite these endemic system problems, Mielke thought that the changes that he had effected in 1982 had improved quality.

He again ordered more attention to fires and other damage to the production of a variety of commodities, but the locals' greatest burden was resisting the exodus of so many Applicants. The pressure on IM handlers was too great, mostly from Applicants and their widespread underground contacts. "There is the problem of knowing Who is Who (in the Opposition)."

Mielke still hoped to refine Chekist methods: "Increasingly the need is to recognize the early beginning of hostility to the state and to prevent its continuing. One doesn't put arrest in the foreground, rather the use of political means to divide, and adopting measures to prevent hostility. Increasingly we must develop operations to oppose the hostile-negatives. The lengthy investigation without proof comes from the lack of necessary IMs who are trusted by the targeted person. One possibility is to work with IMs who wish to emigrate." Bribe productive Applicants with emigration?

The MfS admitted that it was losing that battle: "Ever more Applicants avoid being influenced by the State by working for the church, by living from independent handwork and by the rejection of any legal work position. MfS morale is depressed when with much time and effort they can prove enemy-negative activity, but not enough to enable a criminal case. Even though praised they don't feel successful."[129]

Personnel had still not improved: "The portion of the IMs who can be used on the front line with the enemy has remained relatively constant, that means that we did not gain the desired and necessary access to the IMB [*Inoffizielle Mitarbeiter in unmittelbare Bearbeitung*] who fit our needs. Circa 40 percent of the IMB are used by the county offices. The new recruits added little to the gaining of more significant information. The Minister's commands, 13 February 1987, on how to fill the gaps of FIM [*Führungs IM*] were not followed. The resulting collection of IM shows increasing problems of lack of motivation, increasing professional and social burdens, a lack of perspective and suitability."

The IMs continued to be persons who were willing, not the persons who were able: "The Minister's order of January 1979, was not properly followed. As before, most of the recruiting followed the easiest way. The emphasis was not on the tasks which had to be accomplished, instead the already existent IM willingness was the important factor."

Improvement through education had not occurred: "Clearly the necessary rethinking process of MfS leaders was lacking from top to bottom in this necessary priority. Despite constantly increasing the proportion of persons with a completed university training, there was no visible improvement."

The handlers were not leading the IMs; rather, the IMs were leading the handlers: "The problems continued in setting up the contact, for which the handler did not prepare properly. So the course is set by the IM not the handler, who used only 15–30 minutes in preparation. Often the goals and how the IMs were to be used were not evident. During the interview too little attention is given to objectivity, completeness and actuality or reality of the information. The handlers take too little time, only 1–2 hours, some much less; they know too little about the IMs and they make too little effort to motivate."

Everyone did what came easiest, taking the path of least resistance: "With most of the IMs they utilize only the obvious, immediately recognizable opportunities, those primarily at their place of work. The handlers do not tell the IMs what are the priorities of information, so the IM knows too little, what the cooperation must be and what activities they should develop on their own outside the assigned tasks. IMs should in their free time fight the political underground and stop Emigration Applicants." The problem of remaining secret: "It takes time in small counties to find a place not dangerous to the conspiration."[130]

Mielke took some pride in a Berlin success against Bohley and Fischer, although they remained enemies. The MfS had succeeded in preventing Applicants from organizing. Throwing out leaders had weakened the Applicants' communication system, but they were encouraged by Soviet developments: "The enemies are using Gorbachev's words but their intent is ending socialism. Also they use ecology words for that purpose, using lies and half truths. Church support has increased to those refusing military service."

Church cells of opposition had not cracked under pressure. Of 227 such local opposition groups, 120 still existed. "Despite some successes, we could not reduce that number. The core of such groups is composed of a small number of fanatic persons, driven by a sense of a mission, personal ambition and political egoism, unteachable enemies of socialism. Circa 30 of the 120 alliances go beyond the local level and have the goal of a network of similar groups. Their major activity is their pamphlets. Their disclaimer, 'Only for internal church use,' requires no further comment. One pamphlet concerns uranium mining. Since they have meetings in other socialist lands, we must stop their travel."

Smarter IMs were to solve the problem: "Our major tool against them is our IMs. On them rests our security. That requires that the IMs must know their operative playing field and the boundaries, which they must never overstep. The IMs should be in higher education, in the ecology groups, in community church councils, and important county cultural groups. We have to increase our influence on the more realistic church officials and lay synods."

The strategy was to concentrate at the top and split the organization: "Our best method is to select the persons who represent the greatest dangers: initiators, organizers, and ringleaders. The process is to make them insecure, to soften them up and divide them, isolating the leading forces. The plans should be ready in the drawer, in the law and in measures for working with the public."[131] A special order went out to resist the exit of doctors, along with instructions on how to proceed against persons who used public displays to get permission to leave.[132]

August

Beginning another long speech, Mielke quoted Honecker, who had told the Central Committee: "The economic and social policies are the decisive field for the ever better satisfaction of the constantly increasing material and intellectual-cultural needs of the people and therewith for the inner stability."

Mielke then bragged that the DDR belonged to the few countries that could produce microelectronics. "We must keep this successful aspect of our development always in view. In no decisive area can there be permitted a false development. We have not raised much the proper necessary economic applications of science and technology. The great investment in the key technologies, and I must be frank here, has been at the expense of other necessary aspects of our economy. The quality of the results . . . has not met the requirements."

MfS leaders could be told about the heavy losses: "In 1986 and 1987, we lost 9 billion marks in the export of petroleum products, also from a decline in price in the export of coal, rolled steel, potash. The extreme winter 1986–87 meant an extra 4.3 billion mark expense. The loss from fires, etc., meant a 2 billion mark loss of production, reducing investment. In industry occurred an absolute decline in the work force. Therewith a complicated situation arose, which led to significant economic disproportions [imbalances between various elements of the process of production]."

Investment was not rising enough. "The increase in national income does not suffice to pay for the external debts, to provide for the needs of the people, and provide the urgently needed investment. In 1989, 35 percent of the planned increase in national income must be used to achieve the necessary export surplus." The planned level was not reached in the first half of 1988, "so there had to be 'plan-precisioning' in industrial production of 4 billion marks. These factors, as well as the continuing decline of the rate of accumulation, have meant that in a series of industrial branches the simple maintenance of the production level is not assured."

Part of the problem was obsolescence, and part was inattention: "Interruptions are partly from over-age equipment; 18.5 percent is already written off, 20.1 percent is more than 20 years old. Yet in the first half of 1988, 43 percent of the fires, disturbances and damage came from the false subjective behavior [people did not try hard enough to overcome their problems] and were thus avoidable."

More adaptable IMs remained the Mielke solution: "County MfS units are given the task of improving the IMs to gain information from which operative conclusions can be made. We need IMs who not only know the problems but their sources and the possibilities of solving them. We need IMs who can make their own contribution to changing the situation and who will be involved in clarifying and solving the problem." The IMs must not only inform but also somehow take charge.

He conceded, however, that the people's negative attitudes could not be corrected: "The public reaction about the economy is ever more critical and impatient discussions show the low morale." Complaints concerned the same problems: "Progressive forces are concerned with the increasing skepticism of workers about the feasibility of the goals, an increasing lack of understanding and anger about not solving these problems after so many years. They have noticed the wonderful goals which have not been realized, time and time again. At the same time the fears are increasing that out of the pluralism now in the Soviet Union, certain dangers for the inner stability of socialism are developing, which could have effects in the other socialist states. These problems have led to a reduced worker willingness to work."

Instead, the workers demanded reforms of the system: "Workers get often emotional on that subject. The viewpoint is presented that the time has come to reduce the extent of state subsidies for basic food supplies, in the interest of reducing prices to the consumers and reducing food waste. Among all sectors, the belief is that the relationship of wages and prices must be changed, especially in health concerns."

The public recognized the reality that the system refused to admit: "Increasingly obvious is the disproportion in the development of investment, production and preservation; the hiding of non-fulfillment of the plan by reducing it; the over-concentration on export, which means a negligence of domestic needs, plus the inflexibility in planning and balancing of the national economy."

Everybody, including the MfS, knew the basic problem: "The increasing gap of the DDR technology can not be overlooked, its falling behind when compared to the world class (level of the quality and price of goods produced for the world market) in many areas, because of the slowness of getting the research into production and the insufficient support to research."

Mielke conceded that support was fading on all sides. "The first indications are that representatives of the Friendly Parties, who refer to these old problems that never get solved, will no longer be candidates in the local elections. There is more bitterness among workers and demands that they be better informed and the response of leaders that they can no longer answer the workers' questions."

The man whose job was to prevent the public's speaking the truth is saying to his people that the truth must replace media obfuscation: "The statistical reports are rejected. Progressive forces argue that the only way to motivate workers would be to tell them the truth about the economy. The workers' reaction to the Soviet Party Conference was an unlimited agreement with an open and uncompromising confrontation with the shortages and bad conditions and naming those responsible, no matter how high up."

The Secret Police were saying that more freedom was needed if the economic problems were to be solved: "Our scientists, in teaching and research, economists and public officials, in view of the similar problems they face, the uncompromising fight against bureaucratism, the painting of everything in rosy colors, and the corruption. They hope for the strengthening of the autonomy of the firms and combines and the clear delineation of the tasks and responsibilities between Party, State and economic organs."

Mielke seemed to agree with the public that Gorbachev was right in his efforts in that direction: "They [the public] criticize the SED's distanced position to the development in the USSR. The lack of correct information makes it more difficult to give persuasive answers to the ever-more urgent questions which come from the workers. They are critical of leaders [Honecker] who say, 'Well, that's for Russia and not for us.' Or who avoid dealing with the issues. The general opinion welcomes the Soviet reforms but is afraid that decentralization of trade will make DDR trade with other socialist countries more difficult."[133]

Reinhardt Buthmann's analysis of the MfS impact on computer development noted that the pressure for military development sadly diverted it. The 14 billion marks were simply thrown to the wind, mostly because the major drive was the Soviet military interest. "It was never understood in the DDR, how important for the high technology was the subjective factor of the human being." Especially for the MfS cadre the need for creative colleagues was a blind spot, a misunderstanding of the first order. The MfS massive fact gathering could well assess the security-political value, but not the detrimental implications for the economy. "The chekist and elitist belief in victory and the superiority of communism was so dominant that every diversion from the presumed reality must be the work of the evil and ever-present enemies." Securing the cadre as the means of preventing disruptions of production proved to be false because of its one-sided and warped perspective.

The emphasis on the correct political-ideological motivation also meant in high technology the underestimation of the shortages, which doomed it. Because the MfS control was a disciplining instrument, that distrust grew more and more, and an apathy among the staff deprived them of the necessary courage and willingness to take risks and led finally to a stagnation. The MfS created "the enemies" that it was looking for and thinned out the supply of persons whom it needed.[134]

September

Gorbachev warned Honecker that there would be mass demonstrations in the DDR in 1989 if there were no policy change. Mittag also warned him, "We are at a point where the entire thing can tip over (*Umkippen*)." Labor Minister Tisch blamed the increasing demands by the people, and Honecker suggested reducing the "special needs" by 10 percent. On 15 September the Politbüro ordered measures without consulting the ministers, "the first confrontation of Party vs. state in Honecker's time." It reduced the NVA [National Volks Armee] budget by 2 billion marks and reduced social [civilian] consumption.[135]

A more serious concern was that the shortages were multiplying other shortages. "Increasingly repairs, primarily of autos, are possible only if the customer has the necessary material or parts. Repairmen are constantly forced to spend much of their time trying to find the missing materials. One lives from hand to mouth and is happy if the materials for the next day's production are available. A long-range planning of the work is scarcely possible. It is argued that with 'planned bottlenecks,' one can't produce the necessities for the people."

Therefore, the serious political spin-off: "There is a great public distrust of the regional leaders, their unkept promises, so they won't be candidates, because they can't answer questions and can't change anything." The MfS advised that the SED should open up to the public's discontent: "There should be more talk with the CDU and LDP [Liberal Democratic Party] about price and wage injustices, like rent compared to costs of housing repair, also with missing materials for such repair."[136]

The SED seemed strong with its 2,328,331 members in 59,531 ground (local) organizations; 58.1 percent were workers; 22.3 percent were intelligentsia. The production workers were fewer, and more were quitting. The average age was 45; 51 percent had been to Party schooling, but the Politbüro was told that it must pay still closer attention to the political ideological preparations.[137]

The Battlegroups were supposed in the 1980s to get exemplary military equipment, but there was more money for medals but not for more necessary equipment. The "Effective Stimulation of the Fighters" propaganda was more important to the SED than good transport, communication technology, and the protection from an immense collections of arms. The plan for 1989 was to return the Battlegroups to their original purpose, crowd control, with billy clubs and shields, not the great amount of flak and artillery. There was a shortage of volunteers and of morale, but mostly of money.[138]

A tactical foreshadowing of 1989 was that in Schwerin, Rostock and Magdeburg, silent demonstrations occurred with candles and auto parades with as many as 50 cars with white banners on their antennas. "To create bonds they use grill parties [the report's words] and birthday parties."

People were challenging the authorities in a variety of ways: "Their resistance is by an open rejection of the system, increased personal appeals, many written appeals, seeing the BRD diplomats, four times as much as in 1987. We have been forced into certain compromises and will continue to have to do so. We can't overlook the fact that compromises, which we have been forced to make, have sometimes worsened the problem." People have even used hunger strikes and threatened suicide. The number of meetings in churches increased to 20; planned was the occupation of churches in Saalfeld; such plans in Erfurt and Leipzig were discovered and "prevented."

The emigration problem was becoming ever more serious; the average number was 16.1 persons per 10,000; the highest numbers were in Berlin (37.7), Dresden (24.3) and Leipzig (21.8); the lowest were in Neubrandenburg (5.7) and Schwerin (7.5). University people constituted 15 percent of the Applicants and skilled workers 70 percent. An increase of 214 percent in illegal exit came mostly during "family emergency" trips. "Organized public efforts have increased, encouraged by the BRD program for immigrants. The extortion efforts of the Applicants have doubled in the western diplomatic facilities here and in other socialist countries."[139]

The location that witnessed the breakthrough of dissent was the largest DDR city, Leipzig. As explained by Christian Joppke, it was made possible by the combination of the Applicants (Exits) with Reformers (Rights). "Exits" were mostly a late breakaway from mainstream society and were essentially shunned by the other groups, but the Leipzig civil rights dissidents came to accept them. The dissident movement was in a sorry state of fragmentation and exhaustion; the expulsion of its leaders had practically extinguished the IFM (Initiative for Peace and Human Rights). Schabowski commented, "They annoyed us, but we did not feel threatened."

The 300 Leipzig oppositionists were scattered over some 20 ecology, peace and human rights groups, many living as young dropouts in Leipzig's dark and deserted east end. The city's two most important Initiative groups had formed in late 1987 with an average age well below 25. The ecological group had won some fame from small but well-publicized protest marches about the Pleisse River pollution. The Work Group Justice (AKG), founded in December of former theology students and draft resisters of the university, proved adept in organizing and was able to coordinate the activities of 25 human rights groups in the region.

The most crucial innovation was for these dissidents to work with the Applicants, who were less intimidated than those pushing for rights because they did not want to stay. The collaboration was forged in the Nikolai Church at the peace prayers, which had occurred every Monday since 1982, with rarely more than 30 in attendance. The number of Applicants made a mass of people the dissidents could otherwise only dream of. The dissidents implemented a strict discipline, and the Applicants were not permitted in "the Speaking Circle," which made all important decisions. During the fairs, the dissidents learned to use foreign journalists as protection and amplifiers of their cause.

When Applicants discovered that the church could be their platform, up to 1,000 came every Monday. "Without the would-be emigrants the shift to the public would not have been possible. They were our audience. By surrounding us, they also served as our protection."

The more conservative church leaders, who tried to keep the Applicants out, denounced this, but this did not split the two elements. They shifted to the outside churchyard, where they read protest notes and passed resolutions; a few bricks and planks became a speaker's corner. Gradually, the prayers were only the prelude to what happened outside, and the groups grew each week. Already in March, applicant groups had staged the first silent protest. The courtyard meetings became occasions for similar marches.[140]

Applicants also occupied Berlin's Hedwig Cathedral and the Herder Church in Weimar. "The misuse of churches has caused the realists in the church officialdom to oppose and reject it. These do not treat the Applicants as a group or let them behave as a group in the church." Bishop Leich, head of the Evangelical Church, said what the Applicants did was a misuse of the church.

If the problem was not from Christianity, it was from Communism and was so recognized by the MfS: "We must also trace thoroughly the effects of the massive hostile ideological influence in the direction of *Glasnost* and *Perestroika*, including the publications and actions in the Soviet Union and other socialist countries. I mention here only the many items in the Soviet press, particularly in the German language press, about the treatment and measures taken [by Stalin] against the German communists. These releases are truly not in the interest of increasing the confidence in our policies and strengthening us, rather they damage us seriously. . . . That could mean that demands can come even from functionaries, from the intelligentsia, from block party members with serious effects."[141] In another ominous Gorbachev move, he announced the withdrawal of six tank divisions from the DDR.

December

Mielke denounced "all those forces—some with us—who wish to divert us from our tried and true path." Then he referred to a third front, meaning *Perestroika*, "in a dangerous closeness to our Class Enemy." Mittig described a softening in the MfS ranks, which scholar Walter Süss perceived as a gap in the isolation with which MfS members were surrounded. A higher percentage of those who dealt with IMs were trying to quit, showing that contact with reality was troubling them.[142]

DDR writer Stefan Hermlin described a similar problem at the time in reaction to the Central Committee's seventh meeting: "The DDR leaders are fearful because of the attractiveness of the BRD, the serious crisis in other socialist lands and the revolutionary situation in the USSR. He emphasized it was a serious crisis in confidence." The MfS was concerned: "How precisely Hermlin was informed is shown by the events." Hermlin declined to have his truth broadcast: "If I should make a statement into the microphone, tomorrow the Party newspaper will have a hundred collectives on my neck saying the opposite."

If on the defensive on the ideological front, the SED could attack religion. Mielke told his staff, "More have doubts about Marxism, so there is a flight into the private sphere. The disappearance of religion must be helped by us. Honecker made this the primary problem in his speech to the FDJ."[143]

The MfS reported that the DDR leaders were seizing on the hope that the Bonn government was lamb-like and had moved away from the Cold War policies. If the BRD were to be malicious, the DDR was vitally exposed. "If they [BRD leaders] were to be an instrument of the Cold War, the DDR's internal situation was almost designed for ruining it economically."

The MfS was criticizing the nation's leader: "Honecker made a fundamental mistake when he boasted that the DDR had the highest standard of living in its history and was better than the BRD. This opinion was grotesque to anyone aware of the reality."[144]

This was particularly grotesque to the 1.5 million citizens allowed to visit West Germany in 1988.[145] Then, 195 persons left illegally, 50 percent more than in 1987; the prepared and attempted efforts totaled 2,312, up from the 1,732 in 1987. This included 483 Applicants, 715 persons with police records, and 338 persons not legally employed. In 25 cases, border troops used weapons, and 29 persons were captured; 10 got over despite the use of guns.[146]

The MfS ended the year with its own strong economic critique, which stressed the necessity of moving toward a market economy. "Internal discussions came to the conclusion that basic and quick changes in the economic system are necessary." It must move toward capitalist practices. "In particular were the following demands. The planning should be more market-oriented and the distribution plan more directed to the interests of the producing firms. The ineffective and unprofitable branches of the economy must be reduced or eliminated. The research and development should not be so broadly laid out, rather limited to those products and technologies, which are determined by the world market, based on international cooperation and specialization." The MfS thought that this meant giving up on Mittag's top priority, electronics.

The DDR economy further required a freer, less bureaucratic structure: "The system of economic management must be clearer and competencies better defined, to prevent, for example in a combine, so many state organs and individuals who want to involve themselves, thus disturbing the relationship between democratic centralism and individual responsibility."[147]

The MfS itself was disturbing such relationships, but its advice did not change that "democratic centralism" policy. It wanted a change, but that would require the masses moving in the streets and across the borderlands of Hungary.

NOTES

1. Sch, 18a, Stimmung, p. 4.
2. Sch, 10a, 12.1.8, p. 62.
3. Sch, 17b, Hagenow, 21.1.8.
4. Sch, 18a, 18.1.8, p. 18.
5. Sch, 14c, 31.1.8, pp. 3–14.
6. Sch, 17a, Bützow, 14.1.8, pp. 130–32.
7. Sch, 10a, 2.2.8, p. 63.
8. Sch, 17b, Hagenow, 3.2.8, pp. 3–6.
9. Sch, 18b, 3.2.8, p. 12.
10. Ibid., Sicherheitslage, pp. 5–9.
11. Sch, 49g, 4.4.8, pp. 2, 5.
12. Sch, 10a, 5.2.8, pp. 88–90.
13. Ibid., 8.2.8, pp. 89–110.
14. Sch, AKG, Leiter 2b, pp. 48–49.
15. Sch, 17b, Hagenow, 9.2.8, pp. 134–35.
16. Sch, AKG, 18a, 19.2.8, p. 3.
17. Sch, 17a, Bützow, 12.2.8, p. 154.
18. Sch, 11a, 23.2.88, p. 5.

19. Ibid., pp. 2–7.
20. Sch, 18b, 25.2.8, pp. 24–25.
21. Sch, 11b, 7.4.8, pp. 73–78.
22. Sch, 10a, 18.2.8, pp. 156–57.
23. Sch, 11b, 7.4.8, pp. 73–78.
24. Ibid., 25.4.8, pp. 129–39.
25. Ibid., 16.4.8, p. 93.
26. Sch, 12a, 3.6.8, p. 96.
27. Sch, 17a, 172, Bützow, 18a, 26.4.8, pp. 1–2.
28. Sch, 18b, 27.4.8, pp. 165–66.
29. Sch, 11b, 25.4.8, pp. 129–39.
30. Sch, 17a, Bützow, 27.4.8, p. 191.
31. Sch, 12a, 30.4.8, p. 21.
32. Sch, 25d, 2.5.8, p. 3.
33. Sch, 12a, 25.5.8, pp. 95–96, 100.
34. Ibid., 16.5.8, pp. 69–72.
35. Sch, 10a, 5.2.8, pp. 88–90.
36. Sch, 17b, Hagenow, 20.5.8, p. 50.
37. Ibid., 16.6.8, pp. 174–75.
38. Sch, 18a. 2.6.8, pp. 53–56.
39. Sch, 18b, 10.6.8, pp. 61–63.
40. Sch, 12a, 16.6.8, p. 193.
41. Sch, 17a, Bützow, 1.6.8, p. 206.
42. Sch, AKG, Leiter 2b, 25.6.8, pp. 26, 33–36.
43. Sch, 18a., 2.6.8, p. 144.
44. Sch, 17a, Bützow, 5.7.8, pp. 18–21.
45. Ibid., 25.7.8, Bützow, pp. 24–26, 257–59.
46. Sch, 18b, 28.7.8, p. 176.
47. Sch, AKG, 08c, 11.7.8, p. 101.
48. Sch, 13a, 26.7.8, 130; AKG, 12.8.8, p. 61.
49. Ibid., 3.8.8, pp. 130–52.
50. Sch, 18a, 17.8.8, pp. 76–79, 83.
51. Ibid., 26.8.8, p. 88.
52. Sch, 17a, Bützow, 23.8.8, 260–71; 25.8.8, p. 224.
53. Sch, 18a, 17.8.8, pp. 76–79, 83.
54. Ibid., 2.9.8, pp. 90–92.
55. Sch, 18b, 20.9.8, pp. 73, 77–78.
56. Sch, 14a, 21.9.8, pp. 37, 40–46.
57. Sch, 17b, Hagenow, 21.9.8, pp. 216, 218.
58. Sch, 17a, 29.9.8, pp. 277–80.
59. Sch, 17b, Hagenow, 16.9.8, p. 73.
60. Sch, DOSA, 401135, 30.9.8, pp. 2–3.
61. Ibid., 401131, 4.10.8, p. 5.
62. Ibid., 401132, 002, p. 14.
63. Sch, 18a, 5.10.8, pp. 99, 102.
64. Sch, DOSA, 401132, 244/88, 4.10.8, p. 7.
65. Sch, 18a, 5.10 8, p. 104.
66. Sch, 07, 26.10.8, pp. 187–202.

67. Sch, 17a, Bützow, 17.10.8, pp. 37–40.

68. Sch, 18b, 26.10.8, p. 80.

69. Sch, 17b, Hagenow, 10.10.8, pp. 82–99.

70. Sch, 18b,18.10.8, p. 184.

71. Sch, 17b, Hagenow, 31.10.8, pp. 103–4.

72. Sch, 17a, Bützow, 17.10.8, pp. 37–39.

73. Sch, 18b, 27.10.8, pp. 87–88.

74. Sch, 17a, Bützow, 4.11.8, p. 283.

75. Ibid., p. 302.

76. Sch, DOSA, 4001143, pp. 142–44, 165–68.

77. Ibid., p. 178.

78. Sch, DOSA, 4001143, pp. 173–81.

79. Ibid., pp. 188–200.

80. Ibid., pp. 231–46.

81. Ibid., pp. 247–75.

82. Sch, 14c, 6.11.8, pp. 89, 100–102.

83. Sch, 17a, Bützow, 4.11.8, pp. 299–300; 7.11.8, p. 313.

84. Sch, 18b, 8.11.8, 94, pp. 100–101.

85. Ibid., 23.11.8, pp. 109–17.

86. Sch, 17a, Bützow, 7.11.8, p. 310.

87. Sch, 14c, 11.11.8, pp. 154–57.

88. Ibid., 10.11.8, pp. 19–21.

89. Sch, 18b, 10.11.8, p. 187.

90. Sch, 14c, 11.11.8, pp. 154–57.

91. Sch, 30, 25.11.8, pp. 114–20.

92. Sch, AKG, 15a, 25.11.8, pp. 53–54, 60.

93. Sch, DOSA, 401143, 30.11.8, pp. 25–27, 38, 95–96,132.

94. Sch, 15b, 6.12.8, pp. 2–17.

95. Ibid., 9.12.8, pp. 18–20.

96. Sch, 17a, Bützow, pp. 40–41.

97. Sch, 30, 30.12.8, pp. 171–75.

98. Sch, 15b, 9.12.8, pp. 18–20.

99. Sch, 18a, 23.12.8, pp. 143, 157–58.

100. Sch, 3a, 15.6.9, pp. 141–44.

101. Sch, 30, 30.12.8, pp. 171–75.

102. Wjatschslaw Kotschenmassow, *Meine letzte Mission* (Berlin: Dietz, 1994), pp. 72–73, 83.

103. ZAIG, 5353, pp. 120–25.

104. Alexander Schalck-Golodowski, *Deutsche-Deutsche Erinnerungen* (Hamburg: Rowohlt, 2000), pp. 154–58.

105. ZAIG, 5353, pp. 120–25.

106. Ibid., 11.1.8, pp. 111–14.

107. Ehrhart Neubert, *Geschichte der Opposition in der DDR 1949–1989* (Berlin: Links, 1997), pp. 652, 657.

108. Ibid., pp. 695–96, 707.

109. John Torpey, *Intellectuals, Socialism and Dissent* (Minneapolis: University of Minnesota Press, 1995), pp. 107–8.

110. Manfred Uschner, *Die Zweite Etage* (Berlin: Dietz, 1993), pp. 201–3, 224–27.

111. Elizabeth Pond, *Beyond the Wall* (Washington, DC: Brookings Institution, 1993), p. 83.

112. ZAIG, 3632, 19.1.8, pp. 2–5.

113. ZAIG, 8709, 25.2.8, pp. 5, 11–12, 18–19, 23–25, 35–38, 45–47.

114. Hans-Hermann Hertle, *Der Fall der Mauer* (Opladen: Westdeutscher, 1996), pp. 23, 48–50.

115. Christian Joppke, *East German Dissidents and the Revolution of 1989* (New York: New York University Press, 1995), pp. 118, 126.

116. ZAIG, 4877, Referat 26.2.8.

117. Bernd Lindner, *Die demokratische Revolution in der DDR 1989/90* (Bonn: Bundeszentral für politische Bildung, 1998), p. 19.

118. ZAIG, 5353, pp. 115–18.

119. ZAIG, 8677, pp. 88–99.

120. Alexander Fischer and Günther Heydemann, Hg., *Die Politische "Wende" 1989/90 in Sachsen* (Köln: Böhlau, 1995), pp. 35–36.

121. Uschner, *Die Zweite Etage*, p. 59.

122. Jeffrey Kopstein, *The Politics of Economic Decline in East Germany, 1945–1989* (Chapel Hill: University of North Carolina Press, 1997), p. 102; Peter Christ and Ralf Neubauer, *Kolonie in eigen Land* (Berlin: Rowohlt, 1991), p. 58; Carl Heinz Janson, *Totengräber der DDR* (Düsseldorf: Econ, 1991), p. 104.

123. ZAIG, 4323, pp. 92, 97.

124. Hertle, *Der Fall*, pp. 23, 48–50.

125. ZAIG, 4879, pp. 68, 70, 90.

126. ZAIG, 13659, 10.6.8, pp. 59–68, 82–92.

127. ZAIG, 13659, 10.6.8, pp. 98–112.

128. Manfred Schell and Werner Kalinka, *Stasi und kein Ende* (Frankfurt: Ullstein, 1991), p. 69.

129. ZAIG, 13659, 27.7.8, pp. 115–36.

130. ZAIG, 13659, 27.7.8, pp. 145–49, 158–64, 195–97.

131. ZAIG, 13658, July 1988, pp. 221–48, 297.

132. ZAIG, 13658, 31.8.8, pp. 304–22.

133. ZAIG, 5353, 25.8.8, pp. 126–38.

134. Reinhard Buthmann, *Kadersicherung im Kombinat VEB Carl Zeiss Jena: Die Staatssicherheit und das Scheitern des Mikroelektronikprogramm* (Berlin: Links, 1997), pp. 128–32.

135. Pond, *Beyond the Wall*, 84; Hertle, *Der Fall*, pp. 342–43.

136. ZAIG, 5353, pp. 140–43.

137. SAPMO, DY/30 IV 2/2.039, 57, p. 2.

138. Volker Koop, *Zwischen Recht und Willkür: Die Rote Armee in Deutschland* (Bonn: Bouvier, 1996), pp. 158, 223, 238–41.

139. ZAIG, 8620, pp. 5–15.

140. Joppke, *East German Dissidents*, pp. 128–50.

141. ZAIG, 8620, pp. 26–27, 47–48.

142. Walter Süss, *Staatssicherheit am Ende* (Berlin: Links, 1999), pp. 105, 107, 113–14.

143. ZAIG, 3750, 23.12.8, p. 6.

144. ZAIG, 14414, 7.12.8, pp. 29–32, 37.
145. Pond, *Beyond the Wall*, p. 82.
146. ZAIG, 8676, 21.2.9, pp. 7–18.
147. ZAIG, 14414, 30.12.8; Pond, *Beyond the Wall*, p. 84.

Chapter 5

The Storm Breaking: Spring 1989

SCHWERIN

In the last winter of DDR discontent, the vital technology was failing: "Engineers in the computer center can not complete the new computer, as scheduled for the 40th anniversary, because of a lack of material and technical preconditions."

The workers had come to expect such failures: "Employees of the BVEB Housing Combine say conditions are chaotic, even bankrupt, but nothing is done to get a new director. The workers there blame the failed economic policy. Motivation is lost to the point of resignation, with no belief that we can solve the problem by 1990."

Farmers were also aware of the dishonesty at the top: "Rural people are upset when the Central Committee says that the DDR has a higher living standard than the BRD. The trust in the Party is disappearing."

In particular, limiting travel was creating ever wider waves. "The police are critical that trips to the BRD to their families could hurt their chances of promotion." Most were counting time to the freedom of retirement: "Some teachers are calculating how many years before they can retire and then 'enjoy their full rights as citizens.' They complain again that they who could well represent the DDR in other countries may not go while many politically illiterate are allowed to travel."[1] Older people were envious that young people could go to sporting events in the West and they could not. "They think the youth always have things given to them on a silver platter. The young are particularly influenced by the consumer world of the BRD."

The young were indeed the most skeptical. Vocational school students were asking why the DDR was still recruiting and drafting young men if

Gorbachev was speaking of disarmament. "Many students at Güstrow's Teachers' College consider Poland and Hungary lost to socialism. All agree that Rumanian cultism is wrong and yet the DDR honored Ceauşescu." Youth were critical of the media claim that national income was rising, when they could not see it. "They are also critical of school, they want improvement of the curriculum, no instruction on Saturday and more practical instruction."[2]

Workers distrusted their machines. They knew how old the technology was. "Most of the obsolete technology is liable to break down and repairs are possible only with great use of resources. If one took out the officially obsolete equipment, the plant could no longer function."[3] The problems were increasing of defective machines, cables and even railroad ties.[4]

The workers knew how foolish were the DDR comparisons to the BRD. "So many workers think they must have contact in the BRD to survive, and few think that the living standard is higher here, even with the low prices of basics."

Farmers distrusted the SED and its collectives: "They have also very little identification with their LPGs." When Gadinger told the State Council on 12 January that all LPGs were profitable, many said: "About this they are lying. No one should be surprised that the government does not know what the real situation in the country is."[5]

MfS Colonel Bäcker even distrusted his ill-coordinated organization: "The MfS border officials have scarcely a basis for their work; we don't have our own IMs or operatives in place. Mielke's February 1986, command has not worked. . . . We do not have enough information on NATO's aggressive plans. Our information in the north was only 62 percent in 1987 and 76 percent in 1988. We have some sources in the BRD Customs, but I am not getting all the information, some goes to the county border controls. The [adjoining] North Stendal Border Command does not have an evaluation capacity."

His own personnel could not be trusted: "The IMs are all right, except they are soon to be drafted, and others will come in with less experience. Our IMs mostly watch the border troops. All troops should be evaluated every 3 months so they don't run away. Of each border regiment, 45 had to be transferred as unreliable."[6]

Analysis was lacking. "There is still too much merely passing on information as against analysis and thought." Seventeen operations were described as successful, one of which was to undermine "partner city" Wuppertal's efforts. The MfS described its clever "active" work, although with no apparent relevance to the problems that it had described.[7]

It claimed successes against internal hostiles and "external lovers": "We have achieved an important contribution with an increased commitment of IM forces, to counter the exponents of the underground, and in identifying the agitator." Two IMs broke up a local love affair with a West Berlin girl.

In another case, they stopped a girl from going West, although they knew that both love connections had a firm and intimate character. "We sent in IMs and GMs to prevent a female hairdresser from breaking the law."

They had not controlled a "Concert for the Armenians," at which Stefan Heym said, "The truth is restricted to only a few selected persons and many people have access only to a truth deficit." He used "The Emperor's Clothing" story "to defame the DDR." The singer Barbara Thalheim attacked the MfS and the FDJ. She sang for *Perestroika* and *Glasnost*, and the young applauded her. "We had to take administrative measures." The organizers said they had no reason to suspect the two.[8]

The Party had difficulties in preventing a pro-Soviet protest; workers at the Electrical Combine said they would quit the DSF (German–Soviet Friendship) because *Sputnik* was banned. "This is the least risky way of showing dissatisfaction with developments. If they left the organization, they could lose their wage grouping and their vacation spots."[9]

Even the MfS was criticizing a policy of repression: "Everyone can think differently about Russia, but banning *Sputnik* was a dumb idea." Censoring it did more harm than good. "Students sense insufficient discussion from the authorities, so they discuss among themselves, which leads to errors."[10]

The MfS urged honesty in the coming election and that the DDR would look better if it announced the honest election results of 80–90 percent, rather than the phony 99.99 percent. "Most people know that such an election result can only be achieved by excluding certain groups of people."[11]

Popular dissatisfaction was coming to be expressed in the parties, criticism of the economic, informational and educational policies. Many were saying, "Honecker should go." The National Democratic Party (NDPD) leaders in Wolgast said that the DDR must decide soon whether to take the capitalist or socialist path, in which what was important was only how one could progress, for which the Soviet reforms could be useful to get changes. The LDP was for *Glasnost* at every level and the LDP was no longer being a helper to the SED. [12]

February

The MfS found the reasons that 29 persons had not returned from trips to the West: family conflict, dissatisfaction with their job and the influence of relatives. The explanations for those who did return included having spouses at home and disappointment with the BRD and its housing. The MfS gave no proof of any BRD attack on these colleagues, but the increased travel meant that relatives would try to influence them. IMs were still being wrongly permitted to visit the West without being examined about their honesty.

The Applicants were beating down the fearsome MfS, leaving the officials feeling abused. "Our colleagues in this office, who are exposed to a very high physical and psychological burden, have not escaped without suffering. They conduct 7 interviews daily, some with people who have been trying for years to leave. They get abuse which has led to indications that our staff is giving up the fight. A department head and several assistants have quit." Most Applicants did not quit: "There is some difference in the Applicants' reaction, but most insist on going to the BRD."[13]

Of the Applicants, 62 percent were given the requested documents, of which 50 percent were accepted by the authorities. "The Applicants who are turned down reject absolutely the reasons given. They feel that some change should be introduced in the time they have to wait. The great majority during the interviews remain correct and factual, but make obvious that their decision to emigrate is final. Most continue to cite the Vienna documents. It is clear that most applicants are very well acquainted with the law; and act as though their applications from the previous year are still valid."[14]

The Applicants not only knew their stuff but were fresh: "Those who want to travel know the rules well and are often insulting to officials." As for family travel requests, "Students are less interested in visiting relatives, they just want to experience the BRD. This is partly from the feeling that when they become teachers, it will be impossible to travel."

In addition to travel envy was bonus envy: "Workers at the Hydraulic-Nord plant, Parchim, say the year-end bonus raises questions about the idea of 'produce more, earn more.' They will refuse any overtime because the workers have been lied to and the unions do not represent them." IM "Fred" corroborated the low morale because of the lower bonus. "Even he was angry, getting 385 marks less than the previous year, although the man who only gave out equipment got 1,000; the average was 700."[15]

The workers, getting no answers from the union, were considering a demonstration. "The IM assigned there is politically not firm in the faith and doesn't give the names of the hostiles." To fix it, they called in IME "Wolfgang," who was in a key position.

The workers generally had become a problem. The bosses complained that there were too many accidents and too many workers calling in sick. "There is a declining worker interest in working for society. They openly say they can't expect any change." Certainly not from the union: "In the Güstrow Lewa factory, an entire collective wanted to resign from the union. The manager asked the union to talk, but not to talk political nonsense or the discussion would certainly not have the desired success." Honecker's saying that the Wall could last 50–100 years met with "anger and disgust."[16]

An inspection of a Parchim plant showed that its Plan fulfillment was "not real." Its deficit was 14 million marks. The Schwerin VEB Hydraulic also falsified its production. Similarly, the Home Building Firm in Schwerin ignored "socialist competition," the SED way to create incentive by having firms compete.[17]

Lies and laziness had forced the MfS into all sorts of actions: "We helped solve problems in building railroad bridges and electrification." Physical damage was proven not to be sabotage: "Most comes from poor management."

The report was still positive about the MfS' organization.[18] By using Chekist measures, it was nipping political resistance in the bud. "Political Underground Activity" (PUT) was disrupted or paralyzed, as it had achieved with the Women's Group and the Güstrow Peace Group. "This process of 'differencing' in the churches was also successful but control is very difficult in the Applicant problem. . . . 'Destroyer' [Lietz] is a problem as is his Peace Network."

Yet in responding to the Mielke order of 7 February, Schwerin confessed its failings: "The district has at least 360 operatives but has great problems in preparation. Implementation and evaluation of the contacts, before and after the trip, are often not done at all. Sometimes contacts occur in forest or fields although the subject is complicated. . . . Over 50 percent of IM travel is without any preparation."[19]

Popular cynicism touched more issues. The DDR talked of disarmament but was building a new army base: "How are they going to reduce the military budget by 10 percent if they go on building?" The fear was the harm that it could do: "The people from Marnitz fear that when that project is built, they will not be able to receive television."

Regarding the coming election: "If one sees what the Russians did last week with their tanks, one must simply not go to vote." It seemed reasonable to conclude, "Why vote, the result has already been decided." There was also cynicism about pricing and housing: "There are doubts about our 'stable price policy,' prices do go up and there is ever less to buy. Doubts also exist about the housing Plan." However, "By 1990, the figures will be corrected so that the Plan will again be 'fulfilled.' "

More ominously, "The question is already raised, 'With the developments in Hungary, will we be allowed to visit there?' "[20]

March

When Güstrow welcomed its new partner city, Neuwied, four citizens used the occasion to push for their emigration. "Proper measures stopped this improper behavior." Of these Applicants, "Many were angry that the state is so generous to Applicants, even welcoming them back."[21]

The MfS checked the local election lists and was pleased that two IMs were candidates and that it had removed candidates who had been hostile in 1974 and 1981.[22] It could not create any excitement: "There is not the necessary enthusiasm, too little activity and too few participants. Various mayors say that the county leadership has been very hectic which disturbs the local work. There are fewer volunteers. Many representatives, particularly those with many years in office, were not prepared to be candidates again, with the explanation, 'Nothing changes anyway. We have no input in policy.' "

Few young persons applied. "Every search for candidates among young people meets rejection. The Seehof community, angry that the mayoress and entire council are not working, says they won't vote, but will go fishing. 'All fine phrases but nothing is done.' The deputy mayor said he would like to get up, pound the table and leave the meeting. . . . Every political discussion is linked to problems, whether in health, society or education."

Or machine parts: the great shortage of farm machinery parts had too long relied on getting some in Romania. Or tires: "New tires are not available. . . . There is so much unhappiness that one can't imagine any movement toward commitment."

Discontent was broadened by travel. "This is made worse by those who visit the BRD. One said that compared to the goods available in the BRD, the DDR is 'a nothing' . . . a difference between night and day. One has to see it. Even the unemployed workers have it good. The offerings, the cleanliness and the friendliness to customers are unimaginable. By those standards every meat store in the DDR would have to close." More shocking than dirty butcher shops: "There is even some doubt about Marxism-Leninism."[23]

Primitive conditions plagued Schwerin's new housing complex: "The complaint from Gross Brütz was that the needed drinking water system has been promised for years but always delayed. Water has to be boiled." Elsewhere, antiquated systems meant air and water pollution: "Someone from the district hospital showed slides and said it should not have come to the point that one has to buy water."

The election result: "In Warsow, 8 families live in a New Building, which is improperly insulated and always damp, so they won't vote." Of the reasons given for not voting, 222 persons said housing; 37 gave religious reasons, and 25 gave political reasons; 160 were Applicants. A woman pastor in Rostock said, "The election is only a fraud." There was also anger that the BRD was allowed to dump its garbage in the DDR.

The MfS asserted that the enemy had made little progress with the youth, but the next paragraph admitted, "Youth take everything for granted, and are not enthusiastic or understanding of our problems. . . . Especially critical are pupils, over 16 years, in Parchim, who want high quality youth-clothing and recreational electronics."[24]

The great disillusion was worsened by the year of celebration. "Many people in all circles and classes are saying that this condition in the 40th year of the DDR is ever less explainable and one can not continue to accept the excuses or consolations. The same is said about car parts and the daily fight to keep land machinery working."

Collective agriculture remained mismanaged. "The grain was improperly dried, and lost much value; it could be used only with first class rye, but there isn't any." Some grain sent to Bützow contained glass splinters.[25]

The MfS kept lists of the LPGs who suffered losses from mistakes in feeding, poor leadership, bad hygiene and lack of ventilation. Three swine LPGs were particularly bad because of the lack of qualified leadership, poor control, asocial workers, alcoholism and overcrowding. Getting rid of the animal waste was a great problem. "Some people who raise animals steal most of their feed."[26] Another list added messy offices, bad leadership and lack of discipline, yet LPG leaders complained, "We can't do any producing because of all the security regulations."[27]

A Sternberg factory relied on the requisite improvisation: "There are no parts, we make them ourselves at high cost. . . . The dissatisfaction that the economy doesn't work has in the last two years become decidedly more open and even pupils demand change."[28]

Cadre, too, were angry: "Keeping down bread and rent prices doesn't help, but burdens the economy and food reserves are wasted, like feeding bread to animals. . . . The PWS factory cadre say that with Erich Honecker for four more years, little will change." SED leaders were getting no respect: "The KGW workers said the Central Committee needn't have met because they have no answers." The local leaders were worse: "When and how will the 'no-brains' in the district and local administrations be fired?"

The lack of enthusiasm regarding the election was understandable. "Only a few people come to election meetings. At the Hydraulic plant, the view is that everything is getting worse and the little man who doesn't have connections has to struggle to survive. . . . The State's demands from the economy mean that very little is left for citizens." There was even little left for production: "Carpenters don't have materials. . . . The increased hand-worker problems mean dissatisfaction in all classes." Again the general perception, "Socialism can't solve the problems."[29]

Of 268 complaints in Schwerin, the sorest points were the lack of building materials and housing, the endangered environment, land-ownership conflicts, citizens trying to obtain business approval and telephone connections. Shortages were the most severely criticized, as were the police's tightening travel restrictions. There was still the lack of objectivity in the news and claims of increased production, which were not borne out. "Therefore most citizens listen regularly to BRD radio and TV."

Applicants and clergy were making difficulties in the preelection meetings. Nonresidents asked provocative questions, with personal attacks on Schwerin's deputy mayor and others. A handmade note read, "Imagine there is an election and no one goes." A letter to Christians called for voting "no" and that foreign media should watch the polling booths. "It is clear in Schwerin that the public is much more open and critical than at the last election, making distinctions among candidates." People cited unfulfilled DDR promises from the last election.

In some larger CDU groups the question rose of why they were granted so few seats and why they must follow the SED. "It was not right to vote for candidates who have been inactive in society, only to secure the majority to the SED." Some threatened to strike the nonactive persons from the candidate list. "Rather than being selected administratively, they should be more democratically chosen, voted on individually and not as a block-list."

More questions were being raised about candidates. "People questioned why up to two-thirds of the candidates were new, when some of the old ones had worked hard. Because of their lack of experience and the lack of the necessary contact with the residents, very young mayor candidates were being rejected." In Hagenow, they had rejected the use of county employees. "They also can't understand putting up candidates, whose children in the past year were arrested, or whose wife stayed in the BRD, or who have a bad reputation because of their constant drinking."[30]

Participation, particularly in city districts, was small. "In the work places the attendance at the candidates' meetings is better, but one must remember that these meetings are usually in direct connection with their work hours" (they got off work).

Concerns were local and personal: "Often problems, abuses and questions are brought up in greater openness to the candidates or functionaries." Particularly in Schwerin, questions were asked why promises had not been kept about house repairs, with critical observations thrown in about a trip taken to the BRD.[31]

The MfS could see more enemies: "Increased enemy forces are pushing contact with internal hostile-negatives. Former citizens are working to get their relatives out. Güstrow's partner city Neuwied's mayor telephoned. They want sport contact and use the excuse of conserving the Low German Language and use invitations to church conferences."

Regarding Church law-breaking: "Lietz and Schlaucher expect to be arrested. Lietz and Heydenreich are printing materials without permission." The unstoppable Jehovah's Witnesses were gathering in small groups, "arriving conspiratorially, only pretending to hold study groups."[32]

At church meetings, dissident Ulrike Poppe discussed reforms in Russia and other socialist countries and said that the DDR should do the same. "Hostile-negative forces around the Evangelical Church have announced that they want to put the communal election 'under control.'"[33]

Some Evangelical officeholders commented that the SED's only concern was to have large numbers vote, and the SED must accept the fact that some people do not want to vote and have different ideas. The Friendly Parties also refused to agitate for going to the polls, saying that the SED must respect the right of people not to vote. Other countries do not need 90 percent voting; Russia was satisfied with 84 percent voting and with only 80 percent of the Communist candidates being elected.

Citizens were bitter about Honecker's letting noncitizens (guest laborers) vote: "The foreigners came here to make money . . . being here for 6 months does not give them the vote. They already have more rights than DDR citizens. Some workers say, 'If they vote, we won't.' " There was also a growing reluctance to participate in union elections: "There is a disinclination to accept office in the union; it has no power, at most only to assign vacation spots."

Worse were the conclusions about socialism: "Many think that socialism is dead in Hungary and Poland. Intellectually inclined persons ask themselves, whether Marxism/Leninism is historically obsolete and say that the history of the DDR has to be re-thought. It is clear among many teachers that ideological principles have been replaced by ideological murkiness. Fewer people are willing to make a contribution to society."[34]

There were reports of discontented youth and their teachers: an IM observed Pastor H., who organized a rock group, "Patchwork," in his Stapel Church and told 200 youth of the need for more freedom. He also suggested not voting if one did not agree with some things. The MfS analysis: "The sources of this are mostly in the realm of the subjective, a deficient and partly irresponsible leadership of those in authority. The work with youth continues to be unsatisfactory, with insufficient recreational opportunities near the border. Firm leaders report the shortages instead of solving them."[35]

One youth commented: "If I did not have my girl friend here, I would have been long gone out of the DDR." Another answered: "If I get a chance, I won't think about the girl friend."[36]

Teachers were also angry about Minister of Education Margot Honecker's policies: "They are pressured to quit because of discipline difficulties, the stress and resulting health problems. They feel that without giving pupils grades, there is not sufficient pressure to study. Many think there will be no change so long as she is Minister of Education."[37] Embarrassingly, "The teachers say they have to watch the BRD media to have the information desired by their pupils."[38]

The teachers at convention complained that it had been too long since the last one and that many problems had developed that needed immediate attention. "One still feared to talk, and there was no change in conditions, rather there continued [at the top] the reaffirmation of the correctness of our education policy, describing only successes and praising each other." At the bottom: "A general dissatisfaction dominates, especially among the teachers about their social position and the respect given them." They wanted basic liberal reforms:

1. Permit teachers to give grades without restrictions. "Now a certain

number and percentage have become a fetish, which reduces a teacher's authority."

2. Reduce the extracurricular burden, like the political schooling. "The many indoctrinations negate the personality of the teacher, limit him in his maturity and independent thinking. . . . They should be required only to study what is necessary to keep up in their fields."

3. Older teachers should have reduced loads and never have to be class leaders. "It is humiliating to see how they suffer, and become a plaything of the pupils and of not a few parents. It destroys their personalities." At least inexperienced teachers should be safe. "It is said now that the young teachers can not be exposed to such burdens."

Getting young teachers was a problem. "The profession should be made more attractive rather than pushing someone into teaching, when their further study has been blocked for whatever reason."

Margot's "democratic" ideas worsened the problem: "For many years, the order has been that every student must achieve the class goal. This mistake has become ever more serious. The teachers are forced to be dishonest to meet a statistic ordered from above. That equals a deception to all involved; it makes the student indifferent, they know they will be promoted. It is a torture to the weak student. Strong students are disadvantaged because the teacher has to give extra attention to the weak."

Better students were hurt because so much effort was made with students who should have stopped after the 8th grade; these weak students would be better off if they went into practical jobs instead of being pulled through to the 10th grade. There must be more honesty in school productivity: "We pretend students are behaving well. The official description is increasingly remote from the reality."[39]

Teachers even suffered threats from students: "The ideal is student discipline. The reality, however, is that many teachers barely know how in certain classes to have a calm hour of instruction. Loutishness, insolence, insults, even physical threats to the teacher have clearly increased in recent years. The teachers want to stop Saturday classes, without increasing those of the weekdays because the pupils are already heavily burdened."

Teachers suffered too much stress: "The position of the classroom teacher is increasingly considered a burden and a punishment. There is the mounting administrative work, including regular reports on every student. For 14 days they have to work on Pioneer and FDJ programs. There are 3 class conferences each year and 25 visits with parents."

To get right the political core: "It should no longer be required to be SED." The solidity of the state should mean less preference to the Party: "The school director should no longer have to be 'Comrade,' because this is no longer needed. The foundation of our state is unshakable."

The required conformity was crippling to all concerned. "Ideological education is no longer fitting to the times." Academic freedom is wanted: "It is necessary that every point of view can be expressed without punishment as long as it is not obviously meant to be provocative, so long as the student does not become violent or mean. Students planning to teach feel ill prepared to handle problems when what is to be taught does not agree with the society's developments. One sees that in the work with the youth, numbness dominates, that everything is thematically bound, so that there is scarcely any room for one's own ideas. Teachers are also crippled by their fearful distrust of their colleagues."[40]

Another MfS report described this serious discontent of teachers, their political-ideological weakness, their doubts about SED policies, their lack of understanding of developments, their claim of being overburdened. "They are avoiding confronting the students' doubts. They desire Gorbachev's reforms. . . . They want to liberalize teaching history and political science. They deny the necessity of always talking about 'enemies.' They threaten to quit the SED and refuse assignments. They want to travel."[41] They wanted more money: "The bonuses should stay with the teachers instead of going to the supervisors."

Schools, like factories and farms, sent false reports of productivity: "Problems are leading to the deformation of the schools. Many teachers do not engage themselves politically-ideologically. They discuss openly the idea that the most qualified should become director. They say competition supposedly means the best teachers, which is often not the case. The principle that all students should be promoted is increasingly criticized as a major mistake. Students assume they will be automatically promoted. Some leave the 8th class better prepared than others leaving the 10th. School documents keep saying that the pupils have the best behavior and a high preparedness to produce. This is contrary to the reality."[42]

Part of that reality was evident at a youth club: "Some pupils under 16 got beer; most bring schnapps which has led to fights, breaking tables and chairs." Even in teacher education, "The teachers have real problems at the teachers college in Güstrow in persuading youth of socialism."[43] Of the young men subject to conscription, more rejected the idea of using weapons on the border.[44]

April

Lietz also touched on education, raising the question at an election meeting about military instruction in schools, then shifted to ecology, criticizing the use of fertilizers, which were harming the lakes: "He's going after the top candidates, as is his 18-year-old daughter."

Two villages rejected their mayors because of criminal acts of a son or wife. The mayoress of Gülzow got three telephone threats to her life. Five more signs appeared: "Imagine that there is an election and no one goes."

Also reappearing was Luxemburg's classic quote, "Freedom is always the freedom of those who think differently."

The talk of celebration elicited subversive talk: "Why after 40 years is the DDR so full of problems ... like the lack of deliveries in consumer goods?" District SED chief Ziegner warned the firms to make their deliveries: "In the first 5 months of the year, circa 30 percent of the firms are operating at a deficit." The SED also could not deliver: "The Politbüro has ostensibly studied the core problems for years but there has been no improvement ... There is still talk of raising the retirement age and ending child care centers."

The churches could not stop subversive singing: "The clergy have not achieved any effect on the masses, but they are working to increase their influence with the young." Deacon R. organized a church rock band, and 250 people sang songs of the exiled Wolf Biermann, although told these were forbidden. "Pastor P. attacked DDR dullness and lack of truth in the media; in his group are many doctors, 'interlecktuals' [so spelled] and handworkers in Parchim County."[45]

The LPGs had lost their vitality: "There is often weak leadership and lacking is the fighting and creative atmosphere; only a few members take part in the discussion. The decisions of the leaders are often not explained and discussed, so that often the necessary will to implement the decisions is lacking." They were only going through the motions: "One often encounters formalism and superficiality. The leaders possess scarcely any personal charisma and can not carry out their duties in the daily work process. They don't understand how to motivate politically, how to persuade and do not hold a position of trust among the farmers. So there is often poor work discipline, including alcohol during work."[46]

MfS ordered an "Operative Action" on an LPG member who asked, "How could we have scientific agriculture if the fertilizer and plant protection chemicals are worthless?" Then he observed, "We also have poor and rich. The unemployed in the BRD are those too lazy to work." He knew because he had been there.

An IM reported the scandal of bread's being fed to animals in Gadebusch, where use went from 150 to 230 kilograms per person; one farm community used 25 pounds per person per week.[47]

Some farmers were saying that more elections might be good because then someone would listen to them. On the other hand: "The medical Intelligentsia say the election is only a formal act. According to them the present situation is catastrophic and alarming." The report concluded: "It is clear that all classes of the population display no reaction or activity about the important political points. A public affirmation of our proven policies is scarcely to be seen." Failure came from the many required attendances: "Criticized is having so many parallel meetings, without anything new to convey. So they attend without the desired interest."

More teachers wanted to see the BRD. "They say rather little about the trip afterwards, but will answer questions. They are impressed by the material goods, but note the social insecurity, and the lack of concern with the welfare of people."[48]

More people were refusing to vote: "The youth in Plau are non-voting because the mayor promised but did nothing for them." Nonvoting had actually declined from 1974 with 328, down to 45 in 1986, but was rising again. "By 26 April, 177 have refused the card; 90 more hint they will not vote; circa 70 Jehovah's Witnesses will not vote. . . . Applicants say openly they have no use for the DDR and will not vote."[49] Instead, they organized. "They even want to create a group 'Pro Humanitas' so they can discuss their problems. Their planned ecology demonstration on 23 April was banned."[50]

The MfS admitted losing that battle: "Those applying now are more aggressive and self-confident. Those of us who deal with them are making little noticeable effort to stop them and say that one day they will leave anyway." The MfS expected to fail: "If one wants to leave he should leave; we're wasting too much time on these people. Our measures do no good."[51]

Another report agreed that Applicants were a hopeless case: "A greater effort was made by all of the SED's partners, but the results were completely unsatisfactory, we could dissuade only 25 people." They had succeeded with 80 in 1985, but no more. "Applicants stay out of the way of such efforts made where they work. The police have been nearly no help at all."[52] A report on police problems emphasized alcoholism, including one suicide.[53]

Problems in Bützow included a lack of cooperation between the engineering and technical office; the leader was not competent in technology, and it was not being rationalized. Transition was delayed, because the leading cadre were opposing it. There was a lack of care in preparing export goods.[54]

The LBP (Leichtbauplatten) factory said that it "filled its plan" but was, in fact, 85,000 marks short. "The plan was accomplished in terms of numbers but not in terms of quality. There is a subjective weakness in the leadership, as has long existed."[55]

In Domitz, "The night shift sleeps a lot and often ends after 3–4 hours; 30–50 percent of the time in administration is used to make purchases for themselves and attend to personal matters."[56] The Polish workers also did as little as possible: "The Poles never had wanted to work or were able to work. They would rather go around peddling in the DDR, the BRD and other countries."

There was dissatisfaction with the Russians, too: young people complained of the lack of service on tours of East Europe like those of the Soviet travel agency.[57] An IM described the problems of shipping pork to Leningrad: "Experts there said that Moscow had ordered the sharpest control on meat from the DDR. Every day they look for new reasons to mark down the quality and the price. I told her about the terrible dirt everywhere in Russian facilities."[58]

May

This was the month of the election. Some 240 persons said that they would not vote, their first reason being the housing problem. Or extortion: "People again see an election as a chance to make demands or threaten not to vote."[59] Regarding Bützow, "It was generally said that any government effort to help declines after an election."[60]

To the Party slogan "As we work today, so will we live tomorrow" came the public's weary reaction: "This solution is as old as the Republic."[61] In the last four days there were 17 instances of tearing down DDR flags. "We had to arrest an Applicant because he took the sign to a demonstration: 'We demand freedom and equality for those who think differently.' "[62]

The election was almost its usual nonevent, except that the acclaimed, nearly unanimous success had required some special ballot box manipulations. Although Korth thanked his people for controlling the election so well by clever staff leadership, the results were troubling.[63] Nonvoters had tripled from 2,150 to 7,400; 55 percent were ages 26 to 40; of these, 50 to 60 percent were production workers, and 10 percent were farmers. More voters defaced the ballots, went into a booth, or struck names, particularly of those candidates with bad reputations.[64]

In Rostock, nonvoters were twice those in 1986; 24 were theology students, plus 60 other students. All Jehovah's Witnesses returned their registration without voting. Of 168 Protestant Church officeholders, 116 voted; of Catholic clerics, nonvoters were 91.7 percent; none of the three bishops voted. Pastor Marquardt, former nonvoter, voted "No." In Schwerin, various pastors voting in the booths "very lightly crossed off the candidates with pencil," and it was "overlooked" during the counting; with no negative votes reported, they protested and got a recount.[65] (This was the only MfS reference to the fraud that it admitted later.)

The postelection MfS analysis: the heavy point of nonvoting was small towns, plus those living in old sections of cities, as in Schwerin, with major problems of decaying buildings and places with many ecological problems from industry. "Candidates struck off were long standing officeholders, who have not kept their promises." For that reason in Legde, the mayoress was struck by 150. "They are threatening to continue at the next elections."

A remarkable MfS observation: Gadebusch and Sternberg did not seem different as communities, but Gadebusch had 16 strikings, and Sternberg had 450. The MfS blamed the Sternberg County leader, who did not prepare for the election properly but made arbitrary decisions.[66]

The public reaction to the election, registered by the MfS, not the media, was that there should have been more candidates so the voters had a choice. The persons elected had power only on paper. Policy was determined instead by functionaries who were too old, lacked proper knowledge for the times and were stuck in their old habits.[67]

The MfS reaction evidenced more fear of the hostiles: "The opposition network, even though there are differing political concepts, was showing more organization, with regular central meetings, and a stronger effort to create a web and new groups." They had achieved a wider circulation of information papers and better communication by telephone. Some praise of the opposition had been earned: "Extremely hostile positions are taken by highly qualified leaders. They sometimes work with reactionary church forces. The church has excellently trained legal experts and they are trying to use the breakdowns to make capital with the public."

The West was admittedly winning the battle of the minds: "The election with increased negative votes shows that the greater exposure to the West has not been countered with a similar strengthening offensive by the FDJ, who mostly avoid a discussion of the political questions. There are more hostile discussions in reference to Soviet changes. Artists are trying to present criticism. The class struggle is tough and we know that some SED members can not take it and even change fronts." But the MfS found solace in the old Marxist faith. "The wheel of history is turning forward to socialism and can not be stopped."[68]

Teachers were expressing more doubts: "The real socialism as it operates is forced ever more to its knees, and only the theory is still persuasive and is acceptable to the students."[69] Children were being lost: "The Applicants even take their children out of the FDJ, which organization shows insufficient elan and concern."[70]

Some 22 pages of report described "successes" of the many MfS organizations, then 31 pages of "Operations," with important-sounding accomplishments but nothing of substance. The MfS conceded that it was losing on some fronts: "In the evaluation of the battle results for the past 7 months, there is an increased anger about not being allowed to leave. There is more talk to hostile Western journalists and more use of the church as camouflage to make state action more difficult. Bishop Stier said that our security measures are an infringement on church rights." On 28 April they decided to advocate the cause: "The church leaders raise questions, like how can there be a discussion if the Applicants can not speak? 'So the church must speak for the weak.' The church will help them by getting them work, they have already helped 30 persons."[71]

June

The MfS counted 160 enemy groups in the DDR, and these were making points. In the district, "Over half were started before 1985, and despite our efforts, the number remained stable; some quit but others started." In the Schwerin district there were about 2,500 members, excluding the fringe persons; 600 could be considered leaders, the hard core. About 60 were the real enemies of socialism, like Lietz. Only 12 percent in the groups were workers; some had been SED. "They try to stay within the law, but keep testing it to see what they can get away with. The MfS plan is to use well-prepared 'social forces' [IMs], to take part in the discussions to dissuade and to help security forces. We should go on the offensive with experts on the questions raised."[72]

Six hostile groups were analyzed: an Ecology Circle, the St. Paul's Cellar group, those refusing military service, an Arche group in Perleberg, a Güstrow group and Pastor Lietz's Evangelical Basis. "His Peace Net, although not approved, mimeographs its publications in the church's youth office and uses the idea of *Glasnost*."[73] The MfS added, "He is a fanatic, who feels he has a mission, an unteachable enemy of socialism, with a personal drive to be important and famous. He is close to the Green Party. . . . He and Inge Bräutigam have constant contact with the enemies."[74]

Colonel Kralisch told his agents that enemies were using the economic problems to stir up the people. He conceded that the problems were very serious: 18.5 percent of productive capital was written off; over 20 percent was older than 20 years, so there was an urgent investment need of 500 billion marks; 1987 should have had 20 percent investment, but the state could invest only 9.9 percent.

He was also critical of MfS intelligence work: the first indications of dissidence had been insufficiently recognized. "Too many reports simply convey information, but do not do the necessary analytical and comparative work to realize the political-operative value. The situation reports don't pick up on the changes. They also lack practical methods to react to changes." The IMs were insufficient: "We must use them better and train them better, and know their world better. We must keep improving their bond to the MfS. We must improve reports of the meetings with IMs; they are usually very general. We should prepare IMs in defensive-thinking."[75]

Teachers, although selected as being loyal, were not up to the challenge either but were further softening in their socialism, one factor being events in other socialist countries. "It is evident that many teachers despite recognizable efforts are not in the position to discuss aggressively with students our SED policy or to defend it, particularly when they are confronted by students who have been listening to the West media. Most teachers also listen to it. Many do not make the effort to be prepared, which creates problems. Few can explain the benefits of socialism. Too many take trips to the West and do not return. Many are speaking of leaving the profession for positions of lower qualifications."

A long analysis treated Applicants like delinquents; of 1,510 applications, 471 left with permission, for which 267 gave humanitarian reasons. Of those leaving, 46.5 percent were from Schwerin city, 67.2 percent were skilled workers, and 27 percent were technical school cadre. The new dangerous phenomenon: 65 persons got out by occupying an embassy.[76]

The MfS admitted that the DDR was losing good people: "All those who left lived in secure material conditions; their work was average to very good. None was socially active at work or in neighborhood collectives; the 12 married couples have no criminal record." Despite much effort, only three were persuaded to return.

The DDR's dilemma: "In a Devil's Circle, if people aren't approved for a visit to the West, they use this as reason for becoming an Applicant. If they are permitted to visit and do not return, then they use the humanitarian argument to unite the family. If we deny exit, they threaten illegal action."[77]

A top secret report highlighted the danger of the West media: "Publicity about the Opposition has increased, aided by correspondents and diplomats of imperialist countries. . . . They are trying to bring such persons and meetings under the protection of international public opinion. The meetings are almost always within the structure of the Evangelical churches, with a broad spectrum from the strongly religious to the atheist, mostly young, who have a hostile attitude toward the socialist state and society. There is not much support among workers, but there is among those who have no stable work position."

People continued to express their pleasure with Gorbachev and observe that only on Western TV could they know what is going on.[78] They also had developed skepticism about the Soviets: "The opinion grows that Gorbachev should pay more attention to his internal problems, the anarchistic tendencies."[79]

On his effect on the DDR, the public was also of two minds: "Gorbachev is generally loved, the people favor disarmament and democracy, but fear DDR isolation. The BRD is closer to the Soviet Union than the DDR is. The thought is that the SU will become ever more dependent on the West and therefore less willing and able to help us. At the Party Congress, they should ask how socialism could survive. The prediction is made that in the foreseeable future the Wall and the border will not play a role."[80] The public was more perceptive than its leaders.

Because of the forbidden awareness of Soviet disclosures, the proposed visit of a Moscow chorus brought expressions of anti-Stalinism, so the agreement was canceled. Substituting an SED program evoked little interest, so the organizers turned to the idea of presenting highly honored artists, but the SED leaders or the Schwerin city council did not support this. Nothing was presented, which frustrated the artists.[81]

An artist at the State Theater commented that events in China crushing the student demonstrations showed that socialism had to use violence to stay in power, brutal power, as in 1953, 1956 and 1968 and in Afghanistan. To this "The SED had no real answer." The MfS answer was to permit no more State Theater visits to the West.[82]

A greater danger was a collapsing industry; 297 registered disruptions meant a production loss of 6,369,500 marks. "These derived from a lack of command of the technological processes, worn out equipment, missing workers, a constant decline of qualified personnel and leaders. The steam pipes are a constant danger of serious damage. In the Fiber Glass factory, the obsolescence factor is 80 percent, so it can not function properly, and had 162 disruptions." Thirty-one employees already had health problems and had to be transferred; these were the more qualified. "Of 135 workers, 50 are foreign and probably they will be hurt more. In Wölfen, all of them had to be taken out, which crippled production."[83]

Problems were growing on the land: "The cadre situation in the State-farm in Gadebusch is poor. The director gets no help. . . . The buyer and workshop leaders are incompetent. Housing is lacking, the stalls are poor. There is even a lack of chains for the water buckets. For years, maintenance has been badly neglected."[84]

July

A general malaise persisted. "There is a certain disinterest, even indifference, with the real excess of happenings and in many places a purely material interest. There are shortages, although things are not so planless as in the other socialist countries."[85] The MfS believed the doctors' long list of medical shortages and the farmers' complaint that Berlin was better supplied with food than they were: "Workers are bitter. Communists, like their leaders, strike a pose and then betray everything."

The Teldau LPG-T achieved great personal production, because they gave everyone more free time, like unpaid vacations. Individuals used LPG machines without paying for them, which led to other farmers' becoming upset. In the Baantin LPG-T, the leader, immediately upon his election, changed the picture on the wall from Honecker to Gorbachev.[86]

Gorbachev was more discussed but mostly based on the West media: "It is surprising here that DDR citizens are so excited about him; some say that his only hope to revive the Russian economy is to tie it to West Germany. Hungary and Poland are totally dependent on the USA; socialism there has been sold out. Listening to Gorbachev raises the question whether Marxism-Leninism has any validity now."[87] Clearly, the MfS writer shared this public doubt.

From events had arisen a growing sense of isolation: "Travel in the Soviet Union is mostly rejected, because of the accumulated experiences, poor service, the perception that the DDR citizen doesn't count for much and the conditions in Russia." The isolated DDR was on its own: "There is no longer a solidarity of socialist countries, except for disarmament and peace. It exists no longer in economic questions."

The events in Eastern Europe were also disturbing these Secret Police: "These make doubtful the correctness and the realizability of the entire policy of socialism." In addition to ideology, there was geography: "Our country is too small to go it alone, but events show us being driven ever more into isolation." The examples presented on Western TV "frequently can not be contradicted by our leaders." The sobering discovery: "After 70 years of Socialism, in some places, people are hungry."[88]

A mundane case in point: the warm weather brought a shortage of soft drinks and the closing of the only ice cream shop in Sternberg: "This shows the incompetence of authorities to change conditions; they could at least sell packages of ice cream." The public was withdrawing: "There is a popular disinterest, even doubt about policy. People pull out of social life, resign positions. We have difficulty getting candidates."[89]

Kralisch still blamed "imperialist" tactics for DDR's problems. "They make offers to the Soviet Union in order to open the way into Eastern Europe." The invaders are the malicious guests. "We must also counter 'political tourism.'" Then he followed the official defensive line: "There can be many forms of socialism, we should not use our measuring stick for other countries. The first priority is political stability, then productivity." His solution was the traditional one, making a greater subjective effort.[90]

He claimed that the enemy had increased the level of subversion, which meant that of those who did not return, 70 percent were skilled persons and 16.6 percent were from health services, including two in leading positions.[91] State Theater personnel committed acts of treason by fleeing after giving performances in Duisburg, in Italy and in Bad Hersfeld; four became Applicants on their return. "There is ever less discipline and high alcohol consumption. Ideological conditions are getting worse and worse."[92]

MfS personnel were told to use the law every way possible to block the Vienna Agreement on Human Rights, but the minutes still do not show that the MfS especially worried: "The Alf Klub involves football rowdies, with the usual family and school problems, a group of skinheads linked with Alf football fans."[93]

The most worrisome: "The Applicants have a growing aggressiveness, demonstratively ignoring the effort to instruct them and ignoring injunctions, in a provocative fashion using sit-downs, human chains and walks."[94] Among their "provocative" reasons to emigrate were better chances for a child with severe disabilities; an unsuccessful three-year effort to get an apartment; the problems of being a diabetic in the DDR. "It is clear that they have thought about it a long time and resist arguments."[95]

A touch of MfS sympathy for what Mielke would call enemies: "It is the wrong tactic to call critics malcontents; many feel themselves hemmed in."[96] The Secret Police accepted the general bitterness about police repression: "DDR persons were annoyed by the chicanery of the [DDR] border troops, who constantly stopped them although they were well known. Even IM Udo Stein was stopped and threatened with a gun."[97]

August

The MfS also understood the health professionals' anger: "There are problems with the leader of the health office, his personality, the lack of respect, which means he can not discipline doctors, even in cases of malpractice." In tooth care, "The problems of dentists include the poor quality of false teeth from the USSR. Dentists who get to the BRD praise the health care there."[98]

Intellectuals scorned the less-educated Party leaders: "The SED secretary can not be accepted by the university cadre because he commands no knowledge of their specialized areas. Also among the SED members in the university cadre, there is extremely little willingness to take on Party functions. At SED meetings, no interest is shown in political questions, but when they start discussing material matters, high interest appears."[99]

One had to concentrate one's interest in finding life's necessities: "The consumer goods shortage and repairs are the permanent central point of dissatisfaction. The lack of modern refrigeration means the lack of freshness of fruit and vegetables. Therefore women leave the workplace early and stay away longer, and nothing is said about it."[100] This helped explain to the MfS the increasing impact of the socialist crime of "revisionism and nothing effective is being done to counter it." It was linked to "criminal activity" in dealing with building materials and spare parts. The collapsing of apartment houses was a "national scandal."[101] The same was said of old buildings: "The outright decay of certain buildings is a national disgrace."

Many believed it the worst of times: "The prevalent opinion is that the supply [of consumer items and materials for production] was never so bad as it is now and no solutions are to be seen. It is the opposite of what was promised."[102] A Parchim VEG asked disturbing questions: "Whether the Party itself knows where the development is going. Everyone notes the difference between the success portrayed in the media and the reality of shortages." It could only be lying or ignorance at the top. "Speculation is that the reports from the bottom to the top are manipulated, so the leaders in Berlin do not know."

In the LPGs the need persisted "to do better planning of material deliveries and to replace leaders who are too authoritarian." There was constant deception: "Farmers also think that preparing an LPG especially for a foreign visitor is also a form of deceiving oneself." But then the non-sequitur MfS reassurance: "The farmers are still behind the government."

In Perleberg, 4,000 towels were produced saying "Today we have nothing and tomorrow it will be warmed over."[103] People were saying that those who were living better, functionaries and those with West money, had lost the sense of DDR realities: "There is always the anger that the media are not truthful."

Worse, society was losing its coherence. "As the social, familial, occupational and other binding relationships in the DDR are losing their consistency, many are prepared to leave." Those wanting to flee were no longer outcasts: "The public is generally tolerant of Emigrant Applicants, as long as they do not cause any disturbance. There is no more distancing themselves from them."

The MfS wished that it could keep away from the Applicants: "Those assigned to dissuade them have essentially given up, they just go through the motions. 'Just a waste of time.' " Then the scornful question: "Why do so many leave our paradise, and why don't the million unemployed in the BRD come here?"[104] A part of the answer: "More people are making comparisons to the BRD, like the immediate repairs possible there. The reactionary trend is primarily to be seen in the health service realm."[105] ("Reactionary" meant non-Communist.)

The FDJ-sponsored poet seminar in Schwerin was even worse than before: "The majority expressed openly their distancing from the FDJ and SED policies. Their bourgeois and anti-socialist characters went mostly unchallenged."[106]

Yet the MfS looked for reassurance: "The agitation campaign has found no noticeable resonance, even of the youth, but the concern is about the emigration. That Honecker did not discuss it was taken ill."[107] Emigration had come to mean the mass migration through the gap in the barbed Iron Curtain in Hungary: "That the BRD media described how DDR citizens get out in Hungary is evidence of its sabotage."[108] More accurately, it was the worsening isolation: "With no longer the unity of socialists, the DDR must take its own position."[109]

Mentor Russia was giving shocking evidence of Marxist failure. People could now read that after 70 years, the USSR still had nationality problems: "The thought is that Gorbachev has created an internal chaos. The wonder is how calm and order can ever be re-achieved." The reports of misery there raised the question, "Was there not misery before, which had been kept hidden?" Russian problems, including strikes and national discord, raised the question where DDR citizens would be allowed to travel.[110]

Even in relatively rural and slow-moving Mecklenburg, people and the MfS were well informed and sharing the dangerous thoughts of Berlin dissidents.

BERLIN

Lethal were the political dangers arising within the crumbling walls of the socialist world, accelerated by the liberalization of the Vienna Agreement, which Gorbachev had pushed on the DDR. The critical MfS view: "The USSR is confronting other socialist states with a *fait accompli*."

These other states, by their reforms, were also putting the DDR under pressure to change. In Poland Jaruzelski agreed to a Round Table, which led to the free election on 6 February, which Walesa's workers won. A dangerous precedent.

Still more dangerous: in Hungary in May 1988, reformer Karoly Grosz had pushed out the aging Kadar. A liberal Communist elite began reforming the economy and culture. At the end of 1988, the opposition was legalized. In the spring, to gain acceptance in the West, the Hungarians agreed to follow the civilized practice of open borders. The shocker was the demonstration on 16 June to honor those who had been lost in the Soviet invasion in 1956, heretofore denounced as traitors. Hungary was becoming the weakest link in the Iron Curtain, and it had a common frontier with Austria of the West.

Mielke clearly saw the dangers in the human rights agreement in Vienna, although he claimed that the DDR was leading the way in rights and freedoms: "The DDR fought hard against the imperialists and for the values of each society to be respected, against interference in the internal affairs of socialist states. It had success in getting disarmament included, but it was not all positive for us. Compromises were necessary. We signed the agreement to keep the peace offensive moving forward. We and Rumania led the charge against interference, less so the USSR, Hungary and Poland. In other words, the linking of conventional disarmament with human rights questions was used by the West as extortion. We must frankly admit that they succeeded in large part."

Further, Mielke complained that the DDR had been pushed into a corner and had to sign: "Our position in this question was not supported by the other states of the Warsaw Pact. So that the DDR delegation would not be the only country opposing agreement, we finally did not object to the draft of the document." The DDR was left defenseless: "In their last statements, [foreign ministers] Schulz [U.S.], Howe [U.K.] and Genscher (BRD) attacked the DDR and Shevardnaze did not properly respond. Since then greater efforts have been made to split the socialist states."

The MfS dare not let implementation happen: "The document will mean a regular right to mix in our affairs in order to find some violation. There has been some backing away recently in other socialist states." The enemies must be countered: "The constituencies and the activities under this cover are hostile. Opposition groups in the DDR leave no doubt about their goals. Through the Vienna document, our valid legal order and practice, and basic official regulations will be changed."[111]

Mielke asked Soviet emissary Kondrashev in the early summer 1989: "Sergei, what does Gorbachev think he is doing? Does he realize that if your policy with regard to Poland and Hungary continues the DDR will not be able to contain the social forces it releases? Gorbachev and your leaders should understand that the DDR will be crushed." When Mielke asked how Gorbachev had reacted, he was told, "There was no reaction."[112]

Honecker had signed the Helsinki Agreement without fully understanding its effect, so on 5 January, he told the Soviet representative Kaschlev that he would not accept two conditions of the Vienna Agreement: legalizing counterrevolutionary activity and removing the compulsory exchange by visitors of Western money.[113] Beyond this resistance to Soviet policy, Honecker directly rebuffed Gorbachev, who asked, "What should I tell my people, Erich, if in this situation, you visit the BRD?" Honecker answered abruptly, "What do we tell our people, who are so concerned about peace? Therefore I will make the trip." The atmosphere was "tense."[114]

Another MfS reaction to Vienna was to order on 16 January the creation of a Union of Freethinkers to stop "the abuse of religious and conscience freedom by over 30 religious groups." The rationale: "Their intent is to undermine the separation of church and state and to misuse religion for anti-socialist goals, as well as using human rights, *Perestroika* and *Glasnost*, and demands for a different DDR. Creating this Freethinker organization is not discrimination, but to maintain church cooperation."

The MfS planned the campaign against religious groups in detail, down to the county level, but it should not be conducted in the firms or in armed organizations; there should be 15 members at the district level and 10 at the county level. It was never to be a collection basket for dissidents. "No one with religious ties should be permitted to take the floor. The disappearance of religion must be helped along with a certain structure." Mielke's clinching justification: "Honecker made this the primary problem when talking to the FDJ on 23 December 1988."[115] The real primary problem was the economy.

The Economic Bomb Waiting to Explode

Honecker, ever more out of touch with popular sentiment, boasted on 19 January that the Wall would be there in 50 or 100 years, if the reasons for it, presumably a desire to escape, had not been removed. His economy behind the Wall was not likely to last one more year, and Mittag was trying to persuade him of that.

Mittag saw that the dangers had been multiplied by Soviet demands: their natural gas pipeline required the DDR to provide thousands of kilometers of concrete and up to 15,000 workers. In line with the long experience of dealing with Russians: "The USSR figured it at about half the real cost to the DDR and deliveries of their gas were 13 million tons less than had been promised, which cost us 14 billion marks." The decline in other raw materials from the USSR was 4.4 billion. The cost of the Soviet Wismuth (uranium) project since 1971 had been 7.1 billion marks. The required DDR help to other socialist countries he listed as another 16.9 billion.[116]

His problem with Honecker was that it was taboo to discuss economic reform, which would require more realistic prices, reducing subsidies for consumption, housing or sport, developing joint ventures and using a real production principle. By nature an optimist, Honecker avoided tough decisions and took the path of immediate least resistance in the economy.

He permitted no political change, not even resistance in the Politbüro. A disillusioned member, Heiner Müller, reflected sadly, "Honecker embodies the tragedy of incompetence. His arrogance and his adventurism in the use of power exceeded by far his ability. Lacking understanding of the facts, he could have compensated for it, if he had listened to the counsel of experts and if he had encouraged criticism from his associates. Both he did not do."[117]

Mittag also blamed the Politbüro's push to spend: "Schabowski pushed more housing for Berlin and I could not stop him." There were also "special things like the building of the Palace of the Republic, which was outside the Plan, with its cost being no consideration." Even Mielke was a problem: "There was the MfS headquarters on Normanen Strasse, but we were not allowed to be involved. For the Army in 1989, it was 262 billion marks, for the Stasi 12.7 billion, and for the Interior Ministry [police] 3.7 billion. This did nothing for the economy. I tried to reduce it."[118]

Mittag also evaded the law. Mittag's unscrupulous wheeler-dealer Schalck-Golodkowski had more power than some Politbüro members had. Hired to make deals for the desperately needed hard currency, he was selling whatever possible, including works of art. Much profit came from selling items confiscated by customs officials.[119]

Schabowski and many others blamed Mittag for pushing certain industries like computer chips, whose production required a subsidy of 1.7 billion marks in 1989. That investment had created the technology to spend 538 marks to make one chip, which sold for four marks.[120]

Schabowski observed further that his SED had become unable to react because its personnel had been made eternal. "Logically criticism has to lead to change and democracy is the only way to do that." He thought it "macabre" that the sick, 77-year-old Honecker named the double-amputee Mittag to be his temporary replacement and permitted him the only access. Yet when Mittag wanted to share in a meeting with Gorbachev, Honecker kept him waiting outside.[121]

Disruption within the MfS

There were also increasing conflicts within the MfS, as described in hundreds of pages of trials conducted by its Party organization. "Although all right in most elements, there are personal intrigues and, from time to time, one member will blast the other and describe confidential problems."

Such action occurred when a much-admired Comrade Lessman voted against the decreed Party punishment of a Comradess Grünheid, because he thought not all the problems could be solved by the Party; the judgment against her had been too quick and the punishment too severe. This criticism made the others involved very excited and angry: "He had damaged the collectivity of the leadership." One said that Lessman should be fired, and the Party should not tolerate any "faction-maker." Although others defended him as a good Party man, he could no longer be elected to Party office.

A man wanted to leave the MfS because of the death of his father; instead, he was thrown out of the Party; and when he appealed, he was "lectured." A young officer wanted out so he could have a more comfortable and freer life, and every effort failed to change him; the MfS, ignoring the Party, made him a military instructor on socialism. The Party comment: "No comment necessary."

When some MfS officers stole money, the Party was not consulted, so they stayed in office. An officer sold used cars and bragged that he had earned 8,000 marks. A captain, with "abnormal" homosexual and bisexual drives, had sex indiscriminately with many contacts and with "hostile" men and women. When fired, he said he would not change; he was sent to work in a men's clothing firm. A sergeant twice tried to force a subordinate into homosexual acts, and, as punishment, he was sent to work in a store in Gera.

Drunk driving made up 10 percent of the cases: "A drinking problem had been long evident and they had been punished and elected to office again without changing their behavior. It was hushed up so as not to harm the leader's authority. Such violations went on for years and became a model. Instead, they should be transferred. Some regard themselves as untouchable kings, and do what they like with subordinates, particularly in the large collectives." The report regretted: "The MfS military organizations operate in the military way, no discussion, no criticism, no change."

More seriously, "A relatively high number of old Party members must be brought to trial. They either did not understand the political ideology, or they have deliberately rejected it. The organization should fix it so that no one can avoid the indoctrination."

The MfS admitted more openly that a growing number of its own members had only pretended loyalty to its principles: "There are more pressures now on the MfS and many avoid their responsibilities. There is a failure in inculcating class consciousness and behavior. There is only a superficial knowledge of the correct World View and Party decisions. They had hidden their true views, and are no longer willing to serve the MfS, because of their relatives. They received a civilian education and they try to have these values. They make sharp attacks on the Party, but say they are loyal. They don't realize that the Party decisions are for all members and mean what they say, and that every member must actively support them."

Young IMs, in particular, were backing away from the Party: "Locally the problem is mostly IMs trying to get out. With many young people entering our service, we missed the signals of many of these who have problems, including lacking an understanding of the situation. They lack the close contact to their immediate superiors. They don't accept any responsibility for leadership and avoid Party meetings. There are even leaders who attend only half of them. There are often poor election choices." A member who was assigned to propaganda took the wrong position on *Sputnik*: "One was elected to political leadership, although he had repeatedly been unwilling to do the required tasks; everyone was surprised that he had been picked and elected without discussion."

The MfS had even attracted some fascists: "Some young members joined because they like the military discipline, and these do not reject the neo-fascists, and take on the anti-Semitic and racist slogans; they copy fascist symbols and behavior and joined the EK [right-wing] Movement. This led to some very serious results."[122]

Disruptions among the Public

The cynical reaction to easing the travel restrictions: "Progressive people see it as improving the dialogue with the BRD; the law is now clear, including the right of appeal after 1 July. Those who disagree, like health personnel and church employees, see nothing new. They think it was revised only to indicate the following of the Vienna agreement and for someone to get the requisite court judgment would be as difficult as getting a political judgment."

The MfS admitted a new serious "class" problem: "Even progressives see the division of the DDR between two classes, one with BRD relatives and the other without. Something should be done for those who have no relatives, if not giving them permission to go to the BRD, then subsidies for other travel. Other socialist lands permit travel without family connections. People threaten to petition the central Party and state institutions, to quit the SED or the other parties, to quit social functions to take no part in social activities or apply for permanent exit. These people behave in a disciplined manner, but are determined to leave. The police feel themselves like the buffer between railroad cars."[123]

In 1988, 29,558 such Applicants had left, as compared to 13,785 in 1987; 42,384 had applied for the first time, raising the total to 113,521; by districts: Dresden 6,530, Berlin 5,214, Chemnitz 3,607 and Leipzig 2,138 persons. The MfS kept long lists of emigrant "crimes": 1,291 petitioners committed them as part of the effort, like contacting a Bonn ministry; 5,898 persons remained in the West after a permitted visit, up from 3,233.

Deserting were 14 border troops and 3 sailors.[124] MfS desertions totaled 29 in 1987, 17 in 1988 and 9 already in January, including a colonel. The prepared and attempted efforts to leave illegally totaled 2,312. In 25 cases, border troops used weapons. In 1988, 195 persons had left illegally, 29 persons were captured, 10 succeeded despite the use of guns.[125]

February

Budgetary pressures: The Army lamented Warsaw Pact reductions and defense expenditures being reduced 10 percent: "Our unilateral disarmament can lead to a reduced security, this is particularly felt by the professionals in the tank outfits."[126]

Monetary pressures: "Hostile forces criticize the DDR monetary policy; they think that the subvention policy is to be changed. . . . The Soviet Union, Hungary and Poland are pushing the DDR to have a convertible currency." An MfS admission: "By cleverness, the DDR has kept the rate to DM at 7 to 1; it should be much lower." The official exchange rate was 1 to 1.

BRD journalists' pressures: They perceived that "The DDR hasn't strength to go it alone since other socialist countries look out for themselves, therefore the spiraling costs and shortages."

Pressures to find candidates for the election: The Berlin district needed 260,000, of whom half should be SED; 400 councilmen and mayors were to change. Fewer women and FDJ were available: "There should be more Party friends. We should get the best youth, *but not by having a campaign*; 4,000 were added, 6,000 lost. The exchange is not a cleansing, but we will rid ourselves of those who have become softened."[127]

March

Glasnost reports from other socialist lands continued to disturb: "It was a shock to the DDR to discover that 43 million Soviet citizens live under the poverty line and how many persons are unemployed in Hungary. Things are so much better in the DDR, but people are aware that developments represent a turning away from socialism. The impression is widespread that there has been for years an unreal picture of conditions in the other socialist countries."

The most disturbing thoughts were pressing on the public and even the MfS: "The socialist economies have not proved themselves superior to the capitalist in the scientific-technological domain. The idea that they can catch up to the leading capitalist states is becoming ever more an illusion. In most socialist countries the economy stagnates or regresses. These questions increasingly are discussed in the universities. Students perceive that their teachers avoid a confrontation to their questions. Many teachers are considered unable to argue persuasively."

Nor could the politicians: "SED leaders are bothered that they can not answer the questions of the workers and disturbed that there is no official commentary on what is happening there. Teachers say that such reports make the teaching of socialism very difficult. Some see the Soviet way as the only way out of stagnation." On the other hand, "They believe that the Communist Party no longer is in control in Poland and Hungary. There is also the concern that the economic problems in the east will mean that the DDR will have to make sacrifices to help them."[128]

The MfS itself had problems getting good, indoctrinated youth. The Politbüro was informed that 1,130 MfS candidates had been rejected for insufficient work morale, their social activity or personality development; this was despite the fact that most of those were under 25 and had come out of the FDJ and SED. The Politbüro also heard concern about the decay of old residential areas, street disrepair, protection to the environment and water supply and sewage, particularly in Dresden and Leipzig. One-third of the complaints concerned housing, followed at some distance by traffic and telephones.[129] The DDR could not afford its own repair.

April

Mittag's assistant Janson explained the staggering economic problem: accumulation for national investment had declined from 19 percent in 1971 to 7.4 percent; investment in 1970 had been 22.6 percent productive and 11.8 nonproductive; in 1987 the percentages were 23.5 productive and 22.4 nonproductive; 18.5 percent of production capital was written off, and another 20 percent was more than 20 years old. The capital investment needed was 500 billion marks, which equaled the national income for two years.[130]

The MfS learned of Foreign Trade Minister Dr. Gerhard Beil's frightening dilemma: "We need to increase export . . . to the West, an increase of 8.4 percent, to maintain our ability to pay. Export is the only way to pay for previous imports. This is possible only with basic changes. In our trade with the West, we need cash quickly and must avoid long term credits. We have no alternative to this market. The united west Europe will try to catch socialist lands in its net." This seems like a crippled animal waiting to be swallowed by its enemy.

The worst of it was that DDR exports were admittedly inferior. "We must achieve the West's quality and comply to their norms, we are too small to have our own. In the 30 years of the COMECON, we were unable to achieve common standards." Beil admitted, "The West European standards are objectively progressive. We can not emphasize chemistry or metal, only electronics." Selling cheap would not work: "Export is no longer price based. . . . It is no longer how cheap the crane but how long it lasts and how good the service and how much energy it uses. The Japanese understood that."

Beil saw the dangers mounting. "We can be sure now that Poland and Hungary will buy from us, because they otherwise would need hard currency, but that will not last long. We need the money now, and that does not come from machine tools, which normally require 5 years to be paid."

Beil was also critical of Honecker's snub of Gorbachev: "Without the USSR as economic and political partner, there would not be a socialist DDR. It is not important whether we like what happens there. . . . 40 percent of our foreign trade must be with the SU [Soviet Union], first for gas and oil."

He saw no solution, looking either East or West: "We are too small to produce at three different standards. The West can buy everything we produce somewhere else and usually get it quicker. We do not know what we should sell this year to get the needed 1.5 billion marks. The SU can no longer make the needed commitments." The DDR could not stand alone: "We must react to changes in the socialist world because 80 percent of our raw materials come from there. We must stop thinking, we are the navel of socialism and adjust to their national sovereignty."[131]

Bowing to pressure from Gorbachev, on 3 April the order was issued not to shoot at anyone trying to cross the border.[132]

Mielke was worrying more about the SED's domestic isolation: "The LDPD accepts the leadership of the SED, but wants to be more constructive and critical, not an opposition Party, but to take on responsibilities, not to be just loyal to the SED but to propose policies." That would be altering the system: "They want price restructuring and fewer subsidies; to improve the media, to bring in more reality, to issue any reports of Plan fulfillment only if it speaks to the people."

Capitalist thinking was reemerging: "They want more orientation to the market." Yet more, "There is a growing doubt about the Marx-Lenin teachings. . . . Their young members are not Marxist." Mielke also criticized the media policy: "The reports about the Plan should not be of successes but also of problems which would help motivate the workers."[133]

The MfS observed that the public was much frustrated with the coming election: "The people basically see it intended only to strengthen the government and the Party, but many want better answers from the candidates. The key problem is maintaining and adding housing, plus retail problems, drinking water, streets, roads and ecology. They remember the non-keeping of past election promises and perceive the functionaries' unsatisfactory ability to inform and the insecurity they show. One hears repeatedly that the wrong persons are candidates and that serious failures are being tolerated.

... People have the impression that the representatives avoid any direct contact with the citizens."

There was emotional reaction to letting noncitizens vote, that the Volkskammer had decided it without any public discussion: "Problems and differences in the work-collectives between foreign workers and citizens repeatedly lead to doubt about the correctness of the decision. They refer to the behavior of foreign workers who engage in speculative buying, display little work discipline and little willingness to help, as well as to their provocative behavior. This is particularly the case with the Polish workers, who could spread the ideas of *Solidarnosc* [Solidarity]."

The MfS was conceding the public's criticisms: "Public morale is clearly worse. This is evidenced by the fact that many good candidates are not running, who say that they had had too little influence in communal decisions and that the state has paid too little attention to citizens' concerns. There is too much bureaucratism. There is not nearly enough material and financing for communal problems."

Unhappily, citizens were looking to the Soviet Union as a model: "Increasingly one hears that the DDR should try the Soviet election methods; voting secretly in the polling booth should be obligatory. In the DDR, voting makes no difference, the Party has already decided what will happen. There should be several candidates; the state should not insist on high percentage voting. One hears the rather uncritical repetition of points made on West media." The MfS was also repeating them.

Western journalists were abusing their increased freedom: "The problem is the Opposition's close cooperation with the western media, as demonstrated in the Liebknecht/Luxemburg demonstrations in January in Leipzig, involving several persons who had finished their studies but did not have a job, and who had contacts in Berlin." The correspondents' crimes included publishing the opposition's plans and operations to inspire wider participation. "They say they are prepared to take part in the provocation and through their presence and agitation to heat up the situation. They make a slanderous, deliberately warped presentation. They support escalation to provoke the state and to test and expand their area of freedom."[134]

May

On May Day, the MfS tore down pictures of Communism's leader, Gorbachev! Mass demonstrations were occurring in Poland and Prague, and in the DDR the MfS counted 150 "alternative" groups, of which 35 promoted peace, 39 dealt with ecology, 23 touched on both, 30 addressed Third World issues, 10 focused on human rights and a few discussed feminism and draft resistance. The opposition was not a conspiracy, rather, a diverse minority starting a broad social movement partly with socialist hopes, Green environmentalist ideals and pacifist and neutralist ideas.[135]

The MfS identified a leadership core of some 60 persons; about 600 dissidents could call upon 2,500 protesters. They were mostly ages 25–40; many had degrees from universities; 12 percent were without a "permanent work relationship"; their "intellectuals" held white-collar jobs in the major cities. The groups relied on personal contacts and mimeograph machines, and as many as 100,000 had been in some sort of "action." Some preferred "alternative" lifestyles.[136]

IMs reported that these "hostile-negative" forces, agitating about the election, would demonstrate, with four churches in Berlin and a "Green" group as centers. "Although churches say it is up to the individual, some churchmen have suggested that they vote secretly or tear up the ballot." Included was the Church of Sachsen. "IM information is that in Leipzig they will set up a ballot box for nonvoters to put in the voting cards. We have taken steps to stop it." Thirty similar incidents were reported.[137]

Despite such MfS operations, political realities were admittedly worse: "In contrast to previous elections the attacks of enemy forces, from inside and outside, on the election system have a much greater extent, content, goals, and variety of techniques. This is shown by the numbers of writings, explanations and appeals from unapproved printings, with detailed directions, plus sending information to the West, mostly from Berlin, and getting the protection of the church."[138]

The MfS was gaining more respect for its enemies: "Displaying the greatest energy, they are pushing for a change in the election system, to create an opening for uncontrolled social movements, to destabilize the power relationships in the DDR. They keep their eye on the developments in the USSR and other socialist states. IM information from Berlin, Schwerin and Chemnitz is that they will have their own candidates and watch the ballot boxes."[139]

MfS was mobilizing its traditional forces and tactics: "We have been able to prevent the enemies presenting candidates or gaining positions on election boards. Should they try to agitate in election meetings, progressive citizens will immediately confront them so they can't have an effect. Already in downtown Berlin, the attending citizens attacked a provocative married couple, until they left accompanied by the laughter of the participants." The MfS "forces" would not have the last laugh.

To keep control, foreknowledge was necessary. "We must know of their plans to disrupt. . . . A noteworthy circle of persons have refused the permit-to-vote card, or have announced that they will not vote." In Berlin and Leipzig, via Radio Glasnost, they had announced meetings on 7 May at 6:00 P.M. Incidents of agitation in the first quarter: 23 in Berlin, 3 solved; 7 in Chemnitz, 1 solved; 3 in Potsdam, none solved. "We must watch everyone, including decadent skinheads and punks."[140]

There were signs of election resistance at Humboldt University: of 7,013 registered, 65 did not vote, including 20 foreign and 10 theology students; 377 voted no; in 1986, of 11,449 registered there were only 25 nonvoters and 26 "no" voters. A considerable number of Applicants struck their names from the list. At the Kunsthochschule Berlin, of the 212 registered art student voters, 105 voted no, and only 102 yes. (In 1986 there had been only 1 nonvoter.)

About half of the nonvoters were 26 to 40 years old. There was an increase of nonvoters among Evangelical Church employees. Stolpe voted, but again Catholic bishops did not. Voting were the presidents of the Methodists, Adventists, the Mormons and the Jewish community. Jehovah's Witnesses, as before, did not vote but made no disturbance.

The major reasons for negative voting were consumer goods, ecology, travel, religion, housing; it was particularly concentrated in districts with old residential areas. "It varied with foreigners but probably the majority of them voted."[141]

Election fraud was quickly perceived and later admitted. Schabowski judged: "The local election falsification was not ordered from the top, and was not necessary to Honecker, who had confidence in the loyalty of the Party. Without his knowledge, the mayors were told that the SED wanted certain results. It was not done at the polls but in the mayors' offices, but the examiners of the opposition parties did their work well; they had counted votes at the polls and saw the great difference." Mielke knew about it and ordered stronger measures to suppress the truth.[142]

The MfS commented bitterly on the protests in Leipzig on 7 May: "Everything they do is coordinated with the correspondents, who arranged for a larger circle of western media. They tell enemies in West Berlin . . . in order to gather more enemies of socialism."[143]

Honecker had no better idea than to hold another massive FDJ demonstration. Instead of reacting to the opening of the Hungarian border, he was wasting money and attention on the staged celebration. The MfS reported that people opposed it, "because it costs a pile of money to stage the parade just to cheer at old men. The FDJ itself is seen as a farce which has little to do with the interests of the young."[144]

Mittag warned Honecker on 9 May about the impossible foreign debt problem: in six years the annual interest would be 44 billion marks or 13 percent of national income. He urged a drastic reduction of consumption and of subsidies, increased prices, some relationship of supply to demand. Honecker refused.[145]

Mittag tried again at a conference on 16 May: "When Honecker heard my economic report, he said, 'That is totally untrue. All these calculations are false.' He was saying that 'what dare not be, can not be,' a weakness of Honecker. He cared only about the numbers of new apartments." Mittag was further shocked at how little economics his Politbüro understood.[146]

So was Schürer, who said that the debt was completely out of control and that this meant a necessity of confederation with the BRD.[147] When the "Small Circle" of Party leaders met, he told them that the debt was increasing every month by 500 million marks. Krenz answered in the spirit of Honecker: "We must continue the unity of economic and social policy, because that is DDR socialism."[148]

Mielke passed on Mittag's worried analysis to the Politbüro: "The Minister predicts that the deficit in the plan will increase, in industry, from 258 million to 433 million marks, by the end of July. . . . The major reason was the failure to adjust to the changed demand in the international market and to adjust to the demands of innovation, of quality guarantees, service, etc."[149]

On 12 June Mielke sent Krenz a survey of what was reported to him, although somewhat toned down. Krenz or an assistant read and underlined the important points, for example, the statement, "Socialism has proved itself unable to solve its problems with its own power." Doubts were common about socialism's competing with capitalism. Krenz or the assistant put a question mark next to "Living standards were getting worse steadily." Most angering were the quality and variety of consumer goods, for example, the 18-year wait for a car.[150]

The Krenz file shows that he received sufficient reports as member of the Politbüro from a variety of sources, which should have informed them that something would have to be done soon to avoid bankruptcy and possible revolution.

Yet the MfS blamed the mass exodus on BRD propaganda, beginning 11 May, when it started "to push" DDR citizens toward Hungary by publicizing the border to Austria as open, "little more than a walk through the woods."[151] Mielke alerted his people about problems on the border in Berlin, trouble predicted for 12–15 May: "Don't use guns unless there is no other way."[152]

Mielke set the priorities of what the MfS must do by September: tighten the regulations of 30 June 1980 about meetings and those from 20 July 1959 about printing and mimeo machines, TV and video technique, stopping the export of whatever material could harm the image of DDR. "The information from London will criticize the DDR, CSSR, Rumania and Bulgaria with serious violations of the Vienna agreement, in contrast to the USSR, Hungary and Poland. This shows imperialists are dividing up the socialist countries."[153]

Mielke could not stop Hungarian divergence: "The progressives are increasingly worried, being reminded of 1956. Repeatedly the idea is expressed that these problems in Hungary have been furthered by the changes in the Soviet Union. The feeling is that socialist countries can no longer solve their economic problems, but need capitalist support."

Should DDR citizens be prevented from getting to Hungary? Since the Curtain fell away between Hungary and Austria, rumors among all classes were that travel to Hungary would soon be forbidden. "This means many inquiries at travel offices and banks, plus applications for trips several months in the future. For those not having relatives in the BRD, this would be a drastic reduction of travel, since a vacation in the other socialist countries has become ever more unattractive and the DDR has insufficient supply of vacation places." Rejecting Honecker's reaction: "The people are not satisfied with DDR explanations that each socialist country must find its own way."[154]

Russian experts had already concluded that without basic reform and change at the top, the DDR was doomed, as was the two-state concept of Germany. Gorbachev's policy for European cooperation was being made difficult by the Wall between the BRD and DDR. Shevardnadze and Professor Datschischev said later that Soviet policymakers could see already in 1986–1987 that Germany would be reunited.[155] The Soviet ambassador regretted: "The DDR was swallowing the golden [BRD] hook ever deeper." Soviet expert Falin predicted mass demonstrations, at the latest in the spring of 1990.[156]

Mielke's assistant Irmler emphasized problems in the implementation of the orders of 23 May about mobilizing their "social" forces: "Best results occur when exact orders are given based on IM information. We need influential people in the workplace, housing and leisure areas. Up to now it is primarily at work and we have not achieved the desired effectiveness. The process is still too slow moving."

There were difficulties with the Party: "We have to persuade the SED county leaders, that it is necessary to mobilize all strengths, and it is not entirely our job. This has meant a certain helplessness. Problems developed where the assignment of the forces was not directly under the MfS, where the path of the information was too long and a loss of information occurred. A general agitational assignment of social forces, with examples from all investigated districts, achieved no effect." Something was missing: "It must be judged that not all powers of the state and societal organizations were recognized and applied."[157]

Not all MfS powers could be applied: "A relatively large number of MfS employees (681) were discharged last year, as not suitable and with insufficient qualifications for meeting their duties. The basic reason was their lack of ideological clarity. Their behavior showed a softening of their attitudes, and partly a behavior of capitulation. They showed a deficient willingness for the higher demands of the service. There were moral weaknesses in character, which damaged the MfS with the public criminal acts and an abuse of alcohol."

Among the MfS an abuse of travel was reported: in 1988 a 45 percent increase had occurred in relatives of MfS traveling to the West: "They were no longer willing to break off those contacts; their not coming back has also sharply increased."[158]

In the three months of the new travel rules, 1,230,396 private trips were made to the West, an increase of 24.2 percent, of which 75 percent were retired persons; 159,000 were turned down; 1,416 filed complaints and won in 30 percent of the cases: "The MfS should not question a rejection by our battle comrades, the police. If there is not enough other proof to turn them down, just automatically refer them to Section 13, Paragraph 1, The Protection of National Security Law."

To 31 March, of 88,000 Emigrant Applicants, 90 percent had tried at least once before. The most porous points were Dresden, Chemnitz, Berlin and Leipzig; only 1.9 percent were turned down; only 0.4 percent were persuaded to withdraw. "This is completely unsatisfactory."[159]

In much the same places: "There have been provocations to discredit the election, a widespread agitation in Berlin, Leipzig, Dresden, Cottbus, Chemnitz and Potsdam." IM top secret information described a staff-organized and coordinated movement "that will place our Party under permanent pressure to change the system in the direction of pluralism."

Bishop Leich threatened that the Protestant leadership would have "to concern itself with this question. . . . IM information is that he and the other bishops found general agreement to push it. People openly speak of election fraud and the church assumed the task of getting a proper count." There were reports of effective counteraction: "When an IM told us of a protest in central Leipzig, to force a delay in seating the new council on 31 May, we stopped it with our 'social forces.' "[160]

As the MfS then judged the later controversial church official Stolpe: "Although he seems to be a moderating influence, IM knowledge is that he is encouraging the Opposition. This is helped by the fact that very few pastors or superintendents are willing to criticize this Opposition for 'reason of their reputation.' They fall back on the argument that the church is responsible only to God. They have many contacts with the BRD and many visits or meetings in other socialist lands."[161]

June

The MfS traced the dissident groups to the beginning of the 1980s and to the churches, which were being helped by Western diplomats and correspondents. Of about 160 connections with the non-Communist world, 150 were churchly. The MfS told top SED leaders that a silent march was planned for 7 June from a Berlin church to the Ministers Council to leave their statement about the election manipulation, which was based on witnesses and Western media. "We will talk with them and threaten them with arrest."[162]

The MfS created a 47-page history of these opposition groups, hostile but thorough. Although it had long fought them, it was admittedly not stopping them, including a peace group whose leadership centered on Bohley. "That the Evangelical Church since 1986 has been forcing this activity can be proven. It is primarily an information sheet, which the West media has labeled the underground newspaper of the DDR, in order to inflate the enemy, the opposition and negative forces. It is supported by some pastors who deliberately tolerate the abuse of the attached disclaimer, 'Only for internal church official usage.' About 25 have been produced that were worthy of attention, over half since 1988."

There had been as many as 2,000 copies, up to 100 pages, and they were getting bigger, all printed in church rooms. Some got machines from Western political parties, mostly through the mails. Some sheets had been given to economic and ecology groups. "This has no relationship to church work, discussing such things as uranium mining." The enemy editors included Wolfgang Rüddenklau, Poppe and Eppelman in Berlin and Lietz in Schwerin. "The production is not yet professional but they are trying. Privileged persons get machines across the border, they are planning to send an offset press across in pieces." The MfS reaction was mild: "The State Secretary for Church Questions should tell the bishops what we expect if the machines are misused. We won't be very generous, we might arrest."[163]

IM assured the MfS that excessive actions, such as demonstrations, were not the tactic of the Berlin-Brandenburg church leaders: "The effort for truth and veracity must be done with love. This is not a church action and does not have the support of the leadership."

The MfS preemptive activity was restrained: "We talked to 18 people and told them not to be involved. On 7 June, we talked all day to 160 potential participants, persons who belong to such groups and have been part of such activities. We carried through stronger controls of persons with the goal to keep them away from the gathering. We arrested 48 who were trying to go despite our advice." The fines were 50 to 300 marks, and they were kept until 10:00 P.M.

Stolpe had advised the opposition that their marches would not be helpful, but the popular unrest was pressuring church leaders. After it was clear that the demonstration was not possible, he organized a peace prayer, to which 300 came. A petition circulated against the election manipulation. They tried to leave the Sophien Church to march but were stopped, so they sat down and refused to leave; 140 were arrested and given a stern lecture and released the next afternoon. That evening a meeting was to be held in Gethsemanee Church, so the MfS suggested more strong talks to Stolpe and other church leaders.[164]

Mielke showed ambivalence between loyalty to the Soviets and loyalty to the workers. Although he seemed least affected at MfS headquarters by the criticisms pouring in from places like Schwerin, he gave a speech that was sympathetic to the growing worker discontent: "Some leaders have not listened to workers, ignored them or made empty promises. Lack of interest shown by unions has led to a disinterested behavior, because it seems useless to try to change working conditions: noise, dust, temperatures, problems of shifts, problems of social and medical services, wages, bonuses.

More and more workers are threatening to go to the central political and state authorities because they don't get any local answers."

He seemed to understand the people's miseries: "Retail stores close without reason and have a reduced offering. There is insufficient local transport and lack of housing for families. Citizens threaten demonstrations against state organs because they ignore reports of unused housing."[165]

His MfS urged toughness applying the new travel law but then stressed agents staying within the law: "The aim is to increase political stability, to *secure the power*, to increase the trust relationship and to increase the *socialist state based on law*. All decisions must be based on the law, which makes clear that in some cases it is urgently necessary to refuse." His MfS must rise to the challenge: "Using the legal grounds for refusal demands a high standard. Refusals should be the exception." Suggesting an MfS fear of resisters: "The individual is really in the position to create a dangerous situation."

The MfS should show restraint: "Refusal should involve just those cases of a crime against the state; for example, an IM, recently discharged for dishonesty, who had worked on important cases, if he would give himself to a media campaign against the DDR."[166]

Further evidence of a deeply troubled MfS was its worrying about the economic strategy, even the socialist system: "The concern is mostly with artisans and technicians about the increasing problems. There is more open criticism at meetings, an increasing skepticism that central leaders can bring a positive change. The Forty Year Celebration stimulates the question why in 40 years things are getting worse not better. There are increasing expressions that socialism has proved itself unable to solve problems with its own strength. Therefore it does not offer a feasible way to a solution for satisfying the needs of its citizens."

Dissatisfaction had an objective base: "Worst is the worn out equipment; the basic necessities for fulfilling the Plan are lacking, therefore it is done at the expense of workers and farmers." The problem was more than old machines: "There is weakness in the leading and organizing of production, a lack of cooperation also with socialist states."

The MfS criticized a lack of commitment at every level and saw the leadership weakened in many ways. "Frequently the cadre lack the necessary engagement to solve the tasks, and show their lack of flexibility and incompetence in dealing with the new challenges. Often the problems bring out spontaneous emotional expressions of skepticism, even doubt about the feasibility of the centrally assigned tasks. Among master artisans and technicians is a broadening and deepening criticism, which is leading to exhaustion and resignation. They say the central and state leaders, for reasons of age and health, are no longer flexible enough. The available funds are not enough for the planned development."

The centralized red tape was binding: "Bureaucratism and the demand for constant reporting have reached an extent that is no longer defensible. The reduction of funds for research and delay of resource facilities were shortsighted. This necessarily brought with it a further growth in the gap between the DDR and the world class. All agree that the DDR has fallen behind in the last years."

The MfS understood and shared the growing doubts about the assumed socialist future: "There is also a fear of the effect of the developments in other socialist lands. We must expect an increased unpredictability and unreliability. It is often noted that there is clearly no common economic strategy of the socialist states. The question is how long the DDR can survive this problem. Doubt has grown about the attractiveness of socialism as compared to capitalism. The availability of goods in the west means that visiting there leads to a bitter criticism. Goods that in the DDR were available years ago are today to be gotten only with 'good connections,' or in the luxury shops, and by bartering with goods in short supply. Industry does not respond to consumer wishes, but gives attention only to export."

An MfS speech listed dozens of those missing consumer items: "Worst is the 18 year wait for autos, which are ever farther behind in their features and are overpriced. This situation favors to a decisive extent the increase of corruption and blackmarketing. Used cars are sold for 180 to 200 percent of their new car price. Many citizens see the solution to the auto problem as the measurement of a successful DDR economic policy."

The MfS listed the many DDR inferiorities: "Then come the problems about the variety and freshness of foods, the niveau of the retailing culture in presentation and service, the matter of cleanliness, closing the only store in rural areas, the problems of eyeglasses and false teeth." There were complaints of inflation and lies: "The price explosion combined with the incompetence of economic management will be ironed out at the expense of the workers. . . . Wages don't keep up with prices. The people think that the statistics of increased production reflect only the higher prices charged. . . . Propaganda is ever farther from the reality."[167]

Also growing were the dangers to workers' health: "Increasingly the deficiencies and interruptions in the production process have to be compensated by extra physical effort of the workers, and sometimes violating the laws for protecting the health of the workers and the work place."

On the catastrophic obsolescence of farm equipment: "Workers on the land often say that the working class is not fulfilling its duty *vis-à-vis* the farmers. They argue that the time has finally come when the promises of modern machines and spare parts have to be kept. They cannot understand that the DDR exports modern machines which are so much needed at home. With a certain sarcasm the farmers say that one should first reconstruct the obsolete stalls and therewith improve working conditions before one talks about 'key' technologies."[168]

The MfS writer expressed his personal anger about socialist egalitarianism: "With the breakdown of organization has been the lack of the achievement principle, the lack of ability and inflexibility of the middle cadre. Achievement plays no role with us. This sounds surely bitter, what I am now writing, but it is my experience of many years. Whether one is clever or dumb, lazy or energetic plays no role. Socialism gives everyone nearly the same reward."

An envious MfS described other serious injustices: "There are numbers of people who live from their access to the West, blackmarketing, selling goods in short supply for high prices, toilet-leasers, peddlers, people who avoid paying taxes and drive prices up for autos and land for weekends, those who give services for very high tips in West currency. A society which tolerates such things will quickly be socially unjust. It can not go on forever that the energetic people will happily pull the others through who produce nothing or very little."

The MfS analyzed the false policy of providing needs for the nonproductive: "The subventions of basic foods equal 50 to 60 billion marks, which means 3,500 marks per capita. and almost double that for the workers." It worsened waste and inequity: "The appeal to be careful with subsidized goods had little effect. It is also observed that some social groups receive no or little benefit from subsidies for foods, rents and wages. The talk is of the injustice between city and country. The country gets little."

The MfS understood the general anger: "The Party and the state do not appreciate the change in general attitude and disgust. . . . The problem is also that good products wander off to the *Delikat* stores, and only fat, sausage and meat are available to ordinary customers. Strangely schnapps is amply available in all sorts and classes." The DDR drank 15.5 liters per capita in 1988; the BRD, 7.5 liters.

The lower quality of milk and quantity of fruit and vegetables were added to increasing prices. "Observed is the creeping inflation, which hurts those with lower incomes in buying technical products and clothing. There is also anger that tourists can take advantage of the subsidized prices." Subsidies also damaged the environment: "Very strong in the letters is the connection between environmental awareness and the price policy. The energy and water wastage is widely criticized, in particular the wasted warm water and heat in the [prefabricated] New Building areas."

Even subsidizing rents did harm: "All letter writers like low rents, but say that . . . underused housing does exist at the same time that there is a housing shortage. By using grades of rent each should decide how big the residence they want. Much is built, but we are coming to a painful disappearance of the historic identity of the cities." These MfS reports were not challenging the popular judgments that they were reporting.[169]

Nor did they challenge the popular attitudes toward Gorbachev and Honecker. In late June Honecker had to return from a Warsaw Pact meeting in Bucharest because of gallbladder problems. "Even progressives are bothered that to get details about the Gorbachev visit, they must watch West media. All agree that the DDR is reducing the importance of the visit." Opinion was very positive toward Gorbachev. "We consider the visit a success, in that he is less opposed to increased German cooperation, although he tried to avoid the subject. He saw the technology in the BRD, which the Soviet Union needs and which can not be gotten in socialist lands."

His openness to the West was also seen as a danger: "This could lead to a harmful reduction of Soviet materials to the DDR and the thinking is that the DDR must also open to the West to avoid becoming isolated. The DDR fears that because the Soviet Union is interested in economic support from the West, the willingness is there to make political concessions which are not in the interest of the DDR. In this connection, concern is particularly directed at the security wall on the border."[170]

That border since 1 April had suffered 2,587 cases of "Western attacks," mostly in Berlin; there were 52 cases of entry and damaging facilities and some throwing rocks or bottles at the Wall. The statistics of private trips showed an increase of 11.5 percent, to West Berlin of 20 percent; of the 2,885,544 visits, West Berlin received 1,708,306. If one left out the old and invalid, there were only 829,000. "All of this is top secret."[171] There were fewer difficulties for a retired person's gaining approval to travel, which meant that many counted the days to their retirement.

The effectiveness of border security was 93.2 percent; 61.5 percent of violators were part of a group; 27 persons reached the BRD as against 21 in 1988; 92.3 percent used some material help; 63 percent were from a border county; 29.6 percent were Applicants. Of the 323 arrested, only 10 percent were from a tip from the people; 70 percent were captured before they reached the dead zone. Border crossing succeeded, using darkness, bad weather and isolated places; 40 percent were from 12:00 A.M. to 4:00 A.M. 36 percent from 4:00 A.M. to 8:00 A.M. In Berlin, it was during stormy conditions.

The trick was to have specific knowledge of the terrain, to know how to avoid setting off the signals and to know about the second fence. One needed some help to climb over the fence. "Control failures came from mistakes of commanders and a shortage of devices to prevent crawling under fences."[172] The awareness was dawning that the greater problem was in Hungary, where the fence had been removed.

July

The first panic came from "the misuse of Hungary": in 1987, 314 DDR citizens tried to escape, and 83 succeeded; in 1988, 607 tried, 210 succeeded; to 7 July, 618 had tried, 212 succeeded; 148 more were caught on the way. "The increase is because the West media publicized the tearing down of the fence, despite the agreement of 1963 to stop them." Hungary had joined the Geneva Refugee Commission on 12 March, whose regulations for opening borders went into effect on 12 June. Hungarian officials made a point of publicizing it; its president made a present of a piece of the border to the American president and said that other walls should fall.[173]

On 1 July Hungary sent 34 DDR citizens home. "More should have been returned but they somehow got over the border. . . . We're trying to get Hungary to live up to the treaty and report everyone. We learned that for various reasons they will not be rounded up and sent home, only in exceptional cases if force is attempted. The Hungarian MfS says that border controls will be improved, but concede that there will be more border breakthroughs. We are being told that Hungary will not treat DDR people as refugees and they are interested in sending them home quickly and will create a special office for that purpose. More are expected to avoid repatriation this way. Internal information in the BRD says they think that the DDR has only one solution, ban travel to Hungary."[174]

The MfS blamed BRD propaganda; Radio Deutschland on 3 July broadcast that since Hungary had joined the international refugees' convention, a legal escape hole was opened. "DDR citizens should apply for asylum, they will be immediately accepted as BRD citizens and can leave Hungary."[175]

The MfS had it easier to hamper a Berlin demonstration planned for 7 July. "We successfully stopped it; 124 appeared and we kept 94 more from getting there. At 17:00 after a sitdown demonstration, we fined Schatta 1,000 marks and lectured them." In 11 places graffiti appeared, and there were 24 cases of rowdyism, 16 cases of resistance, 24 public demonstrations. In the Bekenntnis Church, of the 250 persons, half were Applicants; 36 autos came from outside Berlin.[176]

The MfS also compiled a long list of "aggressive" activities along the border, plus a new BRD radio station and a stronger RIAS-TV. "From the BRD come more excursions, trips of classes; from Bavaria, a 400 percent increase. There is pressure for more partner cities."[177]

On 13 July, the West media suggested that an entire family could come West. RIAS-TV spread on 25 July "the lie" that DDR citizens would not be stopped. "Rumors were spread that the border was closing again and that the BRD soon would no longer give full benefits to DDR settlers."[178]

August

On 28 July and 2 August, the Politbüro was given a sharp report on consumer problems and increasing discontent. These papers, written by experts, show some recognition of the problem, but they had to resort to the traditional subjective type of solution: "We must try harder to persuade people to be more productive."[179] The emphasis was still on what should be rather than what could be.

Still in denial on 8 August, the Politbüro minutes mentioned no serious problems in the economy, and things were fine in agriculture. Some concern was expressed about "the 1000 Little Things" that people could not find.[180] In contrast, MfS officer Müller said later that the MfS knew in July–August that the DDR could not be saved. Fellow officer Vogel said that the DDR's collapse had been discussed earlier because the MfS knew the problems. "If they had tried shooting, it could be civil war and the Russians would have intervened."[181] On 13 August, the anniversary of the Wall, BRD television quoted Hennig, BRD Ministry of Inner-German Relations: "The DDR is close to collapse. We must prepare for it."[182]

On 21 August, West TV showed dramatic scenes of flight from Hungary; two days later, 53 DDR autos were seen with an army car racing after them but not catching them. On 29 August, West radio suggested crossing during the day, as the controls were sharper at night. The MfS criticized bitterly: "It was a game with human fates, by agitators and dealers in people. The irresponsible exploitation of emotions and the manipulation of figures remind of the darkest days of the Cold War."

The MfS noted grimly how rapidly a tent camp was built up in Vilshofen in Bavaria, inferring the exodus had been deliberately created. The local efforts were described as part of the agitation against the DDR: *Greed for profits and called Humanitarian.*" It was capitalist cruelty: "DDR citizens will be doing the lowest work, with employers making money exploiting them. Journalists are also profiting."[183] On 29 August, Mittag called a Politbüro meeting to discuss the exodus problem but postponed it because of Honecker's absence.[184]

Mielke was less reticent to discuss the danger with his MfS. On 31 August he held a remarkably open staff conference, during which General Hähnel puzzled, "What is the government going to do to stop the flight through Hungary? People hear on West media the reasons why the persons left and note that they have the same problems. We do so little agitation as a counteroffensive and do not counter with our achievements, in housing, in economics. These don't get the proper respect. They are even taken for granted."

Mielke was also puzzled: "Why do they recognize all the advantages of socialism and all that it has to offer, but still they want to get away? We want to find out here what we can propose so that we can still improve." Technology was a trouble: "A third of the population, by their private initiative, have gotten on cable and see satellite TV. That leads to discussions with those who don't have it." He lamented, "Socialism is good, but the people demand always more and more, and we can't afford to buy bananas."[185]

A Colonel Anders described the large stream of travelers and of hostile meetings. "The peace-prayers do not need organizing or publicity, it has been done for months. The people go to them completely on their own. The churches close the doors afterwards and say they have no responsibility for what happens outside."

Someone of the staff observed, "The head doctor at the Women's Clinic Chemnitz has been promised since 1980 that his roof would be fixed. The nurses have to run about with buckets when it rains." Mielke responded naively, "If you knew this since 1980, you could have organized a few roofers. You can't tell me that that the roof has been leaking since 1980." As though he had not been reading the reports: "One can't conclude from one example that it is that bad everywhere."

General Gehlert dared answer: "In the health realm are many problems, but I must say, they begin with the bureaucratic and formal procedures, above all the management personnel. The work with the people is not what one would imagine in a humanitarian place. There is a hospital room for 12 cancer patients with only one wash counter. The MfS has reported it more than once."

Mielke resisted: "This makes little sense." Gehlert persevered that the MfS information about conditions had been simply ignored. "The First Secretary looked into it. We told them how they could make changes without more funds."

Then the unpleasant truth about the Applicants: "If permitted, Comrade Minister, there are enough instructions and decisions, among which that for every 50 Emigrant Applicants there be one political administrator from the Interior Ministry. But the fact is that the people there run away and scarcely anyone is prepared to work in the Interior Ministry or, better said, to fight there. The work must be one to one, face to face." That was not working: "We figured in Chemnitz, we had only 15 minutes to talk to these people and we think that there are certainly offices where the signs of the times in this connection have still not been recognized."

Mielke countered with the old subjective solution: "It can't be done that way. With all our social organization and directors, we can exert influence, constant influence. Without this influencing nothing can be achieved." Gehlert began by saying that he didn't want to contradict, but Mielke interrupted and conceded limply that there were too few people to work on this problem.[186]

Mielke then rambled on: "You must support Leipzig in these difficult days." He criticized the social democrats: "They want to change socialism. That is only a return to capitalism." More Chekism: "We must exhaust all our operative forces and means, and bring to bear all our experience, to know what the initiators and men in the background are planning. The most important source would be to use the legal possibilities concerning the founding and activity of groups and regulations about holding meetings."

Then the fearful thought: "What will be very unpleasant would be to investigate former employees of the MfS, particularly those who were fired. Many are now applying for travel to Hungary. Many are leaving the Party, but there are thousands of reasons. They don't have our level of understanding."

Then his much-quoted statement: "I tell you, without the Soviet Union, there is no socialism, and we can write ourselves off." Yet Gorbachev had unfortunately criticized Stalin's pact with Hitler, which Mielke defended. He seems then to wander from one vague point to another, rambling on as old ideas hit him. He said defensively about his old age: "The enemy says that we are dying out and are all sick. I am not sick. I am in good condition, I played in senior soccer with the Dynamos. Sadly I don't have the time now to play soccer, but I am in good condition."[187] For an 80-year-old man, perhaps.

Schell concluded that Mielke did not share with his MfS leaders his intent to overthrow Honecker, because he did not trust them.[188] The sick Honecker had made the amputee Mittag his representative to the badly crippled Politbüro, facing a crisis that would have baffled the healthiest leaders.

NOTES

1. Sch, 6c, 3.1.9, pp. 3–8.
2. Sch, AKG 06, Parchim, 16.1.9, p. 50.
3. Sch, 22a, 23.1.9, p. 18.
4. Sch, AKG, 08c, 12.1.9, p. 35.
5. Sch, 5a, KD Bützow, 6.1.9, p. 6.
6. Sch, 59, pp. 13–19.
7. Sch, AKG, 46b, 16.1.9, pp. 1–5, 7.
8. Sch, 49c, 9.1.9, p. 41.
9. Sch, 6c, 3.1.9, pp. 3–8.
10. Sch, 5a, Güstrow, 11.1.9, pp. 110–16.
11. Sch, 22a, 10.1.9, p. 6; Sch, DOSA, 401158, 7, 8, p. 19.
12. Kai Langer, *"Ihr soll wissen, dass der Norden nicht schläft": Zur Geschichte der "Wende" in den drei Nordbezirken der DDR* (Bremen: Temmen, 1999), p. 83.
13. Sch, DOSA, 401160, 32f, p. 37.
14. Sch, 1b, 22.2.9, pp. 10–17.
15. Sch, 6a, Parchim, 24.2.9, pp. 68–69.
16. Sch, 5a, 23.2.9, pp. 129–34.
17. Sch, AKG 09, 15.2.9, p. 19.
18. AKG, Leiter 2b, 15.2.9, pp. 10–25.
19. Sch, DOSA, 401160, p. 28.
20. Sch, 6a, Parchim, 24.2.9, pp. 68–69.
21. Sch, 1b, 2.3.9, p. 47.
22. Sch, KD AKG Sternberg, 4501, 2.3.9, p. 20.
23. Sch, 6c, 6.3.9, pp. 21–24.

24. Sch, 6a, 9.3.9, pp. 87ff.
25. Sch, 5a, 13.3.9, pp. 140–41, 161.
26. Sch, DOSA, 401048, 9.3.9, p. 27.
27. Sch, 49a, Bützow, pp. 44–46.
28. Sch, AKG Sternberg, 4501, 15.3.9, p. 19.
29. Sch, 6a, 9.3.9, p. 79.
30. Sch, 1b, 21.3.9, pp. 153–60.
31. Ibid., 19.3.9, p. 53.
32. Sch, AKG, 48a, 31.3.9, pp. 84–92.
33. Sch, 49a, Bützow, 30.3.9.
34. Sch, 5a, 31.3.9, pp. 163–70.
35. Sch, DOSA, 401222, VVS Swn o002, p. 4.
36. Sch, 49a, Bützow, p. 43.
37. Sch, 6a, 9.3.9, p. 79.
38. Ibid., pp. 87ff.
39. Sch, 22a, Güstrow 6.4.9, pp. 153–66.
40. Sch, 5a, 31.3.9, pp. 179–85.
41. Sch, AKG 48a, 31.3.9, pp. 80–83.
42. Sch, 2a, 20.4.9, pp. 138–41.
43. Sch, 49c, 3.4.9, p. 31.
44. Sch, 10121, KD Bützow, 10.4.9, p. 27.
45. Sch, 6a, 7.4.9, pp. 92–96.
46. Sch, 5a, Gadebusch, 2.4.9, pp. 84–85.
47. Sch, 49d, pp. 2, 6, 31.
48. Sch, 6a, 7.4.9, pp. 102–12.
49. Ibid., KD Lübz, 17.4.9, pp. 11–15.
50. Ibid., 7.4.9, pp. 92–96.
51. Ibid., pp. 98–102.
52. Sch, 30, 10.4.9, pp. 20, 43.
53. Sch, 5, 21.4.9, p. 72.
54. Sch, 10121, KD, Bützow, 2.4.9, pp. 24–25.
55. Sch, 5, 21.4.9, p. 47.
56. Ibid., 25.4.9, p. 46.
57. Sch, 2a, 5.4.9, pp. 84–92, 150, 155.
58. Sch, 22b, 3, 26.4.9.
59. Sch, AKG 06, 3.5.9, p. 102.
60. Sch, 5a, 2.5.9, p. 21.
61. Sch, DOSA, 401048, 4.5.9.
62. Sch, 2b, 1.5.9, p. 85.
63. Sch, DOSA 401060, 10.5.9.
64. Sch, 2b, 5.5.9, pp. 86–87.
65. MfS, ZAIG, 5352, pp. 85–86.
66. Sch, 2b, 23.5.9, pp. 120–28.
67. Sch, AKG, 15a, 7.5.9, pp. 77–78.
68. Sch, DOSA, 400974, pp. 40, 66, 74.
69. Sch, AKG, 46b, 22.5.9, pp. 36.
70. Sch, 5a, 20.5.9, pp. 202–3.
71. Sch, DOSA, 401127, 20.5.9.

72. Sch, 22b, pp. 71–79, 89.
73. Sch, 3a, 15.6.9, pp. 166–70.
74. Sch, 5a, Güstrow, 26.6.9, p. 230.
75. Sch, DOSA, 401192, 2.6.9, pp. 4, 7, 19, 34, 37.
76. Sch, 2b, 2.6.9, pp. 136, 146.
77. Sch, 3a, 15.6.9, pp. 141.
78. Sch, AKG, 46b, 21.6.9, p. 42.
79. Sch, 3b, 15.6.9, p. 165.
80. Sch, 5a, Güstrow, 16.6.9 & 19.6.9, pp. 213, 219–20.
81. Sch, AKG, 48, Leiter 2a, 15.8.9, pp. 7–18.
82. Ibid., 29.6.9, pp. 58–59.
83. Sch, 49b, 30.6, pp. 71–77.
84. Sch, 5a, 21.6.9, p. 91.
85. Sch, 3b, 5.7.9, pp. 89–90.
86. Sch, AKG 06, 3.7.9, pp. 127–30.
87. Sch, 6a, 12.7.9, pp. 13, 117–18, 137–38.
88. Sch, AKG, 46b, 20.7.9, pp. 59–60, 70.
89. Sch, KD AKG Sternberg, 4501, 15.7.9, p. 14a.
90. Sch, DOSA, 401205, 21.7.9, pp. 26, 43.
91. Ibid., 401206, 25.7.9.
92. Sch, AKG, 48, Leiter 2a, 29.7.9, pp. 16–17.
93. Sch, 3a, 25.7.9, p. 164.
94. Sch, DOSA, 401205, 21.7.9, pp. 26, 43.
95. Sch, 5a, 31.7.9, pp. 94, 99.
96. Sch, KD AKG Sternberg, 4501, 31.7.9, p. 13.
97. Sch 49c, 6.7.9, Hagenow, pp. 12, 19, 22–23.
98. Sch, 6a, 4.8.9, p. 25.
99. Ibid., p. 28.
100. Sch, AKG, 46b, 18.8.9, pp. 74, 77.
101. Ibid., 22.8.9, pp. 93, 98.
102. Sch, 6c, 25.8.9, 85, 91–92.
103. Sch, AKG, 48, Leiter 2a, 24.8.9, p. 74.
104. Ibid., Sternberg, 4501, 15.8.9, p. 12.
105. Sch, 5a, 30.8.9, p. 100.
106. Sch, AKG, 48, Leiter 2a, 29.9.9, pp. 24–35.
107. Sch, 5a, 28.8.9, pp. 270–75.
108. Ibid., 30.8.9, p. 100.
109. Sch, AKG, 48, Leiter 2a, 24.8.9, p. 74.
110. Sch, 6a, 8.8.9, pp. 147–50.
111. ZAIG, 5342, Jan. 89, 627, 4046.
112. David E. Murphy, Sergei A. Kondrashev and George Bailey, *Battleground Berlin* (New Haven, CT: Yale University Press, 1997), p. 397.
113. Peter Przybylski, *Tatort Politbüro*, Band II (Berlin: Rowohlt, 1992), pp. 87–88.
114. Günter Schabowski, *Der Absturz* (Berlin: Rowohlt, 1992), p. 214.
115. MfS, 2240, pp. 40–41.
116. Günter Mittag, *Um Jeden Preis* (Berlin: Aufbau, 1991), pp. 263–74, 285, 297.

117. Przybylski, *Tatort Politbüro*, pp. 81, 84.

118. Mittag, *Um Jeden Preis*, pp. 194, 256, 260, 262.

119. Przybylski, *Tatort Politbüro*, p. 326.

120. Peter Christ and Ralf Neubauer, *Kolonie im eigenen Land* (Berlin: Rowohlt, 1991), p. 43.

121. Schabowski, *Der Absturz*, pp. 158, 227, 240.

122. MfS, 15891/SED, Kreisleitung 510, 721901.

123. ZAIG, 5352, 27.1.9, p. 17.

124. Ibid., pp. 13–15, 25–26.

125. ZAIG, 8676, 21.2.9, p. 718.

126. ZAIG, 1072, 2.2.9, pp. 106, 119–20.

127. ZAIG, 14414, 10.2.9, 18.2.9, p. 14.

128. ZAIG, 5352, 2.3.9, p. 3844.

129. SAMPO, Politbüro, Anlage 4, 7.3.9, 14.3.9.

130. Carl Heinz Janson, *Totengräber der DDR* (Düsseldorf: Econ, 1991), pp. 70–71.

131. ZAIG, 14427, 10.5.9, p. 553.

132. Walter Süss, *Staatssicherheit am Ende* (Berlin: Links, 1999), p. 150.

133. ZAIG, 3750, 14.4.9, p. 14.

134. ZAIG, 5352, 26.4.9, pp. 57–68.

135. Armin Mitter and Stefan Wolle, *Untergang auf Raten* (München: Bertels-mann, 1993), p. 540.

136. Konrad Jarausch, *The Rush to German Unity* (Oxford: Oxford University Press, 1994), p. 38; Sigrid Meuschel, *Revolution in der DDR*, p. 107.

137. ZAIG, 3763, 2.5.9, pp. 7, 30.

138. Reinhard Meinel, *Mit Tschekistischem Gruss: Berichte der Bezirksverwaltung für Staatssicherheit Potsdam 1989* (Potsdam: Babelturm, 1990), p. 50.

139. ZAIG, 3763, 367/89, p. 41.

140. ZAIG, 8677, 7279, p. 88.

141. ZAIG, 5352, 7691.

142. Schabowski, *Der Absturz*, p. 174; Przybylski, *Tatort Politbüro*, 104–5.

143. ZAIG, 5365, pp. 2–3.

144. Anne Maennel, *Auf sie war Verlass: Frauen und Stasi* (Berlin: Elefanten, 1995), p. 192–93.

145. Przybylski, *Tatort Politbüro*, p. 211.

146. Mittag, *Um Jeden Preis*, pp. 320–24.

147. Jeffrey Kopstein, *The Politics of Economic Decline in East Germany, 1945–1989* (Chapel Hill: University of North Carolina Press, 1997), p. 103.

148. Hans-Hermann Hertle, *Der Fall der Mauer* (Opladen: Westdeutscher, 1996), p. 343.

149. ZAIG, 14428, 7276.

150. SAPMO, DY/30 IV 2/2.039, 268, 7383.

151. ZAIG, 14393, p. 7.

152. ZAIG, 4882, speech, 5.5.9.

153. ZAIG, 8677, Apr 18 to May 12, pp. 51–55.

154. ZAIG, 5352, 17.5.9, pp. 72–75.

155. Mittag, *Um Jeden Preis*, p. 30.

156. Alexander Fischer and Günther Heydemann, Hg., *Die Politische "Wende" 1989/90 in Sachsen* (Köln: Böhlau, 1995), p. 38.

157. ZAIG, 13642, p. 37.

158. ZAIG, 8677, 10721.

159. ZAIG, 8677, 130138.

160. ZAIG, 5352, 7691.

161. Meinel, *Mit Tschekistischem Gruss*, pp. 57, 63.

162. ZAIG, 3763, 1.6.9, p. 25.

163. ZAIG, 3576, 24, 17, 4960.

164. ZAIG, 3763, 5.6.9, pp. 29, 33–34.

165. ZAIG, 4321, p. 215.

166. ZAIG, 13948, p. 28.

167. ZAIG, 14283, 4.6.9, p. 212.

168. ZAIG, 5352, 6 June, pp. 96ff.

169. Ibid., 95, 11120.

170. Ibid., 26.6.9, 13539.

171. ZAIG, 5351, p. 52.

172. Sch, 26a, 20.7.9, 1119, p. 55.

173. ZAIG, 5352, 12426.

174. Ibid., 12729.

175. ZAIG, 14393, p. 8.

176. MfS, 2240, 45 Anlage, 48.

177. Sch, 26a, 20.7.9, p. 49.

178. ZAIG, 14393, p. 811.

179. SAPMO, DY/30 IV 2/2.039, 268, Versorgung, 28.7.9, p. 91.

180. SAPMO, Politbüro, J IV, 2/2, p. 2340.

181. Dietmar Linke, *Theologie-studenten der Humboldt-Universität* (Neu-kirchen-Vluyn: Neukirchner Verlag, 1994), p. 103.

182. ZAIG, 14393, p. 7.

183. Ibid., pp. 13–24.

184. Gerd Rüdiger Stephan, *"Vorwärts immer, rückwärts nimmer": Interne Dokumente zum Zerfall von SED und DDR 1988/89* (Berlin: Dietz, 1994), p. 8.

185. ZAIG, 8679, 1117.

186. Ibid., 3140.

187. Ibid., 6678.

188. Manfred Schell and Werner Kalinka, *Stasi und kein Ende* (Frankfurt: Ull-stein, 1991), pp. 70–73.

Chapter 6

The Ground Shaking:
Fall 1989

SCHWERIN

On 1 September, the district MfS began to admit that it faced a possible
blowup and empathized with the unhappy masses, which were leaving the
DDR, some physically and most psychologically. "Most people are listening
to West media. That's where one is really being informed. There is much
doubting of DDR policy, therefore the flight to another world. Demands
are for more freedom to live and travel where one wishes. The endangered
persons [to socialism] are those who think like the petty bourgeoisie, those
who feel occupationally held back, and those with many west contacts.
They say, 'The situation has become more acute, everything is getting
worse. We work more and more and are not moving forward.' "

The MfS was taking the rebellious public's side. "People should have the
right to leave and there is a certain fear that no more will be allowed.
Because of the increasing dissatisfaction of all parts of the population, an
uncontrollable reaction is now possible. . . . A powder keg exists for an
explosion."

The Soviets were adding to the danger. "The events in the Soviet Union
are disturbing; statistics and statements won't help." In Parchim, Soviet
officers described the increasing unrest with Gorbachev, which includes a
banditry comparable to the Mafia: "If Gorbachev doesn't change, he will
have to go."

The police were frustrated. "Many want to stand firm in Hungary, but
suggest letting anyone go west if they have the money. Arguments with
them won't help." Perceptive and disillusioned teachers were saying, "For
decades, the USSR was held up as the model. They must have thought we

were stupid. A lifetime we learned something and taught something and today much of that is no longer true. Many teachers say they can not answer students because the Party leaders have not taken a position."

The medical intelligentsia and engineer cadre "greet the liberalization in Hungary and Poland, but don't understand the continued economic crisis and the strikes." Workers were even more critical of DDR leadership: "Events in Hungary show the discontent in the DDR of the masses and the self-satisfaction of the Party leadership, which has led to an inevitable conflict. The DDR has encapsulated itself and dynamic personalities have been pushed away, so the question is whether their concern is about their privileges. . . . The true domestic problems are also pushed away, including the bureaucracy, and a society with two currencies."

The MfS secretly joined the protest against Honecker: "Their leaders ignore the people's wishes and their needs. The SED with Honecker does not have the necessary spirit, niveau or flexibility."[1]

Even in a rural county, people envied the Hungarians in having better leaders: "Not only the BRD but Hungary has consumer goods and travel-freedom. In connection therewith, the idea is frequently expressed that our functionaries are too old and are not at all informed about the real conditions in the DDR. They have many privileges and are very far removed from the normal citizen."

The MfS was scrambling to find out who might go to Hungary or who might be talked into returning home. It conceded, "One can't blame the exodus only on the West media and contacts, there must be much internal discontent." The older generation's reflection about the mass exodus was that the DDR youth had not been trained to be responsible, and they got better jobs so easily in the West. "They have it good, they were offered everything. . . . The youth have not been trained to work, to have the will to achieve, and to have a sense of responsibility."[2]

The field of propaganda had been surrendered almost without a fight. At the teachers college: "They feel that they had been abandoned by the Party newspapers." Again the problem was at the top: "DDR leaders lack the will or the ability to debate western leaders."[3]

Local defenders were also helpless: "Many teachers can not answer questions about developments in other socialist countries. The criticism is about the lack of perspective in socialism now. The path toward socialism has not been able to satisfy the ever-increasing needs of people."

The unanswered bitter question: "Why are exported goods too good for DDR citizens? It has also been noticed that relatively low functionaries, like county department heads are able to get such goods." The inequity of travel: "Young people know that many of their peers want to leave the DDR. Among older people is the sense that if you don't have western contact, you are in fact punished. Some young people have travel possibilities to the West that older people don't have and these young have not worked for the DDR. These views are spread over all groups." And ages.

As so many young left, the old had extra fears. "There is worry about their pensions. Many, above all older people, the party-less, even SED members, see themselves as losing illusions, see their ideals for which they have lived disappearing. As they express it, they don't know what to do, when no clear answers are forthcoming from the Party and government. Even among the old fighters is the opinion that this wave of emigration, if it continues, could determine the existence of the DDR."

The rural analysis was much the same: "The reason for flight is the economic development in the last 10 years. Maybe the government will wake up." So should the media: "We never get the truth on our TV. They are still blaming the BRD."[4]

Farmers also sensed that the lack of freedom was the reason for flight: "Even in the Jürgenshagen LPG, this is discussed because some of their members have left through Hungary. Especially when young people leave everything behind, there must be serious reasons. It isn't because they have it bad here or that they have no money. It is much more the repression of the individual initiative and opinion, of a person's own thinking."[5] This sad repression is admitted by the repressors.

Yet an MfS report was still blaming Hungary: "It is a scandal that Hungary protects those leaving. BRD people in camping places are working to persuade DDR citizens, using newspapers and loudspeakers."[6]

On the other hand, the MfS conceded that the system had to change: "Western TV is defeating Eastern TV, with DDR citizens showing little interest in newspapers. No one has a solution. There is little understanding in particular for the tight bureaucratic corset of our country. More people are saying, the present plight shows again how weak the DDR is. How often have workers, employees and intellectuals been assigned to solve problems and to suggest changes, but they had not solved them and have not been listened to. Now the Party and state leaders have gotten the bill."

The worst of it was that the Western media were telling the truth: "People listened to the worker Kubelt on BRD-TV about why he left and they find his reasons acceptable. . . . The West has so much more, so they can give presents of such things as automobiles. . . . Our leading functionaries live above the clouds and nobody can reach them." Young and old looked for answers: "The high schoolers, who listen only to BRD media, raise serious questions. They don't criticize those who flee but sympathize with them. *People are even talking about the collapse of the DDR.* Old SED members are at a loss and can not explain the silence of the leaders."[7]

The MfS had reported many criticisms for years but had not so obviously taken the side of the critics, particularly of the obsolescence of leaders and their policies: "Basic changes are needed in the entire economy; materials must be there for production; rewards must be based on production. Working conditions must be better; even a 2–3 percent decrease in exports would improve life." They were bitter about the new kind of class conflict: "Two classes exist, those with relatives [in the BRD] and who can travel there versus the others and this must change."

The MfS shared the bitterness about the lie-filled society: "The question of dishonesty, in personal as in the political and social realm, has become an ever greater encumbrance." The MfS was regretting the control that it was enforcing: "DDR citizens already as children are trained to talk with two tongues, one for their private belief and the other for the views they can express in public. The absence of sincerity in the media or in speeches means that they lose credibility. The citizen feels himself to be a plaything of the authorities and the bureaucracy, so that he can never prove that he is an adult and politically mature."

DDR statistics were known to be false: "The constant stories of [DDR] success make the citizen tired and he no longer listens. Prices rise but wages do not; news stories of increased sales mean only increased prices. The statistics of savings means that a few have enormously more money, but most have much less than the average."

Socialism must have honesty to function: "Society should follow the theory about everyone working together, but then everyone should be correctly informed. There is a general agreement that leaders think the luxury they enjoy is the DDR norm." Then came the shock from Hungary: "The mass flight has led to people asking why."[8]

The flight negated the election, seeing so many voting "no" with their feet. "If 99 percent voted SED, and so many have run away, what was the value of our election results? The interviews of those who left have an impact on our young people, who can distinguish very well between the blather and babble about freedom and the answers given by former DDR citizens, who in their personal, private development felt themselves so much fenced in, because our young people are daily confronted with this very same problem."

The promise of technology as the solution had fallen flat: "Their reaction to the DDR claims of computer progress, 'What will that do for me personally, nothing.' " The leaders were too well insulated from the people: "They have the sense that their suggestions are perhaps treated in a friendly way, but they are running against walls of wadding which slow everything down. We can't say it better than a nurse at a meeting: 'I belong here, here is my work, which I enjoy. To run away is not the solution, but the way things are running now can not continue. It has to change fast." [9] The MfS added that it could not say it better!

Another example of technological failure: "The cellulose plant in Wittenberge is badly worn out; their buildings can not be made sanitary and present many dangers. They are constantly exceeding the limits set by pollution controls and pay large fines. . . . They are so close to the border, that it could have political significance."

The MfS had 21 IMs at the factory, including specialists. (Of the laborers there were 113 Cubans, 52 Mozambicans, 75 Poles and 4 Applicants.)[10] At the plant 297 disturbances in production had occurred in the first six months, a loss of production of 6.4 million marks. It occurred from personnel's not knowing how to deal with changing materials, from totally worn-out machinery and the constant lack of qualified personnel and leadership. All was made worse by the lack of air-cleaning machinery for the toxic chemicals; 31 employees had reason to believe that they had a pollution illness in the first half of 1989. "The plant should not use more foreigners as they seem less able to resist the toxic problems; in Wölfen all had to be withdrawn which reduced production by half." The common factory reality: "From many firms the evidence is of bad conditions, a general dereliction of duty and violations of discipline."

Already there were 93 cases with 122 border violators. "It is increasingly of persons not previously noted by police and most act not as a group but as individuals."[11] From the district, 843 had left illegally, 315 via socialist countries.[12] A noteworthy MfS distinction: "The security of the state has been achieved at all times, but it is not the same with the security of the public."[13]

October

An early report, neatly organized in the required pattern, gave less sign of urgency, rather the sense that "We can handle it as before." It described work with various factory directors to restore "the legal conditions."

Yet it also reported more interruptions to production, even treason. In the protection of secrets, the priority objective was to get rid of police who had "conspiratorial" non-socialist world (NSW) contacts. "On the basis of our relevant political-operative information, and the most recent commands of the Comrade Minister for all units in the district, the offensive *fighting of the underground activity has concentrated on the political operative Task Number 1*. The tempo and turbulence have continued to grow. There have been some arrests and assignment of some IMs."

The churches increased their activity, and the MfS continued countering it. "There has been the formation of an inner opposition in the Lutheran Synod. The attempt of the Workgroup Peace . . . to form a partnership with hostile forces from the West has been prevented. We have used a 'differencing process' among the Jehovah's Witnesses and a paralyzing of the influence of selected functionaries of this forbidden sect. We have reduced the contact with former DDR doctors in Bremen and prevented the continued recruiting of doctors and intermediate medical personnel."

The report also listed 15 MfS operations against the ecological Bundes

Arche, BRD information gatherers and state-hostile publications. "We have plans to prevent terror sabotage in 24 selected places."[14]

The MfS recognized the "New Forum," just founded in Berlin, as the new great danger, and it could understand why the public was openly discussing its pamphlets: "The public has the need to experience open and honest points of view and is prepared to support positive changes. . . . Widespread is insecurity and anxiety. . . . The view at the cable factory is that the New Forum is necessary because of insufficient information. Although lacking activists, it has many sympathizers. . . . At the teachers college, the faculty speak against the Forum, but the students are excited."[15] The MfS reports were again supportive of public attitudes.

They intercepted a cautious New Forum message from Berlin: "Dear Friends. . . . Reunification is not up for discussion. . . . Many want to know what is going to happen next. We admit that we did not expect this stream of people who want to join us. We have no organization structure or full time workers or officers. Our goals include a legal political platform for dialogue. We exclude no one."[16]

The MfS reacted candidly the next day: "A thousand persons attended a New Forum meeting in Schwerin. It was clear that many others sympathize, although they didn't go."

The MfS was fearful about the Battlegroups in Crivits: "We must assume that some would not go against the demonstrators."[17] Demonstrators were also fearful: "Those who take part make clear that they do not want to be seen as enemies and clearly fear the consequences. There were obvious signs of dissatisfaction with the meeting. The two leaders lacked the personality to lead."[18]

The unrelenting force was not personality but discontent: "The dominating tendencies are underground activities, pressure on the border, illegal exit, increase in Emigrant Applicants, all directly tied to the BRD campaign and above all, its unrestrained media campaign."

The MfS countered in its practiced fashion: "We have identified some who signed the New Forum list and we are working on the rest. Those who started it knew it was illegal. An art historian in Gadebusch started the New Forum there and by the 27th had 18 persons. . . . The New Forum had 300 in Paul's Church on 2 October. Even if we cannot prove it, the imperialist secret service is directing it, as a test of strength."[19] The MfS commander presented a long list of what he had done, mostly bureaucratic tinkering, but not a single practical action to confront events.[20]

The district's New Forum organized on 4 October: "We could identify many, some from other counties. . . . Two Parchim pastors won't talk to the authorities, one because his sons who had gone to the BRD could not return for their mother's birthday."[21]

The next report continued this remarkable combination of honest insight and DDR talk about agents: "Although we tried to stop them, the New

Forum spread their pamphlet to the transit and construction outfits. . . . At Paul's Church, the participants were mostly under 35. The church holds 800, and it was so full that the authorities [MfS agents] could not be politically effective. They could conduct a counter-offensive only with their immediate neighbors." Chekist crowd control failed because of the numbers.

The enemy was working better together, a unity in diversity: "The rivalry between Bohley and Eppelmann made it necessary to reduce this by uniting in their goals and they have been able to work together without tensions. . . . At the moment no one is wearing the leader's hat, everyone wears his own hat. Everyone finds his own group."[22]

Of the 1,400 participants on 6 October in Paul's Church: "Their ages were 18–40, mostly high school and university students, church officials, even some middle-level cadre, very few workers, no asocial types, except for a few drunken minors; 90 cars which were parked close were identified." Again a put-down: "It was led by a 25-year-old man."[23]

The MfS made an amazingly honest criticism of the state that it was supposed to defend: "This state system, this structure, has tried for 40 years to create roots and is now in the process of internal dissolution. It is strong only toward the outside world, but in its inner substance, it is completely torn apart. *It has no future.* It is only being continued by those who want to maintain their privileges." The MfS regarded the thinking of "The Citizen Initiative" as superficial, "only on the surface and does not go into the substance."

The MfS knew that injustices had made the unprivileged public dangerously angry. "Consumption-thinking is very widely spread." In addition, "The uprising in the DDR shows that all of those who want 'to get out and to break out' come from those circles who do not have privileges. Only 2 percent of the citizens have privileges." The MfS also recognized the crushing of the spirit: "In the DDR, people are turned into cripples, in particular spiritually, in their souls."[24]

The Paul's Church group was mostly intelligentsia and clearly identified with the New Forum. "The organizers did not have concrete results but they regard it as a success. The coordination of Opposition groups is a problem. The leaders of the groups can not stand each other, but despite their rivalries, they have still the common goal."[25]

Applicants, already 1,490 of them, had "the potential for enemy activity."[26] The State Theater group's stated goal: " 'I want to stay, and keep socialism,' then they spoke for moderate changes and more artistic freedom."[27] But the base of discontent was recognized to be much broader: "Most people do not accept the proof offered by the media, because they see the shortages and bad conditions."

Lies had made them bitter. "Young people who are forced to stay at home are not counted as looking for housing. No housing can be taken out of the statistic, because any decrease is not permitted." The DDR had been given enough time: "The people keep repeating that these shortages should have been prevented in the 40 years of the DDR. . . . The gains in peace, in education, job security mean little, because they are accepted as the natural conditions."

Critical was that work had not created the consumer goods: "The citizen has no motivation to produce, because he can not buy what he wants with his money. In 5 to 6 years we could be in the same condition as the Poles." Thereto the indefensible Party privileges: "People ask why leaders buy autos from the West and why they can buy in their special stores where there are no shortages."

The great irony was that real planning was missing: "The DDR does not have a Planned Economy, otherwise there would not be the shortages everywhere. Much happens without plan or contrary to the Plan or those responsible do not have the necessary ability. Young people say, 'We don't know the exact content or the goals of the New Forum but we want to change things and reform, therefore we are for them.' "[28] Even the loyalists were puzzled: "The progressive forces say, 'We don't know enough about the New Forum to argue against it. What is it that makes them enemies of the state?' "

The MfS expressed confidence still on 7 October: "We clearly control the situation, although one border soldier fled."[29] Some flags had been torn down, but 25 graffiti smearings in the district were quickly removed. A few persons were arrested, mostly church employees. Still optimism reigned: "The torchlight parade went well, and removed fears of collapse."

Then a hesitant MfS reaction to the Honecker speech: "It was all right that he and Gorbachev did not discuss the events publicly, but it is assumed they did so privately and will react to them. The public is waiting for answers to the events."[30] The Schwerin MfS saw solutions in Mischa Wolf and Modrow, who said that reforms were necessary. "All classes want more openness and freedom, but there is some fear of riots and a fear of becoming like Poland."[31]

The MfS also stressed the unsolved core economic problems: "Our economy is not working, so we are producing at too high a cost. We must sell on the world market, and sell lower than the value and we are therefore giving away our wealth. All these years we tried to do everything with ideologies and forgot the economy."[32]

The MfS hope was that the opposition lacked leaders: "We can't name a person whom we could expect soon to attempt effective public anti-socialist activities or to lead an action." The MfS fear was the lack of socialist leadership: "Our concern is the public attitude, which is extremely critical. The people are puzzled why the young are leaving. They must be dissatisfied, which means a lack of ideological work. Our media have surrendered to the West's media. People doubt that our leaders could debate with western leaders."[33]

Again a display of MfS confidence: "The situation is stable and is securely controlled. Nothing happening on the borders. We got the flag rippers." Yet on 8 October, in Wittenberge and Perleberg, public sympathy was shown for the New Forum by candles in the windows. Four leaders on 9 October refused to call off meetings; 13 students of theology in Rostock stopped work because of the arrest of 3 fellow students in Potsdam; they sent telegrams all over. When ordered back to the university, they quit the FDJ. A mechanic in Parchim refused to repair the cupboard where police helmets were kept and was charged with breach of contract.

The MfS criticized Party unwillingness to change: "In discussions, the SED response is yes to reforms but only to strengthen socialism and the Plan. The authorities must talk and with the New Forum." The SED briefly made the effort: "Forty persons came from the Party and state apparatus to oppose the New Forum and succeeded in stopping them in Gadebusch. The participants came from the church, fine arts, medicine, schools, cadre and youth. We are working on identifying those present. Beste is the leader and opposes socialism."

The Schwerin MfS reacted negatively to the beatings of demonstrators on 7 and 8 October: "The pictures of police actions in Leipzig and Berlin are disturbing. Does one have to move in with such harshness? DDR television gave 1 minute to these events, the BRD gave 20 minutes."[34]

Police violence had led to more Secret Police worry: "There is the concern that in our 40th year, our success can be destroyed by acts of violence, but we must soon solve the economic and travel problems." They were impressed that six artists in Parchim reacted with an impressive appeal to many offices throughout the DDR.

Although the MfS reported on 10 October a gathering in the Pinnow pastorate and graffiti in Sternberg and Güstrow, it soothed: "The activists are down to 80 persons. The excesses are nearly universally condemned. The people wonder whether it can be controlled. They can see in Poland and the Soviet Union the serious damage."

The "Friendly" parties were slipping away. "The situation in the NDPD is extremely tense, leading to resignations, because it has no independent position, does not criticize the SED and makes no suggestions for change. Their paper just takes the official agency stories, and publishes them a day later." The followers were not following: "CDU functionaries have big problems in arguing with their members. Many are distancing themselves from the SED, the fearful persons. This is also noticeable in the Battlegroups."

Shortages and lies had turned off the workers: "The BRD media campaign has been rejected, but the fact remains that the 'increased' production does not appear in the stores. No one in the DDR admits making mistakes.

Anyone who openly criticizes runs the danger of being described as a mal-
content. . . . Therefore many workers show no interest except for their own
personal affairs."[35]

The MfS again showed anger at the media: "The papers are still talking
about plans which are clearly impossible, particularly with the loss of
young workers." The report reflected further on the limits of indoctrination: "The generation which is fleeing was completely raised by the State.
Now the youth have come to understand that that they will no longer be
given everything and they must be productive."

Another sad truth: "We cannot have a 'Dictatorship of the Proletariat'
against a majority of the workers." The most bitter doubt: "We could have
socialist distribution principles if socialism could achieve a similar high
productivity of labor that capitalism achieves." It undeniably was not.[36]

The MfS praised its own production. Members of the theater in Parchim
wrote the Ministry of Culture, but by tracing the typewriter, the MfS was
able to prevent their posting their statement.[37] It identified other unhappy
groups: church, health, energy and social workers, artists, three soft-drink
firms, the city building combine, five private businesses and handworkers.
"There is increasing discontent, an insecurity, even fear for the future."

Workplace unrest demanded change, and quickly. "The momentary situation has a negative effect on the work morale and work discipline in the
various firms. Some citizens have clearly no more desire to work and only
want to discuss. The situation is getting ever more tense and the people
must absolutely be given some release valve. The masses need some acces-
sible goals." Time was fleeting fast: "The longer one waits, the more trust
will be lost. The Farmers' Party is particularly critical." Then the prophetic
question, "What will the authorities do when suddenly 10,000 or 20,000
people march against the Wall?"

People were looking for new answers to the old problems: "Pupils bring
the New Forum materials to school and ask their teachers. . . . More people
are leaving the SED and say they don't understand its policies. They get no
information, no concrete answers to the outstanding questions."[38] The "politically unfirm" were quitting the Party, and there was a negative strong
"differencing" going on, even in the Battlegroups.[39] To the MfS' chagrin:
"The churches are very active, many come to them with questions because
nothing is happening with the Party."[40]

Dr. Heinrich Rathke, former bishop, led the particular activity in Crivitz:
"He bases his activity on his relatively high popularity, as on earlier occasions (his Swords to Plowshares). Ambition-driven, he shows an excessive
need to dominate, and sometimes he behaves in the presence of the state
authorities demonstratively provocative." He said that forbidding the New
Forum was unconstitutional, adding, "The SED leaders are too old. . . .
Don't we have any politicians who trust the people?"[41] (The MfS was secretly saying the same.) Rathke had many contacts and "intensive com-

munication with all important exponents of anti-socialism," like Christoff Stier, Hannsjürgen Rietzke, Martin Klähn, Georg and Evelyn Heydenreich, Uta Loheit, Messerschmidt and Wolfram Grafe.[42]

On 12 October, from Sternberg: "About 35 percent of the Battlegroups have been to the West; 2 groups are all right, 2 are weak; 75 percent would act against violent demonstrators, but most would not use violence against those who are peaceful."[43]

Confidence in controls was still shown on 13 October. "Security is complete." Various small meetings were being held. "The Central Committee statement on the 11th was fine, but it would be better if a leader would appear on TV's *Aktuelle Kamera*. The hope is that the Central Committee meeting will bring *Glasnost*. The people are pleased that their leaders are not blaming it all on BRD agitation." At the Güstrow farm machinery factory: "The opinion is that the leaders are stalling to calm the masses, but avoiding real changes."

In Hagenow, Vicar de Moor, the son of the Land Church superintendent, organized the New Forum. "There was applause when a not-yet-identified woman artist from Schwerin said, 'The SED was no longer capable of leading.' The audience was mostly nursing students, curious but not impressed."[44]

Very secret: "Lietz commented privately that the Politbüro statement was a compromise of the factions, so one can expect a more attractive socialism." The report goes on and on with criticisms and admits that many people have been influenced by BRD media. The MfS made a shocking comparison: "95 percent of the West media is the truth, while the DDR media is like Goebbels, saying on 3 May 1945, 'We are close to Final Victory.' "

The MfS reported that the SED statement on the 11 October had "stabilized matters" but then sent a long list of necessary basic changes. "The way things are no one can be compelled or persuaded to more production. With plans always getting 'corrected,' all plans have been allegedly filled. After a lightening up of the public, skepticism returns."

Party errors were worsening the situation, and the MfS judged, "The leaders have reacted so late, that this [SED] action must only be a beginning, otherwise the disillusionment will continue. These are getting to be serious criticisms, 'Why is the Party always glorifying itself and appearing so arrogant?' " It was using the wrong tactic: "The SED slogan states, 'What is not in order, we will put in order.' It should be, 'This specific thing is not in order, and we will fix it by a certain time' or admit, 'We can't fix it.' "[45]

The MfS for itself could claim, "We have an almost perfect police state," but then admit, "The worst awakening for most people starts when they have seen the BRD for the first time. For nearly everyone, their world collapses."[46]

The MfS tried to counterattack but was foiled by functionary folly. At the Gadebusch Church, after the New Forum read a Bishop Stier letter: "Our 'social forces' made good contributions and got much applause and prevented the success of the opposition. The positive factor is that leading functionaries are now talking with the people. What is not understood is that these functionaries often act as though they were always in agreement with the people and are now surprised that the reality in society did not accord with what they had always wanted. The people see that a change in leadership is needed."[47]

The situation was again reported as more stabilized on 15 October. "Calm everywhere, but fewer people think that the New Forum is an enemy of the state. The majority of the New Forum are those who had not been active in society before." Schools were not so calm: "At the high school in Boizenburg, students and FDJ demonstrated for the New Forum but were stopped. The senior class put up a wall newspaper. Everyone said they would not be FDJ leaders." Despite such flagrant indiscipline, the MfS advised caution: "The SED should move slowly, no precipitous action."[48]

Every report begins with an assertion of stability, but the New Forum was still growing, as with 200–300 persons meeting in Schwerin's Dom.[49] Pastor Anders said: "A pastor who does not mix in politics is not a pastor," but MfS judged that the New Forum leaders were also against more demonstrations, since they did not have the necessary personnel base. "They also fear acts of violence."

The workers rejected the Central Committee's defiant reaction to the exodus: "We are still 16 million, no tears for those who left." The workers were saying that the DDR had been seriously hurt; some training had already been canceled because so many instructors left. The workers criticized administrators: "There are so many in the administration and they should have to do more work."[50]

In a sad MfS reflection: "We used to be told we must keep secrets so that the West media could not use them as ammunition. They didn't need more ammunition. We have delivered the powder to the West media with our silence for decades and ignoring the problems. Many young people are aware of the problem and willing to express themselves."

More so in Sachsen and Thüringen: "Now 'Red Mecklenburg' runs into troubles in the south. . . . Rumors circulate that northern autos can't get gas in the south, because the north is not supporting New Forum."

Even in the north, SED were fleeing, and the dissidents were rising: "The deputy secretary of the Parchim SED and the Wittenberge FDJ secretary have left through Hungary. In nearly all territories of the district, the New Forum have meetings planned." When 230 persons met in Schwaan, Pastor Kruse read the New Forum statement: "20 persons made provocative assertions, such as, 'Socialism brought us nothing.' 'End military instruction in school.' Ten progressives were there, but raised only two questions, without effect."[51]

The Parchim Metalform plant showed the problem: "The socialist competition has had no effect, because so many parts necessary to production are missing and a plan-based work is not possible. Putting new projects into production takes much too long to achieve." That came from bad organization: "The responsibility must be established at each level of the production process, as is so often not now the case. In principle, four administrators are watching one worker. This much too large administrative structure only hinders the entire process of production."[52]

The SED had blown its chances: "If only SED leaders had changed 4 weeks ago then the masses would have helped. . . . Students are angry that nothing has changed in the Marxism-Leninism lectures." The applicants increased 400 percent.[53] MfS General Korth linked this with the peace prayers in the Dom. Illegal crossings had increased from 206 in 1987, to 358 in 1988, and already to 1,096.[54] Opposition speakers came from Berlin, Leipzig and Dresden to present a list of demands, including term limits. "There is a broad interest in many of the citizens of all classes."

Police were frustrated: "The police can't understand why the New Forum is allowed to operate." On the other hand, some, having made trips to the West, were unhappy with their leadership and media reports that police might be punished.[55]

When Honecker fell, on 17 October, the MfS still praised him but conceded that he had stayed too long and raised the question why the entire Politbüro did not resign.[56] "The popular view is that Honecker should have retired two years ago, as well as Mittag and Hermann. There are other party and state functionaries who are also too old."

As for the successor, Krenz, the MfS observed about twice as many negative reactions in the public as positive. Krenz, considered a pupil of Honecker, had not spoken for change before. "The people question Krenz's health, there's talk of alcohol. He also lacks charisma. Like Honecker, he comes from the youth movement and will continue to spoil them. The young don't want to produce, therefore they leave."[57]

The MfS joined in the call for rapid change: "Mittag should have been fired long ago, the question is, will a qualified man take his place or will they choose again a Party functionary? The change should quickly work itself down to the local level."[58]

By 19 October, the MfS was supporting the demonstrators' position! "What must and can be done to convince the old *Herren* of the Politbüro, so that they understand that they no longer have the trust of the people and that they are talking right past them. Actually we must be grateful to those persons who have left for the West and have the courage to go into the street, in order that our leaders wake up and bring change. As long as the chiefs need only to pick up their packages and their money, they won't be dissatisfied, and so long as they are not dissatisfied, nothing will change." The demonstrators could scarcely be more bitter than this MfS writer!

The MfS was still trying to stop the New Forum, which was making an intensive effort, and the churches were providing it rooms. "It met in the church in Schwaan, and the participants showed themselves delighted. Pastor Kruse was an instant hero."[59]

The MfS officer for the churches said that Pastors Rietzke and Martin Scriba were risking arrest, creating a serious problem of state–church relations. "Bishop [Peter] Müller took a destructive position, saying the meeting was a church matter. 'It was sad that the church was forced into this intermediary position.' He took the same position as the New Forum." People came from all over the area, the BRD and even Norway. " 'Antisocial forces' led the discussions of 200 persons into hostile-negative positions. Some people left and others remained who did not agree, so the organizers did not get any commitments to action. A few said they would leave the church from this misuse."

The MfS misjudged these meetings as failures: "Other than high attendance, such gatherings are not suitable to strengthen the New Forum, so they will go back to regular church meetings. The forces of the Party and city defeated them. . . . The organizers displayed so much explosive power; they irritated the progressive participants. Their resigned judgment of their failure raised the question whether they would try any again. [Dissident] Klähn could only say three sentences and was not able to answer questions."[60]

Despite this alleged failure, New Forum meetings were everywhere but Lübz and Sternberg, with as few as 7 persons in the pastorate in Pinnow and as many as 1,500 in Schwerin's Paul's Church. Almost all meetings were on church property.[61]

The report to Berlin explained well the sources of the New Forum's growth: "They have increased popularity in the communities and have extended and made stronger their structure. They have achieved significant potential with the people that can be used in various activities. The best is the New Forum ability to work in all residential areas in all city districts. They have the contact addresses and speakers, and information is quickly circulated for their cooperation. They have telephones—some private and some church. They are still growing and are unhindered. They have the ability to circulate their materials very widely. They have the cooperation of the various groups. Lietz has links to the Democratic Awakening and the Social Democrats, from long years of working together. The New Forum operates as a roof organization."

Church dissent was "dropping its mask" and was the center of the movement. "From 16 to 22 October, they had almost entirely political meetings, with many more than 100,000 in attendance. These were no longer hidden behind 'prayer meetings,' but directly discussed political concerns. The New Forum does not hide its true purpose."

A top secret report stated: "The 'Democratic Awakening' is taking advantage of the politically desolate condition in some central institutions for art and culture, so Christa Wolf joins in. The New Forum will use artists." Demonstrations were out of control. "From 16–22 October, there were unapproved demonstrations in nearly all districts, totaling over 140,000. It is getting now to Rostock and Neubrandenburg, with candles, chants and signs."[62]

For the Wednesday New Forum meetings, more people showed interest in something new. "The mood is one of awaiting statements from politicians. . . . Most say that if there were freedom to travel, some would leave but not nearly the 150,000. Why has the state been so slow to react to public wishes? The people are opposed to the privileges of high functionaries: 'The leaders preach water and drink wine.' The Party always had problems with the trust of the people and now it has finally lost that trust of those masses." A damning judgment.

The Parchim County Council admitted its defeat: "We were a wretched heap against the multitude. After 'our demonstration' was over, they could have steamrollered us. Such an experience does have an effect on us. What did we do wrong? How is it possible that school children become the tools of the class enemy, so many and so quickly? Many are unhappy with Council President Möller; he possesses no authority, and hasn't changed his style."

Official counteractions fell flat. "The SED demonstration made errors like giving participants little cards telling them what they were to say. . . . Ziegner screamed, but no one heard him." The MfS question: "Why was the New Forum not allowed to speak when it was supposed to be a dialog?"[63] Ziegner tried to seal off from the south and proposed on 23 October a Democratic Block as an offensive. But he achieved the exact opposite: "Ziegner gambled away every remnant of credibility and brought part of the Party apparatus against him."[64]

Again the frustrated quest for a more just system: "There is a demand for just rewards for physical and intellectual production. . . . The public corruption, the 'connections economy,' and other 'capitalistic derailments' are making our economic policy impossible." In another version of the class struggle: "Citizens are treated like third class in the DDR and Soviet Union. There must be no more privileges for those with West money."[65]

In Bützow a group of doctors, previously not active, was allying with the New Forum. "We must invest more in medicine, where we are 20–30 years behind the BRD. Since doctors' salaries have not kept up, no wonder so many are leaving."[66]

Leaders were showing fear: "Anyone visiting a [Sternberg] County Council is accompanied by a guard. Does it have any reason to fear the people?"

The public feared disorder but knew that change had to come: "People are shocked by events in Berlin and elsewhere, by demonstrations and disturbances, but have to agree that conditions never get better. They feel abandoned and doubt the effectiveness of the SED action in September. There is a lack of answers in discussions. All agree that the SED did not help the situation. The people hoped that demonstrations would wake up Berlin and Schwerin. They saw that the leaders would not come to talk unless forced to. The people are prepared to change positions, to make their contribution and are only waiting for the time when their creative cooperation will finally be demanded." The MfS shared the people's disillusion.

The report also picked the Krenz speech apart: "Honecker is only a scapegoat; not only Honecker, Mittag and Herrmann were at fault. Krenz said: 'We now have great problems.' Did Honecker leave a chaos? Krenz said, 'We must talk openly with everyone.' What has the Party been doing? . . . There is no clear line now. The Party made promises before. Some expect a real reformer, like Modrow." It asked suspiciously: "The West predicted the changes. Who told them?"[67]

The MfS joined in the public demand that "The DDR must stop giving away its exports. It should fire those people who don't work, and reduce the administration. There should be a full use of the time at work. Arrogance and anonymity should cease." In short, the achievement principle should be restored.[68]

MfS joined in the attack on the SED's slow change: "The functionaries speak only to functionaries. Rarely does any of them talk to a real worker." In the attack on Krenz: "He can scarcely have any perspective. He is also guilty of the causes of the events in Leipzig and Dresden, for manipulating the last election. We need new leaders, because these can't change their ideas fast enough. Krenz keeps too many functions, and such concentration has been proven bad." The report said that Hager, Sindermann and Stoph should go first. "How can Kurt Hager talk about a personality cult when he was among the worst about Honecker?"[69]

From Sternberg, a similar attack on the SED: "Functionaries did not listen to the workers. . . . They need their daily flattery, like other people need air to breathe. . . . Their talk of reform has become unbelievable." It was also the arrogance: "The party which sings, 'The party is always right' is slapping other people in the face."[70]

The 86-year-old Communist Bernhard Quandt told the Central Committee that "it should create a new Politbüro that had nothing to do with the criminal gang of the Politbüro. . . . We ended the death penalty, but I would re-install it so that we could strangle and shoot those who brought our Party in such a humiliation."[71]

The MfS policy was that the SED should conduct small dialogues and avoid mass meetings. "Popular confidence has been lost by the SED, so the other block parties should increase their input and, where appropriate, speak against SED policy. All privileges of functionaries should be ended so there can be a democracy."[72]

At the Land Youth Conference, New Forum signs were on sale. Speakers were saying, "Don't blame DDR leaders, blame yourselves. . . . Everyone should speak of his or her desires; passivity must become activism." But with restraint: "One should be polite to everyone. . . . The behavior of the Party Secretary [Krenz] showed no sign of re-thinking. Such behavior must meet with resistance from our comrades."[73]

Among small-town demonstrators there was still hesitance: "To the peace prayers in Sternberg came new people and they stood outside the church undecidedly, and seemed to be waiting for something. They were mostly either young or those over 40. Individuals sought, before entering the church, to make connections with others, so a series of small groups were formed."

Pastor Anders expressed the fear that the movement would die out by Christmas, that it was too early for demonstrations, as many were marching without a definite purpose. He spoke against drafting men. "Often during the service occurred strong applause. He said there would be no demonstration today, but also said the church was not there to save the SED." Six more spoke, explaining the new organizations, and mentioned a November meeting in Schwerin. Twenty persons waited outside as though for a demonstration, but they had no candles or signs.[74]

The MfS tried an experiment in Schwerin, trying to get control of the mass demonstration on 23 October, sending in militia in civilian clothes, but the opposition took over when the agents left, and the MfS recognized its defeat.[75]

November

As rural people joined the revolution, Pastor Anders' wife led 130 persons in Sternberg in criticisms of Party and state functionaries. An engineer said that the SED had showed its incompetence. A man who had been an MfS target of operations became quite emotional and said he was ashamed to have been a Communist: "The SED always deceived the people and had become reactionary, not revolutionary." The mayor and representative of the town council were drowned out. Another mayor complained that he was getting no support from the state; he was there entirely on his own. The Blau Bock innkeeper called for the organization of a New Forum at his place.[76]

The next day, 75 sympathizers met there, with the church still the core; some organizers had already demonstrated in Berlin, Leipzig, Schwerin and Güstrow. "The New Forum has gained medical personnel and many construction apprentices." When asked when they should demonstrate, the pastor said it was too early. Then when pushed, he said, "Go and get it approved, if you really want to." His wife again led the meeting, but the local chronicler warned, "I experienced 1953, then they rolled over us with tanks, threw us into prison and now it's starting again." They told the mayor: "Get the Hell out of our village."

About half applauded a former Communist who said that the SED had had a 40-year chance and had failed. "A comrade tried to defend the SED role, but did not succeed for a lack of ability and the many catcalls, such as, 'You're incompetent.' " The county National Front leader described plans for change, but he was shouted down. People called out, "Long ear [MfS informer]. . . . One should shoot the long ears." The mayor tried to say that the church should stay out of politics, but he was also rejected.

The local MfS had only limp ideas for a counteroffensive: "The County Council must do something because the number of potential demonstrators is daily increasing. We should create discussion groups in factories and have talks with church leaders, more City Hall discussions, an improved party newspaper."[77]

The next day, an army officer apologized for a dumb remark about the church. "The atmosphere is substantially less tense, more open than yesterday. There were no aggressive incidents." The New Forum marched from the Blau Bock to the church; the 130 persons included five soldiers, even a lieutenant. On 3 November, the pastor had 170–180 persons, including SED members and army officers. The discussion of local problems in the city hall, with 120 present, was "not hostile"; 150 persons marched to the county Party and police headquarters. Teachers were beginning to quit the SED.[78]

Similarly in small-town Bützow: "Everyone can see a real change in the media; it pays now to follow the news. There is still no real dialogue; most people are still just waiting. Nothing is done about material needs. There is more support for the New Forum, particularly among the young." Pastor Preuss had 1,200 at the church on 2 November; 60 percent were between 20 and 35 years.[79]

In Schwerin's "silent march," the emphasis was on order; 500 candles were placed on the SED steps. Church officials would not accept responsibility and did not call it, although 1,500 persons were at the Paul's Church. SED leaders spoke to 2,000 persons. "All seemed to agree that socialism must be strengthened, but the present leaders must be replaced. They are suspicious about statements of the top SED leaders, who must change themselves."[80]

The church meeting in Sternberg on 7 November attracted 300 persons; those identified were mostly medical personnel. Pastor Anders told them that the movement had started in 1983, and he warned against MfS listening at the service. (Duly recorded by the MfS listener.) He spoke against hatred: "Do not return evil for evil." He commented, "It was not the SED but the people who had brought the Change."

In a moment of exhilaration, "Someone said that government had resigned. This information was greeted with a fanatical applause." The pastor said nothing; he just covered his ears with his hands. All repeated "The Lords Prayer," lit a candle and said a wish or prayer. The pastor suggested carrying candles through the streets, but he stressed that a demonstration was not his idea, and he would not march. He said, "The meetings would be in the church only until the New Forum was legalized. As they marched, they chanted. 'First your TV out, then you come out.' " A modest frustration: "Our IM didn't get any of the 20 pamphlets but we can order one."[81]

Local SED were rising against their county leaders. "Positive persons decided after the Sunday discussion of 200 in the Sternberg city hall that county SED leaders had absolutely not understood the seriousness of the situation and are the wrong persons for their positions. 'They talk exactly as they did before and show no initiative.' " The police were still bewildered: "They can't understand that the security forces do not react to the slander."[82] The district SED told Berlin, "Wandlitz [Politbüro luxury community] means more people are quitting the Party than we can keep up with."[83]

The demonstration in Schwerin on 10 November began with 2,000 and reached 6,000, completely filling the Domplatz. Someone talked of a mass murder by MfS in December 1984; a father demanded its investigation by his lawyer Gregor Gysi. An older man wanted a memorial to that crime. A pediatrician said that teachers had to be schizophrenic and that children had to have two heads, one for school, one for home.[84]

The New Forum had now a BBC film team. "It wants free elections but are concerned that the new travel rules will reduce the pressure for change. There are differences in the New Forum whether they should remain a 'Collecting Movement' or become an independent party."[85]

In Sternberg on 14 November, Pastor Anders properly registered a demonstration and cooperated with the police; "200 were there for the prayers and marched with the usual demands and 50 candles. There were fewer youth than before and fewer at the services." The MfS was resentful: "Lies were being told about MfS privileges, that they were paid partly in Westmarks."[86]

Langer concluded that what was special in the north were the peacefulness and the variety of groups, panels and the procedures. "Peace was an immediate result of the sensible behavior of all participants. Therewith developed a kind of security partnership between the Opposition and the state's power."[87]

The Schwerin District Party reported an increasing fear for the future of the SED and even a call for a new KPD. "There remains a great bitterness, a great fright about conditions. Misuse of power, corruption and lies are having their effect. The loss of trust is growing larger and larger."[88]

The Berlin office was changing fast, and when it was renamed the Office for National Security (AnS), this led to a noteworthy local MfS statement about the necessary Change: "The MfS has represented fear all those years? This raises the question, what is the AnS to do? How many AnS personnel will there be in the county? How will they behave toward citizens? What controls exist to prevent the misuse of power? Are they to be honest? Are they to use force? Are they to join in the discussion?" Remarkable questions for Secret Police to raise.

The Change had begun: "The local commander was agreeable and all was fine. He asked that demonstrators be told of the AnS agreement and it was done. If not only fear is to be reduced, but also confidence is to be increased, it has be actively sought. *We want to offer a bridge between the people and the MfS.*" He politely asked that the old MfS personnel clean up their act.[89]

This fond hope was suddenly doomed. The MfS/AnS, dying from the feet upward, was quickly on its knees. The local unit was being dismantled. On 7 December, after the chief was fired, it was unable to operate. There was a hasty agreement to dissolve, which included the principle to save documents.[90]

On 8 January, the Schwerin office reported that it was sorting and destroying documents, under the control of the military district attorney and the "Citizen Initiative." On 9 January, the district office could not function, and the police secured it.[91] When Manfred Goldmann turned over the building to the Ministry of Justice, he wrote, "Schwerin was the first district to finish the dissolution of the MfS."[92]

This end of the Secret Police in Schwerin had one negative aspect; it was sending no more reports for history. Berlin's would last a short time longer.

BERLIN

September

The MfS remained apparently confident in its strength and in apparent control. Although unwittingly nearing its end, it still had 1,262 properties, of which 1,181 were for "conspiratorial operations."[93]

On 7 September, Mielke re-set its priorities, mostly to deal with the economic problems: achieve production goals, support key technologies and prevent disruptions. "The increased cooperation [with the West] will require more protection of secrets and stopping Greenpeace." A further responsibility: "The MfS should also help agriculture, as with hygienic transport. Most important is that in the competition with capitalism, the

DDR should not be the hare but the hedgehog, the one who is already there, when the competitor gets to the market."

This race would not be won by a trick; rather, the DDR would need a miracle, and all of Mielke's men could not magically produce a solution to the trade deficit. "Over 50 percent of our national income comes from foreign trade; for this year there is a gap of circa 1.4 billion marks."[94] The problem began with the fact that DDR's per capita gross national product was only one-third that of the BRD. To avoid cutting living standards 25–30 percent, economists could only suggest obtaining BRD credits of 2 to 3 billion marks. Afraid of losing power, the SED leaders never dared take the distasteful decisions that might have broken the downward spiral.[95]

Mielke's circular explanation: "The Politbüro is going slowly because the 1.7 billion mark investment in the Plan has not yet been realized nor the increase in production." His Chekist solution was more productive spying: "The MfS can discover the problems and cover up the well before the child falls in. We discovered 970 investment plans outside the Plan and at the expense of its goals. Important objectives were delayed for years, after which many leaders boasted how clever they were and how they fooled the authorities."

The MfS could correctly describe the production problems: "The low morale in the firms, the increased unwillingness and dissatisfaction, expressed in aggressive tones about both consumption and production, a passivity and decline in willingness to produce, and the rise of speculators and corruption."

For these problems SED socialism was offering no defense: "It is hard to distinguish SED members in their attitudes from the others—all increasingly blame leadership, its age. There is a deepening loss of confidence. The SED can not defend the Party line. Only the Opposition talks about the realities. Especially those who understand the economy are critical of the policy, but it is impossible to bring up the problems in Party meetings. Party members feel that they have been abandoned, while non-members ridicule the Party line. Since they get the news from the BRD, they take on the BRD line instead."

An "Only for your eyes" report: "Many old SED are very concerned about the aggressive tone of the demonstrations. There is also a growing apathy and many are leaving the Party, especially in Berlin. . . . Professors can't answer some of the students' questions."[96]

MfS had also come to see the unreality of socialist theory: "All wonder why the young give up security, and the system that they had been taught." The MfS answer: "They had been taught a wonderful theory in school, and then they run into the realities of socialism in the work place, the lack of incentive for achievement. Everyone gets his money anyway, whether he works very much or very little, so they avoid taking any responsibility."

The MfS also sympathized with the reasons for the mass flight: "The young don't want to wait until they get their pension before they can travel." On the lack of solidarity: "Citizens are angry because they are treated like second class in the socialist world. They say they are not to blame if their money is not desired."

The system was exhausted: "One doesn't hear much criticism in the workplace about those escaping. The cadre pull back and don't confront the arguments; they see no chance to change views which are so entrenched. Those who used to be active became tired, then became resigned, then they capitulated. After they see the west, they complain about the lack of cleanliness in the DDR." On the lack of fairness: "There is the growing gap between leaders and the collectives. The members' wages, plus their child-money and marriage money, still do not keep up with the increase in prices."[97]

The MfS analyst made a strong appeal for less ideological reporting: "We can not influence the consciousness of the people and get something moving if we use only the concept of socialism. . . . Journalists are particularly upset with the policy."[98]

The MfS recognized the leadership's failure ("There is a growing criticism of the media, as too slow and too late. The top leaders have not been seen enough. Apparently in the absence of Honecker, no one else can take over."), poor media performances ("Stoph showed his inability to react at the Leipzig Fair") and envy of privilege ("There is a great loss of confidence in the Party, whose functionaries get the western cars").

The MfS worried about the multiplication of hostile actions: a student parliament at the Humboldt University, a Magdeburg prayer meeting, a Halle memorial minute and prayer, in Pankow a New Forum group, in Zwickau a prayer, in Leipzig's Nikolai Church a peace prayer.[99] "Everywhere are critical discussions of the situation. The progressive forces follow it with concern but also with disillusionment. This behavior can not be blamed only on imperialists, it has been around a long time."[100]

The DDR had a vacuum at the top ("For a year and a half, the government has not reacted because the physical and mental ability of the top politicians has been exhausted."), apathy at the bottom ("There is a general shortage of a willingness to work and an escalating indifference. In school, there is also ever less willingness to work and desire to achieve.") and a nonwork ethic ("One can say that there is no unemployment but there are too many 'co-workers,' who might as well be called unemployed."). In the vacuum, if the Party could not effect change, the church would help someone who could.[101]

What the dissidents produced was the New Forum, begun 10 September in the home of Katja Havemann, the young widow of the dissident physicist. The 30 initial signers were almost exclusively less-established intelligentsia, artists and scholars, doctors and, naturally, pastors. The IM report stated: "Most have formed relations with western parties, except for the

CDU, and with the peace movement. Their goal is reforming the DDR and ending the SED monopoly."[102]

As Bohley explained her choice of New Forum founders: "I wanted to transcend the narrow church and dissident circles and appeal to the broader population. So I invited a group of various ages and professions from all over the DDR. No one declined." They wanted to be legal, and any party would be illegal. The New Forum and others provided identification and a reference point, but in no way did they organize and control their followers. Their many ideas of reform struck a nerve when, as a complete surprise, they got 200,000 signatures. [103]

The MfS thought that the New Forum was not given much encouragement at first from the West. "SPD leaders want restraint *vis-à-vis* the DDR, in order to keep contact with the SED, but Ehmke, Voigt, Glotz, Stoppe want a confrontation. . . . The SPD publication accepts the division of Germany because of German guilt in the past."[104] Thus, without direct encouragement, the dissidents "made it happen."

Joppke explained why the revolution happened first in Leipzig, where the Emigrant/Exit movement was strong and more politicized. It had the second highest number of legal and illegal emigrants. When the MfS' harshness to the Luxemburg demonstration left East Berlin's movement in disarray, the fresher and younger groups in Leipzig moved to the fore. In early 1988 the coordination of about 50 opposition groups had moved there.

Only in Leipzig did the "Voice Opposition," the civil rights movement, not shy away from the "Exit Opposition." These "Exits" led the way to mass protest, and "the Voice" offered the organizational ideas.

Thereto came Leipzig pollution. The brown-coal mining had raided whole historic neighborhoods. Strip-mining and smokestack industry had made the city one of the most polluted in Europe. The local sarcasm: "In Leipzig you can see what you breathe."

Worsening pollution was the urban decay. While East Berlin experienced a frenzy of new building projects, Leipzig's long-neglected infrastructure reached a point of near collapse. A substantial portion of the inner city's old housing had become virtually uninhabitable, and its residents were relocated to hastily constructed, shabby satellite cities at the periphery. Thereto the shortages: only during the trade fairs in March was there more than cabbage and potatoes. As a result, in the May election an estimated 20 percent rejected the Unity list.

"The Voice" became more assertive on 4 September, the traditional demonstration for the fair. When the crowd was about to leave the church, a civil rights group, "I.G. Leben [Life]," suddenly set theme banners for freedom at the head of the march. After the banners were taken away by the Stasi, "the Voice" noticed that the Applicants had stayed in the churchyard, where Western TV was registering their protests. The Applicants hissed "the Voice" shouts of "We Stay Here"; West journalists missed the point that civil rights dissidents had tried to take over. Two weeks later their "We Stay Here" drowned out the "Let Us Leave" protests of the would-be emigrants.

On 25 September, 5,000 persons, combining the protesters, marched un-hindered, the first of the demonstrations that catalyzed the collapse.[105] Be-coming quickly worrisome was the traditional Monday prayer in Leipzig's Nikolai Church. To curb it, MfS measures were implemented, including turning back 858 persons who wished to go to the fair at the border.[106] The Leipzigers could not be so easily turned back.

From the Leipzig police already in September came the report that "the fear about confronting the Monday assignment was growing." The police were constantly being attacked when they moved to arrest a demonstrator. "Immediately 10 women and men attacked, throwing the police hats away, pulling at their hair, their shoulder insignia and uniforms and hit them. Particularly aggressive were the women." Süss commented that when the demonstrations involved less risk, loud-talking men pushed the women into the background.[107]

In Berlin the opposition was also impressing the MfS with its vigor: "New Forum leaders claim 8,000 members, half in Berlin, and they rep-resent all layers of the population, although few production workers. This is more because of their program than as a simple accumulation of groups." Ominously, "They are bringing in pop artists on the 18th."[108] On 21 Sep-tember, events included a sit-in at the *Volksbühne* Theater and a hearing in the Deutsch Theater. In an evaluation of "the goals and activities of the hostile-negative forces" in the DDR, the MfS emphasized the Applicants, "who show an increased willingness to take risks and be aggressive."[109]

While thus trying to stop "hostile" change, Mielke sent Politbüro mem-bers, except for Honecker, the noted report of 11 September, with its crit-ical reactions of SED members and functionaries. This was to tell them that the ground was getting hot.[110] Yet his accompanying letter does not show any urgency, any stressing that this was really serious. He sent the criticisms to another list of less important leaders, with a similarly bland letter.[111]

Mielke showed a keener concern about the Republic's 40th anniversary, which required measures to prevent the enemy from disrupting the cele-bration, even keeping them from Berlin. Among the usual charges was that they possessed weapons and explosives.[112] "The West CDU, to help our enemies, plan to meet with Eppelman. He has had close relations with Fink and [Mayor] Diepgen in West Berlin." On 21 September, Eppelman met with three Bundestag members. "Eppelman and Scharrebroich agreed to stay close. Both honor Bohley, which raises the question whether these Bundestag members should be allowed entry."[113]

The Interior Ministry rejected legalizing the New Forum, because it was "hostile to the state." On 22 September, the MfS sent the cold, old-style instructions on how to prevent its growth: "Do not receive a group, only individuals. Each is to be given the following answer: cite the paragraph which says enough organizations exist, then give them a lecture that such activity must be stopped immediately or there will be consequences. Then the conversation is to be closed. A further discussion about reasons, arguments, etc., is not to be permitted."[114] The MfS was laboring under a delusion that its cold-eyed treatment was still possible.

Wolle analyzed Mielke's 22 September message to the Politbüro: "This pathetic picture of helplessness, of political and human loss of orientation, and crippling doubt about the correctness of the Party's policies corresponded exactly to the reality and explained the MfS loss of power which came a few weeks later. Maybe the old men at the top could not have reacted but the middle echelon should have had the youth and intelligence, but over the years with most of the functionaries, the requisite qualities of creativity, fantasy, preparedness to take chances, initiative, civil courage and acceptance of responsibility had shriveled up, because such characteristics would have hindered the desired careers. Whoever had been too tempted by power declined in intellect and in character and whoever reached the top echelons was the result of a long and systematic negative process of selection."[115]

On 28 September, Mielke sent more hard-line orders, but with a soft core: "Use IM to get their plans; threaten them with arrest and break off the talks. If they continue to organize, lecture, warn and take measures against them as disturbers of the peace. If they give interviews to the West media, confer with my deputy Mittig on what to do. Act in similar fashion with church officials. Use your influence with the police for them to use their powers. If you catch them in the act, arrest them immediately. Keep SED leaders informed."[116] Despite such instructions, "old DDR enemies" formed the "Democratic Awakening."[117]

Kratsch, head of Counter Intelligence, opened a discussion among MfS leaders, but only one showed the courage to speak frankly. Department Head Rolf Bauer said, "The Party leadership lies, deceives, falsifies statistics, refuses to accept the true situation, so the country is being led to its ruin." Kratsch told him he was wrong.[118] October would prove Kratsch wrong.

October

Krenz had recognized as early as mid-September that the foundation of the republic was cracking and that an increased repression would not solve it. "Only a political discussion of the complicated questions would bring us forward to perfect our socialist system."

His colleague Wolfgang Herger understood that much more would have to change. The best option was to announce to the country that anyone could leave and return. This advice went to Krenz on 3 October to give to Honecker. Krenz passed on the option to close borders but to promise travel at Christmastime. Honecker took only the repressive part and closed the Czech border, which Herger had predicted would make it impossible to govern.

Thus, in early October occurred the five days of bloody repression and the arrest of 3,500 who, on Mielke instructions, were kept illegally long and subjected to physical and psychological abuse. However, they were not put in the long-prepared camps but released after three days.[119]

A turning point on 9 October: Krenz agreed with the local commander who said that he could not stop so many thousands of people. Krenz had to consider what would have disrupted plans to remove Honecker, a coming together of a crippling of the central regime and the determination and courage of demonstrators. A dialogue was promised, but until the end of October Krenz ordered not recognizing the New Forum with a dialogue, which confused the locals. Those MfS in contact with the masses were not surprised at the failures.[120]

In the Süss analysis, in view of the DDR's catastrophic debt if it had used martial law, it would have precipitated an economic collapse. The foreign policy constellation of military-political dependence on the East and the economic dependence on the West narrowed the options enormously. The battle was lost before it began. The necessity was that there be a pressure from below that was strong enough really to challenge the regime, but the citizens could not have known what the options were of the powerful and whether they would calculate them rationally.[121] Krenz would calculate, and Mielke would be held back.

Mielke's reaction was that if open repression was not possible, use covert measures. At the beginning of November, Mittig's plan was to use IMs among dissident groups.[122] But IMs and their handlers were not the Chekist robots: General Möller complained, "It has become the style to discuss in the units every instruction and every command. It has even gone so far that there are in principle refusals to follow commands.[123]

In the game of DDR survival, Gorbachev was the wild card. Already in July, he had turned away from the Brezhnev doctrine, the Soviet right to save socialism in any of the Soviet allies. He was not for the end of the DDR, but rather its reform, but he would not use force to save it. On 12 September his Central Committee had concluded that neither West nor East Europe wanted German unification, but the idea was not totally rejected, as it had been before.[124] On 20 September, Kotschenmassov warned the DDR leaders, "We support the DDR but not at the expense of our interests in the BRD and in Europe altogether."[125]

When Gorbachev came to help celebrate the 40th anniversary, Schabowski observed the grotesque forms that Honecker used to resist his supposed Soviet partner. When Gorbachev urged reform, Honecker responded that he was shocked at the empty stores in Moscow. The core of Honecker's anger was the Soviet blocking of his ambitions with the BRD and that the West German Communist Party had taken a Soviet-style position. After a tactful Gorbachev speech, Honecker gave a long and painful recitation of DDR successes. When he finished, Gorbachev glanced up surprised, looked around, smiled resignedly and let out the question, "Was that everything?"[126]

The minutes of 7 October recorded Gorbachev's telling Honecker: "If we fall behind, life punishes us. . . . We have only one choice, to decide to move ahead; otherwise we will be beaten by life. Life is a very serious matter, that we know."[127]

As Kotschenmassov described the meeting with the DDR Central Committee, Gorbachev said frankly, "Every party has the right to decide for itself, but has also the responsibility. The SED must decide either to take a new course or be swept aside." Honecker merely repeated himself that the situation was under control. "What did the Politbüro members do? They all sat in silence, not a word was said. They sat. They waited. It was over. They stood up and left. Gorbachev met with us and said, 'What can one do now. It's like throwing peas at the wall. They won't accept anything.' "[128] Ironically that evening, the assembled FDJ no longer was shouting, "Erich" but "Gorby."[129]

In his memoir, "I sensed, particularly as I stood at the podium for the thousands of demonstrators clearly the tension, which dominated, as well as the discontent with the regime. I was surprised at the enthusiasm for *Perestroika* and the obvious lack of respect for Honecker. The Polish First Secretary said to me, 'This is the end.' . . . We were not surprised at the fall of the Wall."[130]

The DDR could counter that the USSR was not part of the solution but part of the problem. Honecker claimed that almost 50 percent of the workers in the DDR were working for deliveries to the USSR.[131] In 1987-1988, the DDR had sent thousands of tons of potatoes to St. Petersburg and Moscow, so that Russians would not starve. The DDR had invested in mining in Magnitogorsk and cellulose works in Ust-Ilimsk and the natural gas pipeline. "The COMECON meant that we had to import things that could have been better produced at home." When in 1988-1989 the promised deliveries failed to materialize, the DDR had difficulties in getting paper, cellulose and much else. They could not explain this to the public because of the necessary friendship with the Soviets. The internal DDR complaint, was that "Gorbachev changed so many leaders, that DDR delegates often met uninformed strangers."[132]

While DDR citizens were trying to flee via Budapest, Prague and Warsaw, Mielke showed more worry about disturbances to the celebration in Berlin: "We are looking forward to the 40 Year Jubilee, which recent events have made more complicated. A sharper confrontation of systems, the

massive increase in the agitation and slander campaign is like a drumfire."
Toughness was ordered: "We must stop the internal enemy. At the least
hint of a disturbance of the celebration, isolate and arrest them."[133]

Mielke continued to order his time-tested but obsolete tactics on recov-
ering those lost to the "hostile/negative forces." First find and concentrate
on the leaders. Remain legal. "Use the laws, first lecture, then arrest and
confiscate materials. Work through the responsible state authorities, and
threaten only those sanctions that are legally permissible and are in accor-
dance with the political principles of the Party."

The MfS defined four enemy groups and their strengths: New Forum,
Democratic Awakening (mostly "reactionary" church leaders), Democracy
Now (begun 12 September) and the SDP/Socialists, put down as mostly
church employees. The perceptive analysis: "The New Forum has the
broadest base, gaining support particularly with the Intelligentsia, students,
and it was trying to reach workers. What has helped them has been the
measured, persistent ideological diversion activity, a new quality of opposition, above all, the electronic media of the BRD; the interest of part of
the population in its contents, which corresponds to their sentiments; the
missing political offensive against them and the missing proof that the New
Forum is hostile to the constitution."

The church's more open stand was attracting the unchurched: "Artists
and 'the cultured' joined them. Important are the mass demonstrations in
dimensions never seen before." A forlorn tactic to regain church support:
"We could adopt a more friendly position, as in the media, toward the
church, conduct a more friendly dialogue and permit more local church
involvement in local affairs."[134]

Pressured by the reality below, even the MfS leaders were raising disturbing questions about the SED and its Politbüro. Had there had been
manipulation or irregularities in the May election? Why was the MfS getting the blame? "Since our information has effected scarcely any results in
the Politbüro, are the information lines functioning? The MfS always reported the truth to the Party but it seems to have had no effect and to have
been a waste of good efforts."

Instead, the Party was failing to communicate with even the MfS. "MfS
members are not kept sufficiently informed, particularly those in constant
contact with the problems. We don't know enough about the New Forum
or about the laws."

They felt themselves being demeaned and unprotected! "Is it necessary
for the MfS to operate at football games? There are those who call out
'Stasi swine' and nothing is done about it. MfS members are not allowed
to visit the West. Don't they trust us?" The feared MfS Security Force was
increasingly insecure itself, evident particularly in the fear about the public's
action against their families.[135]

A major described later how the MfS worked the streets apprehensively:

"We mixed inconspicuously among the demonstrators, accompanied by our IMs. Hundreds of us stood at the sides of the street in order to stop any activity before it got started. We got barely any sleep toward the end." The major later reflected, "Never did I sense that the people were afraid of the MfS. The Stasi was more afraid of the people than the people were of them."[136]

The Leipzig demonstration on 2 October had been up to 25,000, and several times they broke through the police cordons, and violent confrontation loomed. "Everyone knew that the next demo had to be the turning point—the intervening week had been the end game of the DDR." Gorbachev's scorn of the DDR leadership made clear that the Russians would not intervene.[137]

On 5 October the Politbüro received more indications of the popular mood, including the following question: "Where were you [SED leaders] all of these years. Why did you not want to see what the situation really is? If one had listened to the people, the situation would not be this way." The MfS had been deceived: "We were lied to." Its remarkable solution: "There must be guarantees created by democracy."[138]

In contrast, the Mielke orders on that day authorized violence, with talk of class war. The situation could no longer be controlled politically; it was to be the "Chinese solution," meaning a slaughter, like that of Tiananmen Square.[139] Mielke reacted, "Beat 'em up, the swine" [*Hau sie doch zusammen, die Schweine*].[140] The MfS ordered using all force short of shooting.

As the MfS chronicled the events: on the night of 7 October came the worst violence, the beating up of demonstrators at the Dresden train station, through which escapees were on their way from Hungary to the BRD in sealed trains. On 8 October the MfS described the situation as rapidly getting worse and ordered a state of red alert for security forces, to use force to suppress growing demonstrations.

Honecker gave the order to shoot at the next Monday demonstration; troops were deployed around Leipzig in large numbers; hospitals were advised to increase their blood supplies; arrest lists for an internment camp were compiled. The Leipzig newspaper had a story from the local militia that law and order would be restored, if necessary, by force.

Its police said that the situation was as serious as on 17 June 1953. "If clubs aren't enough use your guns." All shops and offices had closed by noon, and heavily armed troops roamed the city—by afternoon the town churches had filled. Saxon Bishop Hempel told them to go home, but no one did, which was the turning point. "Leipzig was thereafter out of control." The MfS report on 8 October shows confidence in its first three pages but described serious provocations, like 5,000 demonstrating in Leipzig, followed by the key message: "Refrain from violence."[141]

In Leipzig, of 4,000 demonstrators, with a core of 1,500, 183 were arrested, and in Berlin and Dresden 129; in Chemnitz, when 600 blocked traffic, Battlegroups and police arrested 28. Some police in Schwerin and Parchim refused to arrest. The MfS listed provocative incidents, page after page, town after town. Entire pages were devoted to theater demonstrations, such as 160 members in Chemnitz, an ensemble onstage in Dresden, at the *Volksbühne* in Berlin, and from theaters in Schwedt and Zittau.

Aware of the extent of the problem, the MfS was frightened by Honecker's lack of political action. "Terrifying was the increasing loss of confidence in the DDR leaders. The chance was lost in the celebration to speak clearly and openly to the people. The Gerlach [LDP] speech was better received as being more to the point." The fort could be lost. "A passive and defensive policy would leave door and gate open to an enemy offensive."[142]

Berlin city representatives met with churchman Stolpe, who said it was necessary to give a sign that the state saw the need for changes. Defense Minister Hoffman talked tough: "It was useless to put the state under pressure. . . . We will not be pressured. In matters of the public order, security and peace of the people, no compromise is possible. The church always wants a sign, and the best sign would be for them to get the demonstrations off the street."[143]

On 9 October the system seemed ready to clear the streets, "the Chinese way," but Krenz forbade violence. The Politbüro stopped the escalation, because it feared a civil war. The force was ready. Around Leipzig were tank troops of the Luftlande Division, the Dzerzinsky regiment in division strength, and the 7th Panzer Division from Dresden, but the Politbüro stopped the escalation, because it feared a civil war.[144] "The people did not want to use force and the rulers could not. If they had, the reaction would have been violent." A revolution occurred despite the fact that "there was no revolutionary class, no revolutionary party, no charismatic personality."[145]

Uschner judged that the initiative to nonviolence had come from below, and Krenz had been pulled along.[146] In Berlin "Young Battlegroups won't fight against demonstrators who have relatives in them." The astounding number of protesters on 9 October possibly persuaded Mielke that he could not use force.[147] The critical mass in Leipzig came after the peace prayer, when Chief of Staff K. H. Wagner was surprised to see suddenly thousands of people coming out of every corner. "It was this unexpected large number of people which broke down the willingness of the armed police."

The next morning, on 10 October, began the long-delayed power struggle in the Politbüro, impelled by reports about the local loss of power. "The reports of the SED districts demonstrated that everywhere in the Party organization there was an expanding and crippling, loss of trust, resignation, depression and confusion." Honecker still wanted to resist, but Krenz made a conciliatory public statement. When Krenz said they must follow election laws and be satisfied with 80 percent, Honecker said there had been a falsification and that an investigation would have led to the fall of those responsible, including Krenz.[148]

Mielke quickly tried to distance himself from Honecker in a remarkable disclaimer of responsibility for the violence: "My instructions were built on false situation judgments. My primary position was based on the principle that political questions can be solved only with political means. From the false security concept came the commands, as on 7 and 8 October, which were false and undifferentiated condemnations of those who think differently. Despite this evaluation there were never any instructions to use violence against persons." A breathtaking plea of innocence. "There is nothing in our basic principles to consider a demonstration as part of a possible counter-revolutionary coup."[149]

Mielke was critical of the Politbüro action of 10–11 October: "We must admit that the Party judged the situation falsely. We tried to tell them the true situation, but not enough was done. That is the bitter truth, with which we must now deal." He continued the argument that he had tried but failed to guide the Politbüro: "We were directly confronted for months with problems that were not solved and bad conditions, which clearly were worsening the public's morale. Serious was the move from bewilderment to resignation, even in the progressive forces, deep in the ranks of the Party. You know yourselves that often with great feeling and bitterness, we discussed the fact that the Party and state leaders in the tense situation did not go directly to the members and the workers to create an offensive against the agitation of the enemy. We could not understand why the leaders were not open with the people and mobilized the Party. I openly urged such things at the Politbüro."[150]

Mielke thus began the MfS defense that it provided the information that should have caused the Politbüro to reform before it was too late. His successors and underlings would blame him, as member of that Politbüro, for not effecting a change.

The record shows his continued effort to find better methods to repress. "That is our political position, with which we in the future will work against all efforts to form an inner opposition. We will and must counter 'the collecting movements' and forces. The Party is led by the firm conviction that all problems in our society are solvable politically. We must so act. This development, the daily increasing of influence and profiling of the New Forum, partly also the other groups as anti-socialist opposition, can not be gotten in hand with the practiced measures and means used up to now. Therefore in the next few days central decisions should be made about how to counter the anti-socialist 'collecting movements.' If demonstrations cannot be stopped in this way, the law about their registration and approval will have to change."

After these perplexing words, Mielke made a confusing concession: "For your information, we must give every DDR citizen the right to travel. With-

out their presenting reasons, they should be given a visa for travel to specified countries. Any refusal of permission should be in agreement with the
international conventions: if it is a matter of national security, if the person
has state secrets or is charged with a crime or if he would violate currency
or tariff laws or if under the age of 26, he hasn't done his military service,
or if he has other financial obligations, or if his property rights are not in
order. We must face the reality that more than a few will leave the republic."[151] Despite all of those limitations?

A "counterrevolutionary," Rüddenklau concluded that when the DDR
rejected violence, the last wall against the tide of the masses disappeared,
the public's fear of beatings. "The people had been observing since 1987,
with increasing interest, the activities of the local groups and the crippled
reactions of the regime. When the SED could not even prevent these groups
from exposing its pseudo legitimacy, that had to have been an important
stimulation point. . . . The SED could not stop the independent demonstrations. Particularly in Leipzig, a snowball was slowly beginning to become
an avalanche."[152]

The MfS report on 12 October began by saying that it had regained
stability but then listed many destabilizing events, many also in the north.
Most SED were "ready to fight, and are waiting for the signal," but the
report admitted, "The fighting power of many local organizations is crippled."

The mass exodus was also crippling the economy. In Dresden, 21 stores
were forced to shorter hours, and 26 had to close; 320 medical personnel
had left; mobilized were 800 persons, mostly intelligentsia, to fill in. In
Görlitz, 400 medical students were put to work.[153]

The public had reacted negatively to a Central Committee statement: "It
was an impersonal publication. If a member of the Politbüro had read it
on TV, it would have made a greater impression. It contained no self-
critical evaluation." The progressives, meaning loyalists, were saying, "If
concrete decisions are not made and implemented soon, the workers will
go into the streets."[154] A top MfS official reacted: "Especially workers were
disappointed. Clearly the Politbüro does not fully understand the seriousness of the situation and the significance of the events."[155]

IM reported that the 40-year voting block was cracking; the Liberals
were finally pushing a long list of liberal reforms. "Gerlach will propose
for the Democratic Block meeting on the 13th: to permit all organizations,
which support democracy and socialism, including the New Forum. To
change media policy and let anyone out who wants to leave. Permit everyone at least one visit a year to the West. End punishment for opinions. Use
the Achievement Principle. Permit private initiative. End the hegemony of
the SED in economic decisions. Cadre selection for reason of suitability not
Party. If the SED is unable to rule, the LDP should take on the responsibility."[156]

The MfS feared that the SED's inability to rule was getting close. "The SED leaders are increasingly regarded as unable to reform. . . . There is a growing disappearance of confidence from a large part of the population. . . . Enemies are showing a much greater activity in spreading such ideas. When the first secretaries of the districts met, almost everyone agreed that the situation is critical. . . . One could no longer speak of cooperation between Party and People."[157]

General Schwarz added evidence thereto: "On the 14th, the New Forum resolution was read by opera artists to heavy applause." In Struth 200 youths shouted, "New Forum! Gorby, Gorby! Throw the Stasi out!" A large picture of Honecker was knocked off the wall. Factory workers at a plant in Erfurt, including many boys 19–22, demonstrated against union leader Tisch. The MfS blasted the leadership's failure with workers: "It is remarkable that no one reacted there. The 'concrete heads' think that elsewhere everyone was happy. It is boiling, but no one has the courage to act."

Young colleagues were telling older workers, "You worked so hard and saved the economy, others went to school and got into politics. Now they sit behind big desks, boss you around and pocket fat salaries. Just think what you will get as a pension and what they will get." Many older workers agreed with that. "Five years ago Party and union leaders came regularly and discussed problems. Now if one sees them, at all, in meetings where they talk and do not want to hear any criticism or an honest opinion."

The MfS saw unrest also in the collectives: "Another state farm wants an immediate Central Committee meeting and immediate introduction of the Achievement Principle. They should tell the public to what extent and at what speed the consumer goods production will be increased and how one will end the laziness and the incompetence at work." As before, the workers could not understand the helplessness of Party officials in the firms and in transport and communications. "Some drivers think the spare parts problem can be partially traced back to Party and union leaders. Various workers say things must change and quickly, propaganda won't do it any more. The DDR can no longer be a welfare state for the asocials and the goof offs." Work (being nominally employed) as welfare must end.

Even high school students were making demands: "We have not expected something all encompassing, rather something concrete, for example a law beginning tomorrow, that the situation in the workplace will be disciplined and to make sure that not every SED functionary can throw out the Plan."[158]

The brutality of Dresden on 7–8 October had deepened the split in the Party, because many county leaders were shocked by what they saw on West TV. Krenz's order was that force could be used only if demonstrators used force. There was to be no use of firearms, but Krenz could not be sure on 16 October that no force would be used. He kept close to Mielke.[159]

The Battlegroups were weakening; by one report, 188 members had re-signed, and 146 refused to follow orders.[160] General Schwarz described other units that were unwilling to use violence: "Our Battlegroups are against building barricades and clearing the streets; 60 percent of the 172 units of Weimar County do not want to implement this kind of assignment; 80 percent of two groups in Wöris County reject the form of training they receive, as do 70 percent of those in Sonderhausen. In the 426 Battlegroups of the railroad, the training had to be stopped because the fighters refused to train with billy clubs. In the group of 120 news-electronic workers in Arnstedt, only 30 were prepared to be sent against demonstrations, 5 re-fused, the rest gave excuses, like being away or craftsmen were working in their house. In the motorized Battlegroup in Eisenach, a relatively high number of fighters are afraid of an eventual confrontation against their own people; 12 quit the SED and therewith the Battlegroup."[161]

An alarmed Mielke told assistant Irmler: "The unhappiness and confu-sion among Party members is becoming evident. . . . They want a united strategy and they want a place in the TV discussions. . . . The Stoph inter-view showed little sign of the desired Change. Many are shaken because for years the information coming from the grassroots has not been consid-ered. Many government leaders don't feel able to take the offensive."[162]

Die Wende—The Change

On 12 October, Krenz, Schabowski, Werner Lorenz and Tisch began the overthrow of Honecker, concentrating on pushing him out and giving little thought to what would happen thereafter.[163] Krenz, since October 1983 secretary of the Central Committee for Security Matters, had the power base to succeed Honecker. He had used the clever Wolfgang Herger to keep informed about the MfS. His similar closeness to Schwanitz meant that Mielke had to appoint him his deputy. Being also the Party link to the Interior Ministry and the army, Krenz had arguably more power than Mielke.

Mielke had earlier mocked Krenz as a Boy Scout/*FDJler* in short pants who would never take chances, but he had a great dislike of Margot Ho-necker. When in August–September, the reports and the Russians made clear that Honecker had to go, Mielke encouraged Krenz.[164] They both believed that the DDR must stay with Gorbachev, to the extent that Krenz's refraining from force was also out of respect for Soviet policy.[165] The mil-itary also recognized it could not use force contrary to the will of the Soviets. The serious social problems also reduced the willingness of the military to use open force against the demonstrators.

Krenz saw no other way but reform, knowing the economic and political problems and realizing that the escalating unrest would have meant an escalation of force. Mielke accepted the ban on the use of force, although it was not easy for him.[166] Krenz showed significant sensitivity: "This violence hurts me . . . Erich did not understand any of what was happening."[167]

Honecker had always been willing to use force but had become helpless to do so. On that fateful 17 October, when he came to chair the Politbüro meeting, he had received the report from Leipzig that the demonstrations were expanding, that nothing could be done to stop the growth of the New Forum, and more such reports were coming from Dresden, Magdeburg, Halle and Chemnitz, as well as Berlin.

He opened the meeting, " 'Point 1,' but Stoph said, 'Erich, permit me?' 'Yes,' said Honecker. 'I make the motion that Comrade Honecker be relieved of his function as General Secretary, and also Comrades Mittag and Hermann.' Honecker's stone face hid his helplessness." He opened the discussion, desperately wondering who would support him, and discovered that no one would. Even Mittag said he must go. "Honecker leafed through the group like a bankrupt looking for a lottery ticket." Even Hermann thought the change could not wait.

Mielke got nasty and hinted about corruption. When he blamed Honecker for mistakes, Honecker answered that Mielke should not open his mouth so much. Mielke replied that he had materials that would surprise them all.[168] Mielke had a file on Honecker, including material about his arrest and an early sex scandal. Abrasunov said Mielke had spread all sorts of dirt about Honecker in the Andropov period in Moscow.[169]

Honecker in his memoirs put down the MfS: "I put little value on these reports, because everything that was in them could be found in the western media. The MfS reports to Party and State leaders were not so reliable and if one compares the reports to the summer of the previous year, you could see that their character had not changed. Their spying system that they had developed left little impact in their reports. That is a self-glorification, a self-flattery of the MfS to make the statement after the fact that we were warned."[170]

Honecker was suddenly out. Krenz was as quickly in and picked up an idea of Gorbachev, calling it, *"Die Wende."* Longtime "crown prince" Krenz had not been popular, seeming to lack ideas, but no one in the Politbüro was popular. Modrow, SED leader in Dresden, was something of an outsider and the most popular of the established politicians.[171]

Conspirator Schabowski reflected, "We had made a palace revolution without offering a real alternative. . . . We had not quickly and thoroughly enough whittled away from Stalin's methods." This was evident in Krenz's first speech on TV—in the old style. The MfS agreed with the public's disappointment with it.[172]

Loser Mittag thought that these rebels had erred. "Krenz like Honecker lived in his illusions. The rebel tactic was to overwhelm the Central Committee by using the fermenting emotions. They did not want the necessary discussion. Above all, they wanted power." Mittag described the rebels' paniclike activity and reflected, "The biggest mistake in judgment was that socialists in the DDR thought that it could be saved despite the world political constellation."[173]

The SED reaction to the speech: "Krenz said mistakes had been made, and it was because they would not listen to us. There are so many leader-cadre that one had to fear that information would not filter down to the bottom." Some local SED expressed their bitterness: "The local organization is the last to know. The West media predicted it 10 days ago, while we were told there would be no change. The West was right again. There must be spies on the Central Committee. While Honecker was sick, could no one else head the Politbüro?"[174]

The MfS guides for change were Gorbachev, Rosa Luxemburg and Markus Wolf. "There is some optimism among the progressives because Honecker stepped down, some skepticism about Krenz, who is thought transitory. The hope keeps returning that stagnation had passed and that the passing of Mittag would end his dogmatic style. There is still a wide skepticism that anything will change."[175]

Mielke reported on 19 October that the situation was under control but then described many problems. "Mittag and Hermann are out, which is fine, but an explanation was needed. . . . The BRD gives quicker and fuller news about the Politbüro than does the DDR." The worry: "There are many meetings and some attacks on officials." The counterattack was restricted: "There is a SED determination to fight, but the stores are closing from lack of help and medical personnel are lacking. . . . We lack transport, so Dresden is 2–5 days behind in its food supply. We will likely close clinics because of a personnel shortage. Gas stations are closing."

Poles were adding to the anarchy: "Their coming to Berlin created problems. They actually stormed the train; 3,000 for 1,000 seats and there are often fights; with 2,500 on the train to Crakow, they had 20,000 pieces of luggage from our stores. They call our officials Nazis and fascists, so proper pass control is impossible."[176]

Visiting BRD politicians were also put down: "They were absolutely at a loss. They were surprised and shocked at the development, showing incredible arrogance and ignorance of the situation in the DDR."[177]

On 21 October, Mielke said force could be used only if people and objects were in immediate danger, "although actually the demonstrators deserve it."[178] He brought in 74 of his generals to tell them that without the Soviet Union there would be no DDR. He also warned them that they could not go against the Soviet wishes and save the DDR with force.

Instead, his Chekist solution was to infiltrate the opposition, but he did not know how. "There must be new ideas on how we can infiltrate with our operative forces the new groups and enlighten them so thoroughly that we can retain control over them. We can take advantage of the fact that they welcome anyone and are not conspiratorial."[179] He meant that they were naive, but an invasion required time, and the groups were multiplying over the landscape.

From 16 to 22 October the MfS counted 140,000 participants in demonstrations, and its IMs reported that the dissidents would keep their actions going. On 23 October, the churches in Berlin and Potsdam had to repeat the service up to five times. "The church is openly supporting the anti-socialists, no longer camouflaging it. These appear more confident in the public and plan to infiltrate the union and CDU/LDP."[180]

Mielke described the effort in the CDU to get rid of the old Götting. "His leadership style is rejected, as is his opposition to any reform. Massive pressure comes from regional leaders. . . . Twelve members are coming 1 November to demand his retirement. If he refuses, these people plan to expose him, so that he would resign." Sadly: "Götting expresses a helplessness toward the many demands."[181]

The dissidents had more linkage with these allied parties than had the SED. "The CDU/LDP think they should join with the New Forum or distance themselves from the SED. The New Forum is not only in universities but also in the factories, although recruits are primarily from the Intelligentsia. They are active in every county."[182]

Yet scholar Mayer concluded that university and older high school students played a sad role in the revolution. Anxious about their careers, most joined only when their reputations would not suffer. "This was probably the first revolution in which the universities—professors and students— stood on the side of the old regime."[183] As partial explanation, being a student had required years of swearing loyalty and chanting that the Party was always right.

The bureaucracy was avoiding confrontations: "The willingness of officials to position themselves against the New Forum is limited." Religion was interfering: "The percentage of those who reject political activity for religious reasons and take no position for or against is still relatively high in rural areas, but in general clearly less supportive than in the confrontations in the past. We are not able to discipline them."

Even the favored elite could not be counted on. "The Intelligentsia want complete equality among the parties. It is incredible how many functionaries suddenly have swung around and say they 'have always fought for the truth.' They turn with the wind to keep their privileges." The usual targets, Hager and Tisch, were attacked, then Stoph; a strike was threatened if Tisch were not out. "Particularly workers in Chemnitz, Erfurt, Rostock and Gera criticize in a massive form the leaders, who do not answer their questions. Excited discussions occurred in the large firms in Chemnitz, whether their managers have understood the demands of the General Secretary. Everyone is still doing the old trot, and no one talks to the workers. One should either fire them or punish them."

Not considering itself among the elite, the MfS was also attacking Party privilege: "Foreign exchange is wasted on western autos for the privileged. They spend large sums for their houses and vacation homes in new locations, then keep people out, their special lands for hunting and the rest. They entertain for free in hotels. DDR citizens could use that money to travel."

Still more system defenders were disillusioned and saw themselves as vulnerable. "The police are upset that the media ignore their problems. They are made the bogeymen. In dealing with the provocations, they must not lose control. They are disillusioned with the Party and state leaders, because they are taking the hit. They would like to ignore future negative confrontation in order to avoid the eventual trouble. They would like to go to their jobs in civilian clothing."[184]

The MfS itself was also troubled that it had become the target of demonstrations. "There are direct attacks on MfS and their families by asocial and criminal elements among the demonstrators. A continued escalation is to be expected, so I order an increase in security."

But the MfS must remain on the defensive. "If they march past our offices, use defensive action according to Article 8, including technical barriers. These are to be used against demonstrators only when there is an immediate danger to persons or our property, and one can not stop it otherwise. The primary goal is to prevent any forcible entry into our offices. That must be done *without* using guns, unless impossible to avoid. Use well-placed IMs. Be prepared for fire. Use clubs defensively, use megaphones, optical and acoustical gathering of evidence." Also strengthen the staff's resolve: "Work to increase the political-ideological preparedness." He attached the Krenz amnesty, of 27 October, for all those arrested in demonstrations, except those who used or encouraged force, endangered health or carried weapons.[185]

Other elements of the DDR were unable to adjust. "The head of the DDR Planning Commission has no concept on how to create a balancing plan. In foreign trade there is no idea on how to solve the problem."[186] Alfred Kleine's report on 27 October said that it would take 500 billion marks in investments to bring the obsolete economy up to Western standards. This equaled two years' national income; the microelectronic level was far behind that in the rest of the world and had impossible costs. "We all know that the workers are increasingly impatient and, in part are absolutely demanding an end to the years-old problems and crippling conditions in the production process and are increasingly open to the arguments of the New Forum and other groups, like the Evangelical Church."[187]

Mielke conceded the enemy's newfound strength: "Without exception, in all realms of society, the New Forum has real power." And organization:

"With so many marches, some youth plus alcohol create a problem, so the organizers have provided their own forces to maintain order." Bohley was also insisting on restraint: "Stay within the constitution." She was reported thinking that the New Forum could disband after The Change, and parties could take over.[188]

On 31 October the MfS admitted a failure, even of its cherished Chekist methods: "Generally there should be no illusions about the effectiveness of infiltration of IMs into the anti-socialist groups. Already the experience of using IMs to fight underground political activity has shown positively that such activities can not be effectively fought or prevented by the means and forces of the MfS."

The MfS would have to break the law to fight political resistance, which it must not do. "The treason of such IMs, or their being uncovered, has a serious political-negative effect in the national and the international arena, as well as a massive discrediting of the MfS that it initiated, organized and guided such an operation."

Central control must be improved and be legal: "Because of the indicated consequences, it should be *fundamentally* voted on and sanctioned at the highest level. They should never involve violence or terror or its provocation. . . . It should not be directed at their top level and involve no violations of the constitution."

The IMs must be better screened and instructed: "One has to consider the IMs' professional and societal position. It should include their participation in meetings and demonstrations, but not their being in the foreground or appearing so publicly, not being the leader, or giving interviews to the West media, or do anything illegal or provoke such action or initiate written materials."[189]

Schalck-Golodowski thought that the true *Wende* occurred in a phone call from Kohl to Krenz on 26 October, with Kohl making clear that there must be easier travel, a release of political prisoners and a positive solution to the embassy occupants. "Then we should cooperate where we can and respect each other so we can work together. That same day we made the catalog of changes."[190]

At the end of October, Krenz gave the Central Committee its most honest report, admitting the disaster of the unpayable foreign debt: "Even when all measures of high priority and quality are implemented, the necessary export surplus to the NSW can not be foreseen. In 1985, with the greatest of effort, it would have been possible. Today this chance does not exist. Just stopping an increase in the debt would mean in 1990 a sinking of the living standards by 25–30 percent and that would make the DDR ungovernable. Even if the people were willing, the necessary export goods could not be produced in the necessary amount." Therefore, the DDR must cooperate with the BRD and capitalistic countries.[191]

November

Krenz must also cooperate with the Communist world, so on 1 November he went to get Moscow's blessing. The minutes of the conference with Gorbachev describe a very human conversation in which Gorbachev commented about his famous statement that the time for changing dare not be ignored; he had spoken about himself. He added that a dialogue with society was essential. One must not fear the people. Krenz responded that the DDR media had created a fantasy world, which the people knew to be false. The loss of trust between Party and people was the worst thing that could happen.

Krenz told him that when he returned from China, he was determined to negotiate and not use force. He and Stoph had wanted to have a discussion of the actual problems, but Honecker rejected a watered-down draft. Yesterday he had given the first honest report about the economy to the Politbüro. Gorbachev remembered a similar experience; his boss, Andropov, had asked him to find out the real economic situation, which he learned, but the truth was withheld from the public.

Gorbachev said the DDR's problem was well known in the USSR. He had tried to talk of it with Honecker but had been brusquely rebuffed. He thought that the DDR could have accomplished the requisite reforms in 1986. Krenz explained that Honecker had lost his sense of reality and relied only on Mittag.[192]

Krenz continued that he had come to understand in yesterday's Politbüro meeting how the effort to keep unity could be an impediment because problems were not openly discussed. Instead, the many studies of scientists had been dumped into filing drawers. Just paying the interest on the external debts would take 62 percent of DDR exports. Gorbachev was surprised at how precarious the situation was. Krenz hoped for cheaper raw materials, but Gorbachev explained his problem that regions of the USSR wanted to get a bigger piece of their production.

Krenz told Gorbachev that if the masses tried to break through, that would compel the troops to shoot.[193] With an implicit note of this impending doom, Mielke wrote all units on 2 November: "All MfS must be informed of this communication. Beloved Comrades, a personal note of thanks to all of you. The situation is very serious. I have complete confidence in you that you will continue to do your duty in this great test, as we as Chekists have always done."[194]

A Chekist move to adjust is evident on 4 November as Irmler sent new rules for the dialogues now permitted. The local MfS should send its best informed; dialogues should occur with only other Party and state officials present. "Don't accept New Forum, or other anti-socialist invitations." To prepare local units for dialogues, he sent questions and prescribed answers, which went on unpersuasively for 30 pages.

Already came the effort to justify the MfS in history: "The MfS always made the effort to inform the Party and State leadership. It also made suggestions on how to avoid the dangers, and to improve economic and health conditions. It also reported the people's dissatisfaction, but obviously it had not been taken seriously enough." Then the admission of an internal MfS degradation: "We must admit that the total societal climate of giving reports had an impact on the MfS. The bitter truth is that the development could not be stopped in time. The MfS principle was not to wait until the constitution-hostile goals had been realized or crimes had been committed. The aim was not to arrest people but to prevent crimes."

The further admission was that the MfS had gone beyond the customary duty of security by assisting the economy, but also within the law: "The MfS helped the Plan by sending people to work in the firms, whereby millions of marks in production were added. Spying was conducted but it was justified. The law was followed in interrogation, with a professional ethic and personal decency acting as restraint." Mielke quoted his beloved Dzerzinsky on proper ethics: "A Chekist must be a human with a cool head, hot heart and clean hands."

Irmler claimed that there had been no MfS compulsory measures or abuses or privileges. "The MfS have had no privileges except to sacrifice life and health for society. They have earned no more than a skilled worker or the average of those with college training and they had no year's end bonus. No special store, we had one once, which 99 percent could not use."[195] (in Berlin for the elite).

As the Revolution Came

From 30 October to 4 November, the MfS counted 230 political meetings in churches involving nearly 300,000 persons, strongest in Gera, Chemnitz and Erfurt. Demonstrators tripled to over 1.35 million in 310 demonstrations; the previous week the participants had been 540,000 in 145 demonstrations. "They now follow the Leipzig model, but with more children, signs and chanters. More skinheads are appearing." There were frequent threats of violence against the Stasi offices. In Halle the SED district headquarters was surrounded but the demonstrators prevented young men from breaking in.

In Berlin the Gethsemane Church group was acting as a coordinator.[196] On 4 November, organizing 26 famous speakers for a mass audience, another SED effort to find consensus resulted in failure. "From their goal to regain the political offensive, the SED was farther than ever."[197]

On 5 November, in a sort of battle report, Jena mobilized 40,000, Rostock 30,000 and Potsdam 20,000. The New Forum was the most significant force behind them, and the MfS conceded that it was finding a broad agreement to their arguments. Targets were consistently SED and MfS headquarters. Almost always they marched past the MfS office and left candles with hostile comments. Some activity was taking place in villages, like Kalbe and Christinendorf. The defense commands were calling up reserves, which were sometimes instructed in possible repression measures.[198]

On 7 November Mittig sent a plan to Schwanitz to pick out the best of the IMs and have them ready for action of two kinds, legal and illegal. IM Günter Hartmann was made leader of the NDPD on 7 November, but he suggested a confederation with the BRD. Three assistants to LDP leader Gerlach had MfS connections.[199] The quick collapse was in part a result of the fact that when the local units were set free to act on their own, their members reacted differently.[200]

Mittig sent Krenz a top secret report describing many dialogues involving state and Party leaders, the highest numbers in Potsdam with 7,000 demonstrators. In Fürstenwalde the mayor's secretary accused the mayor of vote fraud, and the mayor resigned. The mayor of Grünheide offered to resign after his secretary proved election fraud.[201]

The "Friendly" parties were pleased that the SED promised them a greater voice. In return, LDP's Gerlach said that he would question the nature of the government but not socialism. On 3 November, the CDU *Volkskammer* group took a "very aggressive" position,[202] while the CDU applied to cancel the ministerial order of 21 September banning the New Forum. "Its growth was especially in the working class, sometimes entire work collectives go to their meetings. There are cases of worker resistance to the ban on New Forum activity in firms, even a strike of 50 workers to get them permitted."

New Forum recognition, pushed by Gysi, was expected on 8 November; its leaders were planning to use the decision for peace demonstrations. "In contrast is the frequent speechlessness of Party and state functionaries, which is also true in the firms."

IM insiders reported: "New Forum leaders have different views on tactics; some are hesitant to create a power vacuum by challenging the SED's leading role, which is practically gone." In addition, "The acceptance of the constitution is only a New Forum tactic in order to be legalized. The SED policy of 'Change' is distrusted by the New Forum, which has no concrete plans for the economy. They would join in the government because the parties would have the means to effect New Forum policies. The LDP has already met with them. The New Forum idea is that the various parties should not unite now, since there is a certain pluralism, but unite to have elections."

Mielke warned Irmler of impending doom: "This is a very severe tension. The wave of those fleeing has made the citizens very uneasy. The Forums are hostile and filled with hate. Increasingly local leaders say, 'We are not able to deal with the present problems, and are leaving the Party.' The Krenz speech has not reduced the tension. The general view is that the SED has found no concept. The workers are critical of intellectuals who criticize the privileged, but themselves have privileges, particularly the artists. The fear is that with production problems already so severe, a strike would be disastrous. The unions are not united."

The MfS made it unanimous that the Central Committee must change: "The people want the Central Committee's 10th meeting to accept the responsibility for the mistakes and to clean things up quickly. The Central Committee should finally listen to the workers."

The newspapers were out of control. "Many editorials are not following the Party line. The New Forum is getting the support of Friendly parties and not a few SED. It is clear that in the SED there is also heavy pressure for change." Attached to this analysis a handwritten note said sadly, "Overtaken by events."[203]

Süss found it noteworthy that in these weeks he found no documentary evidence of aggressive feelings toward the democratic movement, when but a few weeks before their list of those to be arrested had been updated. MfS feelings of anger were directed only against its own leaders.[204]

The Secret Police was admitting a defeat and blaming the Party, from top to bottom, as unable to confront the people: "The leaders are bereft of strategy and ideas. The Change has had no noticeable practical effect at the ground level, with the middle and local functionaries. It has not been implemented, rather it has been blocked. Everywhere the local SED leaders do not meet with the workers, instead they go on as before. They avoid the public and haven't been seen in the workplaces for weeks. They still talk over the heads of the people. It is their powerlessness, helplessness, incompetence."

The MfS had decided that since the people undeniably supported the New Forum, the Politbüro should accept it. "The progressive forces say these leaders are not willing to change, so the Intelligentsia and middle class see the New Forum as the only social force which is really trying for reform and change. The people do not think of it as being anti-socialist. Because of its resonance with the people, a permission to the New Forum is necessary immediately." The masses knew too much: "People are bombarded by a multitude of media, which makes them react emotionally and this creates disorder."

The MfS was taking a hit from the people and was hitting back at the Party. "Our feeling is that the MfS is being sacrificed and being made responsible. The Party leadership has finally lost the trust of the people. Krenz's major mistake was not to go after the economic problems, although he was given the necessary information to do it. The question is did the old advisers prevent it, those persons who have hidden the problem for years? The precarious financial situation must be addressed, otherwise promises will be empty. The danger is that the comrade leaders have the illusion that imports will save the situation."

The MfS was demanding change from top to bottom. "The old dishonest work style still rules. The Central Committee still has not called in the finance experts to discuss how to get foreign exchange for travel or for Christmas." The New Forum could scarcely be more bitterly critical than these internal reports by loyal Party members in the Stasi.

More such MfS attacks on the system continued by reference to the true socialists: "The progressive forces say that functionaries have forgotten how to talk like workers. They fear for their privileges and getting questions they can't answer. The cadre must be changed. If we stay on the defensive, the Change will be determined by events on the street. All classes believe that with more demonstrations, concrete changes are possible. The necessary preparedness for participating in such demonstrations exists among a broad base of the population. The SED must no longer glorify itself. The progressive forces contrast New Forum behavior with the charge that they are enemies of the constitution."[205] These "progressives," who always reflected the MfS beliefs, were showing respect for the New Forum rather than the SED!

On 6 November Bonn tightened the screws. Finance Minister Schäuble told Seiters that financial help came only with the DDR permission to oppositional groups and the promise of free elections; the SED must give up the #1 position as in the constitution. "Because I needed a credit of 10 billion marks, our internal affairs had become a German matter."[206]

Mielke reported the growing pressures to Krenz on 7 November: "There is increasing popular participation: 100 important dialogue and protest gatherings, with more than 750,000 persons taking part. The signs of rejecting further dialogue are increasing, above all in Leipzig with 200,000, Chemnitz with 100,000, Dresden and Halle with 80,000, Magdeburg and Cottbus with 32,000. In broad circles of the population of the Halle and Schwerin districts, the expectation is that the government and the Politbüro will all resign."[207]

There was still another urge for rapid change: "The demands carry an increasingly radical and ultimatum character." The public wanted new Party and state leaders.[208] It is remarkable that Mielke's MfS stated such demands objectively, with no defense of his SED and its government.

On 8 November the MfS reported fewer demonstrators, but they were chanting against SED and Stasi and for free elections. In numerous gatherings the appearance of "positive forces" was hindered by whistles and shouting. They almost always marched from the church to SED headquarters, passing by the MfS.

In Jena, the council secretary called for a new Communist Party. "The SED had failed and lost the right to lead."[209] The other parties were planning on no longer running as a block and forming a new government.[210]

Demonstrators were in all counties, but increasingly in smaller towns: Wismar had the most with 50,000, Nordhausen, 25,000, Meiningen

20,000 and Weimar 20,000. "The demonstrators were just as aggressive; 2,500 in Berlin protested the election fraud, showing a strongly hostile-negative character. A few broke through the security lines around the State Council." They rejected the new travel rules and election law and were demanding the resignation of the government.

The New Forum was making big plans for a nationwide organizational meeting in Potsdam on 30 November. They were also planning an East European conference with Poles, Russians and Romanians.[211]

When Krenz called for the Central Committee's 10th meeting, he proposed a new Politbüro, but unlike Honecker in 1971, he had no new concept prepared, and one could not be pulled out of the drawer.[212] Markus Wolf and 200 "Perestroikisten" brought a letter of protest; 21 committee members resigned. Modrow entered the Politbüro, weakening Krenz's position.[213]

The reaction among SED functionaries was that the Politbüro resignations were long overdue and an urgent necessity. In Dresden, "Many in all organizations were quite angry about the incompetence and politically false decisions of the district leaders, and the inability of Böhme to conduct a dialogue and his lack of willingness to change with the policy. It was said that the Party leaders had absolutely no political vision. Therefore the SED had lost the confidence of the workers. Numerous members in the factories in the area have already quit the Party."[214] SED leadership instructed locals to pretend to deviate from central policy in order to regain the people's trust.[215]

On 9 November a Mielke assistant, presumably Schwanitz, wrote a remarkable position paper for making the DDR democratic, beginning with the MfS. "Markus Wolf must not be left longer alone in his public defense of the MfS. . . . The Minister [Mielke] should publicly accept the responsibility and *bring to the fore that also in the MfS there has long been a Resistance* to being the implementer of the Politbüro's will. This would be useful for all those who have something very difficult in front of them. The MfS should hold responsible all those who do not have clean hands. Any privileges should be gotten rid of. Everyone should be equal before the law. The MfS must be free from the Politbüro. . . . The sale of prisoners to the BRD must stop immediately."

He admitted that the MfS had been forced into improper and troubling attitudes and behavior: "Following orders as well as following the law has brought many colleagues into a deep conflict. . . . The feeling that one was powerless to bring a basic change had led to a change in [MfS] personality, including the appearance and behavior of resignation, passivity, bitterness and isolation, to a lack of orientation and sense of direction."

The MfS insisted that the SED had declared the task to fight class enemies. "The constant adjuration to be class-conscious because of the allegedly ever greater attack by the enemy, that 'the counter revolution had raised its head,' created a permanent and deep distrust of the workers against the MfS, as well as a greater pressure of punishment against the people. There was the combination of arrogance, insolence, incompetence and compulsion. Anyone criticizing was attacked with unjustified Party-indoctrinating measures."

Admittedly, this authoritarian system had crippled MfS initiative. "The local organizations increasingly lost their activity and creativity. The recognized contradictions between the judgments of the local leaders and that of the Minister were not sufficiently addressed." The MfS was thus forced into a policy of repression. "There was a disciplining instead of a continuing confrontation of ideas. This made a change in the local organization inevitable. There should now be a gathering of local leaders." The MfS was blaming the lack of democracy!

In this remarkable statement the MfS writer was pushing liberal reforms to save socialism and ended with, "We must *think together* out loud and actively *work together for change.*" In stark contrast, the Schwanitz speech to the Collegium on 15 November was mostly nuts and bolts, nothing of this idealism.[216]

A troubled report from the Rostock MfS in conflict: "Although our heart is bleeding and our finger itches, it is not possible that we use our weapons, because if we shoot, we would be destroying the present development."[217]

In Potsdam, Dresden and Rostock demonstrators demanded the resignation of their county SED leaders; in Weissenfels, three youths raised a flag over the county SED that said, "You are guilty." There were increasing resignations from the SED. By IM report, "The dissident groups are planning a declaration for a democratic reconstruction. . . . There is also a small party convention of the reform CDU to get the resignation of its secretariat and presidium." Right-wing *Republikaner* were circulating flyers for reunification.[218]

On historic 9 November [abdication of the Kaiser and Declaration of the Republic] the Politbüro debated the failed travel policy, feeling itself forced into some change. A committee presented a very liberal travel proposal, which was quickly approved unanimously in late afternoon. The economic problems seemed so serious that there were no questions asked about this less important matter of opening the Wall.

Krenz gave a small piece of paper to a tired Schabowski, who at the end of a hectic press conference neglected to read the time on the paper. When asked by reporters when it would begin, Schabowski hesitated and then said, "Immediately." (Krenz later said it was supposed to be the next morning.)[219]

No one was quite sure what Schabowski meant but thousands gathered at the Wall.[220] As Hertle explained its opening, Army Lieutenant General Wagner tried to find out what the policy was. Getting no clear answer, he permitted the exit, not from central policy but from the pressure of the masses. He knew at the time that this act meant the fall of the DDR. Those controlling the openings had lost control "and in contrast to their superiors had enough sense to understand the situation and let everyone back in."[221]

Modrow said later, "It was clear to all of us that something had happened that was actually not intended. We speculated how the mishap could have happened." Krenz at the time wondered aloud who had let it happen. Later he said he had deliberately opened it.[222]

Thus, on the anniversary of the Revolution in 1918, the SED stumbled into the revolutionary breaching of their wall. Berliners streamed through, and by morning the tide of people was overwhelming, never to be reversed. "The real loss of will to rule came only after opening of the Wall."[223]

Kotschenmassov called Krenz that Moscow was uneasy about the situation at the Wall. Krenz answered that the DDR's foreign minister had cleared it in Moscow. Kotschemassov agreed but said that what happened in Berlin itself concerned the Allies. Krenz answered that only military measures could have prevented opening the border in Berlin and that would have meant a terrible bloodbath. Kotschemassov was silent a moment and then said, "You're right. That's the way I see it too." He called back soon with a personal message from Gorbachev, who wished us well, "with our courageous step to open the Wall."[224]

The entire world soon gaped at the famed "Wall of Shame" being used as a dance floor by ecstatic youth. The genie of revolution was out of the bottle and could not be forced back in by the Secret Police.

The irony is that what the world celebrated as a victory of liberty, DDR dissidents thought was more like a disaster. One wrote: "I was sick for three days, lying down with a terrible headache and I couldn't be glad. I took it as an outrageous betrayal *(Beschiss)*."[225]

NOTES

1. Sch, 6a, 1.9.9, pp. 151–58.
2. Sch, AKG, 46b, 2.9.9, pp. 101–2.
3. Ibid., 5.9.9, p. 112.
4. Sch, AKG, Sternberg, 4501, 12.9.9, p. 7.
5. Sch, 5a, Bützow, 4.9.9, pp. 30–33.
6. Ibid., 15.9.9, p. 102.
7. Sch, 6c, 18.9.9, pp. 108–18.
8. Sch, 5a, 18.9.9, pp. 295–300.
9. Ibid., 29.9.9, p. 40.
10. Sch, 49b, 11.9.9, pp. 63–67.
11. Sch, DOSA, 401222, pp. 4–8.
12. Sch, 4c, 3.10.9, p. 172.
13. Ibid., 29.9.9, pp. 132, 143, 149.
14. Sch, DOSA, 401048, pp. 2–11.
15. Sch, AKG, 46b, 5.10.9, pp. 124–30.

16. Sch, KD, AKG Sternberg, 4490, 1.10.9.
17. Sch, 29a, p. 16.
18. Sch, 24c, 2.10.9, p. 24.
19. Sch, 29a, 3.10.9, pp. 2–3.
20. Sch, DOSA, 401221, 2.10.9.
21. Sch, 6a, 10.10.9, pp. 168–89.
22. Sch, 4c, 3.10.9, p. 162.
23. Sch, 6c, 10.10.9, pp. 137, 142, 148–49.
24. Sch, 4c, 3.10.9, p. 165.
25. Sch, 24c, 4.10.9, pp. 8–11.
26. Sch, 29a, 6.10.9, p. 7.
27. Sch, 30, 4.10.9, p. 40.
28. Sch, 5a, 7.10.9, pp. 43–49.
29. Sch, 29a, 7.10.9, p. 19.
30. Ibid., 9.10.9, pp. 33, 38.
31. Ibid., 5.10.9, pp. 13–16.
32. Sch, 5a, 9.10.9, p. 51.
33. Sch, KD, AKG Sternberg, 4499, 9.10.9, p. 42.
34. Sch, 29a, 10.10.9, pp. 40–45.
35. Ibid., pp. 66–70.
36. Sch, AKG Sternberg, 10.10.9, pp. 39–40, 42–43.
37. Sch, 30, 10.10.9, p. 40.
38. Sch, 6c, 10.10.9, pp. 137, 142, 148–49.
39. Sch, AKG, 46b, 11.10.9, p. 132.
40. Sch, 6a, p. 166.
41. Sch, 6c, 12.10.9, pp. 156, 163–64.
42. Sch, 29a, 12.10.9, p. 12.
43. Sch, AKG Sternberg 4500, 12.10.9, p. 38.
44. Sch, 29a, 13.10.9, pp. 77–90.
45. Ibid., p. 102.
46. Sch, AKG Sternberg, 4493, pp. 38, 38a.
47. Sch, 29b, 16.10.9, pp. 33–35.
48. Sch, 29b, 15.10.9, pp. 1–6.
49. Ibid., 16.10.9, p. 22.
50. Ibid., pp. 22–28.
51. Ibid., 17.10.9, pp. 31–32.
52. Sch, KD, Parchim, 5229, 19.10.9, p. 15.
53. Sch, 29b, 18.10.9, pp. 40–41.
54. Sch, AKG, 48, Leiter 2a, 20.10.9, p. 4.
55. Ibid., Sternberg, 4493, 23.10.9, p. 29.
56. Sch, 6a, 19.10.9, pp. 172–76.
57. Sch, 6c, 19.10.9, pp. 171, 176.
58. Sch, 5a, 19.10.9, pp. 308–9.
59. Ibid., 19.10.9, p. 57.
60. Sch, 29a, 20.10.9, pp. 26–30.
61. Sch, AKG, 48, Leiter 2a, 20.10.9, p. 10.
62. Sch, 30, 23.10.9, pp. 1–7.
63. Sch, 6a, Parchim, 24.10.9, pp. 179–83.

64. Kai Langer, *"Ihr soll wissen, dass der Norden nicht schläft"*: *Zur Geschichte der "Wende" in den drei Nordbezirken der DOR* (Bremen: Temmen, 1999), p. 268.

65. Sch, 6a, Parchim, 24.10.9, pp. 179–83.

66. Sch, 5a, 27.10.9, p. 64.

67. Sch, KD, AKG Sternberg, 25.10.9, pp. 23–28.

68. Sch, AKG, 46b, 21.10.9, p. 187.

69. Sch, 5a, 27.10.9, p. 64.

70. Sch, AKG Sternberg, 4493, 27.10.9, p. 25.

71. Langer, *"Ihr soll wissen,"* p. 183.

72. Sch, 6c, 185, 27.10.9, pp. 186–90.

73. Sch, AKG Sternberg, 30.10.9, pp. 18–21.

74. Sch, KD, AKG Sternberg, 4493, 31.10.9 & 1.11.9, p. 20.

75. Walter Süss, *Staatssicherheit am Ende* (Berlin: Links, 1999), p. 367.

76. Sch, KD, AKG Sternberg, 4493, 1.11.9, p. 16.

77. Ibid., 4499, 2.11.9, pp. 2–3, 12–15.

78. Ibid., 4493, 7.11.9, p. 3.

79. Sch, 49a, 3–5.11.9 Bützow, p. 89.

80. Sch, 6c, 7.11.9, pp. 200–208.

81. Sch, AKG Sternberg, 4491, 7.11.9, p. 1.

82. Ibid., 4493 8.11.9, p. 12.

83. SAPMO, DY/30 IV 2/2.039, 317, Schwerin BL, 29.11.9, p. 194.

84. Sch, 5a, 10.11.9, pp. 321–25.

85. ZAIG, 14331, 25.11.9, p. 107.

86. Sch, KD, AKG Sternberg, 4493, 15.11.9, pp. 4–5, 9.

87. Langer, *"Ihr soll wissen,"* p. 271.

88. SAPMO, DY/30 IV 2/2.039, 317, 20.11.9, p. 99.

89. ZAIG, 2326, pp. 103–4.

90. ZAIG, 1992, pp. 69–73.

91. ZAIG, 2240, p. 147.

92. Langer, *"Ihr soll wissen,"* p. 196.

93. David Gill and Ulrich Schröter, *Das Ministerium für Staatssicherheit* (Berlin: Rowohlt, 1991), pp. 79, 91–92.

94. ZAIG, 14428, pp. 5, 9, 33–38.

95. Konrad Jarausch, *The Rush to German Unity* (Oxford: Oxford University Press, 1994), pp. 100–101; Hans-Hermann Hertle, *Der Fall der Mauer* (Opladen: Westdeutscher, 1996), p. 344.

96. ZAIG, 5475, 11.9.9, p. 4.

97. ZAIG, 5351, 13.9.9, pp. 7–22.

98. Ibid., pp. 1–5.

99. ZAIG, 14332, p. 9.

100. Reinhard Meinel, *Mit Tschekistischem Gruss: Berichte der Bezirksverwaltung für Staatsscherheit Potsdam 1989* (Potsdam: Babelturm, 1990), p. 133.

101. Ibid., pp. 135–36.

102. ZAIG, 3576, pp. 83, 94–98.

103. Christian Joppke, *East German Dissidents and the Revolution of 1989* (New York: New York University Press, 1995), pp. 141–43.

104. ZAIG, 3576, pp. 94–98; John Torpey; *Intellectuals, Socialism and Dissent* (Minneapolis: University of Minnesota Press, 1995), p. 139.

105. Joppke, *East German Dissidents*, pp. 144–53.

106. ZAIG, 14435, pp. 47, 52.

107. Walter Süss, *Staatssicherheit an Ende* (Berlin: Links, 1999), p. 303.

108. ZAIG, 3576, p. 130.

109. ZAIG, 14435, pp. 47, 52.

110. Armin Mitter and Stefan Wolle, *Untergang auf Raten* (München: Bertelsmann, 1993), p. 509.

111. ZAIG, 5351, 22.9.9, p. 25.

112. ZAIG, 7314, 27.9.9, p. 15.

113. ZAIG, 3576, 29.9.9, pp. 124–25.

114. ZAIG, 14327, 22.9.9, p. 5.

115. Stefan Wolle, *Die heile Welt der Dikatur: Alltag und Herrschaft in der DDR, 1971–1989* (Bonn: Bundeszentrale für politische Bildung, 1998), p. 317.

116. ZAIG, 13740, pp. 11–14.

117. ZAIG, 3576, pp. 99–102.

118. Manfred Schell and Werner Kalinka, *Stasi und kein Ende* (Frankfurt: Ullstein, 1991), p. 75.

119. Siegfried Suckut and Walter Süss, *Staatspartei und Staatssicherheit* (Berlin: Links, 1997), pp. 256–58.

120. Ibid., pp. 262–65.

121. Ibid., p. 251.

122. Ibid., p. 263.

123. Ibid., p. 268.

124. Wjatscheslaw Daschitschew, "Sowjetische Deutschlandpolitik in der achtziger Jahren," *Deutschland Archiv*, January 1995, pp. 58, 62.

125. Hertle, *Der Fall der Mauer*, 1996, p. 70; John O. Koehler, *Stasi: The Untold Story of the East German Secret Police* (Boulder, CO: Westview Press, 1999), p. 405. Colonel Wiegand sent Gorbachev a secret warning about the conditions in Germany.

126. Günter Schabowski, *Der Absturz* (Berlin: Rowohlt, 1992), pp. 214–18, 241–42.

127. SAPMO, DY30, IV 2/2.035 Büro Axen, 60, stenog. minutes, 7.10.9, pp. 225, 229.

128. Wjatschslaw Kotschenmassow, *Meine letzte Mission* (Berlin: Dietz, 1994), p. 110.

129. Schabowski, *Der Absturz*, p. 180.

130. Michail Gorbatchow, *Wie es war: Die deutsche Wiedervereinigung* (Berlin: Ullstein, 1999), p. 86.

131. SAPMO, DY30, IV 2/2.035 Büro Axen, pp. 60, 252.

132. Josef Schwarz, *Bis zum bitteren Ende: 35 Jahre Dienste des Ministeriums für Staatssicherheit* (Schkeuditz: GNN, 1994), p. 19.

133. ZAIG, 8680, 3.10.9, pp. 4–16.

134. ZAIG, 14336, pp. 11–24.

135. ZAIG, 1072, 9.10.9, pp. 287–96.

136. *Ausgedient, Ein Stasi Major erzählt* (Halle: Mitteldeutsch, 1990), pp. 91–92.

137. Joppke, *East German Dissidents*, pp. 144–53.

138. SAPMO, DY/30 IV 2/2.039, 317, p. 33.

139. Gerd-Rüdiger Stephan, *"Vorwärts immer, rückwärts nimmer": Interne Dokumente zum Zerfall von SED und DDR 1988/89* (Berlin: Dietz, 1994), p. 16; Elizabeth Pond, *Beyond the Wall* (Washington, DC: Brookings Institution, 1993), pp. 112–13.

140. Walter Süss, "Die Demonstration am 4. November, 1989, ein Unternehmen von Stasi und SED?" *Deutschland Archiv*, December 1995, p. 124.

141. Joppke, *East German Dissidents*, pp. 151–53.

142. ZAIG, 5351, 8.10.9, pp. 55–58.

143. ZAIG, 14326, 9.10.9, p. 18.

144. Helmut Zwahr, *Ende einer Selbstzerstörung: Leipzig und die Revolution in der DDR* (Göttingen: Vandenhoeck & Ruprecht, 1993), p. 211.

145. Karl-Dieter Opp and Peter Voß, *Die volkseigene Revolution* (Stuttgart: Klett-Cotta, 1993), pp. 136, 215.

146. Manfred Uschner, *Die zweite Etage* (Berlin: Dietz, 1993), p. 256.

147. ZAIG, 15092, 12.10.9.

148. Hertle, *Der Fall der Mauer*, pp. 81–85.

149. ZAIG, 14409.

150. ZAIG, 4885, pp. 11–14.

151. Ibid., pp. 27, 43, 48, 59–61.

152. Wolfgang Rüddenklau, *Störenfried: DDR Opposition, 1986–89* (Berlin: Basis, 1992), p. 363.

153. ZAIG, 7834, 12.10.9, pp. 36–59.

154. ZAIG, 2326, pp. 243–46.

155. ZAIG, 5351, 13.10.9, p. 76.

156. ZAIG, 3750, 13.10.9, pp. 8–12.

157. Meinel, *Mit Tschekistischem Gruss*, pp. 18, 158.

158. ZAIG, 14326, 14.10.9, p. 131.

159. Peter Przybylski, *Tatort Politbüro*, Band II (Berlin: Rowohlt, 1992), pp. 124–29.

160. Uschner, *Die zweite Etage*, p. 255.

161. ZAIG, 14326, 15.10.9, pp. 80–86.

162. ZAIG, 7834, 17.10.9, p. 12.

163. Stephan, *"Vorwärts immer,"* p. 16.

164. Schell, and Kalinka, *Stasi*, pp. 76–77.

165. Ibid., pp. 78–81, 84.

166. Michael Richter, *Die Staatssicherheit im letzen Jahr der DDR* (Weimar: Böhlau, 1996), pp. 32–33.

167. Süss, *Staatssicherheit*, p. 343.

168. Schabowski, *Der Absturz*, pp. 105–6.

169. Richter, *Die Staatssicherheit*, p. 32.

170. Wolfgang-Uwe Friedrich, *Die Totalitäre Herrschaft der SED: Wirklichkeit und Nachwirkungen* (München: Beck, 1998), p. 113.

171. Stephan, *"Vorwarts immer,"* p. 17.

172. Schabowski, *Der Absturz*, pp. 268–74, 312; ZAIG, 15623, p. 12.

173. Günter Mittag, *Um Jeden Preis* (Berlin: Aufbau, 1991), pp. 25, 29, 34.

174. MfS, HA, ASt Potsdam, 19.10.9, p. 11.

175. Meinel, *Mit Tschekistischem Gruss*, pp. 163, 170.

176. ZAIG, 7834, 20.10.9, pp. 25–27, 30.
177. ZAIG, 15623, 25.10.9.
178. Süss, "Die Demonstration," p. 124.
179. Mitter and Wolle, *Untergang*, p. 532.
180. ZAIG, 3576, pp. 145–50.
181. ZAIG, 3750, 26.10.9, pp. 11–12.
182. Meinel, *Mit Tschekistischem Gruss*, pp. 181–84.
183. ZAIG, 14866, HA XVIII, 28.10.9, pp. 1–2.
184. ZAIG, 1072, 30.10.9, pp. 24–34.
185. ZAIG, 13880, 31.10.9, pp. 4–7.
186. ZAIG, 14866, HA XVIII, 28.10.9, pp. 1–2.
187. Uwe Bastian, *Auf zum letzten Gefecht: Vorbereitungen des MfS auf den Zusammenbruch der DDR-Wirtschaft* (Berlin: Forschungsbund, 1994), pp. 4–6.
188. ZAIG, 3576, 30.10.9, pp. 154, 161–64.
189. ZAIG, 13660, pp. 141–48.
190. Alexander Schalck-Golodowski, *Deutsche-Deutsche Erinnerungen* (Hamburg: Rowohlt, 2000), p. 325.
191. SAPMO, Central Commitee, 02–47/89–666; Christa Luft, *Treuhand Report* (Berlin: Aufbau, 1992), pp. 10–13.
192. Uschner, *Die zweite Etage*, pp. 41, 260.
193. SAPMO, DY/30 IV 2/2.039, pp. 72, 130–41.
194. ZAIG, 7947, pp. 2–3.
195. ZAIG, 2289, pp. 59, 124.
196. Sch, 30, 496/89, pp. 10–18.
197. Süss, *Staatssicherheit*, p. 411.
198. ZAIG, 14418, pp. 187–90.
199. Süss, *Staatssicherheit*, pp. 561, 576.
200. Ibid., p. 604.
201. ZAIG, 8266, 6, 6.11.9; ZAIG, 14418, pp. 184–85.
202. ZAIG, 3750, p. 22.
203. ZAIG, 7834, 6.11.9, pp. 2–6.
204. Süss, *Staatssicherheit*, p. 596.
205. ZAIG, 2326, 6.11.9, pp. 23–27, 36–43.
206. Schalck-Golodowski, *Deutsche-Deutsche*, pp. 326–27.
207. ZAIG, 8266, pp. 10–11.
208. ZAIG, 14331, p. 24.
209. Ibid., pp. 121–24.
210. ZAIG, 3750, p. 22.
211. ZAIG, 14418, pp. 4, 179–80.
212. Stephan, *"Vorwärts immer,"* p. 18.
213. Ralf George Reuth and Andreas Böne, *Komplott: Wie es wirklich zur deutschen Einheit kam* (München: Piper, 1993), p. 153.
214. ZAIG, 14331, p. 119.
215. Uschner, *Die zweite Etage*, p. 261.
216. ZAIG, 2386, pp. 28–36, 79.
217. Richter, *Die Staatssicherheit*, p. 35.
218. ZAIG, 14418, pp. 176–77.
219. Uschner, *Die zweite Etage*, p. 260; Schabowski, *Der Absturz*, p. 307.

220. Reuth and Böne, *Komplott*, pp. 155–58.
221. Hertle, *Der Fall der Mauer*, p. 202.
222. Ibid., p. 7.
223. Uschner, *Die zweite Etage*, p. 259.
224. Siegfried Prokop, *Die kurze Zeit der Utopie* (Berlin: Elefanten, 1994), p. 81.
225. Joppke, *East German Dissidents*, p. 158.

Chapter 7

The Shambles Remaining: Winter 1989–1990

On the day after the Wall cracked, Mittig reported to Krenz that demonstrations were occurring in all districts, except Frankfurt, mostly county seats and larger towns, with a few hundred people; exceptions were Erfurt with 45,000, Rostock with 40,000, and Gera with 25,000. "All behaved in a disciplined fashion and without any excesses. There was a general retreat in aggressiveness. There are more dialogues. . . . Gradually a mutual acceptance is growing."[1]

The public's movement had become not so much political as geographical, across the border to see the long-desired goods of the West; 1,277,392 crossed in Berlin, and 1,178,926 came back; elsewhere 399,788 left, and 196,968 returned. The crowds had gone shopping. In almost every district the fear of a fall of DDR currency led to panic buying and the closing of savings accounts.[2]

The storm of the people to the discount "ALDI" food stores was without a doubt the greatest mass movement of the revolution. Bohley's sorrow was evident on 10 November: consumerism was not what she had worked for.[3] She lamented, "The people are crazy and the government has lost its mind." As Ralf Dahrendorf reflected, the Wall was needed to build socialism: "Utopia was of necessity a closed society."[4]

On 13 November at the Central Committee meeting, Krenz said that he had confronted tens of thousands of people showing dissatisfaction and that thousands of Party instructions were no longer viable. The Central Committee discussion showed confusion unto chaos. It called a special SED meeting for 15–17 December to create a new Central Committee.[5] The MfS was among the first DDR casualties.

THE MfS ON THE BRINK

The MfS first showed pleasure that it had stopped the political underground in the workplace. "The political opposition formed itself outside the world of the workers." The big combines had the thickest network of IMs, who could quickly identify any New Forum adherent.

Yet Henke concluded, "The political will to action was missing, to use the [MfS] information to get rid of the hated enemy had external, that is political, causes, and was therewith outside the MfS competence. Because of the hopelessness of their situation, the Party and State leadership had lost the political will to apply force. When the number of the enemies had become so overpowering, that they exceeded the ability of the many spies to register them, the MfS resigned itself simply to counting the numbers of candles put in front of their offices."[6]

A similar weakness existed even within the MfS: "The insecurity in the organization was so widespread that it was unrealistic to attempt to use punishments and sanctions. It was not long before the internal discipline mechanism was completely out of operation."[7]

On 13 November Mielke was called to the *Volkskammer*, where he claimed that MfS was still in control, to which the deputies began to boo and whistle in derision. Mielke was totally unprepared for such behavior. He stuttered and squirmed and finally raised his arms like an evangelist and shouted, "I love every one of you." Even his staunchest supporters burst into derisive laughter. "Mielke was finished."[8] The nation could see its long-feared minister naked.

Two of his department heads, Kleine and Kopprach, described his speech as "a completely unsatisfactory presentation." They insisted that, "Since 1975, our units repeatedly and openly reported the truth. The MfS informed the leaders about the constantly worsening problems in the economy, including the causes, as well as suggestions for preventing further negative developments." The MfS also reported that it had sent constant reports to both the Politbüro and the Council of Ministers. It traced the list of these many papers back to 17 October 1975.[9]

The head of the MfS Political Organization, Felber, wrote the *Volkskammer* president, protesting Mielke's statement of 13 November. His MfS colleagues were angry: "Through his unsatisfactory presentation and self-defense, he gave a false picture of our views and behavior. We say again that we support the Change and Renewal."[10]

In many discussions MfS leaders expressed "a willingness to support the rebuilding of the people's confidence," but they were bothered that Party and state leaders were not coming to defend them. "Instead these leaders are blaming the MfS, which they had so much praised before, creating a great bitterness because the MfS had sacrificed much for the Party."

The MfS was under attack also from below: "MfS personnel are experiencing psycho-terror right outside their offices in many places, mostly Sachsen, particularly the south fringe of the DDR and Erfurt. . . . Demonstrators are chanting attacks on MfS. The nasty phone calls suggest rough characters are harassing our people." In Plauen, artisans, including a plumber, had pledged not to work for either MfS or the police. In Chemnitz, many Party leaders were quitting, "which further lowers morale."[11]

Further bitter MfS discontent was evident at a staff meeting when Raabe said: "The MfS comrades feel themselves lied to and betrayed by the SED. They demand honesty, no matter where they work in the MfS." Wiedeman added, "There have been MfS refusals to defend the Volkskammer." Sprotte said that a false policy had led to the wrong commands: "We have raised the young comrades to be schizophrenic." None of these MfS discussants indicate a support of the SED; rather, they wander off into "What's to become of us?"[12]

As a kind of confessional, MfS delinquents should be punished. The Berlin Party Control Commission reported on a whole series of violations of Party rules. The courts had let themselves be influenced by Mielke and accepted his arguments that punishment would harm the image of the MfS and damage internal security and that one should consider the past services of the delinquent.

Crimes included a female sergeant who deserted and followed a friend West. An agent had stolen 3,000 marks and when brought to court became angry and quit the Party. Of those brought to trial, "They say they were never really convinced of the Party and joined for other reasons." A MfS captain in a barroom brawl, when arrested, abused the police. An officer committed adultery with a subordinate's wife. A captain protested banning *Sputnik* and DDR media policy; he had been too close to the wife of a man who fled and had used "wrong contacts" and alcohol. A lieutenant had nine years of indiscriminate sex, driving around in his car and an illegal taxi; he also committed adultery with a woman who knew he was MfS. A lieutenant had repeatedly driven while drunk. A sergeant married a woman whose parents were in the BRD; he was told that his marriage should end, he promised but then had two more children with her. A handler had an affair with his IM.

Most cases were of young men who appeared unpolitical and showed little reflection of the Change; many still expressed loyalty; if they promised to behave, they were forgiven. Comradess Sarge noted that the organization was going to be reduced anyway, so one should just say that members dismissed had left on their own request.[13]

According to Richter, on 6 November Mielke, knowing the local offices would be closed, had issued an order for document destruction. On 13 November Irmler said to destroy those that had no more operative value, meaning IM reports. Schwanitz refined this on 15 November: "to destroy what is about to be captured." Orders were so vague that anything could have been destroyed. There was an emphasis on the MfS connection to the SED and on the many SED scandals. Much on microfilm was reportedly sent to the KGB in Moscow.[14]

THE MfS BY ANOTHER NAME

When Mielke's deputy, Dr. Schwanitz, replaced him, Schwanitz was under conflicting pressures to change and confront complaints from department chiefs, such as: "The powerlessness must end. We think we have been abandoned. We must create a new Collegium and county leadership. We are for the Change. We put ourselves in the front rank of this battle and most MfS employees agree."[15]

A new generation of MfS leaders proposed to change the law to prevent more abuses, and they quickly went through the many paragraphs of the MfS policy book, dropping some Mielke policies and altering others. Arrest policy should be liberalized. The MfS held 2,347 persons in prison, and 3,485 more were in investigative arrest. "Except for serious cases on the border, all violators are to be released and can leave the DDR if they wish."[16]

Schwanitz's liberal statement of 15 November had its stimulus in a reform proposal just given him by Wolf and on which Schwanitz had made many marks. Wolf had observed that the DDR had adopted an absurd absolutism, with elements like "Byzantine feudalism," in which Mielke had to know everything. Wolf noted the public hatred and suggested bringing in younger agents and rehabilitating innocent victims. Schwanitz picked up on Wolf's ideas, his intent not as rebel but as savior of the DDR.[17]

Wolf argued that repression would lead to more public hatred and the MfS should work no longer against diversion and keep the public informed. Schwanitz could not completely abandon the "enemy picture" but rechristened it "constitution enemies."[18] Yet Richter had no doubt that the MfS under Krenz was against the new democratic forces. Krenz got daily reports, partly to inform him about who would resist his plan to continue SED dominance.[19]

Written by or for Schwanitz was a remarkable confession of the sins of the past and the weakness of the present: "The goals of the 10th session of the Central Committee are not achieved. The condition of the Party is weakness and inactivity. In the past few days, it has in parts rapidly degenerated. Many members are leaving. Confidence in leaders at all levels is deeply shaken, many district and county leaders have quit or been voted out. The pressure on the party functionaries from outside and inside the Party grows and reaches the level of psycho-terror. The Party is being undermined in the workplace." The rebels had become shameless: "When demands are fulfilled, the demands merely increase."

This added to Security Police insecurity: "There is a fear that the DDR will be sold out. When members learned of the misuse of power and the economic and financial situation, there was a bewilderment, doubt and strong pessimism." On the hopeful side, "Power has shifted from the SED to the *Volkskammer* and the government. The reform of the system will mean more legality, more transparency of the state, and increased awareness of the people."

The MfS would continue with IMs but must sort out the loyal from the disloyal: "We don't yet have a complete idea of where the MfS will fit in, but it must fight the enemies of the constitution and the abuse by the church. It will depend on the IMs, and on our maintaining our conspirative activity, secrecy, and protection of the IMs." But IMs must be improved: "We have learned of many weak spots of the IMs, and we must get rid of the dishonest, unreliable, those lacking in perspective, those who deconspired. The IMs must not be exposed and we must recover their trust." More careful usage: "We should use them only when really urgently needed and when using them clearly makes a contribution. We must create new conditions because there were too many violations. There are things we can't do anymore, at least for political reasons."

The MfS must reconsider what were political crimes: "We must rethink: what does 'constitutional hostile' mean? If we are now to be closer to the BRD and the European Community, what are 'hostile economic activities'? 'Political ideological diversion, political underground, and contact-policy' have lost their justification." Rules must change. "We will soon send you a list of the orders that have been dropped." More freedom but still spying: "There will be the largest possible openness, but we will continue the conspiratorial measures and methods."

The MfS must surrender any privilege and deal more openly with the public: "We MfS will have no special rights and we will conform to socialist frugality." More contradictions in instruction: "We will have direct contact with the media. You should be ready at all times to address the public, but we must coordinate what is said." Public relations are necessary: "We will soon have a press speaker here." Even kindness: "We should be generous with those who fled and return, even for visits."[20]

The Ministry was instructed in the new democratic ways on 16 November: "Actions must not only be legal but the purpose must be given to the public. Actions should aim at extremists, and must be an intellectual confrontation. The most effective protection is an informed public. Having the leader explain it in person to the public is better than only in writing. Without public confidence any 'Constitutional Protection' [modeled on the BRD's *Verfassungschutz*] is an illusion."[21]

The *Volkskammer* on 17 November and the State Council on 18 November ordered a change in name to Office for National Security (AnS). Schwanitz created commissions to restructure his AnS, adding something of a confession: "This is a dangerous situation for Party and State. Already in personal conversations many problems of the societal development were discussed openly, which we naturally reported to the Central Committee and helped to shake them awake, when the true situation could be seen. Yet we did not perform our leadership duties in the necessary way. For that failure, there is no excuse and it dare not happen again. What many of our comrades for a long time saw coming happened in a short time with a sharpness that was not thought possible. It became ever more clear that we were serving a mistaken policy. The basis was a total misjudgment of the situation by the Politbüro."

The Party had misled the MfS. "In June, the county leaders . . . were given a false direction by the Central Committee and the old Politbüro. Now we can see—as painful as it is—that the leadership style was false. For that failure—without any excuse—we must accept the responsibility. Despite efforts for a collectivism, we must separate ourselves in this decisive situation completely enough from the long-standing command style of the Politbüro and the Minister personally, which had its effect also on the Party."

The MfS could have done more on the local level. "We must add that in the Secretariat and among the county leaders, collectivism was always the style and the connections to the Party secretary were close. We should have had a county leadership meeting right after the events of the 7–8 October, but the reason given was about tasks that had to be done and concepts that were not ready."

The problems extended down to the bottom: "The weakness of leadership and the lack of understanding of the depths of the present social process and the changed constellation of power have resulted in the great loss of confidence in the Central Committee, in county leadership, secretariats and sometimes the local political leadership. Many collectives are fine, but others are uncertain and pessimistic. In this situation there have been comrades, and are still comrades, who appear like demagogues, who make the situation worse and increase the tension, instead of responding to the requirements." The sad fact: "We all understand that in this question an appeal to reason will not help."

The AnS must work to regain trust, both inside and outside. "The role of the socialist state security organ requires a critical reworking to recreate honor and trust. The new MfS [sic] leader, Schwanitz, must care for the MfS members and their families. We must consider putting those who leave into a reservist collective. Perhaps not democratically now, new leadership will arise. A core problem of our efforts is viable leaders, although in the present situation one can not elect new leaders. There, where necessary, the Party leaders must be strengthened with cadre."[22]

The Berlin MfS explained to its members the changes at the top, describing the incompetence and halfheartedness of Central Committee and Politbüro, the gap between the Central Committee and the masses of the SED, who demanded a quick change. Seven top MfS leaders declared: "We feel ourselves deceived, we let ourselves become merely receivers of commands. We need a new Party convention and an all new Central Committee." Then an admission of MfS errors: "Mielke must answer for his part in the false analyses. There must be an investigation of MfS crimes."[23]

With whatever ideological movement inside the AnS, the popular movement continued across the border. On 17 November 1,295,000 DDR citizens crossed into the BRD, and 933,000 came from the BRD; the result was a 10-kilometer traffic jam at the Hannover Autobahn Marienborn and 30 km at the Munich Autobahn Hirschberg.[24] On 18 November came another more liberal travel law, but it still lacked convertibility of currency. On 20 November, with so much pressure on the border and with border troops "in danger," several more local openings were made. Demonstration numbers varied from 50 in some counties to 100,000 in Dresden, where the most aggressive were artists, led by a singer.[25]

THE MORE THINGS CHANGE IN THE SECRET POLICE . . .

There was a troublesome decline in discipline: MfS Central had decreed that they could not go to West Berlin or the BRD, but General Möller was shocked to see long lines of MfS, even senior officers who had been seduced by the offer of 100 West marks.[26]

On 21 November at his installation in office, Schwanitz responded to the cascading problems: "We must immediately free the Party from the heavy stress, which was brought on by the increasing pressure on the MfS. The public must be informed."[27] While then introducing the new minister president, Modrow, to the newly named AnS, Schwanitz criticized the old Mielke system: "To know everything that is going on, with such a giant apparatus, can not be supported by any state with our population and economy. . . . There must also be an end to the MfS assuming the responsibility for other organs, and trying to take care of everything, like demonstrations, soccer games and other large gatherings. This led to a great damage when we always tried to take on the task of the police on the streets. We have to separate ourselves from the thesis that politics is the center of our operations and in the application of socialist law.

"Comrades, that policy led to the fact that the MfS became ever more the power-instrument of Honecker. Now we serve the *Volkskammer* and, between sessions, Minister President Modrow." Modrow responded with a warning: "The situation of the DDR is much more serious and much more difficult and complicated than one would think on the outside, in particular the economy. We used to collect hundreds of millions from border crossing. We have been trying to get something out of this but the BRD isn't helpful."

The BRD was part of the problem: "I've been carrying more of the burden of negotiation with the BRD than Krenz who has so many meetings. The BRD negotiator Seitens has been pushing us to change Article 1 of the Constitution, which makes the SED the leading party and he wants to announce the change. My basic belief is that if nothing is left, then we are reduced to begging. History can not go that way. The other party leaders understand this, even Gerlach says, 'Hans, that is to be accepted, but we won't push it, but create a commission, which will take the external pressure off. We can't start slicing away at the constitution.' " (Speaking quite colloquially, he seems frustrated and distracted.)

The LDP had told him that they would raise questions about the new ministers. "I talked with Gerlach, 'If you start this crap, then your ministers are in the drink as much as ours are, then you must not think that everything can be aimed at only one corner.' Anyone like the LDP who hopes that they can use the New Forum is suffering from an illusion. Even the CDU, with their new chief, will stand *vis à vis* the new churchly groups quite differently than before. Gerald Götting knows very well that this machine doesn't run. [The sentence in German indicates his confused syntax.] The necessary coalition will have each doing for itself. This is the only possibility, which I see in my new office as chairman, that I can serve the Party. We are already negotiating and it is like bargaining about cows." He had little leverage: "We must adjust to the new circumstances, which includes millions of people pouring out to see the West. That can no longer be braked."

Schwanitz then emphasized, "It's a true change in the MfS and not just cosmetic. Some here think we can only pretend to change. If anyone is not serious, he should quit now. We must find out what in the MfS went wrong. Most have been good men but operating on false premises. It came from Mielke's perfectionism. One part was to get every possible information, thus many citizens believed we were watching them. Many in our organization also had the idea that, 'We are the greatest.' It criminalized those who think differently, with its operative categories, 'political underground activity,' its 'contact politics' and 'contact-activity.' "

As for the events of 7–8 October: "It was false evaluation, false measures and completely wrong psychological tactics. Because of Mielke, the MfS became a power apparatus of Honecker. Now we are working in a state of laws."[28]

Schwanitz praised the MfS for doing its duty: "No one can blame you if the given line was based on false premises or if you were misused." Power was limited; "We must separate ourselves from the assumption that we can solve political problems and deep-rooted social contradictions with administrative measures, which used to be forced on us by the former leadership. We resisted; we made suggestions for years and repeatedly pointed out that one can not fight a developing oppositional movement with administrative measures." (He meant arresting people.)

The new policy was that they must get close to the people: "We must also free ourselves from being separated from the public, as was increasingly forced on us in recent years. Being close to the public, dear comrades and comradesses, creates trust. Our task is to know all about conditions of the people and of any organization, in particular the SDP [Socialist Democratic Party] and catch any constitutionally hostile activity immediately. There must be more IM activity, the most closely held secrets and conspiration." (This looks like the old way.)

He foresaw that it would not be easy: "The demonstrators are becoming ever most hostile, already some are fascistic. We can be partners with those New Forum who accept socialism. . . . We must face the fact that we have not reached the economic lowest point." On the flood going through the gates: "We must quickly get some control over travel. We must stop the outflow of our currency and works of art." Even so, staff would be reduced: "Some 6–7,000 Chekists are to be assigned to Customs, which is good for your benefits."

An avowed determination: "We remain fighters. We remain communists. We are going forward. We will solve these problems, I am sure." Then a lament: "I must say, comrades, it filled me with great bitterness, that there were some leaders and functionaries, who in this situation did not show the behavior which one would have expected. Many, I say this because it happened, who behaved miserably. Even during the reading of the declaration, they sobbed five times. What kind of an impression is created when the leaders behaved this way and stammered that, 'I will probably be in this chair for only a few weeks?' "[29]

His 64-page document of changes tried to instruct on how members should improve the MfS image, including questions like, "Does the MfS use informers?" "Does the MfS break the law?" He downplayed its privileges, special pay, shops and housing. Again the assertion: "We knew the dangers [of revolution] but our suggestions were not heeded by Party leaders. The truth is that the negative development was not halted in time, the necessary measures were not taken, as the situation clearly got steadily worse. The MfS [sic] must be able to meet its responsibilities better in the future."

Gone was the preemptive arrest: "Our old principle was not to wait until the constitution-hostile actions had started. Because of the political development it has become necessary to examine certain aspects of the law. The changes that have resulted will provide better conditions for MfS work. A judge can now listen to the sound-recording of interrogations." He referred to films and books, which the MfS had secretly furthered.

He stumbled about searching for what would have to change. No one was to be kept in investigatory arrest longer than necessary. "Force is not used in arrest unless the person resists. Use no drugs or threats, no lie detectors as in the West. We do not involve ourselves in other countries, as the CIA does, as in Nicaragua and Angola, or Panama." To redefine hostiles: "Our enemies are those who wish to destabilize and overthrow the socialist state. Political opponents are not enemies unless they are active in destroying the socialist principles of the constitution. In an open dialog, in an objective and fair difference of opinion, we are prepared to join in constructive, differing positions for the continued development of our socialist society, of the socialist democracy, and the improvement of our work."

The AnS would have no privileges: "The MfS [*sic*] have neither priority under the law nor have a special law. For us it is working 9 to 5, and one Saturday a month. Our full earnings equal 1,131 marks a month. There used to be a special store for MfS, but it is closed. There is no special housing or vacation perks."[30]

The Party organization of the AnS demanded that "The group around Honecker that was hostile to the Party be held accountable and fired immediately. They had besmirched the reputation of honest communists." The change was adopted with only one negative vote. A delegate conference adopted reforms similar to those on the Schwanitz list. The MfS Sector Sport was worried that its sport program would be negatively impacted. A more political concern was that students wanted an independent organization: "That's what happened in Poland and Hungary."[31]

A draft paper, by or for Schwanitz, declared for freedom: "The members of the AnS demanded that we must investigate any MfS crimes, and join in the present dialog. The muzzle which was put on us and which isolated us from the people must disappear." Democracy must prevail: "We also can not give this mission to a handful of leaders. The only secrets must be those regarding national security. We can't blame the political decisions any more. A banalization of the problem and a stirring up of revenge feelings are only heating up the present situation." The rule of law: "The deformation of socialism did not leave the criminal law untouched. Real change is necessary. The MfS had forced false testimony, it had used physical and other humiliations."[32]

In a newspaper interview, Schwanitz presented a similar statement of principles: "A government of law; political problems solved with political measures; reconstruction to include the security organization, no longer having to know everything and to have influence everywhere, as Mielke wanted; no longer solving other organizations' problems; no longer political problems solved with administrative means; no more that politics [rather than the law] has the top priority. Persons who think differently do not equal enemy activity, only activities that are hostile to the constitution."

He compared the KGB to the MfS: "In the Soviet Union, the KGB pushed for *Perestroika*; in Germany, the people had to do it. The big mistake was that the MfS took on the job of watching the people, this deformation came from the leaders, including Mielke. I don't know the future of Mielke.

I know only that he had been provided by his colleagues with sufficient arguments and information to have pushed for a Change before the Honecker speech and the important Politbüro meeting on the 10th."

Schwanitz included Mielke as responsible for the violence: "The excesses of 7–8th October were the extreme high point of the false security policy, which considered mass demonstrations not as a breaking out of long-suppressed contradictions but as anti-socialist provocation. Therefore hundreds of MfS employees, without specific training, without any psychological-tactical preparation, and who were made further insecure by the sharpness and the extent of the confrontation in Dresden, were put into a never-before-experienced situation on the street. It was an over-reaction, excessive misuse of power, also by Mielke."[33]

Modrow accepted Schwanitz's organization as necessary. He was going to keep socialism and the DDR, although with some different methods; he would give orders as head of the government, not as head of the Party.[34] He forbade the use of force: "Therefore we have to find a way how we can constructively get around the situation." The term "enemy-hostile" was transposed into "constitution-hostile." Schwanitz on 24 November told his head of Intelligence, Grossman, to operate as before.[35]

Church-based demonstrations had declined, except for Rostock and Gera. "Church meetings have become again almost entirely religious with few participants." The masses were still crossing the border. On 25 November there was up to a 25-km line of cars at seven various border crossings, and the trains were 200 percent filled.[36]

On 27 November, Leipzig had 100,000 demonstrators; Dresden, 30–50,000.[37] In Jena and Gera, transparencies briefly appeared with "Germany United," which disappeared after protests from participants.[38] The question was being raised whether the SED had the right to have its own armed force; its Battlegroups were declining in preparedness. Only verbal attacks on the MfS were reported.[39]

Berlin ordered local units to work on their IMs: "We absolutely need sources in the conspiracy of the enemies. These sources should be in key positions, including people who are active in the church."[40]

On 29 November, the AnS telegraphed the Central Committee: "We support change for Leninist norms, more democratic elections, and a limit to 2–3 terms."[41] It had drawn up a new concept of its task and structure. The plan was to retain 20,000 members in Berlin and 23,000 in the districts; 35,000 must be dismissed, mostly those in the counties. Transfers took care of 12,000 employees. Someone scratched out, "Guard regiment kept as is," and penciled in, "reduction." Closed would be the central office for pass control and search and involvement as travel and traffic police.

The AnS argued that most of its civilian personnel were people whose health had been damaged by their very difficult work, which had taken 25 years away from their trained careers, so that they would not be able to find a job. "They might feel betrayed, which could create serious dangers, like treason or other things that would endanger national security, so they should get a transitional pension." The Berlin office was vague on what help employees in the counties would get.[42]

Reaction from Dresden district leader Horst Böhm, who reported on 30 November: "We have infiltrated 80–100 IMs into leading positions and as members [of the opposition]. . . . 80–85 percent of the IMs are prepared to work with us."[43]

The moral cleanup continued. The Berlin SED Control Commission heard 378 cases and threw out 72 members, and 41 quit. "The West media had caused them to lose their class consciousness and they refused to obey orders." Cases involved 50 leaders, 150 noncoms and 165 officers. There were problems of trusting young officers who were in a position to utilize their (working-) class position. "There were not enough discussions, and they were ignored by commanders and cadre."[44]

Schwanitz on 30 November said that many IMs and MfS full-time employees had fled to the West.[45] He ordered that the destruction of documents be clever and inconspicuous and that "explosive material" be brought to the district offices. Much of the archive on Normannen Strasse was apparently either destroyed or sent to Moscow.[46] The draft of the transition plan reads like the good old days, including opposing enemy activity in the churches and using IMs, but they should not provoke action or become the single leader of a popular movement.[47]

Süss judged that Schwanitz was showing the shortsightedness of the *apparatchik*, still thinking of enemies, working in secrecy and conspiration. "His was a program to continue the repression." Because he was still representing the organization, the real reform had to come from the political side and Wolf understood better the political process."[48] Richter commented that the modest reform brought bitter resistance of top functionaries and military, thus the famous demonstration of MfS employees in the Central's courtyard, reported as a spontaneous popular occupation.[49]

There were 15 New Forum demonstrations and 3 in Cottbus, Berlin and Chemnitz, with more talk of unification. "It was clear that the organizers could no longer control the situation." Even Poles and Russians demonstrated on the Alexanderplatz against "the increased hostility" shown them for their buying scarce goods. In Poland DDR citizens were robbed, which was considered a reprisal against DDR action against smuggling.[50]

The MfS reported a 9.8 percent decline in BRD border passages; the travel on 2 November involved 487,363 to West Berlin and 484,604 to the BRD, 35.5 percent less than on 25 November to the BRD and 18.6 percent less to West Berlin. Yet cars were backed up 10 kilometers on the return. In Andenhausen, some DDR citizens tore down their border. More border communities were demanding an opening. Demonstrations increased in smaller towns, with from 1,000 to 7,000 participants.[51]

THE WHIMPERING END

The scandals about the DDR elite's luxuries during the many years of citizen deprivation had a detrimental impact much beyond their numbers. "The last sympathies for a socialist renewal melted away once the rotten backstage of communist rule had come into view." The hunting lodges and bungalows of Wandlitz became like the diamond necklace of Marie Antoinette.[52]

The *Volkskammer* raised questions about Schalck-Golodowski's supplying the elite's community and buying commodities that were contrary to the law. He had sold artworks and, with Mielke's help, created "Firma Delta," which was a cover organization for importing luxury products for the elite. The Modrow government learned that his job in the Foreign Ministry had really been to get West money, any way possible. He was supposed to make illegal deals, like those in exporting weapons to the Middle East. He was also to get high-tech and to satisfy MfS computer needs. It was thought that he laundered drug money, and rumors were of millions in Swiss banks.[53]

On 1 December, Schalck-Golodowski had contacted Wolfgang Schäuble, BRD interior minister, "about the Amis [Americans]," and then "traitorously" disappeared in the West, to avoid being arrested, as had been Mittag and Tisch.[54] That he remained rich and free was taken as proof that he was thick with the thieves of the West.

An emerging emphasis of the opposition was to end the MfS and expose its past activities.[55] A telegram from the Plauen AnS to the Cabinet demanded that Schwanitz explain immediately to the public that the present AnS leaders had clean hands, were not involved with the Mielke intrigues and knew nothing of them. "If not, we expect an immediate change in personnel. It is important to us who are in the highest degree insecure whether such service can be squared with our political and moral conscience."[56]

The reported anger of the AnS personnel was always against their leaders, not against the people. There were widespread demands for new AnS leadership. An investigating committee and many local units wanted Schwanitz and other leaders fired.[57]

The Leipzig AnS swore loyalty to the new government: "All personnel reported to Modrow and Schwanitz their anger that they had been lied to by Mielke, including his false security doctrine. There is 100 percent support to the Change. One should fine those who are opposed or are passive. . . . We stand entirely behind our government."[58]

On 4 December, an AnS worker reported to the media that masses of material were being burned. The ministry got several angry calls: "I just saw a program on TV, something must be done."[59] Schwanitz telegrams went immediately to all offices. "Immediately stop every destruction and every material transport."[60] AnS offices were being invaded by police and district attorneys, who put in guards, disrupting the work. "Some demanded to see secret documents, which was sometimes not preventable."[61]

Department III reported, "We are on the defensive. The public is not persuaded that the MfS is on the right side. We are no longer in control on the border and in some other areas, there is a tendency to anarchy and chaos. The government organs, particularly at the district and county level, are in a state of self-destruction, with illegal action by outsiders."

The Berlin leaders must act: "There is still no central position publicly taken to the false interpretation of the situation that led to the events of 7–8 October. Still missing is an investigation of the misuses of office. . . . The renewal process is so slow, the central office should publicize some concrete examples."[62]

Walter Süss corrected the AnS story that on 4 December Berlin demonstrators had forced their way into AnS headquarters; they had just asked to enter, and the official covered himself by saying that he had bent to force. "The communication that day shows that both sides were afraid of the other." Süss concluded that the AnS had not seriously changed because it was keeping the IMs; the dissolution of its county offices was to reduce attacks by the local public.[63]

On 5 December Schwanitz ordered the units to try to protect the secrets.[64] "The situation is getting more difficult, in almost every district and county, citizens have tried to push their way in to prevent destruction of documents. I ordered the documents saved. You can expect more to push in. Talk to them and agree to let them in."[65]

The guard regiment was also "under attack" and complained: "The passivity which is forced on us now is unbearable. We are worker children. We should not wait until the enemy is at our gate." The Rostock AnS lambasted Berlin: "Are you crazy? You have had the chance to save socialism. Do something for it! Guarantee that no evidence disappears. There must be not only new structures but also new ideas. Put in honest people." Four AnS local political organizations demanded that Schwanitz be replaced with someone true to socialism and morally clean.[66]

Berlin admitted a moral problem: "There is the failure in clearing up corruption and permitting the disarming of MfS. The problem in the organization has been in the lack of an unequivocal description of the responsibility for the MfS's authoritarian style, and the slow renewal process. We need structure for the cooperation of security forces and military discipline, including keeping secrets."

The Central Office described dangerous local conflicts, more illegal actions and more aggressive demonstrations, with the intent to destroy the SED and the AnS. There was more talk of reunification, strike threats everywhere, already a short strike. "Because of the immeasurable disillusion and disgust of the broadest part of the population about the corruption of leaders and the implementers, the lack of credibility, the public's hysteria making proper and improper judgments of guilt against Party and State functionaries and undifferentiated attacks, there has been a further sharpening by the occupation of various district and county offices. How can we continue? Confusion is reaching the point of being crippling."[67]

The AnS told the National Defense Council of approaching disaster: "The State authority and the legal order are being increasingly undermined. Governmental organs, particularly districts and counties, are increasingly incapable of operating. There are ever more tendencies to anarchy and chaos. Daily grows the danger of a sudden change into no longer controllable and violent confrontations. The basic demands are the end of the SED and the AnS, dissolution of the Battlegroups and reunification."

The AnS concluded that the SED had only itself to blame: "The causes are the corruption, crimes, and misuse of power by the former Party and State leaders. . . . the missing credibility of the policies as well as the lack of evident results in the programs. There are increasing examples that our colleagues, their spouses and children are slandered and discredited, and exposed to a psycho-terror."[68]

During a radio interview of Schwanitz about citizen takeovers to stop the destruction of documents, a reporter from Leipzig asked: "Were there orders to destroy papers? We learned here that mountains of shredded paper were lying in front of the furnace, that allegedly training material was burned. Why have they not shown us such material?" Schwanitz admitted, "We did order such teaching material destroyed." Schwanitz promised no destruction and said he was fully on the side of the New Forum, but people continued to call in to report documents destroyed or taken away by the truckload. The next day he ordered the offices to protect secret documents, like those of IMs and espionage.[69] Protection by destruction? Richter judged that Schwanitz pushed destruction until fired and that almost nowhere did the AnS passively accept the changes.[70]

THE FADING AWAY OF OLD AGENTS

Schwanitz denounced the hostile anarchy and chaos to the *Volkskammer* and the Minister Council: "We are angry to have had our idealism misused in the most shameful way. We were given tasks, which were unnecessary, because of a false doctrine from Honecker and Mielke." Change the law: "Send us quickly a new law for our operations." He also requested security for his security organization.

Hostility erupted within the SED. A telegram from the Gera SED to Modrow: "Go after the catasrophic corruption in the MfS. Fire Schwanitz and the entire Collegium. We have no confidence at all in the leadership and the commander in Gera. It is threatening to become a hatred. Stop the self-destruction of this organization." Other telegrams described shock about the SED corruption.[71]

The Klingenthal AnS protested directly to Schwanitz and about him: "We are writing you from the feeling that we have been betrayed and abandoned, as shown by the daily attacks on corruption, misuse of office, and crimes of Party and State, including leaders of the MfS. We wonder what our leaders think of our situation, where every member, wife, and child is known to the community. There are already attacks, with every week more demonstrations in which 50 percent of the population participate, and where we are massively scolded and slandered. Today there was a general strike here, where firms refused to hire former MfS employees. There is a witchhunt against IMs. Yesterday in a humiliating fashion, the pastor [who has a criminal record] together with the district attorney and the commander of the police went through our office and through desks and files. We must protect IMs."

There was more MfS hostility toward its new leader: "We demand that Schwanitz resign. We lost all our weapons yesterday. When will the delaying tactic stop? We demand a clear position, in 24 hours, we repeat 24 hours."

More telegrams showed local panic and a heavy pressure on Berlin to dissolve these exposed offices. "Various loyal IMs called and asked that their file be destroyed. What should we do with the weapons? They could be dangerous."[72]

A warning appeared in Berlin: "A human chain will form on Ruschstrasse at 17:00. AnS women with children should go home, and up to 50 percent of the personnel." On 7 December 75 percent of the men should stay in the building. Schwanitz lamented, "Our will to non-violence has been misused and this endangers families. It is like the former policy of arrest of relatives."[73]

A Stasi major, when his offices were invaded, was surprised to see some IMs, who were there to get rid of their files, and not a few IMs were on the new citizen committees. "The invaders were surprised how primitively we worked. We were envious of the West with their equipment; with many fewer personnel they could control many more people."[74]

On 6 December Modrow replaced Krenz and had Mielke arrested. Schwanitz dismissed 20 top assistants, including Mittig, Neiber, Irmler and Kleine.[75] At a press conference, he again expressed deep concern about his people and their families. Some offices were no longer functioning. "Our will to end violence in the interest of the DDR and the democratic renewal is being abused. Non-violence requires the responsibility on both sides. . . . I emphasize again that the colleagues of the office can not be held responsible for a false security policy of the former Party and State leaders." He suggested a link to the Nazis: "It reminds of the worst times when harm to families was the practice."[76]

The revolution created on 7 December the "Round Table" of all dissident elements to coordinate reform. It promptly demanded AnS dissolution.[77] This first alerted various levels of AnS that all could end quickly.[78] There were to be no transferring of security organizations to other ministries and no more advanced schools.[79] The Minister Council ordered no more collecting of information, and ordered that the AnS destroy immediately any illegally gathered materials but agreed that secrets should be kept for reasons of national security.[80]

The AnS reported back that most district offices were functioning but that some had been sealed and that the police had taken masses of MfS weapons, materials and vehicles. "AnS offices give their support to 'The Renewal,' with an emphasis on the economy." In return, "They demand that the government express its confidence in the AnS, so citizens can take an objective and humane position to those who are threatened, mostly its young members." They discussed the possibilities of evacuating threatened colleagues and their families.

In Dresden, the demands of militants went far beyond the agreement; mistakes had led to a heated climate, and General Böhm was replaced. "The reasonable forces in Germany are in a bind. The district attorneys are apathetic." On the other side, "the demonstrators show no insight." There were "threats of murder written on the walls of district offices. Comrade Schmidt needed 3 hours to get out of his district office and was followed. Windows were broken of homes near those of our colleagues. Evacuation does not seem possible." Arrest was threatened: "In Gera, the demands are to arrest MfS." Not only external threats but internal rebellion: "There are cases of members refusing commands."

Members feared retribution: "The police have difficulties; the 2,000 prisoners in Bautzen, if amnestied, would want revenge. Four district offices are completely halted. We are getting no information." Under siege, "Our options are to close offices, have them guarded by police, or use our own forces. We need also to protect residences. We need government action."

Schwanitz informed his people that all Mielke's commands and orders for spying on people were revoked. The commander of the Guard Regiment was dismissed: "Its fighting value was zero." More ominously, Modrow had distanced himself from the AnS.[81]

Schwanitz told a *Stern* reporter that he had been MfS since 1951 and had only a four-room apartment: "I have clean hands; most here have clean hands." He blamed the Western press for the false image of the MfS, which had followed the laws. When *Stern* noted that MfS in civilian clothing had beaten demonstrators, Schwanitz blamed "the Policy." When *Stern* asked again about the violence, he answered that it was an illegal gathering. Then surprisingly, he conceded, "Socialism has failed."[82]

At the wish of Bohley, Schwanitz met with opponent Jens Reich, and they agreed to work together against violence and keep each other informed. Schwanitz conceded that the paper shredder had been used too fast; documents should be sealed rather than destroyed; any decision about destruction of documents should come from the Round Table.[83]

The Berlin district office was sealed by the military attorney, as were those at Frankfurt, Gera, Halle, Chemnitz, Leipzig, Magdeburg and Neubrandenburg. Counties showed variety; some were closed, some were sealed and a few were still in partial function, usually under the watch of the police.[84] There were 80 tons of documents in Rostock, where Pastor Gauck was mentioned as the leading resistance person. The AnS concluded that society was not likely to have leaders for the transition if former MfS were not given certain guarantees of integration into civilian life.

Many AnS members were demanding the resignation of Schwanitz and Möller, the head of cadre and schooling: "There is a lack of understanding, anger and disillusionment about the incompetence and the complete misunderstanding of the situation by the Central Office. The ship is sinking and the band plays on." Abuse had led to aberrations: "Fear for oneself and family is felt widely. Individual colleagues and collectives have the idea to use weapons to prevent New Forum access to IM documents and to destroy these documents. Many talk of going to the BRD and selling secrets. Many have been physically and psychologically attacked."[85]

Schwanitz was informed on 11 December that the AnS would be dissolved. Some members could go to the foreign news service and some to "Constitution Protection" in the Interior Ministry, where they could have no executive or arrest power or hold a leading position. There would be no more military titles; the guard regiment was to end by 31 March.[86]

In the Berlin unit, 1,000 members were out; in the districts, 2,200. The border troops would take 7,000; customs would take 12,000; the army, 13,000; 5,000–6,000 were dismissed and looking for new jobs.[87] Richter critiqued that released MfS were given phony papers, usually saying that they had worked in the Interior Ministry, and the former MfS were continuing to work together, which was part of the Modrow plan.[88]

The frequent attorney for dissidents Gregor Gysi became head of the SED on 9 December, which on 16 December changed its name to Party of Democratic Socialism (PDS).

By 12 December demonstration numbers were going down, although conceded "extremely massive" in Leipzig, Dresden, Chemnitz, Zwickau, Heiligenstadt and Halle. Of 12 AnS district offices, 10 had limited capability, and 3 sent no reports; 70 county offices had been given over to local councils.

In the Potsdam District, 13 mayors had been voted out of office; changes were similar in the Schwerin, Gera and Neubrandenburg Districts. "It is difficult to fill offices because the cadre refuse; the cadre of other parties also refuse, so SED have to do it. The campaign against the old MfS raises fear among the authorities that the same could happen to them. The public should be told, that the state must provide order."[89]

The AnS appealed to the public to be reasonable: "Do not do wrong in replying to a former wrong." On 13 December it reported a good experience with citizen committees and state authorities, but former MfS still risked a popular terror.

Actions to open more border crossings had the evident cooperation of BRD citizens, politicians and police. Much lawlessness, particularly on the borders, was reported: "Threats of violence, forced searching of our facilities, violent border breakthroughs, insults, threats of murder, desecration of buildings and the flag, show the fiery potential of the present development. There are more and more contacts of towns in the DDR with towns of the BRD and naturally conversations about how BRD financial measures would 'support' the DDR communities, such as a heating system in Hotel Eisenach. There is already contact of BRD artisans and small firms with the goal of selling."[90]

There was an increasing use of ultimatums for the resignation of local functionaries; there were threats of strikes for wages, bomb threats in Dresden and Schwerin, plus murder threats in Schwerin and Potsdam. "There are more demonstrations with some participants being more aggressive." More intrusion into security facilities was leading to confrontations. Extremely massive were demonstrations in demanding reunification. Daily, 500,000 traveled to the BRD, and on weekends, 700,000.[91] "Human chains [of demonstrators] are created, particularly on the highways."[92]

More AnS were "unfairly" attacked: "They were not responsible and regret the perfectionist spying." Job discrimination was also common: "A resistance exists to hiring former MfS." The DDR would need the AnS to defend it: "If we further reduce AnS, there would be no situation reports nor counter-intelligence against neo-fascists and terrorists. The secrets must be kept; giving out sources would make the patriots insecure and enable lynch justice."[93]

Modrow, arbitrarily, on 14 December, ordered the end of the AnS delayed to 20 June 1990.[94] That day came the famous storming of the Normannen Strasse headquarters, which Fricke thought the least important place to storm. "It is now clear this was initiated by former MfS officers. A MfS colonel said, 'The entire event was organized by the Stasi, and went exactly according to the plan. The mobs included a company of the guard regiment in civilian clothes, who diverted the mob to luxury articles.' "[95] Richter agreed that MfS diverted attention into taking this less important building.[96]

As for the regional headquarters, Schwanitz told Modrow, "With the breaking up of district offices and that which comes from the county offices, we have thousands of tons of written materials. . . . documents with the highest secrecy level and capable of extraordinary political fireworks. Unapproved access would lead to dangers and violence. These could be stormed, therefore I propose destruction of all written material, which does not have immediate importance to the DDR; to keep one copy of central orders and what is of historical importance, anything from before 1945. This act should have the approval of the Round Table."[97]

Five districts were still in pretty good order; in 10 districts, the activity was sharply reduced. Of 209 county offices, 203 were dissolved. "The situation of the former county workers is very critical, there is not always a job for them; a pamphlet in Potsdam says don't hire them, although the New Forum opposed it. Persons in Suhl called loudly for local-justice or even lynch-justice."[98]

Understandably, many AnS were bitter about the sudden dissolution of the county offices.[99] They faced continuing demonstrations. Kamenz and Meißen had up to 2,000 demonstrators, with demands for an immediate unification and liquidation of the state power. "Strikes were increasingly the normal popular outlet, as in Cottbus, Plauen and Görlitz." There was also social rejection: "Completely unsatisfactory is the situation of the re-integration of former colleagues of county offices into careers; often the entire working staff rejected them."

The public was becoming involved in operations: "The ability to work in the local offices is increasingly influenced by citizen group hindrances and demands that the councils and the mayors resign. Sometimes these leaders can not withstand the psychological pressure and resign as a group, as in Rostock, Auerbach, Eisenach, Gransee and Plauen."[100]

The blame was put on the West: "There is increased activity of enemy secret services." A growing darkness ensued: "From the territories we have no reports that would permit an objective judgment of the situation. The closing down of county offices is essentially finished."[101] On 20 December it was generally calm, but one demand was the arrest of Honecker.

From the report on 23 December over 300 offices had turned over equipment, including 190 former county offices; 16,937 personnel had been discharged, of which 12,666 had gone into the economy, 1,303 to customs, 2,968 to pass-control.[102]

The permission for the AnS to take care of its own documents left the door open for further destruction.[103] The chronicle of document destruction is confusing: on 6 December, county documents were sent to the district; on 16 December came a report of destruction of documents about training; on 22 December, reports of the destruction of materials on persons and situation reports and some situation evaluations.[104]

On 27 December the Minister Council, from the pressure of demonstrators, voted to dissolve the AnS.[105] It continued, although much hindered. "The communication possibilities of the districts are much reduced; Erfurt, Suhl, Leipzig are completely turned off." Society must recognize that Secret Police are necessary. "The activity of Constitution Protection, as everywhere . . . is unthinkable without the use of agents. There is much reduced agent work. Citizen groups in Magdeburg, Potsdam, Rostock and Schwerin are opposing IMs." The resolve: "We will have to maintain our members with their highly specialized training and experience. There is an effort to make MfS membership itself criminal." Then in a reflection of the bitter reality: "Finally whatever positive has been created in 40 years would be liquidated and the DDR turned over to the BRD."[106]

Thus ended the year of the revolution with something of a police whimper. Richter concluded that although the MfS included many critics in November and December, almost none really wanted to support the democratic changes. They saw the revolution coming but worked to keep control over how it would be implemented.[107] Hacker thought that the MfS had tried to direct the Change but might not have expected the demonstrations' success.[108]

THE REPORTS OF DEATH ARE PREMATURE

The January 1990 reports were critical of citizen committees' destructive behavior, as in Magdeburg the push to release all AnS.[109] For the hierarchy, the natural solution was to fire those below to keep themselves in office. There were public protests about "transition" money for dismissed state employees.[110]

The New Forum prodded: "It's going too slowly. Do not destroy papers. . . . We do not want any successor organization."[111] There should not be the same offices with different names. On 8 January the AnS coolly reported demonstrations against itself, as well as the SED successor, the PDS.[112] Most of the new political groups publicly forswore violence and reunification, but the AnS was dubious. "Internally leaders of the New Forum and SDP say this for tactical reasons for the next election. New Forum deliberately avoids stating a political program. Instead it just increases its demands to counter government efforts to normalize the situation."

A dire, top-secret report predicted: "There will be increased demonstrations and strikes, leading to a so-called rising of the people to remove SED power before the election. Some groups plan a conspiratorial defense against infiltration by AnS and SED. They plan increased activity with an emphasis on reunification."

AnS survival tactics included avoiding trouble: "There is an increased chance of a confrontation, although talking with small groups has helped. We make no unrealistic promises and make no effort to justify the former activities of the MfS. We avoid big meetings and in churches. We resist violence-oriented forces. Our goal is to distance the sponsors of meetings from the people. We should expose the originators and other illegal and immoral behavior." Divide and reconquer.

The IM basis of power should continue: "We should re-examine our IM base and have an immediate break with any IM who shows a hint of de-conspiration [betraying secrets to the ecomony]. We must persuade them that the AnS is uncompromisingly behind the process of Renewal, that it supports the new regime actively and has separated itself from the deformation of the former MfS."

Yet power had the same basis: "The emphasis is on IMs, that their work can in no way be used against them. Local employees could move away to avoid any danger, for which we could arrange an exchange of housing. Nothing should stay behind which would discredit the AnS."

On 15 January county offices officially ended, and the district offices were to end 31 March. "This will show that we have really changed, and will lead to fewer attacks."[113]

The New Forum and other new groups succeeded in mobilizing the public against the AnS.[114] Some people tried, on 15 January, to get control; 10,000 gathered around the Berlin headquarters. Among them were agents of the BND who made a beeline for Building 2, which had counterespionage material; with schematic drawings provided by Colonel Wiegand, they took what they wanted and disappeared.

The crowd found shocking food delicacies. Shortly before 7:00 P.M., Modrow drove into the courtyard, greeted with shouts of "Red Pig" and derisive boos to his appeal to halt the destruction. Eppelman tried to control the violence, and the crowd left at 8:00 P.M.[115]

Christopher Links observed that when the Round Table learned that Modrow had not enforced the decision to end the AnS, it decided on an appropriate organ from all social forces to supervise its dissolution. This was formalized on 8 February with consultants from former ministries and MfS.[116] Stefan Wolle and Armin Mitter were installed as inspectors and began their 14-month adventure of trying to control the organization. "There was no real political opposition, the reformers were quite surprised to see the SED state diminish day by day. They did not meet opposition, the officials promised full cooperation."[117]

Fricke believed that DDR personnel remained "completely infiltrated with members of the old state apparatus and worse with a large number of former Stasi personnel." When he went to check that MfS weapons had been destroyed, he discovered that they had been secretly whisked away, and the police chief never considered informing the committee. In February finally came the destruction of the physical equipment. In various places, documents were taken directly from the MfS building to the nearest KGB office, of which many had already been turned over as microfilm. Still in early 1990 information went to the Soviets in Karlshorst.[118]

Joppke judged: "The Round Table allowed Modrow to bind the opposition into an attention getting but ineffectual side show while he had free room to maneuver himself." He mostly ignored the Round Table's recommendation and tried to stabilize the old forces, especially the Stasi.[119] Democracy slowly ended the delaying tactics, as when the people voted Modrow out in March, but the New Forum found itself also out.

Only on 31 May did the AnS recall all its officers (OibE) in West Germany, about 300; six days earlier the army told its spies by radio that the game was over. These two broadcasts ended the espionage operations of 40 years.[120]

Yet Fricke thought that the old MfS was not defeated until 7 June, when Pastor Gauck was appointed to head an 11-man committee.[121] Rüddenklau agreed: "The Modrow Government provided an umbrella for the modifying of the structures and until the end of the government of DeMaziére, the Intelligence Department could continue under the protection of Interior Minister Diestel. Large parts of the ruling class in the DDR threw themselves into the wide-opened arms of the brothers and sisters in the BRD."[122] More specifically, the BRD Constitution Protectors absorbed numbers of the DDR "Constitution Protectors."

THE REVOLUTION ABANDONS ITS REVOLUTIONARIES

A disillusioned one-liner read: "The Revolution had won, the revolutionaries had lost." This could be linked to a general public nonparticipation: 3,000 demonstrations occurred by April 1990; of 7,563 communities, of which 649 had more than 3,000 residents, there were demonstrations in 511. "So the majority stayed at home, watching it on TV."[123]

Of the demonstrators, the New Forum had the sympathies of 70 percent at the beginning of November, but at the beginning of December, only 17 percent would have voted for them. The Democratic Breakout at the beginning of December had the sympathy of 58 percent, which rose at the beginning of January to 63 percent; then it was absorbed by the Alliance for Deutschland, which was, in turn, absorbed by Kohl's CDU.[124] CDU and SPD joined the Western party cousins in mid-January.[125]

A speaker for the New Forum agreed that after two months of existence it was not able to govern, only to influence the government. Dresden Mayor Berghofer observed, "Power is up for grabs, yet no one picks it up."[126]

Helmut Kohl picked it up. He had an ally in the DSU Party on the right flank, led by Wolfgang Schnur, later shown to have been an IM. Other leading Western CDU preferred to touch the Eastern CDU only with a 10-foot pole, but Kohl went with his power instinct. He therewith gained 1,000 full-time functionaries, going into every village, the best election instrument. He had also the weapons of quick D-marks and antisocialism. Kohl's meetings attracted ever more participants, and Willy Brandt attracted ever fewer participants, a bitter disillusionment to him, assuming that the DDR in 40 years had created a basis for democratic socialism.[127]

Polls as late as early March said the SPD would get 34 percent, and CDU

22 percent; it was assumed that industrial Sachsen would remain SPD, the only clean party. Consumers followed Kohl's bargain instead. On 18 March the election to the *Volkskammer* gave power to the CDU, which had used the image of Kohl and BRD wealth. Lothar DeMaziére began his six months of satellite significance; MfS papers later showed him also to have been an IM.

Dissidents remained stubbornly on the sinking DDR ship while the people had long jumped into the crowded lifeboat of unification; the dissident party got a bare 2.9 percent. As one said, "We all knew that the majority of the people had quite different goals than to build the true socialism."[128]

Local CDU and SPD activists pushed the intellectual leaders of the revolution aside. Bohley and Reich were quickly again the tiny minority, and the majority was composed of workers, particularly those from Sachsen, who were pro-unity and pro-market.[129]

Therefore, the DDR's Round Table, unlike its Polish counterpart, was not the means to hand over power to the democratic opposition but an expression of the opposition's refusal of power. This was partly because of the Protestant Church environs of most dissidents. "We were deeply distrustful of power. This was something abominable to us." The opposition had been so isolated from the masses that its power would have been *putchist*. "The Round Table became the most vital symbol that both the regime and its opposition had to perish together."[130]

In addition, the Round Table lost the services of some of the stars who worked for the parties in the election. Its significance was that it helped to reduce the SED and to avoid violence.[131]

The New Forum had assumed that the correct program would emerge from discussion. Reich admitted a misjudgment: "Our goal was not to usurp power, but to push for elections. Democratic legitimization was our key concern, not power. In the end the Thermidor would have caught up with us anyway. Yet we missed the opportunity, we ducked in the decisive moment."[132]

Or one can assume that competing, organized political parties are the natural and inevitable power brokers in any democracy.

NOTES

1. ZAIG, 8266, p. 13; 14331, p. 112.
2. ZAIG, 14418, pp. 160, 167–73; 14331, p. 101.
3. Armin Mitter and Stefan Wolle, *Untergang auf Raten* (München: Bertelsmann, 1993), p. 540.
4. Christian Joppke, *East German Dissidents and the Revolution of 1989* (New York: New York University Press, 1995), p. 160.
5. Gerd-Rüdiger Stephan, *"Vorwärts immer, rückwärts nimmer": Interne Dokumente zum Zerfall von SED und DDR 1988 /89* (Berlin: Dietz, 1994), p. 21.

6. Klaus-Dietmar Henke and Roger Engelmann, *Aktenlage: Die Bedeutung der Unterlagen des Staatssicherheitdiensts für die Zeitgeschichtsforschung* (Berlin: Links, 1995), pp. 129–31.

7. Wolfgang Richter, *Unfrieden in Deutschland* (Berlin: Gesellschaft zum Schutz von Bürgerrecht und Menschenwürde, 1992), pp. 44–45; John O. Koehler, *Stasi: The Untold Story of the East German Secret Police* (Boulder, CO: Westview Press, 1999), p. 407.

8. Richter, *Unfrieden*, p. 47.

9. ZAIG, 2289, 14.11.9, pp. 211–15.

10. ZAIG, 2326, 14.11.9, p. 189.

11. Ibid., 14.11.9, pp. 14–21.

12. SAPMO, 15891/SED Kreisleitung 510, 14.11.9, pp. 216–18.

13. Ibid., pp. 157–95, 278, 378, 216–18.

14. Richter, *Unfrieden*, pp. 35–38.

15. ZAIG, 2326, 14.11.9, p. 192.

16. ZAIG, 7834, 14.11.9, pp. 23–24.

17. Walter Süss, "Die Demonstration am 4. November, 1989, ein Unternehmen von Stasi und SED?" *Deutschland Archiv*, December 1995, pp. 132–35.

18. Walter Süss, *Entmachung und Verfall der Staatssicherheit* (Berlin: Bundesbeauftragte, 1994) p. 29.

19. Richter, *Unfrieden*, pp. 40–43.

20. ZAIG, 8682, Hinweise for Dienstbesprechung, pp. 5–20.

21. ZAIG, 2294, 16.11.9, p. 3.

22. MfS, HA, VIII, 636, pp. 47–57.

23. ZAIG, APO, pp. 17, 24–26.

24. ZAIG, 7942, 18.11.9, p. 46.

25. ZAIG, 14418, pp. 142–43.

26. Süss, *Entmachung*, p. 45.

27. ZAIG, 2526, pp. 12, 109–10.

28. ZAIG, 2289, 21.11.9, pp. 791–98.

29. ZAIG, 4886, 21.11.9, pp. 1–47.

30. ZAIG, 7941, pp. 3, 57.

31. ZAIG, 2326, pp. 118–25, 172.

32. ZAIG, 2386, pp. 1–7.

33. ZAIG, 2289, 23.11.9, pp. 252–72.

34. Richter, *Unfrieden*, p. 48.

35. Ibid., pp. 54–57.

36. ZAIG, 14331, 23.11.9, pp. 68, 106.

37. Ibid., 27.11.9, p. 56.

38. ZAIG, 14418, 27.11.9, p. 120.

39. ZAIG, AST 3171, Görlitz, BA, 28.11.9, pp. 2, 8.

40. ZAIG, 13947, 28.11.9.

41. ZAIG, 233, p. 10.

42. ZAIG, 2289, 29.11.9, pp. 5–10.

43. Mitter and Wolle, *Untergang*, p. 533.

44. MfS, 15891/SED Kreisleitung 510, 30.11.9, pp. 126–52.

45. Richter, *Unfrieden*, p. 46.

46. Ibid., pp. 61–64.

47. ZAIG, 13957, 2.12.9; Bausch to Beyer.

48. Süss, "Die Demonstration," pp. 136–38.

49. Richter, *Unfrieden*, pp. 50–53.

50. ZAIG, 14331, 3.12.9.

51. MfS, 2240, 2.12.9, pp. 73, 79.

52. Joppke, *East German Dissidents*, p. 162.

53. ZAIG, 2326, 8.12.9, p. 288.

54. ZAIG, 2240, Sekretariat des Ministerium, 4, 34; Schalck-Golodowski memoired that at the end of November "Schwanitz called to say that I should keep everything secret. On the 27th, an MfS officer came to tell me I was no longer with the MfS as OibE." Alexander Schalck-Golodowski, *Deutsche-Deutsche Erinnerungen* (Hamburg: Rowohlt, 2000), p. 22.

55. ZAIG, 14418, pp. 109–10.

56. ZAIG, 2326, p. 117.

57. Richter, *Unfrieden*, pp. 86–87.

58. ZAIG, 2326, 4.12.9, p. 114.

59. Ibid., pp. 251, 274–78.

60. ZAIG, 2289, 4.12.9.

61. ZAIG, 1992, p. 232.

62. ZAIG, 233, 5.12.9, pp. 21–28.

63. Süss, "Die Demonstration," p. 150.

64. MfS, AGM, 840, p. 12.

65. ZAIG, 2526, pp. 160, 163.

66. ZAIG, 233, 5.12.9, pp. 14–19.

67. ZAIG, 1992, pp. 224–30.

68. ZAIG, 14392, 5.12.9, pp. 2–5.

69. ZAIG, 8683, 5.12.9, pp. 22–33; all that I was given to see in Leipzig were training materials.

70. Richter, *Unfrieden*, p. 105.

71. ZAIG, 233, 5.12.9, pp. 2–6.

72. ZAIG, 2289, pp. 235–40.

73. MfS, 2526, 6.12.9, pp. 174, 182, 185.

74. *Ausgedient, Ein Stasi Major erzählt* (Halle: Mitteldeutsch, 1990), pp. 41, 103.

75. MfS, 2526, 6.12.9, p. 12.

76. ZAIG, AnS, 8683, 7.12.9.

77. Süss, "Die Demonstration," p. 150.

78. Richter, *Unfrieden*, pp. 95–96.

79. ZAIG, 2289, pp. 133, 148.

80. MfS, AGM, 840, 6; ZAIG, 7952, 7.12.9.

81. ZAIG, 2289, pp. 155–64.

82. ZAIG, 2326, 7.12.9, p. 196.

83. ZAIG, 2289, 8.12.9, pp. 165, 168.

84. ZAIG, 14418, 9.12.9, 1, pp. 6–80.

85. ZAIG, 13864, pp. 172–76.

86. ZAIG, 2289, pp. 337, 650.

87. ZAIG, 7942, p. 30.

88. Richter, *Unfrieden*, p. 57.

89. ZAIG, 2240, 12.12.9, pp. 56–59.

90. ZAIG, 2326, 13.12.9, p. 88.

91. ZAIG, 7942, pp. 18–22.

92. ZAIG, 2240, 13.12.9, pp. 65–68, 72.

93. Ibid., pp. 65–68.

94. Richter, *Unfrieden*, pp. 111–12.

95. Karl Wilhelm Fricke, *MfS Intern* (Köln: Wissenschaft und Politik, 1991), p. 73.

96. Richter, *Unfrieden*, p. 164.

97. MfS, 2240, 14.12.9, pp. 156–60.

98. ZAIG, 7942, AnSL, pp. 3–5.

99. ZAIG, 2240, 15.12.9, p. 147.

100. ZAIG, 13864, 25861.

101. ZAIG, 14418, pp. 70–73.

102. ZAIG, 13864, p. 194.

103. Richter, *Unfrieden*, p. 113.

104. ZAIG, 2289, p. 56.

105. Stefan Wolle, "Stasi Auflösung Beginn," in Gisela Helwig, *Rückblicke auf die DDR* (Köln: Deutschland Archiv, 1995), p. 61.

106. ZAIG, 8683, pp. 4–9.

107. Richter, *Unfrieden*, pp. 266, 269, 274.

108. Jens Hacker; *Deutsche Irrtümer* (Berlin: Ullstein, 1992), p. 38.

109. ZAIG, 13864, pp. 98, 105, 112.

110. ZAIG, 2742, 5.1.90, pp. 95–98.

111. ZAIG, 13864, 10.1.90, p. 2.

112. ZAIG, 13864, 9.1.90, pp. 31, 49.

113. ZAIG, 2289, pp. 15–51.

114. Richter, *Unfrieden*, p. 146.

115. Koehler, *Stasi*, pp. 409–10.

116. Anne Worst, *Das Ende eines Geheimdiensts, Oder, Wie lebendig ist die Stasi?* (Berlin: Links, 1991), p. 68.

117. Wolle, "Stasi," in Helwig, *Rückblicke*, pp. 66–68.

118. Friedrich W. Schlomann, *Die Maulwürfe* (München: Universitas, 1993), p. 278.

119. Joppke, *East German Dissidents*, p. 170.

120. Koehler, *Stasi*, pp. 149–50.

121. Fricke, *MFS Intern*, pp. 74, 80.

122. Wolfgang Rüddenklau, *Störenfried: DDR Opposition, 1986–89* (Berlin: Basis, 1992), p. 365.

123. Bernd Lindner, *Die demokratische Revolution in der DDR 1989/90* (Bonn: Bundeszentral für politische Bildung, 1998), p. 89.

124. Ibid., p. 114.

125. Stefan Bollinger, *1989—eine abgebrochene Revolution: Verbaute Wege nicht nur zu eine besseren DDR?* (Berlin: Trafo, 1999), p. 227.

126. Joppke, *East German Dissidents*, p. 163.

127. Horst Ehmke, *Mittendrin: Von der grossen Koalition zur Deutschen Einheit* (Berlin: Rowohlt, 1994), pp. 413–14.

128. Joppke, *East German Dissidents*, p. 213. Of those elected in March, the

academically trained were 85 percent; SPD had the highest percent, 92.8 percent; PDS had the highest percent of Ph.D.'s, 62, mostly scientists and medical professions. John Torpey, *Intellectuals, Socialism and Dissent* (Minneapolis: University of Minnesota Press, 1995), pp. 166–69.

129. Joppke, *East German Dissidents*, p. 166.

130. Ibid., p. 169.

131. Uwe Thaysen, *Der runde Tisch, Oder, wo blieb das Volk?* (Opladen: Westdeutscher, 1990), p. 178.

132. Joppke, *East German Dissidents*, p. 163.

Chapter 8

What We Learn from the Secret Police

WHAT THEY TELL OF THEMSELVES

The public's view of the DDR was of hard-faced officials who had the power of life and death, beginning with arbitrary arrest, a cruel interrogation complete with torture, and a miserable cell, such as can still be seen as cold museums. The perception was that the Stasi had spies everywhere watching, listening and keeping track of ideological misdeeds. As one teacher, Erika, told me, "Somewhere they are keeping a list of your sins and when they want to use it, they will hit you." People felt helpless against such an omnipresent spydom. Or as another, Jürgen, reflected with a grim smile, "There are three kinds of people here, those who have been arrested, those who are arrested and those who will be arrested." Having spent five years in the gulag, he expressed a proper confidence.

On the infamous other hand, the MfS described itself as the discoverer and teller of truths, even uncomfortable truths. Its reports present it as honest and hardworking servants of the state, professionals who were building socialism. Until the change, the assertion was always that the MfS was law-abiding. The internal communication does not speak of any illegal arrest or inhumane treatment. Only in November 1989 do the reports refer vaguely to violations.

With the exception of an angry quote from Mielke in early October, beating enemies was stated as not proper. When confronted by the violence of its armed branch at the Dresden train station, it blamed the "policy" of the politicians. The mass beatings were by those "improperly trained and wrongly led" by the Party.

The belated internal criticism was that Mielke forced the MfS to spy too much on too many people, demanding that he know everything. Citing retired spy-manager Wolf, the new MfS leaders admitted that spying on everybody was neither feasible nor desirable. It had given them a negative image. The twin blame was thus Politbüro policy and Mielke perfectionism.

Although Mielke always honored the Soviets as his Chekist model, his Germans seemed persuaded that they were more perfect than the Russians. Concerning Gorbachev was an ambivalence within the MfS, even some correct projections that his liberal policy would lead to the end of socialism.

The younger, better-educated officials had reservations about their older, more ideological, working-class superiors. They seem more inclined to follow the law than their predecessors, who had been toughened in surviving Hitler and Stalin. This new generation of Secret Police had retreated from violence to an attempt at control by manipulation.

Their "proper" tools were spying on "hostile-negatives," dividing them against each other, arresting, lecturing and occasionally pushing out the few who continued to resist. They came to the reluctant conclusion that those who persisted in wanting to emigrate were incorrigible and would best be permitted to leave rather than haunting the unfortunate police.

Never was there an admission that the goal was not the betterment of society, nowhere a cynical admission that any but a few lower-level employees, mostly in the militarized guard, had selfish motives. Lower-class misbehavior was mostly linked to the Guard Regiment. Sometimes the Party courts dismissed members as insufficiently committed to working-class idealism or having violated middle-class moral standards.

The middle-class civilians considered themselves as making unselfish sacrifices for the common good and being insufficiently rewarded. MfS members were especially offended by stories of their living in the luxury enjoyed by the top Party officials.

They even felt themselves victims, abused by drunken fans at soccer games and more persistently by the obdurate Emigrant Applicants, who were wearing them down. At the end they expressed fear of a public's unjustified discrimination and violence.

OF THE ENORMITY OF THE PUBLIC'S DISAFFECTION

Ehrhart Neubert concluded that the history of the DDR's resistance could not be written without including the phenomenon of the public's adaptation and acceptance. It was not only a retreat when confronted by the state's repressive power but an emotional connection that guaranteed the power of the SED. "By participating in the system one could avoid the always threatening repression. This demanded a reason as justification to oneself and the social environment."

The subjection had to appear sensible. The fear of the superior power must be changed into a positive, which was done by the use of antifascism and socialism, although not so much with the masses as with the more intellectually inclined. Although socialism could not root out individualism and material interests, the inheritance of the false consciousness of capitalism must be denounced, which idealism appealed to the traditional anti-selfish Christian and patriotic ethic. The Marxist "science of history" was also comforting, as it explained any suffering as necessary to the inevitable progress, "the building of socialism."

There were limits to the adapting and connecting, but not so much in the citizen's willingness to adjust as in the construction of society. Whoever was organized was able to avoid further commitments. By "joining in" harmlessly, one could remain internally an outsider.

The masses were always discontented, but everyone knew that suddenly bananas would appear.[1] Life had been made livable by "connections." This supplement to the intellectual persuasion was crushed by the persistent and worsening shortages, which clearly did not exist in the capitalist West.

The MfS documents leave little question about the length and the breadth of the discontent that created the revolution. It existed in the most remote villages of "backward" Mecklenburg. The MfS thus provided ample evidence that the revolution was popular, not an action of a handful of radicals and a street-cluttering minority. By its official description, the regime was not only economically but also politically, intellectually and emotionally bankrupt, and much of this bankruptcy was found within the SED's leaders.

The severe criticisms came to be as sharp from small towns as from the big cities, perhaps even sharpest from the underprivileged collectivized farmers. It is impressive how often workers, urban and rural, were cited as the bearers of discontent and how often workers were more perceptive than their upwardly mobile leaders. They were, in fact, the power of the revolution, although underemployed intellectuals were its vanguard.

The scattered masses yearning to be free needed the few Berlin symbols of open resistance, but demonstrations of rural discontent followed a few weeks after the urban example, even though the small-towners were not protected by a relative anonymity. Nearly everywhere people experienced the similar deficiencies of the system and acted accordingly.

What is further impressive is the consistency of the demands, chronologically as well as geographically, early or late. By November 1987 the essential dissatisfactions that brought on the revolution were being consistently reported, and the MfS did not challenge the validity of the popular grievances.

OF DISCONTENTS LIKE THOSE IN THE WEST

Some of the reaction to social problems was similar to popular complaints in the West: the young had been spoiled by a solicitous system and lacked interest in really working. Many adults were more concerned with obtaining more luxuries than in working. Officials were more interested in their privileges than in serving the public. Politicians were not honest with the public. Men amnestied by liberals from prison were not welcome. Foreign workers were given too many privileges.

The more educated the person, the more likely was the discontent. The privileged intelligentsia were not privileged enough. They were not paid enough compared to managers and entertainers. In the complaint that prices were up and quality down, the DDR did not have the advantage of low price imports from underpaid Asians.

There was, more frequently than in the West, the perception that rewards were not based on achievement, that a kind of welfare existed for persons unwilling to work but nominally employed. This Marxist idea "To everyone according to their needs" was very much resented by both manual and brain workers. Less fear for one's job meant less work, less cleanliness, less courtesy.

The dissatisfaction of teachers was particularly pronounced, although they had been carefully picked and trained to inculcate social values. As in the West, teachers criticized administrators as undercompetent and overpaid, while teachers were overworked and underrewarded.

Students were getting ever more difficult to deal with, sometimes even violent. The teaching of slow students—for the democratic reason of equalizing opportunity—was at the expense of the more talented. Promoting students who had not met standards was regarded as a mistake. It added to the problem of declining discipline and declining value of diplomas.

The DDR teachers had the special grievance that they, like their pupils, must keep personal persuasion out of the classroom. Also, teachers had out-of-class ideological responsibilities to the Party to provide leadership to the compulsory state youth organization. The last blow was that, as "secret carriers," they were prevented from visiting the West, therewith suddenly being among the less privileged.

THE ACCURACY OF THE SECRET POLICE AS REPORTERS AND ANALYSTS

The DDR's Secret Police were more honest than its journalists. As professionals, they valued the truth. They could be honest, in secret, because they could arrest anyone else who wrote or spoke the undesired truth.

The acute danger from DDR discontent had been earlier secretly reported by Gorbachev's Secret Police, who need not show their support to the DDR by looking at the brighter side. An impending collapse of the DDR was predicted in Moscow as early as 1986, when the MfS still had confidence that its clever infiltrating and dividing the opposition could keep them in hand. It showed confidence that it was smarter and better organized than the opposition.

The MfS long did not recognize the potential of the few dissidents, whom it had well identified and isolated. It scorned their lack of popular support, until the sudden numbers of the revolution earned them a grudging respect. It had not imagined a revolution without Lenin-like leaders, and it perceived no credible leaders of the masses. In this it may have been correct because very few of these exerted leadership (or had leadership thrust upon them) for more than a few months. More often those, like Stolpe, who understood power were those who understood power after the change.

The severe criticisms, such as those forwarded from Schwerin, were accepted. There seems to be no time when Berlin told Schwerin, "You must have this wrong. The discontent is not so bad. You're exaggerating. You are deviating from the Party Line."

The MfS rarely judged that the critics had it wrong or that the public anger was unjustified. This would suggest no basic gap between the MfS attitudes and those of the public, which it was supposed to control. Most MfS personnel went shopping and found the cupboard bare. They also resented that as "secret carriers," they were not permitted contact with the West. They were very much frustrated when their IMs applied to go to West and returned beyond their control.

There seems no distinct difference between the MfS Schwerin grassroots views and those of the Berlin headquarters, except for the pronouncements of Mielke, and even he expressed criticism of his incompetent Party peers.

The Secret Police permitted themselves the privilege of describing over and over again the failures and weaknesses of the regime. Clearly evident in their reports is their increasing willingness to accept the popular criticisms as valid. They gradually perceived that the enemy was correctly describing the problems of their "socialist" country and came to the conclusion that socialism did not work.

Even Mielke accepted the validity of popular criticism up to a point. He knew from reports, but not experience, what the shortages meant. His argument in October 1989 with his generals about conditions in a hospital shows that his privileges had isolated him from much of the reality as it had his Politbüro peers. The old Mielke, who had as a young man sacrificed as a Communist, was encased in illusions set in concrete.

The MfS itself displayed a steady increase in concern, reaching the level of frustration in the spring of 1989 that the Politbüro was still ignoring the discontent that the MfS had repeatedly reported. In the MfS mirror, one can detect the gradual escalation of the opposition, bit by bit, hesitantly, then hopefully, then in late summer 1989 with assurance.

One can observe the MfS tactics of divide and control, used at first with confidence and then with some doubts and finally the concession, "This won't help. We have lost." No later than October the MfS was resigned to the necessity of a basic change in Party leaders and basic reforms of the system. Mielke turned on Honecker, but in the opinion of his subordinates much too late, and the MfS quickly turned on Mielke.

THE WEAKNESSES OF THE SECRET POLICE AS ENFORCERS

In his detailed analysis of the limits of the DDR power, Richard Bessel concluded that although the DDR tyranny was much more complete than the National Socialist, "At closer examination it becomes clear that many characteristics of East German history between 1945 and 1989 can be explained only if it is possible to describe the complicated interworkings—earlier one might have used the term the dialectic—between the total power demand of the dictatorship and the many limiting factors, some of which the dictatorship created."

The first restraint was historical continuity. "The indissoluble ties with German history and the soviet hegemonial power could also be seen as the outer limits of the dictatorship. It is certain that certain institutions survived with lesser or greater remnants of their autonomy and logic, church, family and science."[2] Added thereto was the experience of the immediate postwar period, including the uncontrolled Soviet troop behavior and then the artificial West border, which made the DDR only a partial state. With their assertion of humane values, the Communists became more shy about killing than the National Socialists.

For the masses, more important than the real power of the Stasi was the paranoid fantasy of its omniscience and omnipotence.[3] This documentation is not only evidence of what the MfS was able to discover but evidence of how a secret service could fail. Knowledge is not sufficient power.

What is apparent is how dependent the MS was on voluntary and amateur informers. The IMs were used not only to get information but to work on crowd control. Rarely is any other source identified, such as mail or phone intercepts. No repeated assertion was made about the value of any other source of domestic information. IM knowledge was the MfS' strength and IM ignorance its weakness.

Mielke kept complaining that his MfS leaders were unable to recruit the needed IMs, to know them well enough, to assign them correctly, to interview them properly and to analyze critically what had been reported. He constantly insisted that his organization lacked truly knowledgeable and significant IMs; it did not have the right IMs in the right places, and his personnel were unprofessional in using them.

Repeatedly, IMs are cited as the key to power, and as often they are cited for not producing the needed information, particularly about the misbehavior that crippled the economy. Too much of what they reported was admittedly trivial and vague. The more technical and important the intelligence work, the less competent were these spies. Berlin was constantly frustrated when the information required scientific training or being in a high position to observe what had become the worst problem, the economic collapse. The man in the street was better observed than the man in an office of power and much better influenced.

But to these insufficiencies, the prescribed solution remained better IMs. Even when the MfS was struggling to stay above the waters of discontent, even while accepting the Change to democracy, its leaders saw no alternative to their internal spies.

They were frustrated by their inability to prevent foreign journalist "spies," but they were more offended by the obvious dishonesty of the DDR journalism, which ran counter to what they knew to be true.

There was also by 1988 the frequent admission that their "administrative" measures, meaning arrest or threat of arrest, would not suffice, that the power of a Secret Police was limited. More important, the MfS was helpless in dealing with the minds of the masses, particularly in all but a few areas remote from Western TV. The masses, like the few hostiles, could be physically contained, but their thoughts remained free, as in the famous folk song. The masses could be kept from leaving, but their thoughts stayed with those Western automobiles, which were so much superior in every way, including availability.

Its contacts, direct and indirect, with hostile people seem to have made the MfS more hesitant, particularly on the local level, where it was in constant confrontation with skeptics and resisters, particularly those who insisted on emigrating. The MfS prided itself on infiltrating opposition groups, guiding them or disrupting them, but in time it became itself infiltrated, as by a disease of doubt, one based on reality and disproven belief. Infiltrating the emigrant applicants does not seem to have been possible. The documentation shows that loyalty and criticism can coexist and that criticism can defeat loyalty, in this case when the enforcers were aware that the critics had it right.

It is also evident that many DDR citizens risked criticizing the system in strong language at times and places when the MfS spies could hear them. The MfS, unlike the Gestapo, did not describe arresting persons for the crime of criticism, not even hostile churchmen organizing youth. They kept saying that they did not take political prisoners, only those who had broken the law in an action, like attacking the border. MfS tolerance may have derived from its persuasion that the hostiles were not their equals in competence.

The record indicates that the noted arrests of opposition leaders were seldom and brief, in sharp contrast to those of the Soviets, 1945–1949, with sentences of 25 years to the remote gulag. Most arrestees received "instruction," which was supposed to frighten but increasingly did not. As

Eppelmann observed, those restraining their words and ambitions had room to play. This increased as BRD money pried loose the bonds.

The MfS had long lists of those whom they would arrest when danger arose, but, in fact, when danger was clear in 1989, it did not arrest leaders. What is surprising is that the MfS seems to have observed the revolution and tried to divert it but did not send the revolutionaries to available concentration camps.

It did not appear eager to lock up people. It reached the point that the MfS saw the solution in allowing the applicants to leave. There had developed *vis-à-vis* the Emigrant Applicants, a "live and let leave" attitude. Some were permitted to emigrate with their discontent, others stayed and continued flagrantly risking another arrest.

As a rebel who stayed, Jens Reich described the MfS, "The Stasi view was that Mielke was to tell Honecker about the monster [opposition] which they had stopped, having created great amounts of paper for trash about opposition groups who could only argue among themselves. . . . They discovered the truths, which never could be permitted to disturb the SED view. So the Stasi deceived itself and the Party, for which it was supposed to be the shield and sword and at the end it could only provide a paper tiger. The Stasi had turned from weapons to paper."[4]

There is a profound difference between being able to describe the problems (The Secret Police assignment) and being able to solve them (the politician's assignment). The MfS could not win the masses. Its seemingly omnipresent spies, its uniformed army of division strength, and the ubiquitous militias in factories, farms and offices proved useless against the massive discontent that the MfS had long and accurately described.

Diverting from thought control was the high priority given to boost production of factories and farms. There was little that it could do about the obsolescence of the DDR equipment, but with the subjective emphasized as more important than the objective, it spied on officials of the government's economy to find out who was sabotaging and prevent it. It would subjectively defeat the objective problems.

The MfS learned that the managers had to avoid as best they could the "socialist" system of "central planning." The leaders had to beat the system with black market barter deals to get materials and tolerate worker resistance to keep the workers. The workers found their ways to beat the system with work slowdowns, work-time shopping, going home early, manipulating wages and bonuses. Managers and workers pretended to have lived up to the Plan, and the government pretended to believe them.

The collapsing production seems to have been unhindered by the spies, who could describe but not change the system. The masses' drive to earn more and work less was greater than the threat of arrest and the persuasion of ridiculed propaganda.

HOW REALITIES DEFEATED THE IDEALS

Communists had long stressed the "subjective element," which meant using propaganda to achieve harder work. This was in contrast to the "objective element," which meant the material realities, which the subjective was supposed to dominate. (To an "uninstructed," this seems at odds with the Marxist concept of economic determinism.) The irony is that the DDR was defeated subjectively by the media of the West, which came to be accepted as much more credible than the DDR media, which denied the reality known to almost everyone.

The MfS could not keep people from Western propaganda, the most important part of which was the BRD's obvious material success. Watching Western TV had long been surreptitiously common until the state was forced to permit it. The pictures of Western superiority became increasingly compelling, but a visit to the West proved overwhelming and led to the most crushing disillusionment with DDR "socialism," because of not only the amazing plenitude but the cleanliness of the stores and the courtesy of salespersons.

Stopping that travel was a MfS necessity but a near impossibility. Trying to prevent DDR citizens from seeing the other part of the German world was like trying to stop the waves, but the system battled to keep those still working from visiting the seductive West. Letting retired persons visit was permitted first; their defection would reduce consumption but not production. Their staying away was preferable to returning and describing the Western wonders. Many people counted the days until they could retire and travel. Athletes were allowed to travel when still young in order to win gold medals and DDR prestige. Persons thought loyal enough to be "travel cadre" were allowed to go on business trips but had to leave their loved ones behind.

The BRD was able to arrange for ordinary people of working age to get permission to go West for a family occasion, such as an anniversary or death. Restraints on visits to family occasions were taken very poorly. Although the 44 years of division had weakened such ties, particularly the families of the young who had "fled the Republic" were angry that contact was often impossible. Since the DDR could not provide their citizens with West marks, the BRD kindly, or maliciously, gave visitors needed money, which enabled them to see more.

The solution created a problem: permitting some to go West for family reasons led to the serious envy of those who could not find or would not pretend a family justification. This meant yet another new class of those who could visit or obtain Western money from relatives. The more honest the person, the more trouble in getting permission. Those who had gained privileges by a commitment to the DDR became less privileged because as loyalists they should not apply or as "secret carriers" they were forbidden exposure to the dangers of the nonsocialist world.

This widening contact, successfully pushed by the BRD, meant the existence of two currencies. With Western money one could avoid the barren DDR stores and buy in the Intershops, which were a faint but dangerous reflection of Western wealth as advertised on TV. The new Western money class could obtain items, including automobiles, which were nearly unobtainable with DDR money.

Enabled by this overwhelming material difference, the revolutionaries had intellectually won the field no later than September 1989, when the MfS reported that the Party was unable to respond to the opposition's arguments. Teachers could not hope to persuade pupils of the Party line, competing with the pictures on Western TV and the music on Western radio.

The documents show remarkable consistency and tenacity in this public rejection of unbelievable propaganda and of leaders who had become obviously old and apparently incompetent.

Whatever the East German discontent after the Change, the MfS proved that the popular motivation for the Change in 1989 was undeniably long-standing and overwhelming.

THE SECRET POLICE AS DISSIDENTS

Reading the many MfS reports about the frustrating conditions, blamed on the leaders, one could think that the writer was a dissident. The line between critic and supporter of the DDR became blurred. They even expressed the common criticism of the incompetence and privilege of their superiors, including Honecker.

Evident is that the MfS at the local level saw the economic problems, that the collective farms and the state-owned industries were functioning badly, which was blamed on "enemies." Already in the 1950s, it noted the endemic economic problems, waste, inefficiency, laziness and dishonesty, which by the 1980s were nearly catastrophic.

The reader must notice the repeated astounding admissions, particularly in 1989, that the socialist system was not working because it was inferior to that of the capitalist West. The reality did not cause Mielke to waver in his 60-year commitment to Communism, but other MfS leaders expressed doubts, ever more strongly. Then when Mielke was replaced, his successors suddenly voiced a belief in values of the West, albeit somehow combined with the use of IM spies and infiltrators to defend the freer constitution.

By 1989 the strong criticism reported from the masses was obviously what the MfS reporters also felt very strongly. What could be read in MfS secret reports seems more severe than the revolutionaries dared say, except in hushed tones with the very few whom they thought they could trust, some of whom were likely MfS spies.

Consistent in MfS criticism is the missing achievement principle; rewarding people on the Marxist basis of equal needs, not unequal production, meant that many chose not to work or, more importantly, not to think about how to work more productively.

Similar was the lack of promotion for better production; rather, preference was given to those with better Party credentials or contacts. The system was not as productive partly because it did not reward productivity. It did not punish low productivity at top or bottom.

In the middle, MfS members were personally upset that they as the more intelligent and trained were not paid according to their accomplishments. There are times when the MfS criticism is more bitter than that of the opposition that it has been arresting, who as idealists show less interest in extra money and privilege and therewith were sometimes described as the true socialists.

The MfS knew and could communicate more than the opposition could about the faults of the regime. These defenders of the system thus sensed more quickly than its enemies that the system was doomed and that they, its defenders, could soon lose. Some writers have since come to believe that the MfS was itself revolutionary and had the will and the skill to effect the revolution.

THE SECRET POLICE AS REBELS

The obvious fact that the MfS came to demand a removal of old leaders and welcomed "the Change" has led to the interpretation that a powerful and smart MfS created that change. Wolfgang Schnur and Ibrahim Böhme, both IMs, advanced the idea that KGB and MfS worked together on building the dissident bandwagon.[5]

Dissident Rüddenklau advanced an even more remarkable idea about the bloodless revolution: "There is much to indicate that the opponents of the DDR knew exactly what they were doing. The Maltese Hilfedienst had built in spring the camps in Hungary for the refugees who came in the summer. Daimler Benz bought from the West Berlin Senate an obscure property on the Potsdamer Platz, which became soon the most desirable property in Europe. It would appear that a mighty coalition of powers were working to end the DDR. This included the east European secret services, and Egon Krenz, who decided while in the Soviet Union in June on *Perestroika*. And there are many indications that this had been prepared for years by Markus Wolf."[6]

This theory, if true, would have to exclude Mielke, who was the defender of the system until the end, although helping Krenz push Honecker out. MfS internal criticism of Honecker and the Politbüro had been expressed for years. At first the MfS used the phrase "progressive forces," meaning those who believed in socialism and wished the DDR to succeed, to express their own criticisms of the elite. No later than 1987, the MfS displayed a disillusion with policy, although not with the system. Increasingly, disapproval of SED policy and top personnel became internally blatant.

The MfS wanted changes and had the forlorn hope that the powerful Mielke could effect them with his aged peers on the Politbüro. When Mielke would not or could not, he was pushed out and succeeded by the reformer Schwanitz. The MfS press officer Gernknauer observed that the upper-middle layer did want to get rid of the top leadership. That layer began to introduce reforms immediately on his fall from power.[7]

Yet the documentation provides little to support Hendryk Broder's idea that the MfS brought the system down. It kept trying to contain the dissidents until at least early October. Thereafter, the MfS was informed and motivated enough to want change, but it is doubtful that it was strong enough, united enough, in particular well led enough to have created the change. It was smart enough to delay its own defeat but not smart enough to prevent it.

To put it more positively, its advocacy, even before the Wall came down, of more freedom and democracy is impressive. It is amazing how quickly the supposed staunchest of Communists, even MfS generals, could quickly come to affirm internally the necessity and superiority of democracy, albeit one with a strong Secret Police. Their new ideal was that of the Bonn Secret Police as constitution protectors. As professionals, they claimed a needed independence from politicians "to do their jobs."

They retained the fond hope that a democratic socialism would emerge, rather than the selfish capitalism of the West, another Stasi misjudgment. Democratic socialism was defeated by Democratic consumerism.

The core truth was that the Stasi, as fairly ordinary humans, wanted the security of basic needs guaranteed by the state, but like other humans they also placed a high priority on the freedom to obtain something more than the basics. They had the sense that extra freedom, as well as income, should result from their superior work performance. Like many in Western democracy, the MfS spoke of the equality of humankind, but regarded itself as superior and deserving of superior rewards.

Further, a system that not only requires the sacrifice of freedom of expression and travel but does not provide a freedom of consumer goods in its stead can rarely be defended, and surely not by Secret Police alone. For the Secret Police to suppress the truth, the people would have to blind themselves to the very truth that it is their purpose to know.

NOTES

1. Ehrhart Neubert, *Geschichte der Opposition in der DDR 1949–1989* (Berlin: Links, 1997), pp. 18–23.

2. Richard Bessell and Ralph Jessen, *Die Grenzen der diktatur* (Göttingen: Vandenhoeck, 1996), pp. 8–13.

3. Anne Worst, *Das Ende eines Geheimdiensts, Oder, Wie lebendig ist die Stasi?* (Berlin: Links, 1991), p. 111.

4. Jens Reich, *Abschied von den Lebenslügen* (Berlin: Rowohlt, 1992), pp. 85, 87.

5. Armin Mitter and Stefan Wolle, *Untergang auf Raten* (Munchen: Bertelsmann, 1993), pp. 500, 530.

6. Wolfgang Rüddenklau, *Störenfried: DDR Opposition, 1986–89* (Berlin: Basis, 1992), p. 365.

7. Elizabeth Pond, *Beyond the Wall* (Washington, DC: Brookings Institution, 1993), pp. 105, 125.

Bibliography

Allen, Bruce. *Germany East: Dissent and Opposition.* Montreal: Black Rose, 1991.

Ammer, Thomas and Hans Joachim Memmler. *Staatssicherheit in Rostock.* Köln: Deutschland Archiv, 1991.

Aretz, Jürgen and Wolfgang Stock. *Die vergessenen Opfer der DDR.* Bergich-Gladbach: Bastei, 1997.

Auferstanden aus Ruinen und wie weiter: Chronik der Wende in Karl Marx Stadt/ Chemnitz, 1989/1990. Chemnitz: Heimatland, 1991.

Ausgedient, Ein Stasi Major erzählt. Halle: Mitteldeutsch, 1990.

Bahr, Eckhard. *Sieben Tage im Oktober: Aufbruch in Dresden.* Leipzig: Forum, 1990.

Bastian, Uwe. *Auf zum letzten Gefecht: Vorbereitungen des MfS auf den Zusammenbruch der DDR-Wirtschaft.* Berlin: Forschungsbund, 1994.

Bastian, Uwe. *Zersetzungsmassnahmen der Staatssicherheit am Beispiel des operativevorgangfes "Entwurf."* Berlin: Forschungsverbund, 1993.

Beleites, Michael. *Altlast Wismut: Ausnahmezustand, Umweltkatastrophe und das Sanierungsproblem im deutschen Uranbergbau.* Frankfurt, a.M.: Brandes & Apsel, 1992.

Bender, Peter. *Unser Erbschaft: Was war die DDR—was bleibt von ihr.* Hamburg: Luchterhand Literarverlag, 1993.

Bessell, Richard and Ralph Jessen. *Die Grenzen der Diktatur.* Göttingen: Vandenhoeck, 1996.

Bögeholz, Hartwig. *Wendepunkte die Chronik der Republik: Der Weg der Deutschen in Ost und West.* Hamburg: Rowohlt, 1999.

Bollinger, Stefan. *1989—eine abgebrochene Revolution: Verbaute Wege nicht nur zu einer besseren DDR?* Berlin: Trafo, 1999.

Bonwetsch, Gennadij Bordjugov and Norman Naimark. *Sowjetische Politik in der SBZ 1945–1949.* Berlin: Dietz, 1998.

Briefe an das Neue Forum, 3 vols., September to 31 Oktober 1989. Berlin: Havemann Archiv.

Bund Sozialistischer Arbeiter. *Das End der DDR*. Essen: Arbeiter Presse, 1992.

Buthmann, Reinhard. *Kadersicherung im Kombinat VEB Carl Zeiss Jena: Die Staatssicherheit und das Scheitern des Mikroelektronikprogramm*. Berlin: Links, 1997.

Childs, David and Richard Popplewell. *The East German Intelligence and Security Service*. New York: New York University Press, 1996.

Christ, Peter and Ralf Neubauer. *Kolonie im eigenen Land*. Berlin: Rowohlt, 1991.

Czepuck, Harri. *Meine Wendezeiten*. Berlin: Dietz, 1999.

Das Neue Forum und die Stasi: Von der Gründung des Neue Forums bis zur Legalisierung. Berlin: Havemann Archiv.

Daschitschew, Wjatscheslaw. "Sowjetische Deutschlandpolitik in den achtziger Jahren." *Deutschland Archiv*, January 1995.

Davies, Sarah. *Popular Opinion in Stalin's Russia*. Cambridge: Cambridge University Press, 1997.

Dornheim, Andreas. *Politische Umbruch in Erfurt, 1989/90*. Weimar: Böhlau, 1995.

Dümcke, Wolfgang and Fritz Vilmar. *Kolonisierung der DDR*. Münster: Agenda, 1995.

Eberhardt, Andreas. *Verschwiegene Jahre*. Berlin: Spitz, 1998.

Ehmke, Horst. *Mittendrin: Von der grossen Koalition zur Deutschen Einheit*. Berlin: Rowohlt, 1994.

Eisenfeld, Bernd. "Vortat, Widerständiges und oppositionelles Verhalten im Spiegel von MfS Statistiken." *Archiv*, February 24, 1994.

Eltgen, Hans. *Ohne Chance: Erinnerungen eines HVA-Offizier*. Berlin: Edition Ost, 1997.

Eppelmann, Rainer. *Fremd im eigenen Haus*. Köln: Kiepenheuer, 1993.

Findeis, Hagen and Detlef Pollack, Hg. *Selbstbewahrung oder Selbstverlust*. Berlin: Links, 1999.

Fischer, Alexander and Günther Heydemann, Hg. *Die politische "Wende" 1989/90 in Sachsen*. Köln: Böhlau, 1995.

Foitzik, Jan. *Sowjetische Militäradministration in Deutschland, 1945–49*. Berlin: Akademie, 1999.

Förster, Peter and Gunter Roski. *DDR Zwischen Wende und Wahl*. Berlin: Links, 1992.

Frey, Dr. Gerhard. *Prominente ohne Maske DDR*. München: FZ, 1991.

Fricke, Karl Wilhelm. *Akten Einsicht*. Berlin: Links, 1995.

Fricke, Karl Wilhelm. *DDR Staatssicherheit: Das Phänomen des Verrats—Die Zusammenarbeit zwischen MfS und KGB*. Bochum: Universitäts Verlag, 1995.

Fricke, Karl Wilhelm. *MfS Intern*. Köln: Wissenschaft und Politik, 1991.

Fricke, Karl Wilhelm. "Schild und Schwert." Die Stasi, Deutschland Funk, 7 Okt. 1992.

Fricke, Karl Wilhelm and Roger Engelmann. *"Konzentrierte Schläge": Staatssicherheitsaktionenen und politische Prozesse in der DDR 1953–56*. Berlin: Links, 1998.

Friedrich, Wolfgang-Uwe. *Die totalitäre Herrschaft der SED: Wirklichkeit und Nachwirkungen*. München: Beck, 1998.

Fulbrook, Mary. *Anatomy of a Dictatorship*. Oxford: Oxford University Press, 1995.

Gatow, Hanns-Heinz. *Vertuschte SED-Verbrechen*. Berg am See: Türmer, 1991.

Gatzmaga, Ditmar, Thomas Voss and Klaus Westerman. *Auferstehen aus Ruinen*. Marburg: Schüren, 1991.

Gauck, Joachim. *Die Stasi-Akten*. Hamburg: Rowohlt, 1991.

Gegen Das Volk kann nichts mehr entschieden werden: MfS und SED im Bezirk Neubrandenburg. Berlin: Bundesbeauftragte, 1997.

Gerstner, Karl-Heinz. *Sachlich, kritisch, optimistisch*. Berlin: Edition Ost, 1999.

Gill, David and Ulrich Schröter. *Das Ministerium für Staatssicherheit*. Berlin: Rowohlt, 1991.

Golombek, Dieter and Dietrich Ratzke. *Dagewesen und Aufgeschieben*. Frankfurt: Medienentwicklung, 1990.

Gorbatchow, Michail. *Wie es war: Die Deutsche Wiedervereinigung*. Berlin: Ullstein, 1999.

Grande, Dieter and Bernd Schäfer. *Kirche im Visier: SED, Staatssicherheit und Katholische Kirche in Der DDR*. Leipzig: Benno, 1998.

Hacker, Jens. *Deutsche Irrtümer*. Berlin: Ullstein, 1992.

Hammer, Detlef. *Spionage gegen eine Kirchenleitung: Stasi Offizier im Konsistorium Magdeburg*. Magdeburg, 1994.

Hebert, Andreas. *Räumt die steine Weg*. München: Claudius, 2000.

Helwig, Gisela. *Rückblicke auf die DDR*. Köln: Deutschland Archiv, 1995.

Henke, Klaus-Dietmar and Roger Engelmann. *Aktenlage: Die Bedeutung der Unterlagen des Staatssicherheitdiensts für die Zeitgeschichtsforschung*. Berlin: Links, 1995.

Hertle, Hans-Herrmann. *Der Fall der Mauer*. Opladen: Westdeutscher, 1996.

Hollitzer, Tobias. *Einblick in das Herrschaftswesen einer Diktaur—Chance oder Fluch?* Opladen: Westdeutscher, 1996.

Horsch, Holger. *"Hat nicht wenigsten die Stasi die Stimmung im Lande gekannt?" MfS und SED im Bezirk Karl-Marx Stadt*. Berlin: Bundesbeauftragte, 1997.

Humm, Antonia Maria, *Auf dem Weg zum sozialistischen Dorf*. Göttingen: Vandenhoeck and Ruprecht, 1999.

Jander, Martin. *Formierung und Krise der DDR Opposition*. Berlin: Akademie, 1996.

Janson, Carl Heinz. *Totengräber der DDR*. Düsseldorf: Econ, 1991.

Jarausch, Konrad. *The Rush to German Unity*. Oxford: Oxford University Press, 1994.

Joas, Hans and Martin Kohli. *Der Zusammenbruch der DDR: Soziologische Analysen*. Frankfurt: Suhrkamp, 1993.

Joppke, Christian. *East German Dissidents and the Revolution of 1989*. New York: New York University Press, 1995.

Judt, Mathias. *DDR Geschichte in Dokumenten*. Bonn: Bundeszentrale für politische Bildung, 1998.

Kallabis, Heinz. *Ade, DDR!* Berlin: Treptower, 1990.

Kloth, Hans Michael. *Vom "Zettelfalten" zum freien Wählen: Die Demokratisierung der DDR 1989/9 und die "Wahlfrage."* Berlin: Links, 2000.

Koehler, John O. *Stasi: The Untold Story of the East German Secret Police*. Boulder, CO: Westview Press, 1999.

Koop, Volker. *Armee oder Freizeitclub: Die Kampfgruppen der Arbeiterklasse.* Bonn: Bouvier, 1997.

Koop, Volker. *Zwischen Recht und Willkür: Die Rote Armee in Deutschland.* Bonn: Bouvier, 1996.

Kopstein, Jeffrey. *The Politics of Economic Decline in East Germany, 1945–1989.* Chapel Hill: University of North Carolina Press, 1997.

Kotschenmassow, Wjatschslaw. *Meine letzte Mission.* Berlin: Dietz, 1994.

Kurz, Robert. *Honeckers Rache.* Berlin: Bitterman, 1991.

Landtag Mecklenburg-Vorpommern. *Aufarbeitung und Versöhnung.* Schwerin: Landtag, 1996.

Langer, Kai. *"Ihr soll wissen, dass der Norden nicht schläft": Zur Geschichte der "Wende" in den drei Nordbezirken der DDR.* Bremen: Temmen, 1999.

Lehman, R. and Hans Georg. *Deutschland Chronik, 1945 bis 1995.* Bonn: Bundeszentrale für politische Bildung, 1996.

Liedtke, Rüdiger. *Die Treuhand und die zweite Enteignung der Ostdeutschen.* München: Spangenberg, 1993.

Lindner, Bernd, *Die demokratische Revolution in der DDR 1989/90.* Bonn: Bundeszentral für politische Bildung, 1998.

Linke, Dietmar. *Die DDR Kirche zwischen Kanzel und Konspiration.* Berlin: Basis, 1993.

Linke, Dietmar. *Niemand kann zwei Herren dienen: Als Pfarrer in der DDR.* Hamburg: Hoffmann and Campe, 1988.

Linke, Dietmar. *Theologie-studenten der Humboldt-Universität.* Neukirchen-Vluyn: Neukirchner Verlag, 1994.

Lochen, Hans-Hermann and Christian Meyer-Seitz. *Die geheimen Anweisungen zur Diskriminierung Ausreisewilliger.* Köln: Bundesanzeiger, 1992.

Loth, Wilfried. *Stalin's ungeliebtes Kind: Warum Moskau die DDR nicht wollte.* Berlin: Rowohlt, 1994.

Ludwig, Andreas, ed. *Fortschritt, Norm und Eigensinn: Erkundungen im Alltag der DDR.* Berlin: Links, 1999.

Luft, Christa. *Treuhand Report.* Berlin: Aufbau, 1992.

Maaz, Hans Joachim. *Die Entrüstung.* Berlin: Argon, 1992.

Maennel, Anne. *Auf sie war Verlass: Frauen und Stasi.* Berlin: Elefanten, 1995.

Mai, Günther. "Politischer Umbruch in Thüringen und Mecklenburg-Vorpommern." Paper presented at the German Studies Association Conference, Houston, Texas, October 6, 2000.

Maier, Gerhart. *Die Wende in der DDR.* Bonn: Bundeszentral, 1990.

Malycha, Andreas. *Die SED Geschichte ihrer Stalinisierung, 1946–1953.* Paderborn: Schöningh, 2000.

Mampel, Siegfried. *Das Ministerium für Staatssicherheit der ehemaligen DDR als Ideologiepolizei.* Berlin: Duncker, 1996.

Marcuse, Peter. *A German Way of Revolution: DDR Tagebuch eines Amerikaners.* Berlin: Dietz, 1990.

Mathiopoulus, Margarita. *Rendezvous mit der DDR*, Düsseldorf: Econ, 1994.

McAdams, A. James. *Germany Divided.* Princeton, NJ: Princeton University Press, 1993.

Meckel, Markus and Martin Gutzeit. *Opposition in der DDR.* Köln: Bund, 1994.

Meinel, Reinhard. *Mit Tschekistischem Gruss: Berichte der Bezirksverwaltung für Staatssicherheit Potsdam 1989*. Potsdam: Babelturm, 1990.

Merkel, Ina. *Wir sind doch nicht die Meckerecke der Nation*. Berlin: Schwarzkopf, 1999.

Michel, Hans Magnus. *Kursbuch: In Sachen Erich Honnecker*. Berlin: Rowohlt, 1993.

Mittag, Günter. *Um Jeden Preis*. Berlin: Aufbau, 1991.

Mitter, Armin and Stefan Wolle. *Untergang auf Raten*. München: Bertelsmann, 1993.

Modrow, Hans. *Aufbruch und Ende*. Hamburg: Konkret, 1991.

Modrow, Hans. *Ich wollte ein neues Deutschland*. Berlin: Dietz, 1998.

Mothes, Jorn. *Beschädigte Seelen: DDR Jugend und Staatssicherheit*. Bremen: Temmen, 1996.

Müller-Enbergs, Helmut. *Inoffizielle Mitarbeiter des Ministeriums für Staatssicherheit*. Berlin: Links, 1996.

Murphy, David E., Sergei A. Kondrashev and George Bailey. *Battleground Berlin*. New Haven, CT: Yale University Press, 1997.

Naimark, Norman. *The Russians in Germany: A History of the Soviet Zone of Occupation, 1945–1950*. Cambridge, MA: Harvard University Press, 1995.

Nakath, Detlef and Gerd-Rüdiger Stephan. *Die Häber-Protokolle: Schlaglichter der SED West-politik, 1973–1985*. Berlin: Dietz, 1999.

Neubert, Ehrhart. *Geschichte der Opposition in der DDR 1949–1989*. Berlin: Links, 1997.

Neubert, Ehrhart. *Vergebung oder Weisswäscherei, Zur Aufarbeitung des Stasi-problems in den Kirchen*. Freiburg: Herder, 1993.

Neues Forum Leipzig. *Jetzt oder Nie: Leipzige Herbst '89*. Leipzig: Forum, 1989.

Nikitin, Pjotr I. *Zwischen Dogma und gesundem Menschenverstand*. Berlin: Akademie, 1997.

Opp, Karl-Dieter and Peter Voß. *Die volkseigene Revolution*. Stuttgart: Klett-Cotta, 1993.

Pechman, Roland and Jurgen Vogl. *Abgesang der Stasi*. Braunschweig: Steinweg, 1991.

Peterson, Edward. *Russian Commands and German Resistance*. New York: Peter Lang, 1999.

Pirker, Theo. *Der Plan, als Befehl und Fiktion*. Opladen: Westdeutscher, 1995.

Pond, Elizabeth. *Beyond the Wall*. Washington, DC: Brookings Institution, 1993.

Priewe, Jan and Rudolf Hickel. *Der Preis der Einheit*. Frankfurt: Fischer, 1991.

Prokop, Siegfried. *Die kurze Zeit der Utopie*. Berlin: Elefanten, 1994.

Przybylski, Peter. *Tatort Politbüro*. Band II. Berlin: Rowohlt, 1992.

Reich, Jens. *Abschied von den Lebenslügen*. Berlin: Rowohlt, 1992.

Reiprich, Siegfried. *Der verhinderte Dialog*. Berlin: Havemann, 1996.

Reißig, Rolf and Gert-Joachim Glaeßner. *Das Ende eines Experiments*. Berlin: Dietz, 1991.

Reuth, Ralf Georg and Andreas Böne. *Komplott: Wie es wirklich zur Deutschen Einheit kam*. München: Piper, 1993.

Richter, Michael. *Die Staatssicherheit im letzten Jahr der DDR*. Weimar: Böhlau, 1996.

Richter, Wolfgang. *Unfrieden in Deutschland*. Berlin: Gesellschaft zum Schutz von Bürgerrecht und Menschenwürde, 1992.

Riecker, Ariane, Anne Schwarz and Dirk Schneider. *Stasi Intim*. Leipzig: Forum, 1990.

Rüddenklau, Wolfgang. *Störenfried: DDR Opposition, 1986–89*. Berlin: Basis, 1992.

Rutz, Werner. *Die Fünf neuen Bundeslände*. Darmstadt: Wissenschaftliche, 1993.

Schabowski, Günter. *Der Absturz*. Berlin: Rowohlt, 1992.

Schalck-Golodowski, Alexander. *Deutsche-Deutsche Erinnerungen*. Hamburg: Rowohlt, 2000.

Schell, Manfred and Werner Kalinka. *Stasi und kein Ende*. Frankfurt: Ullstein, 1991.

Scherstjanoi, Elke. "Provisorium für längsten ein Jahr." In *Die Gründung der DDR*. Berlin: Akademie, 1991.

Schirdewan, Karl. *Ein Jahrhundert Leben*. Berlin: Edition Ost, 1998.

Schlomann, Friedrich W. *Die Maulwürfe*. München: Universitas, 1993.

Schroeder, Klaus. *Der SED-Staat: Partei, Staat und Gesellschaft, 1949–1990*. München: Hanser, 1998.

Schroeder, Richard and Hans Misselwitz. *Mandat für Deutsche Einheit: Die 10 Volkskammer zwischen DDR-Verfassung und Grundgesetz*. Opladen: Leske, 2000.

Schüddekopf, Charles. *Wir sind das Volk*. Hamburg: Rowohlt, 1990.

Schumann, Frank. *100 Tage die die DDR erschütterten*. Berlin: Neues Leben, 1990.

Schwabe, Klaus. *Arroganz der Macht: Herrschaftsgeschichte von KPD und SED in Mecklenburg und Vorpommern 1945*. Schwerin: Verlagsgruppe, 1997.

Schwan, Heribert. *Erich Mielke: Der Mann, der Die Stasi War*. München: Knauer, 1997.

Schwarz, Josef. *Bis zum bitteren Ende: 35 Jahre Dienste des Ministeriums für Staatssicherheit*. Schkeuditz: GNN, 1994.

Schwarzer, Oskar. "Sozialistische Zentralplanwirtschaft in der SBZ/DDR: Ergebnisse eines ordnungspolitischen Experiments (1945–1989)." *Vierteljahresschrift fuer Sozial-und Wirtschaftsgeschichte*, Beihefte 143. Stuttgart: Franz Steiner Verlag, 1999.

Seiffert, Wolfgang and Norbert Treutwein. *Die Schalck Papiere: DDR Mafia zwischen Ost und West*. Rastatt: Zsolnay, 1991.

Siebenmorgen, Peter. *Staatssicherheit der DDR*. Bonn: Bouvier, 1993.

Staritz, Dietrich. *Die Geschichte der DDR*. Frankfurt, a.M.: Suhrkamp, 1996.

Stephan, Gerd-Rüdiger. *"Vorwärts immer, rückwärts nimmer": Interne Dokumente zum Zerfall von SED und DDR 1988/89*. Berlin: Dietz, 1994.

Stiftung Archiv Partei und Massen Organization (SAPMO) (Archive of the SED Party and the Mass Organizations), Berlin.

Suckut, Siegfried and Walter Süss. *Staatspartei und Staatssicherheit*. Berlin: Links, 1997.

Süss, Walter. *Das Verhältnis von SED und Staatssicherheit*. Berlin: Bundesbeauftragte, 1997.

Süss, Walter. "Die Demonstration am 4. November, 1989, ein Unternehmen von Stasi und SED?" *Deutschland Archiv*, December 1995.

Süss, Walter. *Entmachung und Verfall der Staatssicherheit.* Berlin: Bundesbeauftragte, 1994.

Süss, Walter. *Staatssicherheit am Ende.* Berlin: Links, 1999.

Thaysen, Uwe. *Der runde Tisch, Oder, wo blieb das Volk?* Opladen: Westdeutscher, 1990.

Torpey, John. *Intellectuals, Socialism and Dissent.* Minneapolis: University of Minnesota Press, 1995.

Torsten, Diedrich, Hans Ehlert and Rüdiger Wenzke. *Im Dienste der Partei: Handbuch der bewaffneten Organe der DDR.* Berlin: Links, 1998.

Tschiche, Hans-Jochen. *"Nun machen sie man, Pastorsche!"* Halle: Mitteldeutscher Verlag, 1999.

Unabhängiger Autorengemeinschaft. *Spurensicherung: Zeitzeugen zum 17 Juni 1953.* Berlin: GNN, 1999.

Unabhängiger Verein zur Aufarbeiten der DDR Vergangenheit. *Abschlussbericht.* Rostock, 1994.

Untersuchungskommission zu den Ereignissen vom 7/8 Oktober 1989 in Berlin, und diese verdammte Ohnmacht. Berlin: Basis, 1991.

Uschner, Manfred. *Die zweite Etage.* Berlin: Dietz, 1993.

Vogel, Jürgen. *Magdeburger Kroatenweg.* Magdeburg: Impuls, 1992.

Vogel, Jutta. *Wir haben es einfach angepackt.* Bergisch Gladbach: Lübbe, 1994.

Vollnhals, Clemens. *Die Kirchenpolitik von SED und Staatssicherheit.* Berlin: Links, 1996.

von Sass, Rahel. *"Der Greifswalder Weg."* Schwerin: Landesbeauftragter, 1998.

Wacker, Ulrich. *Entlarven—Begreifen—Verstehen, Auseinandersetzungen mit der DDR Vergangenheit.* Frankfurt: Diesterweg, 1993.

Weber, Hermann. *Grundriss der Geschichte DDR.* Hannover: Fackelträger, 1991.

Weber, Jürgen. *Der SED-Staat.* München: Olzog, 1994.

Wolf, Markus. *Spionagechef im geheimen Krieg.* München: List, 1997.

Wolle, Stefan. *Die heile Welt der Diktatur: Alltag und Herrschaft in der DDR, 1971–1989.* Bonn: Bundeszentrale für politische Bildung, 1998.

Wolle, Stefan. *"Stasi Auflösung Beginn."* In Gisela Helwig, *Rückblicke auf die DDR.* Köln: Deutschland Archiv, 1995.

Woods, Roger. *Opposition in the GDR under Honecker, 1971–85.* New York: St. Martin's Press, 1986.

Worst, Anne. *Das Ende eines Geheimdiensts, Oder, Wie lebendig ist die Stasi?* Berlin: Links, 1991.

Zimmermann, Brigitte. *Ohnmacht: DDR Funktionäre sagen aus.* Berlin: Neues Leben, 1992.

Zwahr, Helmut. *Ende einer Selbstzerstörung: Leipzig und die Revolution in der DDR.* Göttingen: Vandenhoeck & Ruprecht, 1993.

Index

About the Author

EDWARD N. PETERSON is Professor of European History at the University of Wisconsin–River Falls. Introduced to German history through service in the U.S. Army between 1944 and 1948, he later received a Ph.D. from the University of Wisconsin–Madison in 1953. He is the author of seven books on Germany and World War II.